MADAME
SARAH

SARAH BERNHARDT
(Photo Nadar, Collection Yvan Christ, Paris)

MADAME SARAH

Cornelia Otis Skinner

Illustrated with Photographs

PARAGON HOUSE PUBLISHERS
New York

First paperback edition, 1988

Published in the United States by

Paragon House Publishers
90 Fifth Avenue
New York, NY 10011

Library of Congress Cataloging-in-Publication Data

Skinner, Cornelia Otis, 1901–
Madame Sarah.

Reprint. Originally published: Boston :
Houghton Mifflin, 1967.
Bibliography: p.
Includes index.
1. Bernhardt, Sarah, 1844–1923.   2. Actors—France—
Biography.   I. Title.
PN2638.B5S55   1988   792′.028′0924 [B]   87-30354
ISBN 1-55778-107-9 (pbk.)

Manufactured in the United States of America

CONTENTS

INTRODUCTION   xi

1. "GOODNIGHT, LITTLE STAR!"

   *It was Dumas who saw her to her room. At her door,
   he bent his handsome head with its great flaming eyes
   down over Sarah's hand, kissed it and spoke the prophetic words, "Goodnight, little star!"*   1

2. THE SLAP

   *The blow not only felled Madame Nathalie, it rocked
   the House of Molière to its foundations. Never since
   its charter from Louis XIV in 1658 had a first-year
   pensionnaire dared defy a long-established sociétaire, let
   alone use physical violence.*   25

3. GODDESS OF THE LEFT BANK

   *For the first of what would be thousands of subsequent
   times, a crowd of admirers gathered to cheer and toss
   flowers as Sarah Bernhardt made her exit through the
   stage door. "Back in my room that night," she wrote,
   "I felt so rich . . . so rich I was afraid of robbers."*   42

4. SARAH'S FIELD HOSPITAL

   *In her nurse's uniform and flowing white coif with its
   tiny red cross, she must have looked like a ministering
   angel to the weary, pain-ridden men. For once she was
   not Sarah Bernhardt acting a role.*   70

5. WOLF IN THE SHEEP-FOLD

   *"Make no mistake; the engagement of Mlle. Sarah Bern-
   hardt at the Comédie Française is a serious and revo-*

*lutionary fact. Poetry has entered into the house of
dramatic art; or, in other words, the wolf is in the
sheep-fold."* 89

6. THE ROAD WESTWARD

*She may have fallen in love with London, but her im-
mediate concern was whether or not London was going
to fall in love with her. For all the warmth with which
she had been welcomed by high society, she had yet to
prove herself with the British theatre-going public, and
her trial by fire was to be the next day.* 118

7. "THE" BERNHARDT IN AMERICA

*As the ship got closer and closer to American shores,
the habitually taciturn Jarrett grew more and more
elated. "Nobody," he announced with hand-rubbing
satisfaction, "nobody knows better than I how to stage
the arrival of a European star in this country!" He was
quite right.* 146

8. THE SARAH BERNHARDT SPECIAL

*They traveled via the "Sarah Bernhardt Special," an up-
to-the-minute conveyance consisting of three Pullmans
for the personnel and her own private car, known as a
"Palace Car," for Madame Sarah. The scenery, costumes
and heavy luggage went on ahead in a freight express,
also special, and for the passage of both trains, all tracks
were cleared.* 171

9. LA "DAMALA" AUX CAMELIAS

*The moment she set eyes on him, Sarah's divinity de-
serted her and she became all too mortal. Never in the
course of her many love affairs had she made a fool of
herself over any man; but over this despicable rotter,
she was for a time to become a complete and abject fool.* 197

10. ATTACKS AND COUNTERATTACKS

*Mademoiselle Colombier's next intruders were Jean
Richepin and Sarah Bernhardt. The latter stormed in
like vengeance personified. In one hand she flailed the
air with a riding whip given her by Marshal Canrobert,
in the other she brandished the dagger she used in Nana-
Sahib.* 220

11. BELLE-ISLE

*More and more with each passing year, Madame Sarah
looked forward to her Belle-Isle summers . . . her soul
soared with the gulls and she shed her eccentricities, her
off stage play-acting, and became as much of a happy,
unaffected woman as it was possible for her ever to be.*   246

12. LATTER-DAY MIRACLES

*The same thing happened every time she played this
scene. The age discrepancy between actress and character wasn't noticed. Even when she was really old and
minus a leg . . . that latter-day miracle of Saint Joan
took place.*   283

13. THE GLOWING TWILIGHT

*"An old woman heroically and insanely determined to
ignore time, pain and physical laws, smiling and joking
to forestall being pitied, shedding on the public the
warmth of a radiance that never goes out. Greater perhaps in this glowing twilight than in the sparkling days
of her apogee."*   314

PARTIAL LIST OF PLAYS AND ROLES PERFORMED BY
   SARAH BERNHARDT   337

BIBLIOGRAPHY   343

INDEX   347

ILLUSTRATIONS

Frontispiece
Sarah Bernhardt

following page 168
Sarah Bernhardt as Zanetto
The Queen in Hugo's *Ruy Blas*
Doña Sol in Hugo's *Hernani*
In Froufrou by Dumas, *fils*
In Sardou's *Théodora*
In Rostand's *L'Aiglon*
Péléas in Maeterlinck's hit
As Phèdre in Racine's classic
Georges Clairin's portrait of Sarah
Four great co-stars and leading men
Sarah the sculptress
Arrival in New York, 1913
Sarah's private railroad car
On tour in Texas
Sarah in her coffin
In late bloom
Lou Tellegen
Belle Isle
With Houdini
The final American tour

In late bloom
Lou Tellegen
Belle Isle
With Houdini
The final American tour

INTRODUCTION

WHAT DOES the name Sarah Bernhardt mean in America today? To the dwindling number of playgoers lucky enough to have seen her when her artistry was still a powerful enchantment, perhaps a treasured memory. To the average educated adult, merely a figure in theatrical history along with Sarah Siddons or Edwin Booth. To the younger generation apparently little or nothing. I recently mentioned this name to a group of university drama students and was stunned to hear one of them ask, "Who was Sarah Bernhardt?" — a question which to me cast considerable light on that university's drama department.

My impulse was to cry out, "Who was Sarah Bernhardt!" Who, in her prime, was known as The Eighth Wonder of the World and even in her declining years as the greatest personality France had had since Joan of Arc? Who, in every civilized city of the globe, was received with more frenzied enthusiasm than kings and military heroes in her own day or Presleys and Beatles in ours? Who had emperors kneeling at her feet, crowned heads showering her with jewels and adoring mobs throwing their jackets on the ground for her to walk on? Whose opening nights roused more public excitement than all the Hollywood premières of the 1920's and '30's? Whose publicity throughout her long career — it lasted for almost sixty-one years — was so vast, one computation expert figured out that if the newspaper reviews and magazine articles written about her were to be pasted end to end, the streamer would reach around the earth, while a pile-up of her printed photographs would equal the height of the Eiffel Tower? Who was Sarah Bernhardt? Who was Napoleon Bonaparte!

As a matter of analogy, Bernhardt and Napoleon had many qualities in common. Both were conscious geniuses who brooked no contradiction, both colossal egoists. Both had burning ambitions for personal glory which each attained. Both were bold adventurers yet careful organizers. Both had chronic ill health yet boundless, self-renewing energy. And both were supreme showmen.

It was David Garrick who, in the eighteenth century, remarked bitterly, "an actor's name is writ in water," a statement sadly true regarding the great artists who lived before the days of good photography or mechanical reproduction. Who knows what Siddons was like? Or Edwin Booth? Or even Garrick himself? And who in imagination can experience the spectator's spellbound reaction to the uncanny magnetism of Sarah Bernhardt? The jerky flickers of her film *Queen Elizabeth* shot in 1912 when she was sixty-eight can give no inkling of her power and seductiveness any more than do the squeaks and scratchings of her early Victor recordings recreate the magic of her celebrated Golden Voice.

Time is bound to have dimmed the treasured memories of those elderly few who saw her in her autumnal heyday. And as for those of us, not quite as elderly, who were taken by our parents to see her when we were very young and she was very old, our memories are less cherished. For, by then, her haunting face had taken on the spectral quality of an ancient hag, her tiger-like grace of movement had been curtailed by the amputation of a leg and the famous voice was less one of gold than of tin. The theatre-lover who can only read about the acting of Sarah Bernhardt can form no clearer picture of it than can the opera devotee her in his mind's ear the singing of Adelina Patti.

I once asked my father, himself a magnificent player, if he considered Sarah Bernhardt to have been the greatest actress he ever saw. "I don't know," he said, then added, "certainly she was the greatest show woman." And when I asked him how he'd compare her with Eleonora Duse, he replied, "Duse was all thought and poetry," and he paused, then added, "but Bernhardt was an *incandescent light!*" She was a kind of *idol* woman. Max Beerbohm said that she gave an impression of lurid supernaturalness. Another critic said that watching her was as fascinating as watching a wild animal in a cage. Stark Young wrote that there was something mythical about her, like a volcano, that sincerity hardly concerned her "any more than sincerity concerns the sun or the wind . . . she amazed, thrilled, defeated and exalted her audiences." As late as 1915 her American manager wrote, "She will be remembered as the woman whose influence over all who saw and heard her was a psychic mystery that will never be explained." She acted with unerring instinct and with no intellectual approach to any role but with emotional concentration and a fervor that was almost fanatic. The British critic Arthur Symons called her acting "an irresistible expression of a temperament; it mesmerized one, awakening the senses and sending the intelligence to sleep."

The woman's looks by themselves could not have been a major factor in her success. In an era when the ideal of feminine beauty was a rosy Venus all dimples and cushiony curves, Sarah's appearance was the antithesis of the image. Her body was that of a consumptive wraith. Her face, the shape of a young Pharaoh's, was hollow-cheeked and colorless and she emphasized its pallor with slathers of white *poudre-de-riz.* Her eyes were shaped like a cat's, blue as star sapphires when she was in a good mood; when she was angry, they deepened into a brooding slate color with threatening flashes of green. Her nose was straight and Hebraic. Her mouth could be passionately expressive one moment and slyly prim the next. Jules Renard describes the latter aspect, saying, "The llama had a smile like Sarah's." Her hair was a reddish blonde mop, thick, fuzzy and completely unruly. She arranged it in a disordered twist held more or less in place with a single heavy pin of carved ivory. In her heyday, and it was an astonishingly long one, she passed as a beauty. But was she? The author-painter W. Graham Robertson, who knew her well, wrote that he had no idea whether or not Sarah Bernhardt was even passably good-looking. Beauty with her, he says, was a garment she could put on or take off as she pleased. When she put it on, "her face became a lamp through which glowed pale light, her hair burned like an aureole, she grew tall and stately; it was transfiguration." But if Sarah Bernhardt was no true beauty, she could create the illusion of beauty, of great beauty. She moved with the lashing grace of a panther. Her gestures, which at times were so extravagant that in any other actress they would have been dismissed as utter ham, with her became the joy, the wrath or the anguish of Greek sculpture. She gave an impression of weightlessness. When she crossed a stage, she glided as though on little wheels; her very standing still gave an impression of lyrical rhythm; and "when she walks down a spiral staircase," again to quote Jules Renard, "it's as though the staircase turned around her." Her sense of timing was perfect, and when it came to the classical roles in rhymed couplets, there was no actress to compare with her. The poet Théodore de Banville declared, "One can't praise her for knowing how to speak verse. She is the Muse of Poetry herself. Neither intelligence nor artistry have anything to do with it. She is guided by a secret instinct. She recites as the nightingale sings, as the wind sighs, as water murmurs, as Lamartine once wrote."

Apparently at the sound of that *Voix d'Or* every critic forgot to criticize and went into almost mawkish rhapsodies. The impeccably British man of letters, Maurice Baring, likened it to "a symphony of golden flutes and muted strings; a silver dawn lit by lambent lightnings, soft stars and a clear-cut crescent moon." The critic Jules Lemaître called her voice "a caress which strokes you like fingers . . . so pure, so tender so harmonious that if one fine day Mme. Sarah Bernhardt ceased to speak and began to sing it would not surprise me." It could also rumble menacingly or ring forth with the power of a clarion trumpet, especially in those long

passages of mounting vocal crescendo the French call *tirades*.
Lytton Strachey said that in it "there was more than gold, there
was thunder and lightning, there was heaven and hell."

That voice is forever silenced and, in spite of all the writing
that attempts to describe it, the acting of Sarah Bernhardt lies
buried with her body in the cemetery of Père Lachaise. Her
legend, however, lives on. Actually the legend began early in her
career and kept going full tilt up to her death and even after. No
actress in the history of the theatre ever had more written about
her, more gossip true or false told about her, more ecstatic praise
or vicious censure showered upon her. Raising her eyes to the
ceiling or the heavens or whatever was directly overhead, in an
inherent mannerism which her detractors called her act of "posing
for the Assumption," she'd wail in tones of a martyr, "I am the
most lied-about woman in the world!" There is little doubt that
she seldom made any effort to counteract the lies or to reform
the behavior which gave rise to them and which at times was outrageous. With her, to scandalize was a lark. However, she knew
when to scandalize and when not to, for she was a born show
woman and back of all the exhibitionism was the dedication of a
serious artist who realized that notoriety was ephemeral while art
was long. When she was young and enjoying her first success, a
fellow actress, Madeleine Brohan, had sent her a letter giving her
some sound advice:

> If you want to remain the *You* you're creating, be prepared to
> rise on a pedestal constructed of calumnies, gossip, adulation, flat-
> tery, lies and truths. But once you're up on it, stay there and
> cement it with your work and your excellence. Then the mali-
> cious ones who unwittingly furnished the materials for the edifice
> will try to knock it down. But if you are true to your art, they
> will be powerless. That is my wish for you, dear Sarah, for you
> have an ambition and a thirst for glory.

That indeed she had. André Castelot in his excellent book on
Bernhardt says that she was intoxicated by her first success and

remained intoxicated throughout her career. She accepted the fact that she was the greatest actress of her era as logically as Victoria accepted the fact that she was Queen of England. On her initial visit to America, when the crowds went wild over her, one reporter exclaimed, "Why, New York didn't give Dom Pedro of Brazil such an ovation!" Sarah serenely announced, "Yes, but he was only an emperor."

Such arrant egotism, however, in no way hampered her dedication to the theatre. No actress ever approached her profession with more fervor, more serious study, more hours of relentless work. When she was directress of her own theatre and by then in her fifties, it was nothing for her to rise at seven, confer at eight with costume and scene designers regarding a forthcoming production for which she would subsequently rehearse her company at the theatre for three hours, eat lunch in her dressing room with a few chosen members of the cast (usually sitting on the green carpet of her floor and calling the repast a "*pique-nique*"), play a matinee, return to her house on the boulevard Péreire, where at six she'd receive her daily salon of close acquaintances, go back to the theatre for an evening performance, eat supper at home with friends, then study a new role until three or four in the morning. There was never an idle half hour in her day. Once when she was toying with the notion of playing Shakespeare in the Bard's own language, she engaged a professor to teach her English but with the warning, "I can give you only forty-five minutes and you'll have to make it at two A.M. as I'm completely booked up." It need hardly be noted that Madame Bernhardt never played Shakespeare in the original.

And this was a woman whose physical constitution was frail and whose life doctors were constantly predicting to be in a chronic state of impending demise. For her remarkable and frightening vitality she had her own receipt. "Life engenders life," she would say, "energy creates energy. It is by spending oneself that one becomes rich." That she was able to verify this theory was due in part to another quality she had in common with Napoleon. This was the gift of being able to fall instantly to sleep at any time of the day or night and, at a chosen moment, wake up at will. Suddenly, in the middle of rehearsal or any other activity, she'd announce that she was going to sleep for twenty minutes, then she'd fling herself down on a bed or couch or quite often the floor, close her eyes, go immediately off into oblivion and in exactly twenty minutes, as though through some mental alarm clock, wake, jump to her feet refreshed and looking ten years younger and go vigorously back to whatever was under way. There was always plenty under way, both in and out of the theatre. Victorien Sardou, who wrote so many of her biggest hits, declared, "If there's anything more remarkable than watching Sarah act, it's watching her live." Life and its many aspects was a continual passion with her. The critic Jules Lemaître, who is reported to have been briefly one of her numerous lovers, said with admiring amazement, "She could enter a convent, discover the North Pole, kill an emperor or marry a Negro king and it would not surprise me. She is not an individual but a complex of individuals."

No project struck her as impossible. At various times during her restless life she took up sculpture, painting, the piano, writing, pistol shooting, fishing and alligator hunting. During the Universal Exposition of 1878, not content to go up in a captive balloon, she scudded off in a free-flying one. In the course of her first American tour of 1880, she went down a mine in Pennsylvania, fired a cannon at the Springfield firearms factory and in Montreal scared the daylights out of her manager by going with her sister out onto the half-frozen St. Lawrence River and leaping about on the ice floes. Although she was vehemently opposed to capital punishment, she attended four executions, a hanging in London, a garroting in Madrid and two beheadings in Paris. And after each of these depressing spectacles she was sick at heart if not actively at her stomach. One of these last two was the guillotining of the anarchist Vaillant, whom she had known and admired. In fact, during the '90's she gave a donation to the anarchist "soup kitchen meetings." She had once met Vaillant and although in her time she had been an ardent imperialist, she was taken by the man's simple ardor and child-like belief in his misguided cause. She hated cruelty and professed to abhor any form of violence. Yet she was intrigued by the idea of dueling and more than once stated that if she were a man, she'd be fighting every day. Wild animals, especially the big cats, fascinated her and from time to time she collected a number of them as pets. She kept a tame lion in her house until it began to smell up the place, and frequently an ocelot or a puma would wander into her salon to the terror of her assembled visitors. She told one group of dinner guests that she had, that very day, consulted an eminent surgeon to find out if it would be possible for him to graft a living tiger's tail onto the end of her spine as it would be so satisfactory to lash it about when she was angry. It is not surprising that she was occasionally called "The Magnificent Lunatic."

Like Royalty, she was a Presence. The playwright Louis Verneuil, who must have known Sarah well, as he was married to her granddaughter, said that he never saw anyone, famous or obscure, who on first meeting her was not struck with visible emotion. She knew it, of course, and played on it. It was characteristic of her often as not to put the obscure newcomer instantly at ease and gleefully keep the famous one in an awkwardly interminable state of awe. When receiving friends or strangers in her dressing room, the chair on which she sat took on the appearance of a throne; in her living room at home the fur-strewn couch on which she sprawled amid innumerable cushions became the divan of a Byzantine empress, or the barge of Cleopatra; her faithful coterie of intimates was spoken of as "The Court."

Again, as in the case of Royalty, her public felt that she belonged to them. They seldom referred to her by her full name. To them, she was simply "Sarah," as England's ruler was Victoria. To some enthusiasts she was "Sarah the Divine" and occasionally just "La Divine," which was not too exaggerated as there was something goddess-like about her. It was protocol for the members of her company to address her as "Madame Sarah" and the great actor Lucien Guitry, who worshipped her, said it should be spelled *Ma Dame Sarah* because to him she would always be *Notre Dame du Théâtre*. In no other country did a native performer create this feeling of intimate possession by fellow compatriots. No Italian would have referred to Duse as "Eleonora" and had a single Britisher dared such first name impudence in the case of Sir Henry Irving, the Empire would have tottered.

The Bernhardt legend comes down to us in a welter of material, biographies, brochures, press articles. It is preserved in the superb posters by Mucha, in the portraits by Bastien LePage and other artists, whó usually painted her in flowing white, her head and neck emerging like the stamen of a calla lily from the high-standing collar, that well-known *ruche à la Bernhardt*, in the countless photographs which show her dramatically posed in her theatre costumes or her off-stage attire equally dramatically swathed in that voluminous chinchilla cloak she wore the year round, even in July and August. The legend remains in the familiar stories about her vast fortunes, wild expenditures and inevitable bankruptcies, about her numerous lovers, her sudden savage rages followed by periods of abject repentance, about her acts of cold cruelty and her lovely gestures of lavish generosity. We have heard of her ability to faint or to bleed at the mouth (unkind rumor has had it that the former could be brought on through the use of a small phial of chloroform hidden in a scarf and the latter through use of a pin stuck surreptitiously into a gum).

One widely familiar fact about Sarah Bernhardt is that her motto was *"quand même,"* a phrase meaning roughly "even though" or "in spite of everything," a device she adopted early in her career and to whose directive she stuck through the thick and thin of her turbulent life. And of course anyone who has even heard of this extraordinary person has been told anecdotes concerning her skeletal thinness, which was a gold mine for the caricaturists and a source of glee for the wits of the boulevards whose jibes are still quoted: "An empty carriage pulled up at the stage door and Sarah Bernhardt got out." One columnist declared that "La Divine" never needed an umbrella as she was so skinny she could walk between the drops of rain. Another cautioned her against going near any large dog as the creature might mistake her for a bone and start gnawing. One cartoon showed several reporters apparently looking for some object on the ground: the caption reads, "These gentlemen are searching in vain. To escape the press, Madame Bernhardt has hidden herself between two paving stones." At one café gathering of literary cronies, Alexandre Dumas the younger, whose *Lady of the Camellias* was for years on end to be a sure-fire money-maker for them both, remarked, "You know, she's such a liar, she may even be fat!"

She was indeed frequently a liar. It was all part of her exuberance. Even kind Madame Guérard, her close companion for years, had to admit, "She'll say anything for the pleasure of saying it." She knew the value of a good remark as she knew the value of a good scene. It mattered little if both were make-believe. Off stage or on, she never stopped acting, and her statements no matter how exaggerated sounded convincing because she was acting them. She told a group of dinner guests she had it on good authority that the Shah of Persia had been so impressed by the beauty of the Paris Opéra ballet, he had issued an order for all members of his harem henceforth to be dressed in ballerina tutus — a rather appalling idea she'd dreamt up on the spur of the moment.

In his highly entertaining book, *Un Demi-Siècle de Gloires Théâtrales*, the humorist Michel Georges-Michel writes with affectionate amusement of Sarah's melodramatic impulses. Georges-Michel had met her exactly once as a lad of sixteen, and had begged her for an autographed photograph which in time she sent. On it she'd written, "To Michel Georges-Michel, a charming friend to whom I owe all." Bernhardt's promises were as untrustworthy as her statements. Even the members of her devoted "Court" learned not to put much faith in them, and in her own Memoirs she herself admits, "I promise everything with the firm intention of keeping my promise and two hours later, I've forgotten. If some friend reminds me, I tear my hair and invent excuses." Michel Georges-Michel tells of the time an army colonel came backstage filled with emotion over one of her performances. She in turn became filled with emotion upon learning that her visitor was adding to the glory of France not only by serving with the army but by having fathered six children. "There's a colonel who gives his all for the Patrie!" she cried. Bernhardt was a somewhat hysterical patriot, and she insisted that the colonel, his wife and all six children spend their next holiday with her at her Brittany estate on Belle-Isle. She even forced the poor bewildered man to swear on his sword that they'd come. The colonel swore, departed and a month later turned up bag and baggage, wife and children at Belle-Isle only to be informed that the great tragedienne could not be disturbed by tourists, that she had injured her knee, that all rooms in the place were filled with guests and that at the moment Madame was in the midst of a croquet game.

The unreliability of Sarah Bernhardt seems to reassert itself in the numerous books and articles written about her, many of which are widely at variance. Two in particular are extremely contradictory and each professes to be the "as told to" type, the teller having been Madame Sarah herself. Lysiane Bernhardt, Maurice's daughter, writes as though her grandmother were sitting beside her all but guiding her hand. This version is highly laudatory as Lysiane was starry-eyed with chronic admiration. She called her by the pet name of "Great" which was the name Sarah's grandchildren and great-grandchildren always called her, and apparently "Great" readily accepted the modest title. The other book, a work by Basil Woon, is less first-hand. His story was told to him by Madame Pierre Berton, who claims that she had it directly from Sarah herself with instructions that after the actress' demise it be given out to the world. As Madame Berton was the widow of a successful actor-playwright who at one time had been Bernhardt's leading man as well as her lover it is not surprising that this account is very much at variance, and frequently unkindly so, with that of the worshipful granddaughter. Bernhardt's own Memoirs are incomplete. They go no further than 1888 and much is omitted. Her love affairs are politely glossed over and her adored son Maurice suddenly appears as though he had been brought forth from the bullrushes at the age of nine. The present biographer has tried to sort out from a mass of conflicting research what seems most likely to ring true.

MADAME
SARAH

"GOODNIGHT, LITTLE STAR!"

EVEN THE EXACT address of where the great tragedienne was born is a matter of conflicting report. As many streets in Paris claim Bernhardt's birthplace as towns in Greece claim Homer. She is said to have first seen the light at 125 rue du Faubourg Saint-Honoré, at 5 rue de l'Ecole-de-Medicine, at 22 rue de la Michodière and at 265 rue Saint-Honoré.

The locale may be disputed but two dates remain in common agreement, that of her birth and that of her death. In the year of her birth, Louis-Philippe, the "Umbrella King," was conducting his determinedly bourgeois reign in France; in England Sir Robert Peel was minister, the Duke of Wellington was still alive, and Queen Victoria, young and fertile, had given birth to her fourth child; in America John Tyler was President, the Abolitionist agitation was on and Sam Houston headed the independent Republic of Texas; while in Prussia, a young man named Otto von Bismarck had barely come of age. The year of her death, Warren G. Harding was President of the United States; in England, Stanley Baldwin was occupying No. 10 Downing Street; and, in Germany, French troops were occupying the Ruhr. During her long life span this woman, in her own country, existed through a monarchy, an empire, two revolutions, a commune and two major wars. For Sarah Bernhardt was born October 23, 1844, and died March 26, 1923.

Sarah, or Rosine, which was her actual given name but used only during her early childhood, was the illegitimate daughter of a

Judith Van Hard, a Jewish Dutch woman, who lived for a time in Berlin. The Van Hards were of bourgeois middle class although one romantic rumor has it that Judith was the love-child of a Belgian Marquise, Thieule de Petit-Bois de la Nieville, who ran away from a chateau named Saint-Aubin-de-Corbier with a German oculist — which sounds suspiciously like a legend Sarah herself might have thought up. Judith was a milliner — that is, until she came to Paris and switched to a less respectable but more lucrative profession.

Judith, known to her friends as Julie or Youle, was exceptionally beautiful and a conqueror of men. Gay and pregnant she came to Paris with one of her conquests. As to who he was, accounts, as always, differ. The majority say that he was a law student named Edouard Bernard, who later became a successful notary in Havre, and that is as good a supposition as any. The only possible interest he can have is the fact that he sired Sarah Bernhardt. After the baby was born, and very likely in his Left Bank student quarters, he is said to have been called back to Havre. He seems to have had a commendable sense of responsibility for he settled the sum of 100,000 francs on the child as a dowry when she would come of age and he saw to it that Youle had enough to tide her along for a time. Youle, in turn, saw to it that before such time was up, others would tide her further along, and elegantly tided she was.

In the Paris of the 1840's, for a smart young woman without husband, family or fortune, there were just three ways of making a living: by being a milliner, by being a governess or by being kept. Youle was fed up with millinery, she could never have endured the dreary life of a governess and she had all the equipment for the third career which the French glorify by the dashing name of *galanterie*. This was an era when the successful *courtisane* was looked upon with interest and guarded admiration, when infidelity, as long as it was not publicized, was, among a certain class, taken as a matter of course. Morals were anything but rigid and although a dull, paternal king sat on the throne, smugly setting his subjects an example of marital fidelity (as Louis-Philippe was by then entering his seventies, he must have found little difficulty in maintaining such fidelity), only the respectable bourgeoisie followed his commendable example. The world of fashion and the arts paid little attention to the Seventh Commandment. Among the literati, even the immortals were not above indulging their mortal proclivities. Victor Hugo's mistress was the actress Juliette Drouet, whom he kept quite openly in spite of the propinquity of his wife Adèle, and Adèle Hugo, in turn, found solace in a highly charged if unfulfilled affair with the critic Sainte-Beuve. Alexandre Dumas the elder, not content with one, had practically a harem of ladyloves, and George Sand bestowed her favors on many, including Chopin and Alfred de Musset. Every young dandy of the day, who might have stepped out of the pages of Balzac's Parisian novels, had his kept woman. As for the professional *demi-mondaine*, if she were clever enough to rise to the top of her precarious profession, she found herself in a position as enviable as that of a popular actress or a famous ballerina.

Youle's appearance was one of great distinction. She carried herself with dignity. It was said that she had the head of Raphael's Madonna of the Chair: perfect features, limpid eyes, dark hair parted demurely down the middle. There was apparently a piquant attraction about a madonna of easy virtue which some men found irresistible. Youle risked her stakes on capitalizing that attraction, and in a very few months she became so successful that she had little or no time for baby Sarah, but placed her in the care of a Brittany wet-nurse who took the little thing off to her cottage near Quimperlé and looked after her with a peasant's rough kindness. There was one hair-raising moment when the world might have been deprived in a hideous fashion of the future glory that was Bernhardt. The tiny creature, learning to turn herself over, rolled off her straw pallet-bed and onto the open hearth where a flying ember set her clothes on fire. The nurse, who was out tending her cabbages, hearing screams, rushed inside, grabbed up the flaming bundle and plunged it into a large bucket of milk, a maneuver which apparently did neither the child nor the milk any appreciable harm except that it might have been the start of Sarah's life-long obsessive terror of fire.

In a year or two Youle, who had become very elegant indeed, feeling that a Breton peasant's hut was hardly the proper setting for a child of hers, rented a little suburban cottage in Neuilly, where she installed the nurse and her charge. Neuilly was only an hour from the center of town, near enough for Youle to pay an occasional duty call on her daughter, not from motives of maternal concern, but to impress some current swain who might drive her out in his smart trap and enjoy the pretty scene of the beautiful young mother making solicitous inquiries and briefly fondling the peaked little bundle of bones whose well-being could not have concerned her less.

Youle had taken to the *demi-monde* and Parisian life as a duck to water. The French capital was a paradise for the fashionable, the frivolous and the pleasure-loving. The daily amusement routine delighted her. There was the noontime "hour for the Bois" when everyone owning a smart equipage, or renting one, would join the parade up the Champs Elysées and into that enchanted forest for a brisk trot around the lakes and down the Allée des Poteaux, in a pageant of luxury horses gleaming like their polished harness, pretty women with stylish escorts in landaus, traps, tandems and cabriolets looking as though they were driving directly out from the lively sketches of Gavarni or Constantin Guys, equestrians on caracoling mounts, dandies from the Club de l'Union, flashing *cuirassiers* and jingling dragoons, and the prancing tandem of Baron de Rothschild. The crowd was made up of the wealthy, the well-born, the cream of Orleanist society, along with the Bonapartists soon to come into their own. This was the hour for the high-priced women of easy virtue. It was also the hour for theatre celebrities to exhibit themselves and remind the public of their importance. Here one might pass the great star Rachel enjoying the air with her current lover the Prince de Joinville, sporting son of Louis-Philippe, gaily unaware that Rachel was about to jilt him for a man who within four years would become Napoleon III, Emperor of the French. Afternoon was the time for those great arteries of worldly and intelligentsia Paris, the Grand Boulevards with their brilliant cafés, the leading one of which, Tortoni's, was the gathering place for important journalists, patrons of the ballet, clubmen, critics and those charmers of biting wit, the *boulevardiers*. The Café de Paris, then on the corner of the rue Taitbout and the boulevard des Italiens, catered to writers. Here might be sitting Balzac, Eugène Sue, the poet Heine, who was then Paris correspondent for a German newspaper, or that illustrious voluptuary Dumas *père* with his kinky hair, handsome features and irresistible allure. While at the Café de la Régence opposite the Théâtre Français, one might have observed the song bird of youth and love, Alfred de Musset, quietly getting drunk or, as one wit put it, "becoming absinthe-minded."

At night the streets swarmed with theatre or opera-goers. These were the days of Mendelssohn and Meyerbeer, and Monday was the fashionable night for the Opéra. Tuesday was when *Tout Paris* turned out for the Comédie Française, and on evenings when Rachel was billed for *Phèdre*, the venerable house was packed to the rafters. The late supper scene enjoyed an attractive atmosphere of glamor and agreeable sin. The smart restaurants specialized in excellent food and *cabinets particuliers*, elegantly appointed private dining rooms situated on the mezzanine floor and reached by a special stairway. In some establishments the row of discreetly closed doors resembled those along a hotel corridor. The most famous late supper rendezvous was the Café Anglais, and the most famous *cabinet particulier* in all of Europe was the Grand Seize, private dining room No. 16, outside of which was stationed Isabelle, a flower vender to whom gentlemen patrons paid at least two gold louis for an insignificant bouquet and the assurance of her silence. If, in their day, the walls of the Grand Seize could have talked, the world of society, of high finance, even of Royalty would have rocked. Its patrons were clubmen, bankers, sportsmen, South American millionaires and certain of the more amorous crowned heads of Europe. The patronesses were mainly those delicious creatures of easy virtue and exorbitant price who were known as "The Great Lionesses" or more candidly as "The Grand Horizontals."

Judith Van Hard, who now called herself Madame Bernard — the "h" and "t" were added later — now had a stylish flat in the rue de la Michodière and plenty of admirers to pay for its upkeep as well as for her clothes and jewelry. Being both Jewish and Dutch, Youle was clever with the money she acquired. She knew just how much to spend on the ostentation necessary to her profession and how much to save or entrust to some gentleman friend from the Bourse to invest for her. For her the primrose path became so profitably paved, she persuaded one of her sisters to leave Holland and come join her on the pleasant thoroughfare. This was Sarah's Aunt Rosine, the only relative who was kind to her and whom the lonely girl loved dearly. Tante Rosine was pretty and vivacious. There was always a delicious scent of orris-root sachet about her and Sarah called her *Tante Sentibon*, or "Aunt Smell-good." Rosine came to Paris, took up her sister's chosen trade and also did very well for herself. Within a few months she too had her own little flat, her own fashionable horse and carriage and her own string of beaux to foot the bills.

The persons who footed most of Youle's bills were a wealthy banker named Régis Lavolie and a Baron Larrey, the son of the surgeon-in-chief of Napoleon's army. There were other bill-footers as well as a number of non-paying gentlemen-in-attendance who got into the habit of calling merely to be amused by the hostess' entertaining gatherings. During the '40's and '50's a top-flight *courtisane* was in a position of importance and could, if she played her cards well, surround herself with a brilliant coterie.

Judith Van Hard was a skillful card player and her circle included dandified club men, some of the Tuileries Court set and even a few current celebrities. There was Camille Doucet, director of the Beaux Arts. Alexandre Dumas the elder was a constant visitor and good friend. The composer Rossini, who at the time was a popular figure in fashionable society, frequently stopped by for an afternoon glass of malaga. One person who also dropped in regularly was that charmer of wit and distinction, Charles de Morny, later the famous Duc de Morny, half-brother of Louis-Napoleon, being the love-child of their mother, Queen Hortense, and the Comte de Flahaut. Morny was to personify much of the Second Empire, as Philip Guedella has said, "with his elegant patronage of the stage-door and his faint flavor of the Bourse." He lived in great style and one of the sights of the Bois was that of the duc in his driving equipage, a four-wheel *quadrige* with an outrider, postillions and footmen in red and gold uniforms. Rumor has it that Monsieur le duc de Morny not only dropped in but occasionally stayed on after the others had left. It is said that he paid a number of Youle's expenses. But then it is also rumored that he concentrated his amorous attentions on Rosine. Who knows? Perhaps the two worldly sisters shared his favors much as the two literary brothers Goncourt shared those of their mutual concubine.

Sarah lived on in Neuilly until she was four. Then her Breton nurse, a widow and still lusty, met up with a fellow who had the job of concierge in a rundown apartment house at 65 rue de Provence. The man proposed marriage to her, a proposition the woman accepted with alacrity. All she had to do was return little Sarah to her mother. She took the child to the rue de la Michodière, where Youle had been living, only to be told that Madame Bernard had given up her flat, had gone on a trip to Switzerland with Baron Larrey and had left no forwarding address. The nurse tried to get in touch with Tante Rosine but was informed that she too was off on a sentimental journey to Baden-Baden with another rich gentleman and no one knew when she'd be back. The woman married her man. He had to stay on his job in the rue de Provence and there was no one with whom they could leave small Sarah. The newlyweds were obliged to keep her with them in their concierge quarters. Those quarters consisted of a single room, damp, dingy and unheated. There was no breath of ventilation and the only daylight filtered in through the filthy panes of a small oval window high overhead. During the day the child played as best she could in the building's doleful courtyard or out on the street with neighboring urchins. At night, she slept on an ironingboard covered with a quilt and set up between two kitchen chairs. Only a flimsy curtain separated her from the nuptial bed of the concierge and his bride. The small girl, pale and pitifully thin, developed a hacking cough. There is little doubt that as a child and teen-ager, Sarah Bernhardt had tuberculosis, or "consumption," to give that scourge of the nineteenth century its more romantic term. She spat up blood, ran a constant temperature and her body looked as though a hearty sneeze would carry it away. Doctors predicted that she'd never live to be twenty. They administered vile-tasting medicines and prescribed snail soup, a popular panacea for consumptives.

For two or three months small Sarah existed in the dismal squalor of the concierge quarters. Then one day, by a remarkable coincidence like a farfetched trick of melodrama from one of the inferior plays the actress was later to produce, Tante Rosine happened to be driving along the rue de Provence in an open landau accompanied by a stylish beau when something went wrong with a piece of harness and the coachman had to stop. Where he stopped was right outside No. 65 at a moment when Sarah was sitting on the curb idly sailing a dead leaf in the open sewage. The child looked up, recognized her aunt, made a dash across the gutter and into the landau, flung her grubby arms around Rosine's taffeta bonnet-strings and started begging her to take her away. She cried out that she was a prisoner, that she had been abandoned in this horrible place to die. She sobbed, she moaned, she screamed. In short, she put on her first big emotional act which impressed everybody on the block except Tante Rosine, who had no intention of allowing her filthy little niece to defile either her pretty frock or the tan whipcord upholstery of the elegant landau. Her escort had drawn a scented handkerchief from his pocket and was holding it over his nose as he ordered the coachman to hurry up with the harness repair. The concierge and his wife rushed over, yanked the yowling little monster out of the carriage, back to their quarters and locked her in. The coachman jumped onto his seat and cracked his whip to start the horses, only to pull them up with a violent jerk to avoid trampling the body of a small girl who had hurtled down seemingly from the sky and was now lying inert on the paving stones. After being incarcerated in the hated room, Sarah managed, heaven knows how, to clamber up to the oval window, force it open and fling herself out and onto the street, thereby winding up her act with a dislocated shoulder, a slight concussion and a shattered kneecap, which may have been the start of all the suffering she was to have with her leg in later life.

There was nothing for Rosine to do but to have the child placed in the landau and driven to her apartment while her escort continued to hold his handkerchief up over his nose. For a time, Rosine cared for her wretched little niece as best she could, then the moment Youle returned to town, she rushed the fledgling back to the maternal nest, which was now a chic flat at 265 rue Saint-Honoré. Youle was anything but a solicitous mother bird. Her daughter's presence interfered with her activities, and for her livelihood she was largely dependent upon certain of those activities which, heaven knew, required no third presence. Moreover, she was expecting a second baby, which turned out to be Jeanne, the child who became her mother's favorite. Who Jeanne's father was is neither here nor there. It is doubtful if Youle herself knew.

In Paris that winter there was much unrest. The people, tired of their pear-faced king, revolted and Louis-Philippe fled his over-stuffed throne. The Bourbons were gone for good and the Orléans lilies were once more replaced by the tricolor. If the child heard the momentous decrees read out on street corners to the rolling of drums, or the distant gun fire, she paid little attention. Even to her mother and to Tante Rosine, the Revolution of 1848 was merely a bothersome interruption to their daily rounds of gaiety, the barricades in the streets a deliberate blocking of their carefree way to the Café Anglais and the occasional pool of blood something to be gingerly stepped around on satin-slippered feet.

For the next three years, Sarah moped indolently about her mother's flat. Occasionally she was sent to Tante Rosine, who somewhat reluctantly housed her for a time in the rue de la Chausée d'Antin. Here and at her mother's her only contact with the world was through talk with the second-rate servants. She didn't do much of the talking. She was a morose child, given to moody silences. Now and then she'd throw a sudden tantrum or burst into a fit of wild glee over nothing at all. Sometimes the sight of Youle, beautiful and exquisitely dressed to go out for an evening, filled the little girl with a strange, sobbing emotion and she'd rush to clasp her mother by the knees and bury her head in her lilac-scented taffeta skirts, only to be reprimanded and pushed abruptly aside.

At the age of eight, little Miss Bernhardt could neither read nor write. Her mother, prompted less by concern over her daughter's literacy than by finding it a means of getting her out of the way, sent her off to Madame Fressard's pension for young ladies, in Auteuil. Here the child spent two more or less happy years. She learned to read and write, count and sing *Frère Jacques* with the other small pupils. She played supposedly instructive games and was taught to embroider handkerchiefs for her mother, who undoubtedly passed them along to the cook. She acquired a few good manners and a few Christian prayers. For the first time in her life, she had the companionship of girls her own age, not that the companionship was always idyllic. In the brutal way of children, the other young barbarians made fun of her eccentric appearance. They laughed at her uncontrollably kinky hair and called her "the blonde Negress." When they did, Sarah would go into one of her terrible rages, kick, scream, scratch and end up rolling on the ground in convulsions so nearly cataleptic, it would take the headmistress and the school gardener to get her under control.

During her two years at Madame Fressard's, Sarah's mother came to see her exactly twice. On one of these occasions, it was too bad that she did. This was for an evening of theatrical entertainment in the form of a play acted by the children for the questionable pleasure of an audience composed of teachers and parents. The dramatic offering was a one-act gem called *Clothilde* concerning a little girl of that name and the Queen of the Fairies. Sarah was cast as the Queen. The plot was a simple one, the final denouement coming when Clothilde, a realistic child, proclaims that there are no such things as fairies, at which cruel announcement, the Queen falls dead from shock. (This was the first of those death scenes which were to become such a Bernhardt specialty in later years.) Sarah, peeking out through the flimsy curtain at the assembled mothers and wondering if hers might be among them, was in an agony of fear. On being assured that no member of her family was present, she relaxed, went on and played the first scenes with grace and remarkable assurance. Then suddenly, she saw coming through the door at the back of the hall, four fashionable persons and realized, to her horror, that they were her mother and Aunt Rosine with two dashing escorts. Every line fled from the agonized head of the Fairy Queen, her body started shaking like an aspen and she ran sobbing from the stage.

This was the initial attack of that excruciating terror the French call *le trac* and we call stage fright which was to plague the actress throughout her long career. Biographers with a tiresome proclivity to trace every ill back to a traumatic childhood experience have

said that Bernhardt's future attacks were due to a subconscious
memory of this first theatrical disaster. That, of course, is a lot of
psychiatric gobbledy-gook. All actors worthy the name suffer
from this particular form of emotional torture which, when it hits,
makes them wonder why in God's name they ever went on the
stage in the first place. Bernhardt never overcame hers. It grew
worse with the years as more and more her acting advanced to
perfection and more and more she learned the hazards of her
craft. Like any serious artist, she was always critical of her own
performances and never completely sure of herself. The uncer-
tainty was especially gruelling before going on to play her greatest
roles. It would be at its worst before her first entrance in *Phèdre*.
Magnificently costumed for Racine's terrible heroine, she'd stand
in the wings, ashen beneath her make-up, teeth chattering, her
hand clutching the arm of whatever actress played the companion
Œnone, with such an icy grip the poor woman would all but squeal
as the star muttered, *"Quelle horreur! C'est atroce!"* The story
is told of her once overhearing a giddy young soubrette boasting
to a group of players over the fact that she didn't know the meaning of stage fright. The great tragedienne patted the little creature's
shoulder and remarked consolingly, "Wait 'til you get to be a
good actress, my girl, and then you'll know."

At ten, small Sarah could read, write and count beyond ten.
Meanwhile nothing had been done about her religious education.
Youle, in whatever faith she had, was steadfastly Jewish; but she
realized that the Parisian smart set was mainly Catholic. If she
thought at all about her daughter's future, it was to hope for her
a worldly marriage or a successful amorous career, the chances for
either of which commendable goals would be enhanced by a
grounding in the pious doctrines of the Church. Through the
endorsement of the Duc de Morny, Sarah was admitted to the
convent of Grandchamps at Versailles, a select institution and
proudly pro-Royalist. On the same wall as the portrait of Pius

IX was another of a handsome young aristocrat to whom the little girls were taught to refer as "Henri V, our King." The fact that the current Sovereign of France was the Emperor Louis Napoleon was stoutly ignored.

The nuns were kind and most of them were patient with their new boarder. They needed patience, for she was still given to violent rages. One day when Sister Marie was trying to comb the snarls out of her kinky hair, Sarah broke into such yowls of fury and used such shocking language, the gentle sister rushed for a dipperful of holy water and poured it over the wicked brat. The one person who had a quieting influence over her was the Superior, Mother Sainte-Sophie, a saintly and understanding soul for whom Sarah formed a fervid, almost hysterical devotion. Catholicism appealed to the sense of drama that must have been inherent in the girl. She loved the ceremonial, the incense, the chanting, the whole mystery of the Mass. Recalling her convent days in later years, the actress would raise her eyes in her "Mary going to heaven" manner and, quoting from her own Memoirs, say in her best on-stage voice: "The Christian legend took over my spirit. Later the Son of God became my cult and the Mother of the Seven Sorrows my ideal." Yet for all her professed Catholicism, and it was undoubtedly sincere, she never lost sight of the fact that she was of Jewish origin. She never allowed a word of anti-Semitic talk, and during the hysteria of the Dreyfus case she had the courage to take a steadfastly pro-Dreyfus stand. Once when a reporter asked her if she were a Christian she answered, "No. I'm a Roman Catholic, and a member of the great Jewish race," then added with a sweet smile, "I'm waiting 'til Christians become better."

During her first weeks at Grandchamps Sarah went in for Catholicism with the exaggeration she was always to have for any new enthusiasm. One morning at school assembly, Mother Sainte-Sophie announced to the pupils that Monseigneur Sibour, Archbishop of Paris, was coming to pay the convent a visit. Sarah, at the news, emitted a scream of anguish, cried out, "How can I

look his Eminence in the face? I who have never been baptized!"
and fainted dead away. She was revived by a drop of *eau de
mélisse* on a lump of sugar and several firm slaps on the cheek.
When Monseigneur Sibour paid his visit, she had the consolation of
appearing before him on a rickety little stage in a terrible dramatization of the story of Tobias and the Angel. Hers was the role of
the archangel Raphael while the sea monster was interpreted by
César, the large convent dog who lumbered on, none too happily,
in a jacket covered with paper fish scales. Little Bernhardt performed her archangel role with great charm and disarming simplicity, and after the finish the eminent prelate called her over to
congratulate her. At this the child fell on her knees before him and
confessed that she had never been baptized in the sobbing tones of
one confessing to having leprosy. The kindly Archbishop placed
a hand on her small bowed head and promised that on his next
visit, he himself would perform the ceremony. Unfortunately the
promise was never fulfilled, for a week or so later the good man
was assassinated by a maniac.

Some other cleric christened Sarah. It is said that the arrangements had been made by that elusive individual, her father, about
whom so little is known. He was not present at the ceremony.
However, her mother and Tante Rosine came out for the occasion
and they brought with them Sarah's half-sister Jeanne. They also
brought another half-sister. This was little three-year-old Régina,
who seems to have turned up as an afterthought in Julie Bernhardt's
amorous career. Youle's purpose in bringing the other daughters
was to have them baptized also. It seemed a practical measure for
the joint purification of the three children with which she had
been blessed, each by a different progenitor. Youle's party also
included the requisite baptismal sponsors in the persons of three
fashionable clubmen. These were Régis Lavolie, who was to
stand as godfather for Sarah, a Monsieur Meydieu, godfather for
Jeanne, and a General Polhes, godfather for tiny Régina. Meydieu
and Polhes may easily have also had a less spiritual parental relation-

ship to Jeanne and Régina, but there seems not to have arisen the slightest rivalry between any of the gentlemen and things went as merrily as though to the sound of wedding bells.

Sarah received her First Communion early in 1856 and after this the child became a religious fanatic. She still gave vent to occasional tantrums of rage and violence, but they were followed by stretches of repentance almost as spectacular as the tantrums. One chilly night, she slipped from her bed in the dark and after telling her dormitory mates that she was going to the chapel to offer a nosegay of mignonettes to the Blessed Mother, then have a talk with the archangel Raphael, pattered away barefoot and clad only in a nightgown. She and the upper echelon angel must have had a good deal to talk about for it was daybreak when the sisters discovered her in a frozen state of ecstasy and the beginnings of a case of pneumonia. She was nursed through the attack by the sisters, then sent to recuperate in the Pyrenees at Cauterets.

On this trip south she was accompanied by her mother and another aunt, a Madame Félix Faure (not to be confused with the subsequent French President) whom Sarah didn't particularly like. Madame Faure was an austere, smugly respectable woman who highly disapproved of her frivolous sisters and their choice of profession. Perhaps if she had chosen it herself, she might have been more indulgent. In compensation for the wet-blanketing presence of Tante Faure was the heartwarming company of Madame Guérard, a youngish widow who lived in the apartment above Youle's in the rue Saint-Honoré. Madame Guérard was gentle and lovable and from the first moment they met, Sarah formed an attachment to her. She in turn was devoted to the girl with an unwavering devotion which was to last through the years until the dear woman's death in 1890. Madame Guérard was eventually to become the actress' constant companion, social secretary, chief lady-in-waiting and bosom friend. She was a permanent fixture of the star's entourage, living in the various Bernhardt houses, going along on all the tours, her room usually adjacent to Sarah's.

If Madame Guérard had a first name, no one seems to have known it. At the age of fourteen, Sarah had nicknamed her *mon p'tit dame* and everyone called her that.

During the late '60's, Cauterets was a small but smart resort where fashionable Parisians, jaded by the season's social whirl, came to wash out their livers and kidneys in the waters of the thermal springs and to clear their lungs with the mountain air that blew from the surrounding Pyrenees. Here the young convalescent's health improved although the scenery depressed her. Throughout her life mountains, chasms, shadowy valleys were to fill her with a deep melancholy. There was enough Dutch blood in her to make her love the sea, vast sweeps of sand, flat meadows, wide marshes and endless stretches of open sky.

What didn't depress the girl, however, were the local animals — the dogs, the cats, the sheep and little goats, the calves and now and then a tamable squirrel. It was her first contact with four-legged creatures and they filled her with rapture. Youle had never bothered with any household pets, which were also tabu at Madame Fressard's. At Grandchamps, she had made her first and passionate contact with a canine in the form of César the convent dog. There her innate love of live things had found outlet in the collecting of lizards, crickets and spiders. Her schoolmates had run screaming from the spiders, the sisters had exterminated the crickets, and most of the lizards had suffered the unpleasant fate of losing their tails due to Sarah's too precipitate closing the lid of the tin container in which she kept them, after which disaster, the child would weep and try to glue the tails back on again. But Cauterets for her was animal heaven. Every day she would wander off into the fields and village byways to return with some doleful trophy, a mangy cat, a filthy dog, a mud-caked goat or an open-beaked fledgling, only to be met by shrill protests from Youle, who would drive the wretched things away.

Countless stories, most of them absurdly untrue, have been circulated about Sarah Bernhardt's household menageries. It was said that she kept two lion cubs in her dressing room, to whom she fed live quail; that she picked up stray cats and hurled them screaming into the stove — ridiculous inventions of her enemies, about as true as their other scabrous reports. There was, certainly, a primitive streak in the woman and she could shed on an animal the same magnetism she could cast on an audience. She could handle a supposedly savage beast such as a lynx or a cheetah with fearless ease. Even reptiles held a fascination for her. When she played Cleopatra she more than once insisted upon using a real snake for the final scene. It was all part of her love of challenge. However, she would never have brutalized an animal. What flashes of physical savagery she had were for people, and only when in her own opinion she had been justifiably provoked, as when she'd hurtle a paper weight at the head of a bungling servant or when, armed with a horsewhip and dagger she went after an authoress who had written a vilely libellous book about her. Wild or domestic creatures in distress roused her to mawkish pity and extravagant gesture. Her summer estate in Brittany was a haven for all sorts of rather dreadful stray dogs, and one cold winter in Paris she spent 2000 francs for rolls with which to feed the starving city sparrows.

After her convalescence in Cauterets young Sarah returned to Grandchamps for a few more terms, then she was taken out at the age of fifteen. The formal education of Sarah Bernhardt lasted a scant six years. Further schooling was apparently never needed, for although she was not a highly literate woman, all her life she gave the impression of being a cultivated, at times even a learned one. She seemed responsively intelligent even when she listened to things she couldn't remotely understand. Had Pierre and Marie Curie chosen to discuss with her the complexities of radium, she would have appeared to comprehend every word they uttered. Sarah Bernhardt's adult education came through the conversation of the brilliantly informed persons with whom she surrounded herself. Talk for her was a game of mutual excitement. Through it she learned avidly what she felt would be of use to her. At the same time her interlocutors seems always to have experienced tremendous mental stimulus, if not actual inspiration. One writer, Jules Renard, said after a day spent with her and her friends, "One feels renewed and enlarged: this overexcitement is a good thing and if the next day one hasn't talent, one is a cretin." Dumas *fils* spoke less fatuously. "When I am with her," he said, "she exasperates me to death but when I get home, how I can write! How I *can* write!" Her life-long friend the painter Georges Clairin gained inspiration from her very silences. Once while working on a canvas, he found himself at a certain point where he was creatively stuck. It was one of his immense murals so there was plenty of space on which to be stuck. Rushing from his studio, he hailed a fiacre and hurried to Bernhardt's house, the doors of which were always open to him. The actress was in her main salon, characteristically sprawling amid the pillows and fur throws of her great couch. Wordlessly Clairin drew up a chair and sat staring at her. Sarah stared quietly back and, being sensitively perceptive, said not a word. For a full fifteen minutes Clairin sat studying her face, then, still silent, departed and ran back to his studio where he painted like mad. "It used to be absinthe," he told a friend, "now it's Sarah."

At fifteen the girl's religious devoutness was still strong. She longed to return to the convent, no longer as a pupil but to take solemn vows. The mental picture of herself in nun's habit, piously observing her devotions, was about the prettiest image she could dream up. She brooded over the prospect with melancholy fervor.

Life for her at her mother's was dismal. When Youle was off gallivanting with her frivolous friends, Sarah would wander about the place listless and moody. Her younger sisters were not companions for her. Baby Régina was a giddy tot given to dancing jigs and using rather shocking language which she picked up from the servants. Sarah adored the child but would get deathly tired of her prattle. Jeanne, the next older, was her mother's favorite and Youle lavished on her the love and concern she denied her other two daughters. As a girl, Sarah was insanely jealous of Jeanne and, with her terrible temper, it is a wonder she didn't do her some bodily harm. In later years, as Sarah reached maturity and with it success, her jealousy softened into the protective attitude of an understanding older sister, but at the age of fifteen, Sarah bitterly resented Jeanne and avoided her company.

One member of the rue Saint-Honoré household was a self-effacing Mademoiselle Brabender, who came in daily as a tutor. Mademoiselle Brabender had once been governess to a Russian Grand Duchess and had never gotten over it. She was a pious, somewhat melancholy soul with a pronounced and slightly drooping mustache. Sarah was very fond of her and, with that loyalty she had for old retainers, kept in touch with her in later years after the lady had retired to a convent. In her own Memoirs, Sarah tells of being summoned to the convent at the time of Mademoiselle Brabender's death and, upon arrival, finding the nuns in a state of hysterical agitation. It seems that in death not only had Mademoiselle Brabender's mustache grown considerably but a definite black beard had begun to sprout all over her face, a horrid phenomenon which had set the sisters repeatedly crossing themselves and enquiring if they shouldn't call in a priest.

During Sarah's adolescence, her one consoling companion was Madame Guérard. The love-hungry girl would go up to *mon p'tit dame's* flat to spend hours in her gentle company and they were the happiest hours of her lonely years. Her mother's gay parties and receptions held no attractions for her. Occasionally if she needed an extra person to fill out her dinner table, Youle would press Sarah into service, but seldom successfully. At the last minute her rebellious daughter would resort to some desperate measure such as spilling a bottle of ink over the front of her dress, or going into one of her fainting acts. The sight of a number of strangers in a room sent her into a panic. In later life after she was extravagantly installed in her own sumptuous house, she herself was to give countless dinners, luncheons and afternoon receptions, bril-

liant occasions whose guests were carefully hand-picked. Any
stranger lucky enough to be admitted had been brought by a
friend with Madame Sarah's special permission — or rather at her
royal command. But this was to be far in the future. At fifteen,
little Bernhardt was shy, gawky and painfully anti-social.

She was still frail, still subject to a hacking cough, still occasionally spitting up blood. The doctors still despaired of her existing
beyond a few more years and quite callously discussed with her
family, and in her presence, her doomed condition. One medic
who fancied himself a wit joked heartlessly about her state of
physical emaciation and said the girl was so thin, if she swallowed
one of his pills she looked pregnant. The prospect of an early
demise filled the poor child with a dramatic gloom. Death became
a melancholy obsession with her. In those days the Paris morgue
was open to the public and Sarah paid it frequent visits for the
ghoulish solace of communing with the corpses of derelicts that
had been dragged up out of the Seine.

It was probably around this time that she acquired her much
publicized coffin. Lysiane Bernhardt quotes her grandmother as
saying: "From the day Dr. L. condemned me, I begged Maman to
buy me a pretty coffin. She, quite obviously, refused. But I wanted
not to be laid away in an ugly bier. I pestered her and her intimate
circle so persistently she finally got me a rosewood coffin lined
with white satin." She occasionally slept in it in order to get used
to her final resting place. That coffin crops up time and again
in the Bernhardt legend. While still in her teens, she had herself photographed lying in this cheery piece of furniture. It is
a naïve photograph, crudely taken and showing her looking pitifully young. In subsequent years she must have had a more up-to-
date photographer immortalize her in such all too mortal a pose.
For in this picture there is more attention to detail, the tapers burn
at the correct angles and the flowers and palm branch lie prettily in
becoming arrangement. In America, *Theatre Magazine* for December, 1903, reproduced the latter picture with the legend:

When Mme. Bernhardt is world-weary, she gets into this coffin
. . . and covering herself with faded wreaths and flowers, folds
her hands across her breast and, her eyes closed, bids a temporary
farewell to life. A lighted candle on the votary table at her left
and a skull grinning on the floor add to the illusion. It is only
when dinner is announced that the tragedienne languidly opens
her eyes.

One afternoon, Sarah was summoned to appear in her mother's
salon for what was announced to be a "family conference" — the
conferees being, in addition to a notary from Havre, her mother,
two aunts and four gentlemen whose intimacy with the lady of the
house seemed to have warranted their inclusion as part of the family. Sarah came in and dutifully sat down on an indicated chair.
Youle in tones which she tried to make impressively portentous
stated that the two aunts and these distinguished gentlemen had
given of their precious time in order to meet and decide upon Sarah's future. Sarah said quickly that she had already decided upon
her future — she was going to be a nun — a decision which set
the assembled gathering off into gales of laughter. Youle, still
laughing, protested that in order to join a religious order in those
days, one had to have money, to which her daughter countered by
reminding her of that 100,000-franc legacy she would eventually
inherit from her father.

"But that's for your dowry when you marry!" cried the mother.

Sarah, raising her eyes to heaven, replied in the voice of a child
martyr: "I shall marry God." This was too much for the notary
from Havre. "The silly fool should be sent to a house of correc-
tion!" he snorted. And at that, Sarah put on the greatest tantrum
scene to date of her young life. With the yowl of an infuriated
animal, she sprang at the notary, pommeled his chest, scratched his
face and tore out a fistful of his pomaded hair. It took two of the
gentlemen present to rescue the wretched man from his attacker,
after which order was restored. And at that moment there unex-
pectedly came the decisive words which were to eventuate in the

creation of Sarah Bernhardt. They were spoken by the Duc de Morny who, calm and suave, had sat silently by, watching the comedy with an amused eye. "The girl's a born actress," he said quietly, "she ought to be sent for training at the Conservatoire." Everyone was stunned by his announcement — everyone except Sarah, who was horrified. "An actress?" she exclaimed. "Never!" She had seen an actress once, she said. It was the tragedienne Rachel, who had paid a visit to Grandchamps. Rachel was by then a pitiful shadow of her former self, pale, hollow-eyed and racked by the tuberculosis that was soon to end her brief and comet-like career. One of the convent sisters had pointed her out to Sarah and had whispered that this hag-like creature had been a great actress and that it was her wicked profession which was deservedly killing her. The Duc de Morny's proposal filled Sarah with such alarm, she fled from the room.

Whose decision it was to invite her that evening to attend a performance at the Comédie Française is not known. The girl had never seen a play and what with her preconceived notions about the horrors of theatre life, she had little desire to go. The party consisted of Régis Lavolie, the Duc de Morny, Alexandre Dumas *père* and Youle, with Sarah tagging along balefully behind. They were to occupy a dress circle box as Dumas' guests.

It was a Tuesday, *the* night at the Théâtre Français. During the Second Empire, the spectacle of a Tuesday night audience at the Comédie Française vied in glamour with the spectacle being presented on the stage. Formal dress was *de rigueur* and the circles and parterre flowered with the fashionable elite dressed by Worth and the best London tailors. On the gilt chairs at the rear of the red plush boxes bearded dandies with ruffled white shirtfronts and satin waistcoats, some still wearing their gleaming black toppers and scarlet-lined opera cloaks, formed a distinguished background for a dazzling foreground of lovely women who, when stared at through a lorgnette from an orchestra seat, appeared to be clad solely in their jewels. The Empress Eugénie, best-dressed woman in Europe, though herself rather a prude, had set the mode for an evening gown with a crinoline bottom so wide, it took up a good five feet, and a top so low, it was referred to as a *décolletage à la baignoire*. *Baignoire* means both "bath tub" and "opera box" and a lady sitting in one of the latter with well-exposed shoulders and bosom often gave the effect of being about to perform her daily ablutions. Now and then, in the case of the tightly corseted and overdeveloped female, the exposure might get startlingly out of control, in which case a husband would nervously hold up a shielding program while his blushing wife hastily shoved the little mischief back into place.

On this the occasion of Sarah Bernhardt's first presence in the Comédie Française, who might not have been in the audience? Princesse Mathilde, patroness of authors and niece of the great Napoleon, might well have been, or her rival hostess, Pauline Metternich, that most Parisian of Austrians, brilliant wit and championess of Richard Wagner. Perhaps one might have enjoyed the dazzling sight of Madame de Castiglione, the notorious beauty who was currently sharing her favors with the ineffectual Emperor. In her book, based on the information she received directly from her grandmother, Lysiane Bernhardt writes that the audience that evening included the Baroness de Rothschild, Céleste Mogador, dancer and belle of the Bal Mabille, George Sand, mercifully unaccoutered with trousers, and the man-about-town poet and dandy Barbey d'Aurevilly.

Whoever were the notables, they were of no interest to Sarah. She looked in stupefaction out over this crowd, this intangible thing called "the public," and suddenly it turned from an assemblage of several hundred individual human beings into one fascinating and terrifying entity — a sacred monster. Throughout her career she was always to call it *le monstre bien aimé*. The gas lights of the great chandelier dimmed, those of the foots glowed on, the three hammer blows announced the opening act and slowly there started to rise the red curtain of the House of Molière. In her own Memoirs Bernhardt wrote, "It was the curtain of my life which was rising." Her baleful mood vanished, to be replaced by one of wonder, then of rapture, then of raw uncontrollable emotion. The play was Racine's *Britannicus*, and she experienced every mood of every character. The rhymed-alexandrine sorrows of Junie and Britannicus reduced her to tears, which in time gave way to sobs so loud that a good portion of the audience said, "Sh!" Barbey d'Aurevilly stared disgustedly through his monocle, Youle turned purple with shame and Régis Lavolie walked out of the loge, slamming the door behind him. The Duc de Morny sat characteristically silent enjoying the scene in the box better than the one on stage. The person who came to the girl's aid was Alexandre Dumas. He moved his chair next to hers and put a protective arm about her heaving little shoulders. He later told Morny that he was right, the girl seemed destined for the stage. She was still in a highly emotional state as they returned to the rue Saint-Honoré. On reaching the flat, Youle, still outraged, dispatched her overwrought daughter immediately to bed. It was Dumas who saw her to her room. At her door, he bent his handsome head with its great flaming eyes down over Sarah's hand, kissed it and spoke the prophetic words, "*Bonsoir, petite étoile!*"

2

THE SLAP

D ESPITE THE FORESIGHT of that prophecy, it was not Dumas *père* who launched Sarah Bernhardt on her space flight to stardom but Morny. The dapper duke, still amused by his notion of turning the tempestuous child into an actress, spoke about her to the composer Auber, who having succeeded Cherubini as director of the Conservatoire had for twenty years presided over that "National Conservatory of Music and Declamation." Auber was a person of wit and charming kindness. His operas, especially *Fra Diavolo*, had gained him the position of grand old man of French music, and Napoleon III had given him the title of imperial *maître de chapelle*. Morny as half-brother of the Emperor and President of the Legislative Corps was about the most powerful man in France, and Auber readily agreed to give young Bernhardt his special attention. He did, however, remind Monsieur le duc that the director alone could not expedite the entry of an aspirant into the Conservatory. Like any other candidate she would have to try out in the annual auditions before the admissions committee. This was a formidable jury made up of the faculty who were all leading artists from the Comédie Française. Auber even went so far as to invite Morny to bring the protégé by his house for a special interview, which the duke obligingly did. The aging composer must have been slightly baffled when, after inquiring in paternal tones, "And so, dear child, you want to become an actress?" the "dear child," casting her eyes to heaven, demurely replied, "*Ah non, Monsieur*." Morny leapt forward to explain that such a blunder was due to the girl's excessive modesty and quickly whisked her away to deposit her with her mother.

That lady, who did not at all go along with Morny's inspired suggestion, had other plans for her daughter's future. The wretched little creature, she decided, was far too skinny and eccentric-looking ever to make a success as an actress, even less of a success in Youle's own line of self-employment. A comfortable marriage seemed the best solution, and oddly enough she had come up with a likely suitor who, more oddly yet, was sincerely attracted by the strange, cadaverous girl. This was a Mr. Berentz, a silk merchant from Amsterdam who had an enormous amount of money. He also had an enormous amount of hair. In fact he appeared to be fairly pelted with it — on his chin and cheeks, in his nostrils, on his neck, his hands and presumably his entire body. The only attractive thing about him were his eyes, which had the appeal of a wistful Saint Bernard. According to Lysiane Bernhardt, who had it directly from "Great," Mr. Berentz was deeply, hopelessly in love — so much so that instead of asking the mother for the customary *dot* or dowry which went with the marriage transactions of a daughter, he was prepared to make his own settlement of 500,-000 francs on Sarah the moment she said "Yes." But Sarah said "No." In fact, she practically laughed in his face. Then suddenly, in one of those characteristic changes of mood, with regret for her callousness and a quick compassion for the poor man, she grabbed his paw-like hand, patted its furry surface and told him that although she was extremely fond of him, from now on she intended to be wedded only to the art of acting. Mr. Berentz said that he was willing to wait and, to Sarah's relief and her mother's fury, he walked sadly out of their lives — whether to wait or not, we don't know. We do know that he gave her two lots of his best silk, one blue and one black. Youle ordered her *couturière* to make up the black one into a *robe de ville* as smart as her daughter's bony figure would allow. The voluminous crinoline skirt then in vogue concealed her pitiful inadequacy of hips and some judicious padding worked the same effect for her bosom. Sarah felt forlorn in the outfit, maybe because at every fitting her mother complained that it was not a wedding gown which was being created.

Very possibly there were other suitors besides Mr. Berentz in Sarah Bernhardt's young life. In Basil Woon's account, which is based largely on material supplied by Madame Pierre Berton, Sarah herself is said to have stated that she received one thousand proposals of marriage and that she could remember the name of every proposer and the date of every declaration. It would perhaps be unkind to speculate as to how much with tongue in cheek Sarah uttered this statement or how great was Madame Berton's gullibility. One can only surmise.

Little Bernhardt was now determined that the theatre was to be her career and she attacked the project with fervor or, to use her own words, "that vivid exaggeration which which I embrace any new enterprise." The auditions for Conservatoire candidates were to be held in a month's time, and she spent much of the intervening days perfecting her speech. Her chief instructor was her mother's friend Monsieur Meydieu, an insufferably pedantic bourgeois fond of whist, good wine and pretty women. Laboriously he coached her in diction exercises which were the Gallic equivalent of "how now brown cow" or "prunes and prisms." To perfect the rolling of her "r" 's he made her repeat over and over *un gros grand rat rongeait trois gros grains d'orge.* And he gave her the lip-pursing exercise of *petit papa, petit popo, petit pupu, petit pipi* in order, he explained, to shape her mouth *en cul de poule,* which meaning as it does "a hen's rear end" seems an interesting objective. Much more valuable coaching came from Dumas *père.* The huge man would stride magnificently into her room and put her through a rigorous rehearsal of the scene he and she had selected for her competition piece. Dumas was a stimulating task master. He was aware of Sarah's potential power, of her intelligent sensitivity, of her "otherworld" allure. Dumas was the first to praise her extraordinary voice. He called it a spring of clear water, "a spring that ripples and leaps over golden pebbles," and he gave her some vocal advice which any player of any era would do well to follow: "Don't drop the end of a line, keep up the tempo, learn to breathe especially when you have some time before the final point, contain your breath so as not to 'die' on the last word like an asthmatic."

The day for the auditions came around and the family coterie gathered in the salon: mother, two aunts, Uncle Faure, Mademoiselle Brabender, Madame Guérard, Régis Lavolie and the unbearable Monsieur Meydieu. They were there presumably to "help" in the way of offering unsolicited counsel, fussing over her clothes and hair and generally driving the girl to the point of screaming. Youle had decided that the dress for Sarah to wear should be the black one made of Mr. Berentz's silk — an unfortunate choice, for the frock was somberly severe. Moreover the maid, in pressing it, had burned a crack in the bodice which Youle covered up with a lace fichu. The effect was tatty, and Sarah looked more like a mournful little widow than a fragile fifteen-year-old. Forlorn and deathly pale, she stood apart while everyone else in the room chattered, laughed and completely ignored her. If ever a young person needed affection and encouragement, it was Sarah at this moment.

Youle was too much involved in herself to be concerned about her daughter's emotions. The lady had a delicate heart and any situation of tension or over-excitement would set it fluttering. In such a crisis she would sink half swooning onto the handiest sofa as she held a curved and provocative hand over her left bosom. That day she had no intention of going with Sarah to the auditions. Her heart, she declared, would never stand the strain, and she added that her nostrils would never endure the atmosphere of the students' waiting room.

The person who supplied the needed warmth and support at this time, as always, was Madame Guérard. It was the gentle and understanding *mon p'tit dame* who took Sarah in a hired fiacre to 15 fabourg Poissonière. The Conservatoire green room was indeed, as Youle had predicted, a milling crowd of youthful aspirants,

nervously mopping their histrionic brows and frantically muttering the lines of their recitation pieces — those hackneyed selections
from the classics, Racinian and Molièresque equivalents of Hamlet's
soliloquy or Juliet's Potion Scene. In addition to Auber there were
five jurors, top-flight members of the Comédie Française: three
men, Beauvallet, Provost and Samson, and one woman, Augustine
Brohan, who though now in her fifties was still alluring and continued to play the leading coquettes at the Français. She was known
off stage for her biting wit and her series of lovers, among them
Alfred de Musset.*

It was an awesome panel for any contestant to face. Sarah, waiting her turn, stood stock still, a strange wraith-like girl with glowing eyes and proud Biblical features, watching her fellow victims
as one after the other was summoned out through a door which
led onto an adjoining stage. Eventually the head usher, a Monsieur
Léautaud, called her name. The girl in a near faint stepped forward
and Léautaud asked what she was going to recite.

"*Phèdre*, act 2, scene 2, Monsieur," she managed to answer. "The
role of Aricie."

"And who will give you your cues?" asked Léautaud.

"My cues?" croaked Sarah.

"Your cues," he repeated impatiently. Léautaud was the official
prompter at the Comédie and he had all the self-importance of the
French minor official. As Sarah continued to stare mutely at him
he snapped, "The lines of the character Aricie is talking to, who
will read them?" Sarah blanched paler than she already was. It had
not occurred to her to bring anyone along and she told Léautaud
so. He suggested that she ask one of the other contestants to hold
the book, which, incidentally, she had also neglected to bring with
her. Sarah looked over the disheveled and perspiring throng and
shuddered. Then she made the decision which in time made the-

---

* According to Goncourt's Journal, some years after the supposed de Musset
affair Augustine Brohan ran into the poet and accosted him with, "Monsieur, I
hear you have boasted that you've been to bed with me." To which Musset with a
courtly bow replied, "Non, Madame, I have always boasted the contrary."

atrical history. "I shall recite," and her voice no longer croaked, "la Fontaine's fable of *The Two Pigeons*."

Léautaud, making no effort to conceal a smile, announced, "Mademoiselle Sarah Bernhardt, *Les Deux Pigeons* par Jean de la Fontaine." The little creature glided onto the stage, not without hearing Beauvallet snort, "A fable! The child must think she's still in school," and Augustine Brohan counter, "Never mind. It will take less time." Sarah curtsied jerkily and started:

"Deux pigeons s'aimaient d'amour tendre."

She spoke in a trembling undertone and a couple of the jurors tittered. Auber called them to order and asked Sarah to start again. Augustine Brohan protested, ah no, that it would now take as long as a scene, and Auber silenced her. Sarah faced her judges. Her stage fright, that terrible *trac*, had given way to defiance. She would show these barbarians *quand même*, and in a voice as clear as a crystal bell she recited la Fontaine's touching account of the restless pigeon who leaves home and mate to seek happiness in an unfriendly world. She recited with delicate fervor and infinite pathos. The five jaded jurors sat up to listen and gradually they become transfixed. The exquisite little fable ended with the prodigal bird, battered and repentant, returning to find true happiness in the downy sanctuary of his nest, and the young voice stopped. Augustine Brohan put down her lorgnette to wipe away a visible tear and old Auber blew his nose in a blast like a trumpet. Without a curtsey, without so much as a nod, the girl turned and dazedly walked from the stage. She would probably have walked on out of the building if she hadn't been stopped by Auber with a yank at her shoulder so abrupt it increased the split in her dress. He was followed by Provost and Beauvallet. "You were very good, Mademoiselle!" the venerable composer exclaimed, "very good indeed!" Sarah's blue-green eyes looked into his with incredulity. "Do you mean I'm accepted?" she asked. Auber assured her that he did mean to say exactly that and added, "I'm sorry that that voice of yours isn't destined for a musical career." Years later

Bernhardt told a reporter that Auber's chance remark had given her the inspiration to bring music into every sound she uttered. Then Auber further staggered her with the information that Provost and Beauvallet each wanted her in his class, and which teacher would she choose? Sarah looked them both over and shyly stated that she would like to be the pupil of Monsieur Provost.

It was an unerring choice. Provost was one of the best actors of his day. He had started out at the Porte Saint-Martin playing melodrama villains and playing them so convincingly audiences hissed his every move and on one occasion the police had to be called to protect his exit from the theatre. Later at the Comédie Française, where he remained for thirty years, he won the public's affection appearing in more sympathetic roles. Théophile Gautier wrote of him: "He's a great, a very great actor, Provost. What naturalness, what good humor and at the same time what *finesse!*" Provost thanked little Bernhardt for choosing his class and kindly shook her hand. Speechless with excitement she rushed to join Madame Guérard, who hailed a fiacre, and jubilant the two hurried back to the rue Saint-Honoré to tell the great news to the mother who in no way shared their elation. Judith Bernhardt always underestimated her daughter's extraordinary gifts. To be precise, she didn't even estimate them. She died at the age of fifty-three in 1876, by which time Sarah Bernhardt had become the leading luminary of the Comédie Française and the most talked-about actress in Paris. Jeanne was Youle's favorite child and Sarah's spectacular success left her unimpressed.

At the Conservatoire, the new pupil worked with fanatic zeal. Having made up her mind to become an actress, she was determined to be the greatest actress in the world. She practiced her diction exercises hours on end, memorized many more roles than those assigned to her and fairly acted her heart out in classroom recitations. She also put on an occasional non-curricular performance. Her mother supplied her with daily money for luncheon and transportation on the horse-drawn *imperiale* omnibus which thun-

dered its way along the Grand Boulevards. Sarah, going without
lunch for a few days and walking the sizable distance between
home and the Conservatory, would save up enough sous to hire a
cab for the simple satisfaction of pulling up before the Institute in
a style to astonish the other students.

Halfway through the two-year course Provost fell ill and Sarah
was transferred to Samson's class. This was by no means a disastrous move, as Samson was a superb teacher. He himself had studied under Talma, Napoleon's favorite actor, and he passed on to
his pupils what he'd learned from that great tragedian. For fifty
years Samson was in the front ranks of performers, seldom appearing in the grand roles but bringing such distinction to the secondary
ones it was said he played a valet as though he were playing the
master. The dramatist Legouvé wrote that "as an actor and author
Monsieur Samson was a man of true talent, but as a teacher he was
a man of true genius." He had taught many contemporary players
at the Français and years earlier had been one of the first to recognize the latent genius of Rachel when that extraordinary artist had
hardly emerged from being a street singer. Samson was her adviser throughout her all too brief career and Rachel would never
tackle a new role without his intensive coaching.

Sarah found Samson superbly stimulating as an instructor. The
one way in which he let her down, and it was a big letdown, was
in his choice of the two selections he assigned her for the *concours
de sortie*. This was a commencement competition in which each
member of the graduating class was called upon to perform two
scenes, one of tragedy, one of comedy, to vie for prizes awarded
by the faculty. The prizes were desperately coveted. A first in
tragedy might easily lead to a beginner's engagement at the Odéon
or possibly the Français, and even an honorable mention in comedy
could open doors in the Boulevard theatres. For Sarah's competitive numbers Samson chose as a comedy selection a scene from
l'Ecole des Vieillards, and for tragedy an excerpt from *La Fille du
Cid*, both by Casimir Delavigne. Sarah was crushed. Although she

was only seventeen, she had an instinctive sense of what was good theatre and what was bad. As a dramatist Casimir Delavigne wasn't exactly bad but he wasn't exactly good either. His plays, written in stilted verse and celebrating noble moments in history, had been extremely popular in their day but it was a day that had ended some twenty years before. Young Bernhardt sensed their outmoded quality and told Samson as much, but her professor stuck stubbornly to his choice. Sarah considered the choice nothing short of disaster and, sick at heart, studied up on the dismal parts.

Further disaster fell on the morning of Prize Day. Youle in an impulse of maternal concern suddenly decided to raise Sarah's morale by improving her appearance. To this end she called in her own coiffeur and ordered him to do something about her daughter's hair. What the coiffeur did was to make a complete botch of that unruly mane. The wretched man did his best to smooth out the kinks with oily pomade, an effort which gave it the appearance of a floor mop which hadn't been washed in months. He tried to arrange it into the falling ringlets so popular in the '60's. Sarah's hair was not only thick and fuzzy, it was stubbornly short, and the coiffeur himself was the first to admit that the curls looked like small sausages. He cursed, Youle scolded as though the state of her daughter's hair were an act of deliberate insubordination, and Sarah broke into racking sobs.

All the way to the Conservatoire her sobs continued and when eventually she stepped out before the faculty jury, she looked a holy horror. Having made a last-minute attempt to comb out the sausages, her hair now rose wildly up like Streuelpeter's. Her eyes were red-rimmed and when she started to speak her voice was a forlorn foghorn. Her first recitation, the bit from *La Fille du Cid*, was for tragedy, and she acquitted herself lamentably. Without having to glance at the glum faces of the judges or the bored expression of her mother stifling a yawn in the visitor's row, she knew this only too well. Then she started her comedy test and that inner spark of indomitable determination which whenever her spir-

its and circumstances were at rock bottom flashed like a self-renewing dynamo seemed to kindle her entire being. Her head rose
high, her voice rang clear and she played the little excerpt from
l'Ecole des Vieillards with such delicious delicacy and humor she
completely captured her audience. She also captured a second
prize. The first was won by Marie Lloyd,* a pretty young thing
about whom little is known other than that she went on to the
Comédie Française, where for thirty years she played soubrettes
with verve and no particular distinction. Marie Lloyd's chief
claim to immortality rests in her having won a prize ahead of the
country's most celebrated actress.

When little Bernhardt walked off the stage Samson uttered one
of those prophetic remarks the subsequent biographer has either
quoted or invented. "That young person is going to be either
sublime or execrable!" The young person, clutching her citation
of honorable mention, went off to the Green Room to join Mad-
ameame Guérard and Mademoiselle Brabender, who were waiting,
and immediately fainted. In a few moments she came to, her mother
joined them and the four of them returned in silence to the rue
Saint-Honoré. Only the clop-clopping of the horse was heard.
Youle was exasperated that any daughter of hers should not have
won two first prizes instead of one contemptible *accessit*. Sarah
too was exasperated, not with the jury, whose judgment she was
honest enough to recognize as being perfectly fair; her resentment
was aimed at the hairdresser, on whom she laid the entire blame for
her flop.

During the next few days, she lolled about the house, a listless
young tragedy queen. Youle, at a loss to plan her child's future,
brought up the name of the hirsute Mr. Berentz. Sarah, with a
dramatic shudder, asked her mother whether she, in similar circumstances, would have married Mr. Berentz. Judith Bernhardt
had the good humor to laugh and go on her pleasurable way. Then
one afternoon the clouds of gloom were magically dispersed. A

---

* Not to be confused with the later Marie Lloyd of English music-hall fame.

letter arrived delivered by hand. It bore the seal of the Comédie Française. If Sarah had received a personal message from the
Emperor, she could not have been more incredulously excited.
The communication was signed by Edouard Thierry, adminis-
trator-in-chief of the Théâtre Français, who requested her to appear before him for an interview on the following day.

The Duc de Morny, due perhaps to a little prodding from Youle
or Rosine, had been busy. Still amused by his idea of the Bernhardt girl becoming an actress, and possibly a very good one, he
had put in a favorable word about her with Camille Doucet, National Minister of Arts. Doucet had recommended her to Thierry,
who, glad to do a favor for the duc, had agreed to sign up his
protégée as a *pensionnaire*. That is the term for any beginner at the
House of Molière who must go through a number of probationary
years, during which time dismissal is possible. Then, if lucky and
talented, he or she may attain the status of *sociétaire*, or veteran
performer of high merit, who automatically becomes a share-
holder in the profits and has a voice in the governing administration.

Mademoiselle Bernhardt set forth for her interview and she set
forth in style. It was only a short distance to the Français, but to
get there she had wangled the use of Tante Rosine's *voiture à la-
quais*, a luxury eight-spring model with cockaded coachman and
footman on the box. It was a bright spring day and the tables outside the Café de la Régence were crowded with men in gleaming
toppers and women whose huge crinolines billowed like tents
about the tiny chairs. They must have looked up from their glasses
of bock, their ices or their games of dominoes to watch the passage of the stylish barouche with its strangely appealing occupant.
Bernhardt says in her Memoirs that she wore a cabbage-green dress
with black velvet trimming, a mantle of black grosgrain and a
broad-brimmed straw hat. Madame Guérard loaned her a frilly
sunshade and her mother gave her a turquoise ring. The carriage
pulled up before the noted stage door marked "Administration,"
the footman hopped down to offer his forearm and the young girl

jumped to the curb at the same moment that Beauvallet, the *doyen* or senior member of the Français, arrived to pick up his mail. Beauvallet vaguely recalled her having been a student at the Conservatoire and she had the satisfaction of hearing his thundering voice boom out, "My God, young lady! What an equipage you have!" The young lady, who didn't realize how overostentatious she was being, thanked him jauntily and tripped into the Administration office, where Thierry signed her up as a *pensionnaire* at a salary which was barely adequate to pay for three good meals a week.

During the Second Empire, a girl starting out on the stage was presumed to have the financial backing of a "protector." Beginners at the Français like apprentices in the Opéra ballet often as not formed a sort of stable to be looked over by Paris' leading *noceurs*. No doubt Edouard Thierry thought that the duc was "interested" in little Bernhardt. After all Morny was known as a leading rake himself. One of the more racy rumors concerning his "interests" has it that his valet made a small fortune in blood money after stealing a casket in which the duc kept a treasure trove of photographs of his many conquests, all taken in the nude except for some tasty floral arrangements covering the more erotic portions of their anatomy — at least such is the assertion of Edmond de Goncourt in his occasionally outrageous journal.

There was, of course, no photograph of Sarah in that collection. She was barely eighteen and she had as yet no "protector."

On a hot day in August, Sarah Bernhardt stood in the cool arcade of the Français staring up at the yellow playbills which advertised forthcoming productions. One of them bore the unbelievable announcement that the program for August, 1862, would include: "*Iphigénie* by Jean Racine. For the debut of Mademoiselle Sarah Bernhardt in the role of Iphigénie."

The debut was by no means sensational. It wasn't even good. Before she made her first entrance, she was seized with one of her terrible attacks of stage fright. Provost, her former Conservatoire

professor, was in the wings to give her encouragement and his terrified pupil asked him if it ever happened that *le trac* could para-
lyze an actor into speechless immobility. Provost smiled and said,
"No, never," then as her cue came up he gave her a reassuring shove.
She went on stage shaking like an aspen and all through the first
act she rattled off her lines at such speed she turned most of Racine's noble alexandrines into so much gibberish. The audience
was coldly indifferent. The only aspect of the new debutante that
impressed them was her extreme and, to them, grotesque thinness.
She had pleaded with the official costumer to put sleeves in her
gown but was firmly told that sleeves in a classical robe would be
a rank anachronism. When at one given moment, the suppliant
Iphigenia stretched out her skinny little arms toward Achilles, a
wag up in the gallery called out, "Watch out, Monsieur, or you'll
inpale yourself upon her toothpicks!" a comment which brought
down the house. The act came mercifully to an end and Sarah
ran from the set. Provost, still standing off stage, was dolefully
shaking his head. All he could find to say was, *"Pourquoi? Pourquoi?"* Sarah, shattered with shame, asked if he could ever forgive
her. "Yes, I can forgive you," he said, "and you'll eventually
forgive yourself. But Racine in his grave never will."

Provost was wrong. Sarah Bernhardt was to be the most thrilling interpreter of France's sublime tragedy writer, not excepting
Rachel. And when she performed his tortured and terrifying *Phèdre*, "Racine," as her granddaughter has written, "always stood
watch in the wings."

But that was to be far in the future. On the present painful occasion, Sarah, with a mental picture of Jean Racine heaving up the
sod at Père Lachaise, stifled a sob and fled to her dressing room.
Grabbing a stick of grease paint, she scrawled a defiant *"quand
même!"* across her mirror. The gesture released some pent-up
adrenalin and she played the remaining acts adequately though by
no means remarkably. The press, the next day, was indifferent and
the powerful critic of *Le Temps,* Francisque Sarcey, who in Paris

was as much feared as in New York George Jean Nathan was to be, wrote that the new *pensionnaire* "carries herself well and pronounces with perfect precision. That is all that can be said about her at the moment."

During the ensuing weeks she appeared as Henrietta in Molière's *Les Femmes Savantes* and as Hippolyte in his *l'Etourdi*. She also played the title role in Scribe's *Valérie* opposite Coquelin, who was then one of the younger players and yet to come into his magnificent own. None of these performances was particularly good. The directors and *sociétaires* thought that Thierry had made a mistake in hiring the girl and Sarcey dismissed her as being pretty and insignificant and added: "It is quite natural that among the debutantes we are forced to see there should be some who do not succeed."

Sarah's sensationalism manifested itself in two off-stage performances. Basil Woon says that one day, arriving for a matinee, the stage doorkeeper addressed her as "Little Bernhardt," a flippancy which for some reason outraged her, and she broke her parasol over the man's head in a blow that opened his scalp, making it bleed profusely. At the sight, Sarah, in dramatic remorse, ran for a glass of water, then tore off strips of her own petticoat with which to dress and bandage the wound. Some twenty years later, the doorkeeper, because of age, was forced to retire. Heartbroken and penniless he sought out Madame Sarah for help. It is characteristic of this uncharacterizable woman that in an impulse of magnanimity she instructed Pitou, her secretary, to purchase a cottage for the old boy in his native Normandy and to set him up with a trust fund for the remaining days of his life.

Sarah's second performance of off-stage melodrama resulted in her eventual dismissal from the Français. This occurred during the ritual known as *La Cérémonie*, which was held every January 15, the birthday of Molière. In this traditional function the bust of the beloved comic writer was set up stage center and two by two the players of his House each in the costume of one of his characters came on to pay tribute by placing a palm leaf at the foot of the shaft and performing a brief scene from one of the comedies. Sarah as the youngest member of the company was given the duty of merely walking on with a laurel wreath which Beauvallet, as dean of the troupe, was to accept from her and place reverently on the marble curls of the Founder.

Little Régina Bernhardt, who wanted to be in on everything her older sister did, had for days begged, nagged and implored to be allowed to watch the ceremony, and Sarah, who adored the child, had finally agreed to take her along. Either the regulations regarding backstage visitors were lenient at the Français or Sarah invented her own for she arrived to take her place in the line-up of tribute payers with the laurel wreath in one hand and the nine-year-old led by the other, it being understood that when Sarah walked on stage Régina would remain quietly behind in the wings. Standing directly in front of them was Madame Nathalie, a formidable actress of colossal build whom a contemporary writer described as "Nathalie the fat, the solemn, the old and wicked Sociétaire of the Comédie Française." For her appearance in the ritual Madame Nathalie wore a voluminous garment of purple velvet which looked more like a Good Friday cathedral drapery than a seventeenth-century comedy costume. Time came for her entrance and the monumental lady started majestically forth only to be yanked into sudden immobility. Régina, in all innocence, had taken a firm stance on her train. Nathalie turned ponderously, saw Régina, grabbed her by the shoulders and shoved her wrathfully off the train and into a stucco pillar whose sharp edge cut a gash in the child's forehead. Terrified, Régina called out to her sister that she hadn't done it on purpose, that it was the big cow who had pushed her, and began yelling, "*Vache! Vache!*" at the top of her lungs. As that term in French bears the same opprobrium as the shorter English term for a female dog, one wonders where the little angel had picked it up. Madame Nathalie then started to vent her homeric wrath on Sarah, who silenced her with a well-aimed and violent slap on her multiple jowls.

Madame Nathalie toppled and fell in a seeming dead faint onto a nearby actor who, at the impact, buckled under as gracefully as possible. The backstage commotion was something worthy of Molière himself. Actors and stage hands gathered about the prostrate Nathalie. Someone started pouring water on her lofty brow, at which she sat up to scream that her make-up was being ruined, then went back into her prone position, whether still on top of the actor or not we do not know.

The blow not only felled Madame Nathalie, it rocked the House of Molière to its foundations. Never since its charter from Louis XIV in 1658 had a first-year *pensionnaire* dared defy a long-established *sociétaire*, let alone use physical violence. If the members of the Français were outraged, the members of the Paris press were delighted. They wrote gleeful accounts of the fracas, cartoonists pictured it and *La Gifle* became the talk of the boulevards. The public had at last taken notice of Sarah Bernhardt. It was not exactly in the fashion on which she had counted and she was amazed, not agreeably, yet not altogether disagreeably. At barely nineteen the showman in her sensed that even adverse publicity was better than no publicity at all. This was her first press story — the start of a vast coverage that was to continue increasingly during the next sixty years.

The following day Mademoiselle Bernhardt was summoned to report to Monsieur Thierry in his administration bureau. Peremptorily he ordered her to make a public apology to Madame Nathalie, and peremptorily she refused unless Madame Nathalie were first to make a public apology to Régina. Worse, she laughed in Thierry's face. Hoping she'd come to her senses and that the whole affair would blow over, he kept her on in the company for a week or two. Although he would have been the last to admit it, the report of the fracas had centered fresh attention on the revered old house. The general public were coming in droves and the *gratin* were sending their footmen to enquire when the new young actress would next appear.

She didn't appear there again — that is, not for ten years. Thierry had cast her for a part in a forthcoming and not too important production, but on the day of her first rehearsal, Madame Nathalie descended upon the manager demanding that he withhold any further appearances of this insolent upstart until she had made her public apology. Madame Nathalie was a powerful woman and Thierry acquiesced. Sarah, however, did not apologize and without further discussion Thierry demanded her resignation.

3.

~~~~~~~~~~~~~~~~~~~~~~~~~~~~~

GODDESS OF
THE LEFT BANK

FOR ALL Sarah Bernhardt's stubborn pride, her enforced resignation from the leading theatre of France was a bitter blow.
Her family, who during her term there had made little effort to attend her performances, thought her conduct had been
disgraceful. They and all her acquaintances for that matter kept
repeating, "One does not walk away from the Comédie Française,"
until it sounded like sing-song. For nearly four years she was in
the situation which jobless actors, as a sop to their wounded self-
esteem, call "being available." She was restless, footloose and anything but fancy free.

It was probably about this period of her life that she started
taking on lovers. It seemed the thing to do. To her there was
nothing immoral in such behavior. After all, her mother and aunt
had hardly set her an example of shining virtue. They had even
at one time discussed training her for their gainful but precarious
profession at which she could never have been a success. She possessed none of the requisite qualities for a *grande courtisane*. She
would never have developed a kept woman's sense of maneuvering
nor her calculated submission, any more than she could have followed the advice of Tante Rosine, herself an expert at keeping her
keeper, who exhorted her to "remember that a lover is a lord and
master. It's a lucrative form of slavery." Sarah Bernhardt could
have been a slave to no one. Her lovers may have given her jewelry and other expensive gifts, even occasional funds, but she
never took one on for mercenary purposes. Moreover her liaisons

were not primarily with men of wealth or influence but with persons of distinction in intellect or creative activity. For any idle drifter no matter how rich or of how exalted a social position, she had nothing but the utmost contempt. To her an affair was a matter of the mind and heart. At least she pretended to the lucky man and doubtless to herself that such was the case. And she may well have pretended, for few of these fleeting adventures meant very much to her. She has been called a female Don Juan, but the lists of her amours have been grossly exaggerated.

Possibly her first lover was Emile de Kératry, an officer of hussars, a gentleman who was at home in politics, the best clubs and the Court circle. He was good-looking and amusing and had the added attraction of an irresistible uniform. After a brief liaison she and Kératry remained good friends, as she was to become with many of her subsequent lovers.

Even at eighteen, Sarah Bernhardt was not one to waste much time on amorous dalliance. Acting was her life's purpose and she was determined to make a success of it. She had given herself a tough assignment. Everyone in town knew about her assault upon Madame Nathalie, further stories about her outbursts of savage temper had gone the rounds and no manager would have anything to do with her. Eventually through some wire-pulling on the part of her godfather, Régis Lavolie, she was able to land a job at the Gymnase, a popular Boulevard theatre which under a clever director named Montigny was presenting a series of highly successful, light-weight comedies.

The atmosphere at the Gymnase was as frivolously fashionable as that at the Comédie had been solemnly traditional. Backstage the cast talked gossip and paid scant attention to the Bernhardt girl. She understudied the two leading ladies, Blanche Pierson, a blonde beauty, and Céline Montaland, a luscious brunette, both of whom, though hardly older than she, were already launched on their way to stardom, Blanche Pierson in particular, who was to become one of the most popular actresses of the Français. Sarah appeared in two inconsequential comedies in which she was hardly noticed. As before, it was off stage that she gained public notice. The setting was at the Court of the Tuileries, the occasion a reception for some visiting royalty. As entertainment the Imperial Chamberlain had asked Montigny to send in a group from the Gymnase, each to give a recitation before their Majesties and guests. The kindly Camille Doucet, who had been instrumental in getting young Bernhardt into the Théâtre Français and who still believed in her talent, had requested Montigny to include her in the group. For her bit in the performance, Sarah had picked out two poems by Victor Hugo.

To recite Victor Hugo before the Bonapartist Court at that time was the equivalent of what today would be reciting Karl Marx before the Colonial Dames. Hugo was a highly controversial figure, a hero to the liberals, anathema to the imperialists. Violently outspoken in his opposition to the existing regime, he was living in self-imposed exile on the island of Guernsey, writing his scathing denunciations of the Emperor and calling his fellow citizens to revolt against the papier-mâché Empire. "Sons of France!" was his cry, "you elect who suffer for the Patrie!" His poems were brought out in Paris under the title of *Les Châtiments* (The Chastisements), which the authorities did their best to suppress. A pamphlet in which he satirized the reigning colorless Bonaparte as *Napoléon le Petit* was actually banned by the censor — which meant that forbidden copies sold by the hundreds. Sarah, who at the age of nineteen knew as much about politics as she knew about higher mathematics, had no remote idea of the implications her selections might convey. She merely thought Hugo's poetry was pretty and very moving. When her turn came, she stepped onto the platform, made her reverence and started *Oceano Nox*, a turgid lament about sailors drowning at sea. At her announcement of the poem and its author, the Emperor and Empress froze and remained frozen. The members of the Court also dutifully went into deep freeze. Sarah thought their silence was due to the sadness of the subject and blithely announced a less tragic number, *Feuilles d'Automne*, again by the proscribed exile. Without giving her a chance to start, Napoleon rose, offered his arm to Eugénie and walked out of the ballroom, followed by Court and guests.

Sarah, in complete bewilderment, stood stock still — but not for long. The stage manager in charge of the Gymnase group descended upon her and, grabbing her brutally by the wrist, vented on her such a tirade of invective and blasphemy the crystal pendants of the giant chandeliers fairly jangled. According to Louis Verneuil, he was cut short by the appearance of a distinguished-looking young man, handsome as the day, who in a voice of ringing authority demanded that he let go of the girl immediately and shut up. He would not, he declared, tolerate anyone using such vile language in the presence of a lady — especially a young and pretty lady. He turned out to be Prince Henri de Ligne, scion of a noble Belgian family. After silencing the stage manager, he kissed Mademoiselle's slender hand and departed. It is a pretty account, maybe spurious, of Sarah Bernhardt's initial encounter with the future father of her child.

The young actress' final appearance at the Gymnase was in *Un Mari qui lance sa Femme*, a silly comedy by Ernest La Biche, author of *The Italian Straw Hat*, and Raymond Deslandes, author of nothing noteworthy. In this she played a giddy Russian princess named Dumchinka, a role in which she had to dance, skip, sing, eat, giggle and behave in a generally idiotic manner. Her performance was embarrassingly bad. Unfortunately Julie Bernhardt happened to attend the show that night. She was horrified to think that people in the audience might realize she was the ingenue's mother. Her only comment as they drove home that night was, "My poor child, you were ridiculous as your absurd Russian princess!"

Sarah was plunged into despair. Alone in her bedroom she brooded over prospects of suicide. She went so far as to run up to Madame Guérard's flat to ask *mon p'tit dame* for some laudanum. Needless to say, the dear startled lady refused to give her any.

Back at her open window, she stared down at the paving blocks below contemplating a death leap. These morbid speculations were cut short by the unexpected appearance of Dumas *père*. He had been present at her lamentable stage performance, had sensed her state of desperation and had felt a sudden compulsion to go talk to the girl before she did anything rash. Realizing she was on the verge of a complete emotional breakdown, he is said to have told her she must cut her stakes for the time being and start off immediately, that very night, for some other country, preferably Spain. It was the sort of reckless decision which appealed to Sarah's spirit of adventure. She scribbled a note to Montigny telling him not to expect her at the theatre any more, winding up with, "have pity on a poor crazy girl." Victorien Sardou, who was to become the almost exclusive Bernhardt playwright for many years, was in Montigny's office when the note was delivered. With a snort, Montigny passed it over to him. "What's this?" said Sardou, "the little madcap who slapped a *sociétaire?* She's very amusing." "Perhaps," growled Montigny, "but not for managers."

In her memoirs, Sarah Bernhardt says that she did set forth for Spain then and there, determined to change her course of life and perhaps marry a bullfighter, that in Spain she encountered bandits and was befriended by the Vice-Consul and his lady, who gave her letters to the fashionable set in Madrid, where she was wined and dined and escorted by grandees to *corridas* — a colorful narration with a suspiciously Munchausen flavor.

Maybe she did go to Spain. Most biographers agree that wherever she first went, she ended up in Belgium. Her granddaughter says that the very night of her decision to escape from Paris, the elder Dumas put her on a train bound for Brussels armed with an introduction to some friends named Bruce. Lysiane Bernhardt's report of her first encounter with Henri de Ligne is even prettier than Verneuil's. She claims that they met at a masked ball given by the Bruces, Sarah costumed as Queen Elizabeth, the prince gotten up as Hamlet. There was the usual operetta scene in a con-

servatory to the accompaniment of distant music, de Ligne en-
treating her to take off her mask and she coyly refusing. At the
finish of the final waltz, he is said to have handed her a single perfect rose, its thorny stem wrapped in his own fine lawn handkerchief which, upon later inspection in her hotel room, she found
bore an embroidered coronet and below it the letter "L." Next day
she rode in an open victoria down the fashionable Avenue Louise,
wearing a billowing gown, a wide-brimmed Winterhalter hat and
pinned to her lace fichu the perfect single rose. On a gleaming
pure-bred, who should ride up and rein in alongside but the handsome Hamlet of the ball! He dispatched his groom to fetch
his runabout, into which he lifted the blushing Queen Elizabeth,
and drove her directly to the palatial house in the Avenue de la
Toison d'Or which he shared with his family who, most oppor-
tunely, had gone for a month to their country estate. Across the
events of that day and the ensuing ones, a velvet curtain is discreetly
drawn. Lysiane Bernhardt reprints a letter written to the elder
Dumas by Mr. Bruce which reads in part:

> And so, my dear Dumas, your young friend Mlle. Sarah Bern-
> hardt has conquered Brussels. At our ball she captured the heart
> of the Prince de L. . . I think they've been meeting. Do you re-
> sent my offering the girl too much to distract her from her trou-
> bles or do you congratulate me for giving an actress a means of
> freeing herself from prejudice? . . .
> P.S. I have just returned from her hotel. Sarah has not shown
> up for eight days. It seems that she is traveling with "friends."
> I fear these "friends" merge into one person and that they have
> not traveled further than the Avenue de la Toison d'Or. That's
> what happens when you let a dragon-fly loose with a butterfly.

The idyll, wherever it took place, was cut short by a dispatch
from Madame Guérard saying that Judith Bernhardt was seriously
ill with a heart attack. Sarah in frantic concern took the next train
for Paris, concern over leaving her prince and concern for the
mother who, in spite of Youle's indifference, Sarah loved with in-

termittent bursts of fierce devotion. She found her mother over the attack and well on her way to recovery. She also found, after a few weeks, that she herself was pregnant. She told no one. She didn't even write the news to her lover for fear he'd feel trapped into sharing the responsibility.

In spite of all mounting complications, her ambitions for the stage were undiminished. She haunted the theatrical offices, in each and every one of which she tasted the bitter humiliation of being peremptorily turned down. Her shockingly unprofessional flight from the Gymnase had added to her reputation of being un- reliable, if not slightly demented, and most managers wouldn't even grant her an interview. None of these brush-offs weakened that spirit of *quand même*. She still gave way to outbursts of anger or moments of affected bravura, but her general bearing was one of proud distinction. Someone called her "a *cabotine* [ham actress] cast as a gipsy but pretending to double as a pampered princess."

For five months she was jobless. Eventually, her state of preg- nancy becoming more and more apparent, she realized she'd have to tell her mother. Judith Bernhardt, who by now had taken on that curious bourgeois respectability of the retired *courtisane*, was outraged. She screamed that she would have no little bastard born under her roof, ignoring the fact that she herself had borne three little bastards each by a different father. She ordered her sinful daughter to get out of her home and the sooner the better. Sarah found a small flat in the rue Duphot for which she departed, taking Régina with her and leaving no address. The mother was glad to be rid of the two of them. She could now lavish her full attention on Jeanne. Madame Guérard also moved into the rue Duphot. There on December 22, 1864, attended only by her faithful *mon p'tit dame* the twenty-year-old actress gave birth to Maurice Bern- hardt.

Soon after, too soon for the good of her health, she started forth to find work for the support of the baby she adored. Her funds were depleted and although Madame Guérard helped out as best she could, it was not enough. A job finally came up at the Porte-Saint-Martin, a theatre specializing in melodramas and extravaganzas which were of a superior quality due to the clever producer-director Marc Fournier. It wasn't much of a job. She played parts which were practically walk-ons and understudied the other actresses. A break came with *La Biche au Bois*, a musical billed as a *vaudeville feërique* with scenic effects as pretty as a candy box, a Madame Debay as the Princesse Desirée and a Madame Ugade of the Opéra Comique as the Fairy Prince. Halfway through the run, Madame Debay fell ill and Marc Fournier took the risk of putting Sarah on as substitute. It was quite a risk, as the Princesse Desirée was called upon to sing a few numbers including a duet with the Fairy Prince. Madame Ugade was a trained singer and Sarah was not, but through some vocal trickery of half speaking, half intoning the words in a manner which she herself admitted sounded at times like a provincial actress reciting Racine, she got by and her name appeared on the bill posters.

Fortunately her financial problems for the time were solved by the arrival in Paris of Prince Henri de Ligne. Through the theatre he had found out her rue Duphot address and had immediately moved in with her. Far from being horrified over the arrival of his infant son, he was filled with happy emotion, for he was still deeply in love with Sarah. She was still deeply, passionately in love with him. A month or so passed blissfully, so much so that de Ligne made up his mind that the bliss must be permanently and legally continued. He went to Brussels and faced his family with the shattering announcement that he wanted to marry an unknown half-Jewish actress by whom he had had an illegitimate child. One can imagine the impact of this thunderbolt. There were the expected horrified refusals, parental tears and threats to disown and cut him off without a sou.

The young man pointed out that Madame Tallien, a turn-of-the-century *courtisane*, had been socially accepted when she became the Princesse de Chimay and that La Païva, a contemporary "grand horizontal" had attained respectability by marrying the Count of Donnersmark. The fact that Madame Tallien had gone to bed with every important man in the Directoire and that La Païva was not only notorious for her erotic activities but was suspected of being a spy for the Germans hardly strengthened his argument. He protested that anyway his beloved was *not* a *courtisane* and never had been — all of which left his parents unmoved. He hurried back to Paris still determined to marry Sarah no matter what the consequences. After a few days, he was called away on business affairs and during his absence there arrived Henri's distinguished uncle, General de Ligne, who had been dispatched to break up his nephew's shocking liaison and save the honor of the family. The impressive old gentleman strode into Sarah's sitting room prepared to confront a bedizened huzzy and found instead an exquisite young mother, simply gowned, serenely playing with her baby.

Anyone can improvise the ensuing scene or, failing a gift for improvisation, let him read the libretto for the second act of *Traviata*. The outcome was that although completely captivated by Sarah's candor and charm, he was adamant in regard to the family stand and he took his leave with Sarah's heartbroken promise to give up her lover for the sake of his future. Henri returned to Paris and the renunciation scene took place. (It might perhaps be uncharitable to point out that when Madame Sarah related these events to Louis Verneuil and subsequently to her granddaughter, she had already performed *La Dame aux Camélias* well over a thousand times.) Sarah reminded the prince that marriage with her would mean loss for him of position and fortune. He protested with a noble variation of "all for love and the world well lost!" She then found courage to say that much as she adored him, she could never be happy with domesticity in a garret. Moreover her aim in life was to be a great and successful theatrical star, and she added that she already had an offer from the Odéon. The young man listened with incredulity which changed into fury. He didn't, as in the play, fling a pack of cards in her face, but he flung a stream of bitter invective. He called her a worthless *cabotine* who cared for nothing but sensational notoriety, a vulgar harlot and further unfortunate epithets. At the finish of his tirade he stormed from the room slamming the door behind him and Sarah fell senseless onto the floor. For several days she lay in a *bona fide* coma cared for by Madame Guérard who despaired of her life. But then, Madame Guérard was the apprehensive type.

There are other versions of the Bernhardt-de Ligne affair too numerous and some of them too preposterous to repeat. To give a brief résumé of Basil Woon's, he states that the prince remained Sarah's lover until he found out she was pregnant, at which awkward disclosure, he immediately jilted her. After little Maurice's birth she is said to have sought him out in his Paris apartment, babe in arms, to beg for assistance, sent in a note via the footman and waited miserably in the outer lobby. The prince is credited with having scribbled a reply on the back of Sarah's card reading, "I know a woman named Bernhardt but I do not know her son." Sarah persisted in her entreaties to see her demon lover, who finally appeared and coldly disclaimed any responsibilities of parenthood. Sarah swore by all she held sacred that he was indeed the father, to which he retorted with the remark Augustine Brohan had already made famous about sitting down on a bundle of thorns and being unable to know which one has pierced you. Woon's account is obviously lifted from Marie Colombier's libelous *Memoirs of Sarah Barnum*, a vindictive and scurrilous book which for the most part is a collection of distasteful lies and of which more will be told.

It would be senseless to attempt to prove which account is the true one. The great show-woman told hers directly to Louis Verneuil and to her granddaughter. At least, she told them what she wanted told in turn to posterity. I prefer, in respect for her wishes, to stick by the *Lady of the Camellias* version.

There is no question that Sarah Bernhardt's adventure with the father of her son was the great love affair of her life, which remained sacred and nostalgically painful in her memory as her "abiding wound." If she romanticized it over the years, who can blame her? What woman doesn't romanticize her better amorous recollections?

She never discussed Maurice's parentage with anyone although she never tried to pretend that his birth was legitimate. To people tactless enough to express curiosity on the subject, she had been known to remark, in her usual reckless fashion, "I could never make up my mind whether his father was Gambetta, Victor Hugo or General Boulanger." As late as 1917 she told one starry-eyed young actress in her company — whom she swore to utmost secrecy — that the true father of her son was not the Prince de Ligne but the Duke of Clarence. The fact that the Duke of Clarence, like his supposed son, was also born in 1864 adds color to this statement.

When Bernhardt told de Ligne that she had received an offer from the Odéon, it was partly true. She had gone after it following her interview with the General and her heartrending decision to break with his nephew. In desperate need to find an immediate job and bury herself in work, she had gone to the Ministry of Fine Arts and her old friend Camille Doucet begging him to bring pressure at the Odéon as he had at the Français. This she knew would be a big step forward in her career.

The Odéon on the Left Bank near the Luxembourg was known as the Second Comédie Française. It too was a National Theatre but far less tradition-bound and more enterprising than the grand old establishment across the Seine. It too was a repertory house presenting the classics but in more experimental style, and new plays were constantly being tried out. The ticket price was cheaper and the clientele less fashionable but composed of knowledgeable theatre-lovers. To have a job at the Odéon was regarded as an enviable distinction. When young Bernhardt made her urgent request, Doucet had looked grave. It would not be easy, he said. The entire theatrical world who knew nothing about her talent, knew at least about her forced exit from the

Comédie, about her skipping her obligations at the Gymnase. The only name she had made for herself was that of an irresponsible flibbertigibbet with a temper so uncontrollable as to be at times phrenetic. He scolded her like a grieved but tender father. Sarah shed a torrent of repentant tears and promised that once in the Odéon, she'd be the model of good behavior and Doucet with considerable misgivings gave her a letter to Félix Duquesnel, who, with his partner Charles-Marie de Chilly, ran this excellent theatre.

Duquesnel was a gracious gentleman and a spirited director who handled his actors with tact and warm good humor. Sarah found him completely delightful, and he must have found her so for he wrote of their first meeting:

> I beheld before me the most ideally charming creature one can dream of. Sarah at twenty-two baffles all description. She was not pretty, she was better than pretty. It was mid June . . . She wore a China silk blouse of a delicate shade with beaded embroidery, her arms and shoulders thinly veiled, a feather fan at her belt and on her head a fine straw "skimmer" trimmed with tiny bells that tinkled at the slightest movement.

He wanted to give her a contract on the spot but said that the ultimate decision would have to be up to his senior partner, into whose office he conducted her. The young woman's heart sank when she recognized Chilly, who all too clearly recognized her. He had been present when she had tried out for a part at the Ambigu Theatre and under unfortunate conditions. The part was that of a shepherdess in something called *La Bergère d'Ivry* written by Lambert Thibout, a friend of hers who had recommended her to Faille, the doddering old director of the Ambigu. Faille called her to give a reading on a bare stage lit only by a smoking kerosene lantern which served as a work light. At the finish, Faille shook his head and said, "My child, you have no qualifications for the theatre." Chilly, who had an interest in the show, had been watching from the darkened house. His single comment was, "Whoever saw a shepherdess so thin?"

Chilly was as loutish and disagreeable as Duquesnel was courteous and affable. He listened to Duquesnel's recommendations, glanced through Doucet's letter, then insolently looking the girl up and down snorted, "If I were alone in this, I wouldn't give you a contract." "If you were alone in this, Monsieur," she retorted, "I wouldn't sign it."

She did sign and for the sum of 150 francs a month. Her opening role was that of Silvia in Marivaux's *Jeu de l'Amour et du Hasard*, and she was not good. The playing of eighteenth-century comedy offers a problem of trifling but precise stylization which was never her forte. That was to be based on an inner power of fundamental sincerity which was out of place in period frivolity. Moreover in Fragonard costume she looked ridiculous. Dumas, who still took a fatherly interest in young Bernhardt and who was attending the performance, commented, "She has the head of a virgin and the body of a broomstick." Chilly wanted to cancel her engagement immediately but Duquesnel still had belief in her, so much so that he volunteered to pay her salary out of his own pocket if Chilly would give her a further chance. Her next appearance was as Armande in Molière's *Femmes Savantes*, again stylized comedy and again she was not good. But she was better, and Chilly was a bit less contemptuous, although he still made cutting comments about her skinniness, referring to her as "a needle automated by four pins." Sarah more than once was tempted to give him a sock in the pudgy face, but she remembered her promise to Doucet and controlled herself. In *King Lear*, Sarah proved an exquisite and touching Cordelia and her prospects brightened.

Her first personal hit was as the young boy Zacharie in Racine's *Athalie*. This was to be a special production using Mendelssohn themes in the background and, as a startling innovation, the lines of the Greek chorus, which is usually omitted, being semi-chanted by a group of music students from the Conservatoire. It was an interesting idea which didn't exactly work out. The students couldn't seem to come in on the proper cue and when they did, they sounded rather like a class of medical graduates reciting the Hippocratic oath. The Comédie Française actor Beauvallet, who had been brought over as director, gave up trying to get the desired effect, dismissed the students and entrusted all the words of the chorus to Sarah. Standing apart at one side of the stage, this wisp of a girl in her young boy's tunic spoke the words in a voice of pure music, and the result was magical. The audience picked her out for special applause and next day the press was warm with praise, the sour Sarcey writing that young Mademoiselle Bernhardt "charmed her audience like a little Orpheus."

Her big break came with the 1868 revival of *Kean*, the elder Dumas' drama concerning the colorful and periodically mad British tragedian. Sarah was cast in the leading feminine role of Anna Damby. The opening night before the play began, a demonstration was staged in the audience which all but grew into an uncontrollable riot. This was a period when Victor Hugo, still an exile on the island of Guernsey, had become, in the eyes of the radicals and the liberals, a hero and the torchbearer of democracy. The fact that his plays were banned by the imperial government merely fanned the fervor of his supporters. That night a delegation of students and other ardent "Hugolians" had bought out a large portion of the house for the purpose of putting on a noisy demonstration to protest the fact that the Odéon, a state theatre, should be giving them Dumas instead of a work of the Master. To add to their indignation, Dumas himself appeared in a box accompanied by his current mistress, a highly unpopular creature named Ada Montrin. There were boos and catcalls and cries of "Down with Dumas! Give us Hugo!" The three hammer blows signaling the moment for the rising curtain failed to quiet the uproar. Sarah, listening in the wings, was shaking with apprehension. The play started and the speeches of the beginners were inaudible above the din. Sarah's cue came to go on and she was sure she could never brave it. But somehow she did. Ashen under her make-up and fragile as a reed in Anna Damby's 1810 costume, her appearance made no impression on the demonstrators out front, who continued to whistle, stamp and demand their author. Then all at once terror gave way to her extraordinary zest for meeting a challenge. The young actress stepped artlessly down to the footlights and held out her hands in a gesture of disarming appeal. Gradually the audience grew quiet and in a clear, candid tone she said: "Friends, you wish to defend the cause of justice. Are you doing it by making Monsieur Dumas responsible for the banishment of Monsieur Hugo?" It did the trick. The audience broke into good-natured laughter and applause. The rioting stopped and the play proceeded without further interruption except for occasional bursts of spontaneous appreciation for the remarkable performance Sarah found herself giving. She played like a dream, fluid, exquisitely moving and with a simplicity which for those days was startlingly "natural." At the finish, Duquesnel sent her out to take a solo curtain call and she heard for the first time the intoxicating thunder of a personal ovation.

Duquesnel was rapturous. Even his surly partner was impressed. "You were good," he exclaimed, "wonderfully good!" and he went so far as to address her by the intimate second person singular. Sarah, also employing the *tu*, responded sweetly, "You find I've grown plumper, Monsieur?" The management informed her that her salary would be increased to 250 francs a month, and Chilly told Duquesnel he need no longer pay anything out of his own pocket; he furthermore could get back his previous payments from the theatre treasury. Old Dumas came puffing backstage to kiss Sarah's hand over and over and declare he would write a new play especially for her. But he was to die in two years before doing so. For the first of what would be thousands of subsequent times, a crowd of admirers gathered to cheer and toss flowers as Sarah Bernhardt made her exit through the stage door. "Back in my room that night," she wrote, "I felt so rich . . . so rich I was afraid of robbers."

From now on she was one of the most popular actresses of the

Odéon. Her rapidly growing public was largely composed of students, artists and Left Bank literati who began claiming her as "Our Sarah." When her name appeared on the bill posters, the house was usually a sell-out. And her name appeared often, as the members of the Odéon rotated in many roles. Nine or ten different bills were presented every week at the Odéon and some fifty or sixty new productions a year. It was a tough schedule but the troupe was made up of ambitious young enthusiasts and diligent seasoned "pros" who thrived on creative work. Bernhardt gloried in every one of the six years she was there. She wrote of those days as a member of *Le Théâtre des Jeunes*:

> Ah, the dear Odéon! It was the theatre I adored the most. And I left it with regret. We all loved one another, everyone was gay. And Duquesnel was a director full of wit, courtesy and youth. I thought back to the few months I had spent at the Comédie Française surrounded by people who were stilted, gossipy, jealous. At the Gymnase one talked nothing but dresses and hats, frivolities . . . matters miles from art. The Odéon was a dream come true. We thought only of producing plays. We rehearsed morning and afternoon . . . all the time. I adored every moment. And I worked hard . . . always ready to go on as a replacement for I knew every role.

Sarah Bernhardt's prodigious memory was receiving its early training. She could memorize a part merely by reading it through four times with complete concentration, planning her interpretation as she went along — "here I do this" and "here I speak in such and such a manner" — and after a fifth reading she knew every word. Even in her later years and old age, she kept letter perfect in mind at least twenty-five roles of her vast repertory and could start reciting a speech from any one of them without needing once to refer back to a script.

What man or men contributed to the young woman's love life during her Odéon days is neither here nor there. As one writer put it: "Her private life does not matter for it had no true reality."

The biographical reports read like so much guesswork. Some claim that Félix Duquesnel took more than a managerial interest in her and he may well have. He was exceptionally attractive and he had, what would especially have appealed to the actress, a brilliantly stimulating sense of theatre. Whether Duquesnel was her lover or not, he remained her close friend and adviser. Madame Pierre Berton asserts, and with a certain surprising pride, that her husband, then a handsome young lead at the Odéon, was the only person at that time to receive what is euphemistically called her "favors." Pierre Berton was gifted and intelligent, a fine actor and a moderately good author. He was later to write the highly successful play, *Zaza*, if it may be said that such distinction constitutes a claim to fame.

As Sarah's success grew, so did the rumors about her. One which went the rounds linked her name with that of the Emperor's cousin, Prince Napoleon, son of King Jerome and known to his friends by the skittish name of "Plon-Plon"! Although a direct heir to the Bonaparte succession, he was a liberal member of the National Assembly. He was also a popular clubman and an enthusiastic patron of the *demi-monde*, one of the beneficiaries of his patronage being Cora Pearl, who has gone down in history as the lady who, at a stag dinner in the Grand Seize, was borne in on a mammoth serving platter, stark naked and blowing kisses. On his less giddy side, "Plon-Plon" was, like his sister Princesse Mathilde, keenly appreciative of music and the arts. He got into the custom of crossing the river to the Odéon evenings when Sarah was playing and he attracted with him a fashionable clientele from the Right Bank curious to see the new young actress in whom Prince Napoleon was interested. Whatever constituted "Plon-Plon's" interest, he was a frequent caller in Mademoiselle Bernhardt's dressing room.

The story went the rounds after an incident during one of his visits when a certain Paul Deshayes, an outspoken anti-imperialist who had been calling previously, burst in without knocking to retrieve his gloves which he had left behind. He recognized Prince Napoleon and without any apologies remarked boorishly, "You are sitting on my gloves, Monsieur." The Prince, outraged at his impudence, pulled the gloves out from under his somewhat ample posterior and contemptuously flung them on the floor saying, "I thought the chair was clean!" Sarah picked up the gloves and handing them to Deshayes said to "Plon-Plon" with a delivery as though quoting a noble line from a noble drama, "Courtesy was always the privilege of kings, apparently it is not taught to princes!" And "Plon-Plon" departed in an imperial huff, but after a week or two he renewed his visits.

He had been brought first by George Sand, in two of whose plays, *François le Champi* and *Le Marquis de Villemer*, Bernhardt had successfully appeared and whom she had grown to know and venerate. The writer in turn became warmly attached to the young actress. Madame Sand was in her sixties by then. A quiet gray-haired woman, she'd sit in Sarah's dressing room night after night, smoking incessantly, and Sarah thought her wonderful. In fact, she had a sort of schoolgirl crush on this eccentric authoress who had led such a brilliant life of trousered independence, defying all the conventions, clearing a dauntless way for free love, "which," as she wrote, "strikes its blind brow against all the obstacles of civilization" — a phrase which impressed Sarah as being exceptionally beautiful. Alfred de Musset had been dead for ten years, but the aura of her long and passionate affair with the love-obsessed nightingale still hovered about her in Sarah's eyes. The two took lengthy strolls together in the nearby Luxembourg Gardens, the older woman listening while the younger one poured out her fervid ambitions. "Oh, Madame Sand!" she once cried, "I would sooner die than not be the greatest actress in the world!"

Along with her growing professional success, Sarah Bernhardt's social life was beginning its own remarkable career. More and more distinguished visitors were arriving in her dressing room. Among the authors she received was Gustave Flaubert and among the politicians who came was a young firebrand then gaining controversial importance as leader of the Opposition Party. His name was Leon Gambetta. There were journalists, too, such as Arthur Meyer, editor of the Royalist paper the *Gaulois*, as well as a few members of the fashionable *beau monde* such as Charles Haas, close friend of the Prince of Wales and the only Jew with the exception of the Rothschilds welcome in the exclusive clubs. Haas was also to be Proust's model for Swann.

The Odéon kept open all year round, and for the summer of 1868 Sarah rented a cottage with a garden out in Auteuil. She made the trips to and from the theatre driving herself in a small carriage known as a "Little Duke," which Colette once described as a cross between a fairy chariot and a child's pushcart. It was a gift from Tante Rosine, as were the spirited ponies which drew it. The latter, it must be said, had recently frightened the daylights out of Tante Rosine by bolting during a drive in the Bois.

Now that Sarah was becoming famous, her family had begun to take an interest in her. Her daughter's success had thawed the maternal heart and Youle would pay her an occasional call, enquire disinterestedly after the health of little Maurice and leave a few hundred-franc notes on the table for the education of Régina, who was still living with her sister. Youle by now had brought her own mother down from Holland to stay with her but found her not only a crashing bore but dowdy and embarrassingly bourgeois, so when in the autumn Sarah took a somewhat spacious flat in the rue Auber, Youle sent her over to live with Sarah. Mevrouw Van Hard was a crotchety old lady, a strict Orthodox who disapproved of her granddaughter's non-Kosher cuisine, her non-Jewish friends, her wild extravagance and her haphazard way of life. Her presence must have been a constant irritation, but Sarah, who always had a strong sense of family obligation, accepted the situation with good grace and made a certain use of her by letting her take care of little Maurice. Madame Guérard also lived with Sarah periodically and was more and more to take up permanent residence in her household. In addition to these incumbents, she had her maid and cook and the beginning of an ever increasing collection of live pets. A dog, sometimes two dogs, accompanied her wherever she went, while Chrysagère and Zerbinet, a pair of turtles with gold-encrusted shells, crawled freely about the flat, which the major part of the time was a whirlwind of mess. The latter report came from the actor Pierre Berton, who went there to call on her exactly once and refused ever to meet her again in the untidy premises for fear of becoming completely disillusioned in regard to the woman whom at the moment he worshipped.

Sarah Bernhardt's expenses were mounting to what, during the greater portion of her career, would be their chronic degree of being far beyond her salary. This had, to be sure, been increased to 350 francs a month; moreover she had recently received a generous legacy from her father's estate, and she set about spending every sou to say nothing of a number of sous on credit. Finances, debts, even an occasional bankruptcy were of secondary importance. What was of paramount importance was her adored son, whom she spoiled outrageously, and her art, which she never permitted any person or circumstance to spoil.

One of the leading actresses of the Odéon some twelve years older than Sarah and still alluring was Madame Marie Léonide Agar, a dark beauty who, according to one contemporary, "incarnated all the loveliest types of ancient Greece." She was an excellent actress and had a deeply luscious speaking voice. Madame Agar also had a recurrent propensity for serious and passionate love affairs. The Goncourts, who knew all the gossip, tell in their Journal that Louis-Napoleon, before whom she recited at the Tuileries, was so enchanted by her rendering of Gautier's verse he paved the way for getting her into the Comédie Française. When kindly Camille Doucet warned her that if she went under those conditions, there might be talk, she answered, "I'm not worried. If it were ever said that I'd gone to bed with the Emperor, they'd have begged me to come to the Français long ago!"

After one matinee, Madame Agar called Sarah into her dressing room to introduce her current flame, the poet François Coppée, at the time unknown and as shy as a schoolboy. Agar explained that the young man had just finished a little masterpiece in verse which would be ideally suited for the two of them. Blushing with embarrassment, Coppée handed over a slim manuscript which Sarah started reading in her carriage on the way home. Halfway there, she called excitedly to the coachman to turn around and return to the theatre, where she walked directly into Duquesnel's office and announced, "I'm going to read you a one-act play written for two characters. It's good."

"Not you!" said Duquesnel. "You with your deceptive voice, you could make anything seem good!"

"Then you read it to yourself. Right now while I wait," and she sat down. The piece was *Le Passant*, Coppée's little love duet taking place on a terrace in Renaissance Italy, all moonlight and nightingales and a plot as charmingly improbable as a ballad. Francisque Sarcey said, "It's no more than a dream, but a charming dream: idyllic shadows which glide in the poetic regions of blue." It concerns a Florentine lady named Sylvia and a strolling boy troubadour named Zanetto, the lady bewailing her fate in having a heart of stone, the boy in search of a beauty named Sylvia whose loveliness conquers whoever beholds her. Sylvia conceals her identity but has the satisfaction of feeling her heart melt. Zanetto wishes to be her minstrel slave and remain with her forever and, on being gently turned down, swings his lute over his shoulder and sadly takes to the road again to sing his lays from now on with more poignancy, while the lady, for the first time in her life, weeps. It is as simple as that. But Coppée's graceful verse gave it delicate appeal and Duquesnel was as charmed with it as Bernhardt and Agar. However, Duquesnel had to consult his difficult partner, who wasn't charmed in the least. Grudgingly Chilly agreed to let it be put on for a single performance as part of a benefit but he refused to build a special set for it and he stipulated that the two actresses must supply their own costumes.

Sarah drew the sketch for hers with taste and period authenticity. Photographs give us an idea of how appealing she must have been as this slip of a youth. The average actress in masculine costume can be acutely embarrassing to behold, and a hippy lady in man's tights is material for the cartoonist. But Bernhardt's extreme slimness gave her the ethereal quality of a choir boy whose voice has not yet changed. Except for her Zacharie in *Athalie,* this was the first of many boy parts she was to play over the years (I have counted some twenty-five) culminating, of course, in her triumph as the ill-fated young Duc de Reichstadt in Rostand's *l'Aiglon.* For a woman to impersonate a young man was nothing new in the French theatre. The convention has come down from the time when Beaumarchais created Cherubin in *The Marriage of Figaro,* and as late as 1923 the fresh and lovely Yvonne Printemps enchanted audiences with her performance of the youthful Mozart.

Le Passant opened January 14, 1868, and was an immediate raving success. Sarah's Zanetto was irresistible. She looked like an angelic Donatello musician. She moved with eloquent grace and spoke Coppée's verse in a voice less of gold than of silver . . . fresh as a brook, pure as a child's. The press was ecstatic. Théophile Gautier wrote after seeing *Le Passant:* "it recalls the jewels of the Renaissance . . . so preciously, so delicately worked . . . It is only a dream, but it is an enchanting dream. . . . With what delicate and tender charm Mlle. Bernhardt said those delicious lines." The little drama ran for one hundred and fifty performances. It became a "must" with the Parisian public and every night the broughams and coupés of the wealthy and aristocratic were lined up in the Place de l'Odéon. Zanetto the little lute player became a figure as popular as Peter Pan. Sarah Bernhardt had definitely arrived, and her salary was increased to 500 francs a month.

The most eminent *Passant* enthusiast was Prince Napoleon's sister, the Princesse Mathilde. Princesse Mathilde was a redoubtable lady who went in for a variety of hobbies, her current enthusiasm being sculpture. Her sculpture was fairly redoubtable too, the subjects being of a heroic nature. At the time she was working on a bust of Minerva using Madame Agar, who was her close friend, as model. Agar persuaded the Princess to come see the hit at the Odéon, which Mathilde did and immediately fell in love with the play and its cast of two. Being a power at Court, she arranged for a command performance at the Tuileries. It was given after a banquet held in honor of the Queen of Holland and her son the Prince of Orange, jocularly known as *Le Petit Citron*. Sarah, Madame Agar and a stage manager waited some time in a salon adjoining the ballroom where the play was to be given. Sarah kept practicing the deep reverence she would have to make upon being presented to the Emperor and Empress and was interrupted by Louis-Napoleon himself, who had come in unnoticed and remarked with amusement, "I liked the way you did it the first time, Mademoiselle!" To her intense relief he failed to recognize her as the tactless Gymnase ingénue on whose recital of Victor Hugo he and the Empress had walked out five years earlier. The play went enchantingly. At the finish, there were three curtain calls which, coming from a Court audience, was considered an ovation. There was a slight hitch to the imperial exit from the ballroom owing to the fact that Eugénie, who was vain about her tiny feet and always wore shoes a size too small for her, had surreptitiously kicked off her torturous little slippers during the entertainment and when it was over couldn't get them back on. She had to order a lady-in-waiting to retrieve them, then walked out majestically, her giant hoop skirt concealing her swollen arches.

A few days later by way of appreciation the Emperor sent Mademoiselle Bernhardt a magnificent brooch bearing the imperial initials in diamonds. Word of the gift got about town and again the rumors flew — all of which gossip was of course nonsense. Madame Agar doubtless received a similar thank-you token from the Tuileries, but Madame Agar was not news and Sarah Bernhardt was.

Much of it she brought on herself. She was young and irrespon-sible and at times her behavior was that of someone slightly de-mented. One evening just before curtain time her maid, who had come back from an errand, entered the dressing room to find her mistress prone on the floor, pale as wax and seemingly not breathing. The woman ran out screaming incoherently that Ma-demoiselle Bernhardt was dead, and the stage manager rushed with her to find out what on earth she was jibbering about, took one look at the lifeless body and raced out to the box office to summon Duquesnel, who galloped to the dressing room, knelt down on the floor and inspected the inert form as best he could. To all intents and purposes she was indeed quite dead. The commotion had taken some time and the waiting audience was stamping and whistling in impatience. There was nothing for Duquesnel to do but step before the curtain and announce the cancellation of the performance due to certain dreadful circumstances. He spoke with such obvious emotion the house instead of leaving remained seated in stunned amazement. The name of Bernhardt was whis-pered about, someone said she'd suffered a violent seizure, someone else speculated that she might even be dead. Backstage the cast, management and stagehands, most of them weeping, crowded into the mortuary dressing room and at that the defunct rose like a lively Lazarus, burst into peals of shrill laughter and asked how they liked her impersonation of a corpse. Duquesnel, fuming with rage, had to return before the curtain to inform that there'd been a misunderstanding and that the play would go on. It was an idiotic prank and one that hardly helped Bernhardt's public image.

There was additional talk after her apartment was destroyed in a fire that nearly ended in stark tragedy. She was at the theatre when word of the conflagration was brought, she rushed to a waiting cab which dashed to the rue Auber as rapidly as the coachman could whip up his horse. By the time she arrived, smoke was pouring out of her front windows. Frantically she looked about in the gathered crowd, spotted Régina but failed to see her grandmother nor, to her horror, any sign of little Maurice. By now the front doorway was a sheet of flame. Knowing of an entrance off the boulevard Haussmann, she ran around the corner, fighting off the people who tried to restrain her, and plunged into the building. Choking and nearly blinded, she made her way to the room in which her grandmother and son were sleeping, shook the old lady awake, wrapped the four-year-old in a blanket and with the aid of two firemen who had come up a ladder, made an escape in the nick of time. Her action was especially heroic in view of her psychotic fear of fire. The firemen eventually got the blaze under control but not before it had gutted the two overhead floors and seriously damaged a third. Her own apartment was a ruin with its contents incinerated, including a diamond and pearl tiara given her by a certain Kabil Bey after she recited at one of his soirées. Who Kabil Bey was, other than a Near Eastern millionaire, is not a matter of record.

News of the conflagration and the Bernhardt losses made the headlines, and the columns — which as she became more and more conspicuous were inclined to print more and more malicious stories about her — implied that she herself had started the blaze in order to collect the insurance. The story was not only malicious, it was ironically untrue. There was no insurance. Sarah, in her careless fashion, had put off signing the policy and not only had she no claim, she was held for damages to the rest of the building as the disaster had been caused through one of her servants who carelessly left a lighted candle near a muslin curtain. The amount for which she was sued was 40,000 francs — a king's ransom, and kings came high in those days.

She was, not unnaturally, in despair. Her rich friends were sympathetic but did nothing about coming to her rescue. Those who eventually did were Duquesnel and Arthur Meyer, the editor of the aristocratic *Gaulois*, who together arranged for a benefit. Meyer was a kindly man, also a bit of a snob, who liked nothing better than to busy himself prominently in some fashionable event. He was a friend of Adelina Patti, whom he admired inordinately, not only because she was the greatest singer of her time but had, through marriage, become the Marquise de Caux. He approached her with the request to sing in the proposed benefit for the bankrupt young actress and the diva graciously agreed to take part. The name of Patti on the announcements was a magnet to attract *Tout Paris,* and although the tickets were exorbitantly priced, the house was a complete sell-out. This, which was the singer's first participation in a benefit for a French artist, endeared her to the public more than ever. Their ovation was almost overwhelming and she had to repeat Rosina's aria from *The Barber of Seville* four times. "Una voce poco fa" was to become as much of a theme song for Patti as the *Pagliacci* "Vesti la giubba" would be for Caruso.

The admission price for this benefit was not printed on the tickets. Whatever anyone paid was in the nature of a donation and Sarah cleared 33,000 francs, which was sufficient to pay her debts, if not her current expenses which were mounting in their carefree fashion. She had now taken a flat in the rue de Rome which she equipped at random with furniture donated by friends or purchased on credit, tributes from admirers in the way of paintings and statuary, some of it good, much of it awful, fur rugs, second-hand Oriental carpets, potted palms and always a profusion of flowers. Here she entertained with a lavishness which her finances hardly warranted. Here she started the nucleus of her loyal coterie which was to develop into her famous "Court."

Here also she started the creation of that baffling and fascinating enigma that was to be Sarah Bernhardt: a woman of unpredictable facets and moods, one day a legendary Faraway Princess, the next a hearty comrade. She could take a warmly sympathetic, even intimate, interest in a friend one day, and a week later greet the same person with the cold detachment of someone being introduced for the first time. Her temper was as volatile as ever. It was nothing for her to hurl a hairbrush at a maid and, next moment, by way of atonement to hand her a piece of jewelry. Sometimes she seemed a thoughtful adult, almost a scholarly one. Another time,

she became an irresponsible child, almost a delinquent one. How
many of these kaleidoscopic shifts of behavior were off-stage acting, it is doubtful if she herself knew.

In spite of her boundless energy, Sarah Bernhardt's health was
never robust, and during her first thirty years it was fragile to a
degree that would have made an invalid of the average person. She
was still subject to fainting spells — some, to be sure, were brilliantly contrived acts. But others were quite genuine, often
brought on by extraordinary causes, one of them boredom. Once
at a dinner party she found herself seated between two excruciat-
ingly tiresome table companions and actually fainted dead away.
After a highly emotional scene on stage, she was known to fall
unconscious in the wings — not, to be sure, before she had ac-
knowledged the applause of the audience. She also suffered from
the far more frightening affliction of attacks of bleeding at the
mouth. Whether these came from latent tuberculosis or whatever
the cause is not known. After she reached the age of thirty-five,
they gradually ceased.

Her precarious state of health never for a single day slowed
down her dedication to work or her exuberant way of living until
one summer when a severe oral hemorrhage so depleted her, the
doctors and theatre management ordered her to go to Eaux Bonnes
for a couple of months and take the cure.

It was early summer and the year was 1870. Back in Paris one
heard talk of a man named Bismarck. The words "Prussia" and
"Berlin" were on everyone's lips. Flags fluttered from windows,
patriots boasted of the invulnerability of "Our Glorious Army,"
rallies were held on street corners and the *Marseillaise* was played
at every public gathering. On July 19 France declared war
on Germany and the city was in a ferment of hysterical elation. Crowds rushed senselessly through the streets shouting "À
Berlin!" They stood in droves along the Champs Elysées to cheer
the lines of marching soldiers who might have doubled as the
regimental chorus in *The Grand-Duchess of Gerolstein* when

Hortense Schneider sang, "Ah! How I love the military!" Gay in their bright red Zouave trousers, their sweethearts' flowers stuck in the visors of their kepis, they filed jauntily out through the Arc de Triomphe to meet the oncoming ranks of Teutonic drab and steel. The story of that tragic encounter and of the ensuing debacle is a matter of familiar history. On September 2, the white flag of truce was hoisted up over the conquered town of Sedan, 82,000 bitter and exhausted Frenchmen laid down their arms and the Emperor of France surrendered his sword to the King of Prussia.

4.

~~~~~~~~~~~~~~~

SARAH'S
FIELD HOSPITAL

THE FACT that the Emperor had surrendered his sword did not mean that the rest of the country had given up to the enemy. Military and civilian, they fought on with the ferocity of Frenchmen defending their Patrie against the wave after wave of invaders advancing inexorably onto their precious soil. On September 4 a Republic was proclaimed. In the capitol the imperial eagles and laurel-encircled "N's" were ripped from the Tuileries and the tricolor again flew from the public buildings. Any rejoicing over the welcome change was short-lived as worse and worse news poured in from the front. Actually there was no front. The lines of the army of France were broken everywhere, its battalions scattered, the officers lacking all word of top command. Although there were a number of deserters, most companies put up a desperate but ever retreating fight clear back to the fortifications of the city itself. There were countless instances of heroism, such as Marshal Canrobert's stand at Saint Privat, but the cause was hopeless. By September 19, 160,000 Germans were encamped in the outer Bois and immediate suburbs, the crack troops of the Crown Prince of Prussia posted to the north, the regiment of the Crown Prince of Saxony cutting off approaches from the south. In almost a complete circle, cannon bearing the ominous name of Krupp were trained on the city. The Siege of Paris had begun.

During the initial weeks, except for more and more recruitment of a growing number of volunteers, life continued as usual, but people went about as though in a daydream. There was a sense of unreality, a complete inability to grasp the situation. It became the smart thing for intrepid citizens to drive out to the barricades for the sport of watching the batteries firing away at galloping Uhlans. The more cautious climbed to the summit of Montmarte to follow through opera glasses the sorties and skirmishes against the besiegers which, at a distance, looked no more actual than battle scenes on a painted panorama. At first it all seemed make-believe. A soldier's wife or girl frequently walked to the ramparts with her man cheerfully carrying his gun, or came out during the afternoon with cheese and a litre of wine. Often as not, officers of the National Guard would leave their posts in care of their subalterns and go home for dinner. There were, to be sure, the wounded and the dead, but the wounded were cared for by pretty women in Red Cross uniforms and the bereaved consoled themselves with the thought that their loved ones had died gloriously. Then the enemy demolished the bridges of Saint Cloud and Sèvres, every approach to and from the city was blocked and the people were jolted into a harsh awareness of their situation.

It was a time of ignorance and alarm, of blind patriotism and hysterical suspicion. Anyone reporting an unsuccessful sortie or a defeat for the provincial armies was branded a traitor. The telegraph wires had been severed and all communication with the outside cut off. Gambetta in October had made an escape over the enemy lines in a balloon and was organizing a Resistance and Government of National Defense in Tours. The mails, reduced to a minimum, also went out and returned via balloon, that is when their pilots succeeded in dodging the volleys from German machine guns. Official dispatches between city authorities and Gambetta's forces were effected by carrier pigeon and not always successfully. Many of the gentle creatures served as target practice for the Prussians, others fluttered back bloodstained and injured. Not a few were snared for food. For by November, provisions were strictly rationed and the citizens were feeling their first hunger pangs.

Earlier in Eaux Bonnes, Sarah Bernhardt had been in a frenzy of anxiety. At the news of the French army rout, she tossed to the winds all prospects of completing her cure and, against the orders of her doctors, rushed back to Paris. The Siege, though imminent, had not yet begun and she managed to send her small boy with his nurse, her mother, sister and grandmother and the servants from the city, presumably to Havre. Then she settled in her apartment with only her cook and Madame Guérard, to face what might come.

Most theatres had shut down. What few struggled to remain open did little business and none at all after cold weather set in. There was neither heat nor gas and the only illumination came from petroleum lanterns which sputtered and stank or from candles substituting for footlights. The Odéon along with the Français, being state owned, had been officially closed. Then the latter was opened up as an emergency military hospital for the casualties who, as time wore on, were becoming more and more numerous. Sarah made up her mind that if the First National Theatre could help care for the wounded sons of France, so must the Odéon, and that she herself would organize and run the enterprise. She wrote to the Prefect of Police, who at that time was the Count de Kératry, her former friend and possibly first lover:

> I hope that in remembrance of the little girl you once knew, you will listen to the young woman who, having known suffering now wants to ease, as much as possible, the sufferings of others. I request in my name and in those of my companions a permit to install an emergency hospital with thirty-two beds in our foyer and lobbies.

She got the permit. That was not the only thing she got out of de Kératry. Shortly after the opening of her hospital, she called to thank him for the permit and to ask for further favors in the way of government supplies. The weather was bitterly damp and chill, a precursor to the icy cold that was shortly to seize the city in a relentless grip. Kératry's office being unheated, he was keeping himself snug in a fur-lined overcoat. At the finish of the interview, Sarah had his promise for food and medical supplies. She also had the overcoat. She wanted it, she said, for one of her ambulatory cases, a Breton mobile guard with a hand shot off, whose bed was needed for the more seriously wounded. A week or so later, with fresh casualties begging for admission and provisions running short, she called again on her friend the Prefect. As she entered his office, the harassed gentleman was in the act of locking the door of a large wardrobe and pocketing the key. In a tone of pitiful pleading he said, "My dear and beautiful friend, when you last were here, you appropriated my one adequate overcoat with the result that I shortly came down with severe bronchitis. My only remaining outer covering is a battered old number which I have locked in that cupboard and you can't get the key!" This started the word of warning that went around town: "Don't go near the Odéon in any warm clothes. Sarah Bernhardt will rip them off your back for her *invalides*." Kératry did, however, come through with an official order for forty cases of biscuits, one thousand jars of preserves, one hundred bags of coffee and ten barrels of wine, most of which came out of the Empress Eugénie's larders in the Tuileries.

Young Bernhardt paid numerous calls on influential acquaintances and acquired any amount of excellent loot. Her singleness of purpose plus, when she chose to turn it on, that irresistible charm had more persuasive potency than the point of a gun. Baron Rothschild saw that she was supplied with two hogsheads of brandy. The chocolate magnate Monsieur Meunier sent her five hundred pounds of his nourishing product, the grocery czar, Félix Potin, contributed one hundred boxes of sardines and through the Dutch ambassador she received bolts of Holland linen for bandages and three hundred night shirts. Due to her efforts the Odéon *ambulance*, as the French call a field hospital, was the best stocked in the city. This was during the earlier stages of the Siege, when

there were still provisions to be had and Paris had not yet begun to
starve.

The twenty-six-year-old actress took over complete management
of her project. She also performed the duties of head nurse. She
was quick to catch on to medical techniques, her instructor being
Dr. Duchesne, an eminent physician whom Sarah through some
magic had commandeered and so won over he gave unstintingly of
his time to attending her wounded men, leaving most of his fashionable clientele to the care of his assistants. A stove was installed
outside one of the first tier boxes and Sarah's personal cook kept
making soup and tea all day long and frequently into the night.
Her two steady workers were *mon p'tit dame* and an older Odéon
actress named Madame Lambquin, a loud-mouthed, somewhat
coarse person, fond of calling a spade a dirty spade but blessed with
a heart of gold. There was one volunteer gentleman assistant who
served as orderly, porter and general factotum and a military in-
spector who came daily to receive reports and, with the help of
two stretcher bearers, perform the grim task of moving out the
dead. Most men civilians were doing daily duty at the ramparts
but after dark when the firing and sorties had let up for the night,
business friends would stop in to help balance the ledgers.

Sarah Bernhardt, the creature of fragile health, worked with the
vigor of ten peasants. Guérard and Lambquin ran her a close
second. The three women rotated their sleeping hours, each taking
every third night for what respite they could catch while the other
two stayed on duty. Sarah, with her extraordinary ability to fall
asleep at will and a few minutes later wake completely refreshed,
took occasional catnaps in her dressing room, usually flat on the
floor as often she moved out her couch to serve as an extra sick
bed. Her endurance, her fortitude were phenomenal. She who
normally fainted at the sight of blood staunchly held a basin while
Dr. Duchesne amputated a limb or probed in raw flesh to the
length of his forceps for scraps of shrapnel. She who abhorred unpleasant smells to the degree that she would dismiss anyone who

smoked in her presence (with the exception of Gambetta, who was given occasional permission to light up his well-known cigar) now unflinchingly dressed wounds which reeked of infection and gangrene. She who except during midsummer had an abhorrence for outdoor air spent an entire night along with a detachment of Sisters of Charity and the Brothers of the Ecole Chrétienne out on the battlefield of the Chatillon Plateau administering brandy to the dying, in a cold so bitter many only moderately disabled men froze to death.

Winter had set in, the severest on record, with the thermometer below zero and the Seine choked with ice. Throughout the city coal had run out. For some vestige of heat, the Odéon burned the wooden benches of the top gallery. Sarah and her workers ransacked the cellars and storage rooms for further fuel, and crates, platforms, throne chairs, balustrades and old scenery flats were flung one by one into the furnace.

Conditions throughout the city became daily more desperate. Disease was rampant. The cold took its toll of some, starvation of others. By the last week of December 3280 citizens had died along with 4000 of the military, which now included among its volunteers old men and young boys. Food was almost impossible to obtain. Cab horses and the black funeral chargers of the Cuirassiers were requisitioned for the markets. Animals in the zoo were slaughtered and a boulevard Haussmann profiteer made a fortune out of selling choice cuts from two giraffes, three zebras, six donkeys and a buffalo. One heartbreaking sacrifice came with the official shooting of Castor and Pollux, the two beloved elephants of the Jardin des Plantes who for years had borne the Parisian small fry for slowly dignified rides on their patient backs. Famished families tearfully took their domestic pets to the butcher. The price for a dog was according to its size and whatever flesh it had on it. A cat sold for twenty francs, a rat for two, a sparrow brought one and a quarter. Edmond de Goncourt killed his own in his yard and for a New Year's treat, feasted on a pair of larks.

In spite of the appalling hardships, morale was high, fortitude and heroism plentiful. Parisians could still joke to keep up their exhausted spirits. Street hawkers sold cheaply printed songs, one about an elderly spinster apologizing to her parrot for being obliged to wring its neck. A cartoon by Cham shows a line of men and women on their hands and knees outside a rathole waiting to grab their prey the moment it emerges.

Sarah and her valiant little staff made out as best they could, often going without food themselves in order to feed their patients. All told more than one hundred and fifty men were cared for at the Odéon hospital as well as two women civilians, one who, with frostbite in both feet, was unable to walk further, the other a starvation case who on entering the lobby collapsed and died. One day a prisoner named Franz Mayer, an officer of the Silesian Landwehr, was brought in. Although seriously wounded he had all the arrogance of the Teutonic conqueror which he considered himself to be, for when the other men in the ward made the sort of derisive gibes at which the French soldier is an artist, Mayer snorted, "Joke while you can. In less than forty-eight hours Paris will capitulate, as we know you're reduced to eating rats and mice." Sarah, overhearing his remark, that evening herself brought the German his supper saying, "This is how much we are starving, my man." On the tray was a breast of excellent chicken. It came from the last of a small barnyard of live fowl and geese she'd bought at the beginning of the Siege and had housed in the boudoir of her rue de Rome flat.

Another day a man, injured but still able to walk, arrived at the *ambulance* asking for admission. Madame Guérard, who was on duty, told him regretfully that there was no spare bed, not one. He was blond, blue-eyed and very young, still an undergraduate at the Ecole Polytechnique. He repeated his request, this time piteously. Please, he implored, he'd just be there a few days, as all he had the matter was a shrapnel wound in his shoulder. Then he added that it would mean so much to him even to be under the same roof as Mademoiselle Bernhardt. She was his goddess and for two years now he had worshipped her from the topmost gallery of the Odéon. This was enough persuasion for his goddess, who had walked out in time to catch the conversation. She immediately ordered an extra cot to be put up for the "gallant young defender of his country." During the short period of his stay, his worship deepened. He followed her every move as though he were watching a celestial vision. Actually Sarah Bernhardt as she went her round of duties did have a visionary quality about her. Working to the point of utter depletion, existing on starvation rations, she was the shadow of her anything but substantial former self. Her body had the weightless grace of a lovely wraith and her face, hollow-cheeked and pale, had taken on a new beauty that seemed unearthly, even spiritual. In her nurse's uniform and flowing white coif with its tiny red cross, she must have looked like an ministering angel to the weary, pain-ridden men. For once she was not Sarah Bernhardt acting a role. She was a compassionate humanitarian losing her own identity in selfless dedication. The day the young *Polytechnicien* was discharged as being again fit for duty, he approached his goddess and, blushing like a schoolboy, shyly begged for a photograph with her signature. She smiled, went to her desk to get one and, dipping her pen in the inkwell said, "Your first name is Fernand, isn't it?"

"No, Mademoiselle, Ferdinand."

"And your last?"

"Foch," he said.

In 1918 when Sarah Bernhardt, old and minus one leg, was again giving selflessly of her patriotic services by going into the trenches to recite for the *poilus*, she was reminded of the incident by the great officer who accompanied her, Marshal Foch, commander-in-chief of the Allied Armies.

In early January during the sixteenth week of the Siege, the indiscriminate bombardment of the city itself commenced. The hospitals immediately put up their flags but the Prussians trained

their gunsights on the Geneva cross, and many of their shells made
direct hits. The worst raids being made at night, Sarah and her
staff moved their patients down into the cellars where the poor
wretches had to suffer the further horrors of water pipes which
freezing had broken, flooding sewage and rats that ran over the
beds and even tried to gnaw at open wounds. Conditions for maintaining an effective *ambulance* became impossible and Bernhardt
was forced to close it down. The more serious cases were moved to
the military hospital of Val-de-Grâce. For some twenty remaining
convalescents, Sarah at her own expense rented an empty flat in
the rue de Provence where she, Guérard and Lambquin nursed the
men to recovery.

The people of Paris withstood the shell fire with fortitude. It
was only starvation, disease and the complete lack of supplies which
at the end of the nineteenth week brought about a capitulation.
Bernhardt in her Memoirs tells of that January 29, 1871. She had
gone for a walk with two friends:

> Suddenly one of them turned pale. I looked to see what was the
> matter, and noticed a soldier passing by. He had no weapons.
> Two others passed and they, also had no weapons. And they were
> so pale too, these poor, disarmed soldiers, these humble heroes.
> There was such grief and hopelessness in their very gait; and their
> eyes, as they looked at us women, seemed to say: "It is not our
> fault!" It was all so pitiful, so touching I burst out sobbing, and
> went home at once, for I did not want to meet any more disarmed
> French soldiers.

She did not remain in the capital to witness the yet more galling
sight of the German flag hanging from the Arc de Triomphe and
the conquerors goosestepping down the Champs Elysées to the
strains of Schubert's *Marche Militaire,* but fled from town, her
destination being, of all places, Germany. Late in the Siege, a
minuscule communication, written on transparent paper and
brought in by heaven knows what post, informed her that her son
and family were safe and well in Hamburg. Her reaction was one

of mixed emotions, relief over the news of their safety and where-abouts and rage that her son had been taken for refuge into the country of the hated enemy. She blamed it to the possible maneuvering of her Aunt Rosine, who looked back nostalgically on her past giddy sojourns of love and gambling at Baden-Baden. She made up her mind to go to Hamburg and bring them all back as soon as possible. The prospects of such a journey during those hazardous times would have discouraged the doughtiest of men, but not Sarah Bernhardt. To obtain a pass beyond the city limits was next to impossible, but the determined young woman got one through Paul de Rémusat, a deputy in the Chambre. He was a good friend and, according to the inevitable rumors, possibly a lover, and de Rémusat arranged an introduction to President Thiers himself. Sarah must have switched on an extra voltage of electrifying charm, for that sardonic Chief of State gave her a *laissez-passer* as well as some stern warnings about the perils of travel for a young and pretty woman during the prevailing conditions of confusion and lawlessness. The trip to Hamburg, which indeed was a nightmare of overcrowded trains, twelve-hour delays in rural stations, drunken German soldiers, lay-offs in filthy inns, inedible food or none at all, took over seven days. The return journey, which was equally arduous, took five, the last fifteen kilometers being made in a peasant's milk cart. But the hardships were quickly forgotten. She was at last reunited with her adored and pampered son and back in her own home.

She didn't remain there long. The war and the Siege were over and the hateful peace terms agreed to, with France handing over Alsace and Lorraine to Germany. Paris, on the other hand, was in a ferment of uprising, and soon the Commune erupted, that second terror of fire and bloodshed in which twenty thousand men, women and children lost their lives without knowing why. The government fled to Versailles, leaving the capital in the ruthless hands of the Communards. For a time Sarah stayed on in town, but her days were made miserable by petty persecutions and threats from the Prefect of Police. This was the Communard Raoul Rigault, who had been her vicious enemy ever since he sent her an atrociously bad play he'd written which she returned with the none too diplomatic comment, "Monsieur, your play is unworthy to touch let alone to read." Rigault's threats becoming seriously alarming (it is interesting to learn that the man was subsequently shot as a traitor), Sarah with Maurice and her staff also fled the city to Saint-Germain-en-Laye to sit out this latest national crisis. She didn't do much sitting but vented her anxieties by riding them out, for among her varied interests and activities, she had an intermittent enthusiasm for riding and was an excellent horsewoman. She went for daily canters along the surrounding bridle paths with her good friend and, who knows, possibly a *pro tem* suitor, a Captain O'Connor, who later as general was to be the hero of the Tunisian campaign.

One afternoon as they were trotting through a glade in the Versailles forest, a Communard who'd been lurking behind a tree sniped at them, but the bullet went wide of its mark. O'Connor whipped out his gun and shot the man squarely between the eyes. Sarah's odd reaction was to cry out at her escort, "Assassin!" slide down from her saddle and hold the assailant's gory head in her lap until he expired. Then she returned to her horse and O'Connor and rode back to her house in stony silence, doubtless enjoying every moment of the melodrama. Next day she generously forgave O'Connor for saving her life and the two of them stood together on the terrace of the Saint-Germain chateau watching the horrifying spectacle of the burning of Paris by the Communards, with the Tuileries and countless other buildings going up in flames.

By the end of May, MacMahon's Loyal Army had liberated Paris and the Commune was overthrown. The Republican government was back in power and Sarah reinstalled in the rue de Rome. Her building had escaped the holocaust, but her flat reeked of the smoke which for days had hung like a pall over the city. It must have reeked even more interestingly after Sarah, in an effort to ameliorate the aroma, doused the rugs, velours hangings and massive furniture with the heady perfume she habitually used.

Her mood was one of black despair over everything: the defeat of her beloved country, the wreckage left by the Communards, the theatres still closed and no prospects for the future. To intensify the air of doom, she ordered all shutters closed and all curtains drawn — which must have made a curious atmosphere for little Maurice to play in — while she lay prone on one of her fur-strewn couches, feeling not long for this world about which she no longer cared.

After a few days, this Werther-like self-indulgence was interrupted one afternoon when her butler announced that Monsieur Chilly of the Odéon was calling. Sarah, still prone on her couch, wearily said to show him in. Chilly groped his way through the encircling gloom to the chair she indicated with a wan hand-wave, cleared his throat and informed her that he and Duquesnel were reopening the Odéon early in October with a double bill featuring André Theuriet's one-act *Jean-Marie*, in which they would like her for the feminine lead. Sarah, her face muffled in pillows, moaningly replied that she had no further interest in anything — the theatre, her career, nothing. She was going to retire to Brittany and start a farm, what sort of farm she did not specify. Chilly rose and said very well, if that was her decision, he and Duquesnel would have to sign up another actress and, naming Jane Essler, a potential rival, quickly walked out of the room. Sarah, like a panther released from a trap, was after him in a bound. She grabbed him by the coat collar in a jerk which almost toppled the little man over backward. "Chilly!" she cried, "when do we start rehearsing?"

Jean-Marie was well received. The title role, that of a middle-aged Breton, was excellently played by the actor Porel (he had been one of Sarah's *ambulance* cases, was later to be director of the Odéon and to marry the delicious actress Réjane). But it was Bernhardt's touching performance of his child-wife which made

the hit of the little play. In her Memoirs it is her modest assertion
that the success of *Jean-Marie*, due, of course, to her, "carried its
author straight into the Academy." It would be unkind to question this assertion in spite of the fact that André Theuriet did not
gain his entrée into the Academie Française until some twenty years
later.

After the strain and horrors of the past year Bernhardt was happy
again. She was not yet a star but she was once more the pampered
leading lady, the goddess of the Left Bank. Best of all, she was
back in the theatre she adored, the dear old Odéon with its Doric
temple columns sheltering friendly arcades with little bookstalls and
cheap flower stands where her Latin Quarter adorers bought their
small string-tied bouquets to toss in her carriage. She was back
in the milieu she delighted in, the hard-working, zestful repertory
company, all good companions. Her time spent there, she recalled,
"was like existing in a happy provincial village."

During the early '70's, the grand old man of Paris, in fact of
France, was Victor Hugo, who had returned from exile shortly
after the overthrow of the Empire. He was welcomed home like
a conquering hero — a long-lost Messiah. Such national adulation
could not have been motivated solely by the fact that he was one
of the greatest poets of nineteenth-century France, or that his
plays and novels, ponderous as they may seem to modern readers,
in their day threw over stultifying convention and spearheaded the
way for liberating romanticism. Many of his worshippers had never
read a word Hugo had written. It was because in France there had
grown up a Hugo legend with the public; he symbolized all that
was implied in their burning words of *Liberté, Egalité, Fraternité*.
For some curious reason he was welcomed as a sort of savior of his
country although other patriots had worked more actively to save
it. There was a nation-wide "apotheosis of Victor Hugo." Poets
sang his praises, eminent lecturers made him the subject of their
discours and when he gave audience to friends and admirers in his
house in the Place des Vosges, it was said that one couldn't see the

Master for the incense. The Master was also known, by his few detractors, as the Monster, and the morally prudish were shocked by stories which periodically cropped up concerning his private behavior. Although well in his '60's, the grand old man was known still to have much of the grand old satyr in him.

Late in 1871, the Odéon management felt it was time to produce one of Hugo's plays. They decided upon *Ruy Blas,* the verse drama based on the story of Don Cesar de Bazan, who in vengeance on the Queen of Spain, who has spurned his advances, sends Ruy Blas, his valet, in the disguise of the absent Don Sallust to make love to her, a ruse which proves all too amorously successful for both of them and ends in utter disaster. Bernhardt did some deciding on her own and that was that she was going to play the Queen. Her decision was not completely shared by the management. Her friend Duquesnel was all in favor of Sarah, but Chilly had set his mind on engaging the popular actress Jane Essler. While the matter was under discussion, Sarah wasted no time but went about pulling wires and when Sarah Bernhardt pulled a wire, it was a live one. She turned her persuasive charm on Paul Meurice, Hugo's manager, Auguste Vacquerie, a relative, and his close friend the actor Geoffroy, who was to play Don Sallust. The three managed to maneuver the *Maître* himself into requesting her for the part. He had seen her performance in *Jean-Marie* and had thought her good though not great, but adequate to interpret his Queen.

Sarah herself almost ruined her chances through an idiotic gesture of petty egotism. The great author asked that the first reading of his play take place not on the stage or in the Green Room of the theatre as is customary, but at his house in the Place des Vosges, a demand which Sarah chose to consider an outrage to professional tradition. Back in her salon at the daily five o'clock gathering, she discussed the proposition with her faithful and all too doting "Court." Most of them agreed with her and she was about to dash off an indignant note to the management flatly refusing to attend a first audition of any play no matter how famous the author anywhere but in the theatre when Marshal Canrobert, who was not only a brilliant general but a tactful diplomat, arrived in time to advise her to plead indisposition as the excuse for not going to Hugo's house. Her note, one of her few legible ones, read, "The Queen has taken a chill and her *camerara mayor* forbids her go out. You know better than anyone else the etiquette of the Spanish Court. Pity your Queen." Hugo's terse reply was, "I am your valet." The first reading of *Ruy Blas* was held at the Odéon.

The author himself attended every rehearsal, sometimes sitting on a chair in the wings, sometimes standing at the back of the house. Sarah's first attitude toward the *Maître*, of which she was later ashamed, was one of elaborate indifference, a sort of "Who does he think he is?" bravura. Hugo took her childish behavior with friendly irony. He quite disarmed her one day when, during a scene in which she did not appear, she chose, during the wait, to perch on a table, swinging her feet with gamine nonchalance. Hugo scribbled something on a bit of paper and solemnly handed it to her. He had written:

> Une reine d'Espagne, honnête et respectable
> Ne devrait pas ainsi s'asseoir sur une table.*

Sarah, upon reading it, burst into peals of laughter, jumped from her unqueenly perch and all but flung her arms around the neck of the illustrious master. From that moment on she joined the ranks of the worshipful *Hugolâtres*. Suddenly she was aware not only of the greatness of this man but of his essential goodness. "When he arrived for rehearsal," she wrote, "the place took on a new light."

On the night of January 16, 1872, Sarah Bernhardt became a star. Her performance of the love-stricken Queen was a thing of lyricism and beauty. She wore a tiny coronet of silver lace and pearls and it seemed to symbolize her regal youth and fragile grace. The public, her "beloved monster," fell completely under her spell. It

---

* A queen of Spain, honest and respectable
  Should not sit in that fashion on a table.

was as if every man, every woman in the audience were breathlessly in love with her. And at the finish, the house went wild. In addition to her Left Bank following, the fashionable of *Tout Paris* were attending this opening. After the last curtain call, friends, admirers and any number of celebrities came crowding into her dressing room. Among them was that genial royal Francophile, the Prince of Wales. He too had fallen under the Bernhardt spell, a happy condition of emotion which he was from time to time to re-experience in the future. Suddenly a hush came over the hubbub of visitors as a white-haired, short-bearded man appeared in the doorway, and the heir to the British throne stepped aside to make way for Victor Hugo. For once, the master of words was at a loss for them. He dropped on one knee, kissed his Queen's delicate hand, able only to murmur, *"Merci! Merci!"*

She could hardly make her way past the stage door and out through the cheering crowd jamming the rue Vaugirard clear across to the palings of the Luxembourg Gardens. Once safely in her carriage she received a further gratifying if hair-raising tribute from the delirious students who unharnessed her horses and, taking the shafts themselves, ran her all the way to the rue de Rome at breakneck speed shouting, "Make way for Our Sarah!" It was a question of whether she or the students would have the first heart attack. Once back in her flat, she stayed up for what remained of the night talking with her dear Guérard.

Due to Bernhardt's performance of the Queen, *Ruy Blas* was the hit of the season. It had been running some months when she received one morning a hand-delivered envelope bearing a single engraved circle enclosing the words, "Comédie Française 1680." Her heart leapt but she was afraid to open it. She knew it would contain an offer and she knew she would have to accept it. Yet she knew it represented the end of the happy freedom and security she enjoyed at the Odéon and could continue to enjoy for years to come if she chose to ignore the road ahead. But that road was opening up and she had a clear intuition that it could lead her in triumph around the globe. She had told George Sand that she would die if she could not be the greatest actress in the world. Should she die comfortably here in the Odéon or use the First Theatre of France as a stepping stone to that greatness and the rest of the world? She opened the envelope.

Emile Perrin, the brilliant *Administrateur Générale* of the Français, offered her a contract and 12,000 francs a year. The Odéon was paying her less than 10,000. She consulted her friend and manager Duquesnel. Or rather she didn't consult him so much as inform him what she thought she must do. He reminded her that her contract with them held for another year. All Bernhardt ever needed to stiffen her determination were obstacles put in her way. She stated bluntly that unless they paid her 15,000 francs a year, she'd accept the Français offer. Duquesnel, taken aback, said that it would be up to Chilly whether or not they'd release her, that she'd have to take the matter up with him but at least he offered to pave the way. Duquesnel's paving was not very extensive. All he told his disagreeable partner was that their leading actress was toying with the idea of leaving their playhouse. When Sarah walked into Chilly's office, she found the little man in an apoplectic rage. Only recently she had had a vitriolic altercation with him after one performance when her dog, an unpleasant toy griffon named Hamlet, had escaped from the dressing room and trotted morosely after her onto stage center, had taken fright at the roar from the audience and had run off yipping. Chilly called the incident a deliberate misdemeanor on the actress' part and slapped notice of a fine on Hamlet's owner which she, with no intentions of paying it, slapped right back onto the manager's desk. Now he wrathfully demanded to know whether or not she had taken leave of her senses. What other theatre in Paris, he shouted, could offer the advantages she was enjoying here. Sarah in the voice of a lisping little girl mentioned the name of the Français. Chilly shook with sneering laughter. He knew at first hand, he told her, that no one even remotely connected with the Français could bear so much as the sight of her. She whirled out of his office, hailed a fiacre and in tones of Racinian fury thundered at the startled *cocher*, "À la Comédie Française!"

Once in the dignified, impersonal Administration office of that higher temple of drama, her fury gave way to sudden misgiving. Perrin was the antithesis of Chilly. Glacial, polite, he impressed the young actress as a distinguished automaton. She told him she had made up her mind to sign his contract. Perrin bowed distantly, pushed the contract across his desk and handed her a pen. It was one of those traditional French pens, with nib splayed and corroded, the sort which makes one wonder how some of the greatest prose of all time ever got written in France. Sarah, in her sudden nervousness, dipped the wretched point too deeply into the inkwell and a large black blob dropped onto the contract. Her first reaction was to tell Perrin that his pen was no good, which was quite true. Her next was one of childish superstition. "Wait!" she cried, "let me fold the paper and we'll see what comes out. If I make a 'butterfly' it's good luck and I'll sign. If it's just a smear, you can tear up the contract." Painstakingly she made a fold across the wet blob. When she opened it out, there appeared the silhouette of a perfect butterfly complete with antennae.

Sarah dashed back to wave the contract in Chilly's pudgy little face. She would finish out the run of *Ruy Blas*, she said, then leave for the Français in the autumn. As she made a sweeping exit, Chilly screamed that he'd bring action against her for 6000 francs. It is in keeping with this woman's complex character that it never occurred to her to tell Duquesnel what she had done. She could be inconsiderate with her friends to the point of cruelty, yet take for granted that they would still remain loyal and loving. She never apologized, never retracted. When Duquesnel, hurt to the quick, reproached her for not informing him, her reply was a shrug and an indifferent, "Yes, I suppose I should have. But it's done now!" And with a dazzling smile, she dismissed the matter. Duquesnel forgave this baffling, infuriating woman whom he could never resist. But Chilly avoided speaking to her for weeks until one day she flung her arms around his fat, red neck, affectionately called him an imbecile and demanded his forgiveness. Chilly softened somewhat but added that he was sticking by his 6000-franc suit for breach of contract. After this, there was an armed truce between the two for which Sarah was later thankful.

After the hundredth performance of *Ruy Blas*, Victor Hugo gave a sumptuous supper at his house for the cast, management and a number of literary friends. At the finish of the meal, the grand old poet rose, glass in hand, and praised his "adorable Queen and her Golden Voice." He spoke of her harmonious movements, her irresistible enchantment and wound up, "She has more than beauty. She is something better than an artist. She is a woman." All of a sudden, everyone at the table was staring at Chilly. His face ashen and beaded with cold sweat, he tottered to his feet and gasped out that he had pains in his chest. He was helped into the adjoining room by friends and the host, who had already dispatched a servant to fetch a doctor. The guests tried to carry on while nervously sipping champagne. The doctor arrived and was rushed into the other room. In a few minutes Hugo came out. "What a wonderful way to go!" was his only announcement.

Sarah, looking as though she'd be the next to go, emitted a racking sob and called for her carriage. It was all a bit like the sort of scene she herself was later to stage in one of her Sardou productions. For several days she put on a great show of grief over the loss of this grumpy little man who had hardly been a close friend.

Ironically, it was Chilly who had the final say in their dispute. The suit he had filed for breach of contract was pressed and Sarah Bernhardt was obliged to pay the Odéon 6000 francs of damages.

~~~~~~~~~~~~~~~~~~~~~~~~~~

5

WOLF IN THE
SHEEP-FOLD

SARAH BERNHARDT's re-engagement at the Comédie Française
had been due largely to the urging of Francisque Sarcey,
whose powerful opinion had great influence with Perrin. The
exacting critic was changing his attitude toward the young actress
whom he had treated so harshly. Now Mademoiselle Bernhardt's
"talent" had become an "art" and after *Ruy Blas* he had written
that it was a pity the Français could boast of no one to equal her, or
the presence of such an artist in their ranks might go far to pick
up their recently lagging box-office receipts. Such comment hardly
endeared her to the members of that august assemblage, any more
than did the outburst of congratulations from the poet-critic,
Théodore de Banville, who, after the announcement of her re-
admission, wrote:

> Make no mistake; the engagement of Mlle. Sarah Bernhardt at the
> Comédie Française is a serious and revolutionary fact. Poetry has
> entered into the house of dramatic art; or, in other words, the wolf
> is in the sheep-fold.

When Sarah showed up for her first rehearsal, she had the feeling
of walking not as a wolf into a sheep-fold but as a victim into a
lion's den. The *sociétaire* lions had the attitude that it was less a
Daniel who had entered their midst than a bony nonentity not
worth eating — although doubtless Madame Nathalie kept her own
cautious distance. A few friendly lions, however, went out of their
way to make her welcome. There was Madeleine Brohan, the

daughter of Augustine Brohan, a witty and *bonne camerade*, and Marie Lloyd, who had beaten her to first prize at the Conservatoire and who, though long established in the Français, had risen to no great heights. Then there was the dear, the wonderful, the glorious comedian Constant Coquelin, the baker's son from Boulogne who was to delight the world with his *Cyrano de Bergerac*. Although only three years older than Bernhardt, Coquelin had entered the Comédie ten years earlier, had become an immediate celebrity and made a *sociétaire* at the unprecedented age of twenty-three. In spite of all his success, Coquelin was a modest, adorable person who immediately won Sarah's heart and she his. This result was a warm and sincere friendship which lasted until the great comedian's death in 1909.

One other person who made Sarah Bernhardt feel welcome was Sophie Croizette. Blonde, smilingly pretty and fresh as a Latour pastel, Croizette was currently the most popular actress of the Français. She played with gay animation and a coaxing charm which, according to Sarcey, "could lure a crocodile." She had a bonny nature and her fans spoke of her as "La Belle Croizette" and sometimes "La Bonne Croizette." She was the pet protégée of Perrin in more ways than theatrical — as it was politely put, she was *trés liée* with that coldly formal administrator. Croizette in no way regarded Bernhardt as a notorious intruder. The two of them had been good friends since childhood and were to go on being so.

The other players, however, continued to turn the cold shoulder, and rehearsal days for the newcomer were strained and difficult. She missed the exuberant stimulation of the Odéon, where the preparation of a play was a matter of excitement and joyous hard work. Here, the dignified regulars reported for duty with the solemnity of board members turning up for a committee meeting. Sarah was further disheartened because she cared for neither the play nor the first role to which she had been assigned. She would have been better off if Perrin had followed the advice of Sarcey, which was to introduce this controversial new *pensionnaire* unobtrusively in some supporting part such as that of Aricie in *Phèdre*. Instead he chose to present her right off in the title role of *Mlle. de Belle Isle*, an uninteresting heroine of a mediocre work by Dumas *père*. Bernhardt felt she was not going to be at all good and her intuitions were correct.

On November 6, 1872, she opened to a full house. The audience was of a very different calibre than had been that of the Odéon. It was composed of the chic, the sophisticated and a number of those elect whose names are listed in the *Almanach de Gotha*. The majority had come out of curiosity to judge for themselves this young actress about whom there had been so much gossip. Even before the curtain went up, Sarah sensed the none too friendly attitude of the audience. She played the first acts lamentably. It was only in the last that her paralyzing trac released its grip on her and the Bernhardt magic began to glow. But by then it was too late to make up for her earlier inadequacy, and Sarcey's review was regretfully unfavorable. He spoke of her disappointing appearance, of her voice which though delicious was a complete failure in passages that demanded power, and wound up admitting that "roused by the coldness of her public, Mlle. Sarah Bernhardt was entirely herself in the fifth act. This was certainly Our Sarah once more . . . the Sarah of *Ruy Blas*."

She attributed her personal fiasco to the fact that shortly after the start of the play, she saw her mother, who had been sitting in a stage box, suddenly rise in an obvious state of pain and, her escort supporting her, stagger out from the parterre. Sensing that her parent was having a heart attack, she played the first act distractedly then, during the intermission, sent *mon p'tit dame* off to find out what had happened. At the beginning of the last act, Guérard returned and standing in the wings signaled that all was well and Sarah played the final scenes with her customary artistry. Such, at any rate, is her version and any actress must be excused for establishing an alibi for a bad performance. It turned out that Youle Bernhardt actually had suffered a heart attack and Sarah is honest enough to write that it may well have been brought on by chagrin upon overhearing a nearby spectator's estimate of her daughter, "Why, she's like a dried bone, this little Bernhardt!"

A few nights later, "Little Bernhardt" retrieved herself with a glowingly exquisite performance of Junie in Racine's *Britannicus* and after this, three or four personal hits in the Français repertory brought her back into the ranks of stardom. The Paris *beau monde* granted her its fashionable patronage and her loyal Odéon following streamed across from the Left Bank and were so vociferous in their applause, her enemies accused her of employing a claque.

Oddly enough, her only professional rival was her good friend Sophie Croizette, although the rivalry in no way affected their warm comradeship. The public, however, chose to build up a bitter feud between the two, the factions dividing themselves into the "Croizette-istes" and the "Bernhardt-istes." The "Croizette-istes" were composed of the bankers, the smart set, the club men, while the "Bernhardt-istes" included the intellectuals, the students, the members of politics and the arts. Both actresses took the situation as an enormous joke. The playwright Octave Feuillet, observing the friendly rivals, said, "There was nothing more amusing than to see them leaving after rehearsals . . . They'd be off like two startled goddesses, noses in the air . . . swinging their little umbrellas, talking and laughing at the tops of their voices so that passers-by turned to look; then they'd go into Chiboust's pâtisserie and stuff themselves with cakes." It is surprising that this pleasant relationship continued, as Sarah Bernhardt might easily have resented Perrin's marked favoritism of Sophie Croizette. He continued to cast her in most of the best parts and Croizette frequently appeared three and occasionally four times in a week while Bernhardt usually played only twice. No two women could have been more disparate in appearance and character. Croizette was all curves and dimples. Bernhardt all exotic slenderness and sultry pallor. Croizette was outgoing and good-natured, Bernhardt eccentric, moody and unpredictable. Edmond de Goncourt describes Sophie Croizette's dressing room as being decorated in "serious luxury": silk paneled walls, rich but conservative hangings and elegant Directoire settees and cabinets. Sarah Bernhardt's *loge*, like all her subsequent ones, was a mishmash of unmatching furnishings, profusions of flowers, a few yapping dogs and almost the year round a crackling fire going in the grate.

Her apartment in the rue de Rome was also a hotchpotch of objects, some admirable, others quite dreadful. Fine Louis XV chairs and tables mingled with mausoleum-like Second Empire cabinets and cupboards. Dominating the main salon was her much publicized divan on a raised platform. It was canopied with Oriental hangings upheld by velvet-covered spears and strewn with immense satin pillows and a variety of fur throws. She loved the smell and the feel of fur and she'd stroke the fine pelts and nuzzle them with her nose. The Persian carpeted floors were ankle-deep in bear, lion and tiger-skin rugs and the red damask of the walls hardly showed up between the jumble of ornaments attached to them: paintings good and bad, Byzantine gewgaws, antique weapons, Japanese fans and brocade chasubles. There were a good many potted palms and always a regular hothouse of flowers, many of them wilting dolefully. They exuded their fragrance in every room and the hangings gave off the further scent of the heady perfume with which the mistress of the house periodically doused them.

This potpourri must occasionally have been interestingly infused with a few less ethereal aromas, for Sarah's home menagerie had been enlarged with the addition of parrots, any number of dogs and now and then a wild animal or two. Their owner insisted that her creatures were all quite tame but her friends and visitors were not so sure. Alexandre Dumas *fils* experienced his introduction to the Bernhardt zoo one summer afternoon when he called bringing with him the one and only copy of a new play he had just completed. While waiting for his hostess to appear, he became aware of a curious crunching sound and, looking in the direction from which it was coming, beheld a puma serenely eating his boater hat and apparently savoring every straw. At a whistle from somewhere out back, the beast bounded from the room. Dumas' relief was short-lived. A gray parrot suddenly landed squawking on his shoulder and started biting off the buttons of his waistcoat. It was stopped only by the leaping entrance of two gigantic collies, one of whom grabbed the precious script of his play while the other hurled joyous paws onto the terrified man's chest and started licking his face with an impact so violent it knocked Dumas back onto the divan with a fall in which he knocked over a large vase filled with water and peonies. At this awkward moment, Sarah appeared, "diaphanous and golden, in a white gown . . . her hair catching the sunlight." Seeing the wreck her pets had made of her caller, she went into gales of laughter so uncontrollable, she toppled down onto the couch beside him. This was the somewhat disordered beginning of the twenty-year friendship there was to be between Bernhardt and the author of *The Lady of the Camellias.*

That divan was the one on which she posed for the portrait by Georges Clairin which today may be seen at the Petit Palais. The picture is romantically idealized. Wearing a flowing white teagown, a snowy Russian wolfhound at her feet, a hand held up to one cheek, she stares dreamily straight out from the canvas, half reclining against an exotic background of cushions and Persian hangings. A typical Academy chef d'oeuvre, it made a popular stir at the 1876 Salon. The fashionable magazines reproduced it and society Parisiennes, those frivolous *petites femmes* of Paul Bourget's smart novels, copied the provocative pose when receiving their clandestine gentlemen callers.

Clairin, who at one time had been briefly one of Bernhardt's lovers, became one of her closest life-long friends whom she always called her "dear Jojotte." He was an attractive man, tall and handsome, who had the *bonhomie* of a *grand seigneur.* A hopeless romantic, he dressed the part of a painter in the most expensive of bohemian clothes. His corduroy trousers came from a well-known tailor, his ties from Charvey, his carefully casual shirts were made to order by the smartest Boulevard haberdasher. For over forty years Georges Clairin was to be a favorite member of the Bernhardt "Court" and hardly a day passed that he didn't call or come for a meal. She had other artist friends, among them Bastien-Lepage, who made the much reproduced profile study of Sarah, her hair down the back of her neck, her throat swathed in filmy ruchings, holding in her slim hands a figurine. She saw quite a lot of the Belgian painter Alfred Stevens, and a great deal of the brilliant illustrator Gustave Doré.

Bernhardt's taste in art was as haphazard as her taste in household decoration. It was the high noon of the Impressionists, but she had no interest in their painting. Instead she patronized the extremely inferior work of Louise Abbéma, who produced pretty-pretty pictures on pretty-pretty subjects which were cheaply popular and, reproduced in color, sold sucessfully in the stationers' shops. Sarah thought these embarrassing canvasses were just lovely purely because Louise Abbéma was a good friend. Louise Abbéma was also, according to rumor, an avowed lesbian, but such a defect of character didn't bother Sarah in the least. Along with Clarin, Abbéma became a fixture in the Bernhardt "Court."

It was around this period that the actress discovered she could do some plastic creating of her own. To amuse herself, she tossed off a few water colors along with some crayon drawings, and upon seeing them, Alfred Stevens advised her to take up painting. It struck her as an excellent idea. Her Français appearances were limited to hardly more than two a week and she was chafing with impatience over having so much enforced free time. She indulged a brief enthusiasm for landscape and went on occasional sketching trips in the nearby countryside with Georges Clairin or Gustave Doré.

Basil Woon in his book *The Real Sarah Bernhardt* — which on the whole is highly unreliable — recounts one incident which, whether it be true or not, is characteristic of Sarah's sense of adventure. He says that she and Doré had gone for a sketching trip on foot outside of Barbizon. They lost their way back to the town, it had grown dark and they had to put up for the night at a farm house. Sarah on these jaunts always dressed the part, wearing corduroy trousers, a loose peasant jacket and an artist's broad-brimmed felt hat jammed down over her head. Doré was shown to a room and his companion was led away, he supposed to hers. Next morning Doré looked out his window and beheld Bernhardt washing her hands and face in the farmyard pump, her hair matted with wisps of straw. The farmer, taking her for Doré's boy apprentice, had shown her to the hayloft, where she apparently snuggled down cozily and had a more comfortable rest than Doré had on his cobblestone mattress.

A more serious artistic pursuit was modeling, and at this she found herself to be amazingly proficient. Her instructor was Mathieu-Meusnier, a popular sculptor of the day who specialized in storytelling or public-monument-type works which have hardly classed him with Rodin. He is to be remembered, according to Larousse, as the creator of a statue entitled "The Death of Laïs," which about sums him up as an artist. Meusnier had taken a long look at Bernhardt's sensitive hands with their tapering fingers, and had pleased her no end by telling her they were meant to caress works of art.

She was an apt pupil and quick to catch on to a facile technique. Her own sculpture was strictly Academy style in the vein of "Love Triumphant" or "The Fatal Reaper Cutting Down Youth" and further rather dreadful allegorical figures. However she was surprisingly successful at it. A representative gallery exhibited and immediately sold a high-relief plaque she did of the dead Ophelia (very pretty and not too believably dead) and her allegorical Figure of Music was eventually installed in the Monte Carlo Casino, where it must have fitted in nicely with the pastry-shop ornamentation of that establishment.

She won an honorable mention at the Salon of 1876 with a life-size group called "Après la Tempête" depicting an old Brittany woman holding the drowned body of a boy. This had been inspired during a brief holiday she'd taken in Finisterre. Every evening she had watched a half-crazed crone totter out onto the storm-battered cliffs and toss pieces of bread onto the churning waters below. The local villagers explained that the poor soul had lost all three sons at sea, and had been left with one small grandson whom she had raised to be anything but a fisherman. But the lure of that life was irresistible to the boy and one day he set out in a rowboat to join the sardine fleet and was never seen again. Day after day his heartbroken grandmother came out onto the windy promontory to toss down bits of bread, calling out to the waves, "Take food to my little boy."

Sarah modeled busts of Georges Clairin, Louise Abbéma and the journalist Emile de Girardin. Her study of Victorien Sardou was said to have been a striking likeness and her touching head of her sister Régina, made shortly after that poor girl had died, won a prize at a further important exhibition.

Her head of Baron Adolphe de Rothschild did not turn out so successfully. That multimillionaire had commissioned it at a very large fee. After he had given her a few sittings, she put on the finishing touches in his absence, then sent word for him to come see the clay model before it was sent to be bronze cast. Rothschild arrived, check in hand, took a critical look at the head and asked bluntly, "Is that supposed to be me?" Bernhardt, with a yowl of rage, seized the check, tore it up, then grabbing her work, she hurled it to the floor where it shattered into fragments.

Discriminating art connoisseurs, of course, hardly took Sarah Bernhardt's sculpture seriously. Rodin railed against its banality, calling it "old-fashioned tripe" (at this same time the majority of the Paris public was railing against Rodin's "immoral modernism"). Among the public there were many who resented Sarah's extracurricular activity and the press, for some reason, took particular offense that a leading Comédie Française actress should exhibit her non-theatrical creations. The resentment was especially acute a

few years later, after she had had a highly successful show in
London. The champion who rushed hotly to her defense was, of
all people, Emile Zola. That author was a member of her coterie
if only an off-and-on member, as the two periodically quarreled.
During one of the "on" interims he wrote with customary verve to
one paper: "She is reproached for not having stuck straight to
dramatic art . . . to have taken up sculpture, painting, heaven
knows what else. How droll! Not content with finding her thin,
or declaring her mad, they want to regulate her daily activities. One
is freer in prison. To be accurate, she is not denied the right to
sculpt. She is simply denied the right to exhibit her works. This
is the height of farce. Let a law be passed immediately to prevent
the cumulation of talent."

Her studio was at 11 boulevard de Clichy, and she made an
enthusiastic attempt to infuse it with a *vie de Boheme* atmosphere.
At least it was in Montmartre and at least its casement windows
looked out over the rooftops of the outspread city below. Like her
apartment at home, the place was a cluttered jumble of unmatching
furniture, exotic wall hangings and *objets d'art*, not all of which
were *art*. One visitor likened it to a salesroom prior to an auction.

Here she sometimes received her "Court" and, to augment the
bohemian atmosphere, served them execrable tea which she herself
brewed over a gas-jet. As she was utterly cavalier about her social
appointments, the "Saradoteurs" never knew whether to find her
here at five o'clock, or in the rue de Rome flat.

The inevitable rumors went the rounds. It was whispered that at
11 boulevard de Clichy there were held orgies of an immoral
abandonment to equal those of the *Quat'z Arts* Ball. The sculptress'
costume only helped to confirm belief in these stories. This, like
the tea gowns in which she received at home, was all white: white
silk trousers, white satin blouse with white lace neck *ruche* and an
enormous student *lavalière* tie of white tulle. It was hardly what
one would call a very mannish outfit and yet it was considered as
scandalous as the short hair and men's pants worn by Rosa Bonheur.

She allowed a photographer to take a picture of her in this studio attire and that enterprising gentleman had the result reproduced on postcards which sold like hot cakes in the souvenir shops. The dignitaries of the House of Molière were not amused.

By now Sarah Bernhardt was the most talked-about woman in Paris. Her name had become a cliché. One biographer says that Bernhardt couldn't take a spoonful of castor oil without it being reported in the papers. She seems to have had a genius for infuriating the public and at the same time fascinating it, adored one moment, bitterly resented the next. A eulogistic article would appear on one page of a periodical and, on the next, a vicious caricature. Dumas *fils* told about being at the death bed of a certain elderly man-about-town whose final words were, "I depart this life willingly, for I shall hear no more about Sarah Bernhardt." One of her many biographers, Binet-Valmer, claims that she never denied the slanders and calumnies but accepted them rather in the spirit of an idol accepting incense. "Was this the exaction for glory?" he wrote, "it was indeed, but Sarah imagined it to be glory itself." The stories, as always, were grotesquely exaggerated. It was said that she wore male attire because she was planning to take on the *jeune premier* roles at the Français, or that in the interest of her sculpture, for anatomy study, she occasionally undressed her guests (it is to be assumed that the said guests disrobed voluntarily). Because the only form of outdoor exercise she ever took was horseback riding, it was reported that, in the early morning, she was to be seen riding bareback in the Bois on young racehorses to get in training as a jockey in the Grand Prix. Sarah laughed and let them say what they liked. The only time she disclaimed a rumor was when a journalist named Jouvin questioned her nationality, accusing her of being half-Prussian and pro-German. Furiously indignant, she wrote the following letter to Jouvin's paper:

I am French, absolutely French. I proved it during the Siege of Paris and the *Société d'Ecouragement au Bien* awarded me a medal. Would the *Société* have done this for a German? All my family is of Dutch origin. . . . If I have an accent (and I regret it very much), my accent is cosmopolitan, not Teutonic. . . . In a word, Monsieur, I demand the rectification of an error prejudicial to my son's future and painful to my heart, which is that of a Frenchwoman.

And always there was the prevalent gossip about that coffin. This was still the model her mother had bought for her when she was a girl, and which she continued to keep in her bedroom. Actually she did, for a time, sleep in it, but not for purposes of notoriety. Régina, whose health had been declining, took a marked turn for the worse. Sarah, who loved this sister as though she were her own daughter, took personal care of her, overdoing her solicitude to the point of having her share her bed. Régina was running a constant fever, had a hacking cough and was vomiting blood. The poor girl was obviously in the final stages of tuberculosis and the doctor forbade Sarah to sleep close to her. There was no space in the room for an extra bed. The rosewood coffin was satin-lined and, with the addition of a few extra quilts, served as a perfectly good cot and one which appealed to the actress' bizarre imagination. Moreover her attitude toward the coffin was no longer one of morbid brooding. She regarded it as a familiar piece of furniture to which she had become affectionately attached. Contrary to the popular and preposterous rumor, the actress never took it along on her travels.

She may have once or twice allowed a few intimate friends to see her lying in it, but if she did, it was in the spirit of a humorous act. Robert de Montesquiou spoke of an occasion when he conducted a mock funeral service over Sarah as she posed in her coffin, which sounds as though Sarah had good-naturedly indulged a sudden whim of that eccentric poet-dandy. Montesquiou is remembered as a Royalist snob, an aesthetic dilettante and a partial model for Proust's Baron Charlus, although Huysmans' fantastic Des Esseintes in *A Rebours* comes closer to being a direct portrait of this absurd decadent. Montesquiou, who was much younger than Sarah, had adored her ever since her Odéon days. He wrote her elaborately esoteric poems, ordered a duplicate costume to her *Passant* one in which he fancied he looked just like her, and had the two of them photographed together. Sarah accepted this ridiculous exquisite's infatuation, which could hardly have been of an over-poweringly carnal nature as the man was a homosexual. How-ever, he is reported to have had a twenty-four-hour love affair with the lady, followed, alas, by a week of vomiting. But in spite of this unfortunate interlude, if indeed it took place, theirs was a warm friendship.

Escapades such as Montesquiou's intoning the burial service over Sarah's coffin were silly larks not to be taken seriously. But ac-counts of them with variations and exaggerations spread about town. It was said that seated in it she received her guests, that lying in it she received her lovers, and some wag referred to it as "a sepulchre built for two." The press took up the "coffin subject" with indignant censure, one journalist writing, "This gruesome joke crowns her other eccentricities. There is a limit to bad taste. It is, of course, true that this artist of the Comédie Française is so thin the coffin contains nothing but bones."

Young Régina died, and Sarah was genuinely heartbroken. The girl had lived with her and been her responsibility for some time and her loss left a large gap in her life.

One never-failing topic for the scandalmongers was Sarah Bernhardt's love life. This currently centered itself upon a de-licious affair with Jean Mounet-Sully, the handsomest actor in France and its greatest tragedian since Talma. Born in Bergerac, he had the dashing allure of the Gascon of romance. Mounet-Sully and she had both been members of the Odéon company at the same time but each had regarded the other merely as a pleasant acquaintance. He entered the Comédie shortly after Bernhardt and their initial encounter was in the nature of a sudden mutual revela-tion. According to Louis Verneuil, Sarah stared at this perfect specimen of manly beauty and was completely stunned.

"It's not possible, Mounet!" she gasped. "What's happened to you?"

"What do you mean?"

"But you're very handsome!"

"So I've been told."

"But you weren't like this at the Odéon."

"I believe I was."

"Come on, now. I'd have noticed it!"

"Perhaps you didn't have the time to notice me."

She noticed him now, all right, and he noticed her in an instant and mad infatuation. It was what the French call a *coup de foudre*, and their affair lasted for many months. The Paris public, far from disapproving, was delighted and considered this liaison between the two most celebrated players of the Français as being quite in keeping with theatrical tradition. They were spoken of as *le Couple* and when their names appeared jointly on the billboards the box office was sure of a sell-out.

Mounet-Sully for many years was the male theatre idol of France and famous throughout Europe and Great Britain. He has been described as "a Jupiter of a man with a voice of distant thunder and eyes of lightning." In her memoirs Marguerite Moreno, that fine actress who was first to create *The Mad Woman of Chaillot* wrote her impressions of Mounet-Sully at the time when she was one of his pupils in the Conservatoire. "He lived in a world of gods and demi-gods. When he came down from this empyrean he must have found us poor mortals as small as we found him great." His art was indeed genuinely great, his forte being the classics, the grand roles of Racine and Corneille. The creation which is recorded as being one of the most magnificent in theatre history was his Oedipus. Whoever saw him never forgot the impact of the terrible scene when that luckless king, after discovering that he has unwittingly married his own mother, has ripped his eyes from their sockets. (It might have come as a shock to his adoring public to have learned that, for this gory scene, to give his make-up a more realistic touch, Mounet slathered his eyelids with strawberry jam!)

Sarah Bernhardt and Mounet-Sully first appeared opposite one another in Racine's *Andromache*. She was twenty-nine and he a glorious thirty-two and their joint success established them both as the Français' leading tragedy interpreters.

However, Sarah Bernhardt was not immediately allowed to play the great classical heroines. Perrin, the cold disciplinarian, kept her for a time in secondary parts. She was put on as Aricie, the touching ingénue of *Phèdre*, and she gave such a moving performance, people who saw it said the title of that drama should be changed to *Aricie*. Next she was cast in Octave Feuillet's *Le Sphynx*, supporting Croizette, who was given the star role. Sarah accepted the lesser position with good grace. Then night after night at home she studied her interpretation with serious concentration, secretly determined in the eventual performance to outshine her friend Croizette. Yet in a flash she could switch from diligent work to giddy frivolity. Feuillet, the author, recalling rehearsals, wrote: "She turns up dressed in the height of fashion, or at least dressed carefully in her own fashion; she is all in velvet . . . and always with a high *ruche* collar . . . generally clutching a few bunches of fresh flowers. She rehearses her part with considerable care and with the sober gravity it requires . . . When the act is over, she breaks abruptly into a ballet-step, hops about the stage, sits down at a piano and accompanies herself in a bizarre Negro dance-tune which she sings in a very pretty voice. Then she rises and begins to march about, taking long steps like a clown, laughs in your face as she munches the chocolates with which her pockets are stuffed, takes from her reticule a little rabbit's foot which she passes over her lips, shows her teeth, white as fresh almonds, and goes on munching chocolates." For all such foolery at rehearsals, the hit of *Le Sphynx* was not Sophie Croizette but Sarah Bernhardt.

A hot summer had set in. The Comédie Française, in those days, did not shut down with their present *clôture annuelle* during July and August. Sarah was tired and wanted some time off for a rest. Her health was still precarious. In fact, during her seven and a half years at the Théâtre Français she never felt completely well.

She continued to have periodic fainting spells and she still occasionally bled at the mouth. She approached Perrin and asked for a few weeks' vacation. That unfeeling autocrat flatly refused her. He was putting on Voltaire's *Zaïre* in a special production and he wanted Bernhardt for the title role. The actress pleaded ill health. She said that she could never live through the strain of rehearsing in mid-July and August. Perrin impassively ordered her to report for work on an appointed day and added that if she failed to show up, he'd impose an exorbitant fine on her. Sarah was wild with frustration. For all that Voltaire might be France's immortal philosopher-critic-poet-historian, she abominated his play.

One can hardly blame her, for it is indeed a rather preposterous work. *Zaïre*, a Christian child, is stolen by Turks and brought up as a Moslem in the seraglio of the Sultan Orosmane. She is about to marry the Sultan when, after a lot of intricate and somewhat idiotic plot, a long-lost father and brother appear most inconveniently and convert the girl to Christianity, after which everything ends in utter woe and a double death by dagger. Sarah hated the part. Perhaps the subconscious realization that Madame Nathalie's first name was Zaïre aggravated her attitude. Even Mounet-Sully's excellent portrayal of the Sultan Orosmane didn't help.

They opened on a sweltering August 6, and Sarah made up her mind that getting through the show would actually kill her. She was determined to die as a revenge on Perrin. To this mournful aim, she acted with violent abandon, giving whatever was her "all." She let out cries and shrieks that fairly ripped the fly-loft. She emoted with an intensity which she felt certain would burst her blood vessels, and when Mounet-Sully as the jealousy-maddened Orosmane made the gesture of stabbing her, she grabbed the dagger and gouged her own breast until real gore trickled forth. Then, in those writhing death throes for which she became so noted, she collapsed onto the ground, fully convinced of the immediate demise through which she was going to get even with Perrin. The curtain came down and she found to her astonishment that she was anything but dead. In fact, she felt gloriously alive. She jumped to her feet with the vigor of a young athlete to take her curtain calls. Instead of tottering off-stage half swooning onto Mounet's arm, she fairly skipped to her dressing room, where she felt invigorated and ready, if need be, to go through the entire performance all over again. At this moment she realized her own extraordinary sources of self-renewal. Much as she regretted not being able to carry out a revenge on Perrin, the realization was joyously gratifying.

Zaïre was followed in that same year of 1874 by a personal triumph in the role which has for two centuries been the greatest challenge for any French actress, Racine's tortured and terrible Phèdre. She got the part through a fluke. It had originally been allotted to an actress named Mademoiselle Rousseil, who was already billed and rehearsing when she and Perrin had a bitter altercation, Rousseil demanding that she be made a *sociétaire* before appearing as Phèdre and Perrin, who was not one to be pushed about, giving her the choice of biding her time before that promotion or else taking leave of the Français. The lady chose to leave and she did so just three days before the scheduled performance. Perrin sent an urgent summons to Bernhardt and nearly bowled her over with the information that she was to go on as substitute for Rousseil. She had exactly seventy-four hours in which to memorize the lines, rehearse the action and think out the interpretation of one of the most difficult roles in classical tragedy.

The cast was a fine one, with Mounet-Sully playing Hippolyte, Phèdre's handsome and virtuous stepson for whom this fascinating and unprincipled heroine conceives an overpowering physical passion which in those days was looked upon as horrifyingly incestuous. And yet if a stepmother-stepson erotic relationship is not regarded as incest, the tragic aspect of *Phèdre* makes very little sense. Having Mounet as co-star was of inestimable support. She needed support badly, for on opening night she was weak and sick with stage fright. She thought of all the actresses whom this monumental role had either broken or carried to glory. The ghost of Rachel seemed to hover near and she anticipated with dread the comments of the old-timers out in the audience: "You think this woman is good? You should have seen the sublime Rachel!" She knew hers would be a widely different performance, that Rachel's art was of the grand, classical tradition, noble but severe, whereas hers, belonging to no so-called school, was completely her own. Her acting had been termed "modern" because there was no other way to categorize it. Suddenly she heard her cue to go on. With a whispered *"quand même!"* which with her was becoming a form of Hail Mary, she made her first entrance in the role which was to be her greatest. From the very start it was one of those magical evenings, all too rare for any actress, when she felt not only inspired but *right* in every word she spoke, every gesture she made, when, as she herself put it, "The god was there." Her Phèdre was a creation of consummate artistry. At one moment she was all weakness, fever and fragility, at the next her movements were those of a wounded panther and again of a salacious voluptuary, as when, with hands clutching her inner thighs, she cried out her desire in the line *"C'est Venus toute entière à sa proie attachée!"* Racine's women had hitherto been deprived of their sex by two centuries of falsely noble interpretation, but Bernhardt's Phèdre was all sex, a female devoured by insatiable lust and abject guilt. Sir George Arthur, who saw it often, wrote of the "terrible mixture of triumph and self-loathing; and her grief and horror of herself were so poignant as to turn, for those of us who heard the agonized tones, horror for the sin into something like pity for the sinner." She acted with her entire body, and when she tried to seduce the stubbornly virtuous Hippolyte, she entwined him in the coils of a snake. The audience sat fascinated and aghast. Everyone was immeasurably moved emotionally, even physically. Their ovation was thunderous, and after the last curtain call Sarah fainted effectively into Mounet's arms.

The critics raved. Most of them spoke of her spellbinding femaleness. Jules Lemaître wrote that she put in her role "not only her soul, her spirit and her physical charm, but her sex. Such bold acting would be shocking in anyone else; but nature has deprived her of so much flesh and having given her the looks of a chimeric princess, her light and spiritual grace changes her most audacious movements into exquisiteness." Sarcey was a little more realistic. "This is nature itself served by a marvellous intelligence, by a soul of fire, by the most melodious voice that ever enchanted human ears. This woman plays with her heart, with her entrails."

This was the first of what were to be many triumphs in the role. Over the years Sarah Bernhardt as Phèdre was to become a sort of national institution which the French claimed as uniquely their own, along with Notre Dame and the Eiffel Tower.

Throughout her long career, *Phèdre* never had the box-office popularity of her *Lady of the Camellias* nor the drum-rattling appeal of *l'Aiglon*, but artistically it was her masterpiece. It was also, of course, her most difficult creation. Because it was so emotionally exhausting, she didn't play it as often as she might have and always before she did, she would sit alone in her dressing room with the lights dim for a solid hour of silence and concentration. And yet for all her perfection in the role, she was seldom satisfied with her performance in this or in many of the others, for that matter. Hers was the inner misgiving, the torturing self-criticism, the "divine unrest" of the great artist, and because she never outgrew this she remained a great artist to the end of her many days.

Her *trac* was always at its most torturing before *Phèdre*, especially because she knew the house was predisposed to be warmly receptive. A friendly house scared her to death because she was afraid of not living up to their expectations. A cold or antagonistic house offered the sort of challenge on which she thrived. Maurice Baring knew this and many years later before a London matinée of *La Dame aux Camélias* he went backstage and deliberately told Bernhardt, who was a good friend of his, that he was seeing the play with a well-known Russian actress who had seen her some time

ago in that play and had found her performance careless and un-
convincing. This was all Bernhardt needed. That afternoon she
acted her heart out. The audience including the Russian actress was
dissolved and one could hardly hear some lines for the blowing of
noses. After the final curtain the very members of the cast were
so undone, their make-up was running in rivulets down their cheeks.

In October of '75, the Français put on a single performance of
La Fille de Roland, a patriotic play that was to be revived from
time to time on national occasions. The action takes place in the
days of Charlemagne and the text is full of heroic speeches about
country, victory and just revenge. The bitter defeat of 1870 was
still fresh in Frenchmen's minds and the chauvinists read into *La
Fille de Roland* a stirring plea for the much-talked-about *revanche*
against Germany. This was an official performance with Maréchal
MacMahon, then President of the Republic, seated with his wife in
the box of honor. When Mounet-Sully as Charlemagne thundered
forth the line *"La France a besoin d'un bras!"* the audience spontaneously rose and, turning toward the presidential box, applauded
le Grand Soldat who had put down the Commune. MacMahon
rose in acknowledgment and as the ovation died down, he took his
wife's bouquet, tossed it at the leading lady's feet and called out
"Vive Sarah!" at which she made a graceful reverence almost to
the floor and in tones of a golden trumpet cried out, *"Vive la
France!"* and the house went into happy Gallic insanity.

By now Bernhardt realized her powerful position as the leading
woman star of the Paris theatre and she accepted as a matter of
course one journalist's statement that "there are only two celebrities
in France today . . . Gambetta and Sarah Bernhardt." She knew
that if she chose she could, should occasion arise, tell Perrin where
to get off. Perrin knew it too and was careful never to let such occasion arise. He still put up a cold façade of having the upper hand.
When she defied him in minor matters, he openly called her
"Mademoiselle Révolte" and he still made periodic gestures of casting her in secondary parts.

In one production, Bernhardt arranged to have herself cast in a non-leading role. This was for Parodi's *Rome Vaincue*, a turgid drama about a Vestal Virgin who carelessly loses her virginity, for which misdeameanor she is condemned to be buried alive. At the last moment her blind old grandmother brings her a dagger to plunge into her own heart rather than face the more hideous death. On learning that the girl's hands are tied behind her, the desperate old woman herself strikes the fatal blow.

Bernhardt, with her unerring sense of theatre, asked to be cast, not as the errant Vestal, but as Posthumia, the blind grandmother. She was thirty-two years young but she played the pitiful crone with convincing reality. The scene in which she fumblingly laid bare her granddaughter's left breast and felt for where the heart was beating was almost unbearably poignant, and when she plunged in the dagger, "The audience," wrote Sir George Arthur, "was as if electrified . . . Sarah's whispers, Sarah's gestures and Sarah's hoarse cry in this grim episode must be burnt into memory." This cheerful dramatic offering ends with a scene outside the tomb of the slaughtered Vestal with the old woman groping her way to knock piteously on the door and beg for admission. Sarah managed the effect "in that whisper which could be heard right across the house . . . after which she seemed to disappear into the shadow of the grave as the curtain came slowly down."

Bernhardt's outstanding role of 1877 was her Doña Sol in Victor Hugo's *Hernani*. That revered tragedy at its opening forty-seven years previously had been considered so avant-garde and such an outrage to classical convention that it had roused a controversial riot which has gone down in dramatic and literary history, and which today is hard to believe for, as reading matter, one would recommend *Hernani* for sleepless nights. It had long been a regular, almost yearly item of the Français repertoire, but Bernhardt brought to it a new freshness with her special magic as the luckless Castilian noblewoman who loves the bandit Hernani, endures for his sake dire complications of plot, and at the finish dies jointly with him, both sharing the contents of a phial of poison. The role of Charles V was played by Worms, a brilliant actor despite the unfortunate English connotation of his last name. Mounet-Sully in all the glory of his looks and talent played Hernani. By now, the love affair between the two brilliant artists was common knowledge. At the end of the last act when the popular "Couple" fell dying into each other's arms, the audience wept and applauded with appreciation that was downright fatuous. The author was in front that night and he was genuinely elated. He told the friends who were with him that, for the first time, he had seen his Doña Sol properly acted. (It is to be hoped that the ghost of Mademoiselle Mars, who had triumphantly originated it, was not within earshot.) The following morning, Sarah received a small box with the accompanying note:

> Madame, you were great and charming; you moved me, me the old warrior, and, at a certain moment when the public, touched and enchanted by you, applauded, I wept. This tear which you caused me to shed is yours. I place it at your feet,
>
> Victor Hugo.

The "tear" was a single perfect diamond drop attached to a delicate gold chain bracelet. Some years later in England while staying at the country estate of the Sassoons, she lost the exquisite little trophy and was heartbroken (Sarah was notoriously careless with her possessions). Mr. Sassoon, in an effort to repair the loss, sent her a magnificent jewel which she returned to him, graciously explaining that nothing could ever take the place of Victor Hugo's tear.

Hernani was the Comédie's hit of the '77–'78 season and Sarah Bernhardt was referred to all over town by the pet name of Doña Sol.

By now she had moved from the rue de Rome and had built herself a smallish but elegant *hôtel particulier* or private house designed by the fashionable architect Félix Escalier on the corner of the rue Fortuny and the avenue de Villiers. To say "built herself" is not completely a manner of speech. During its construction she went often to the site to talk with the workmen, offer suggestions to the masons and plasterers and sometimes climb up to dizzy heights on the scaffoldings, terrifying the friends who accompanied her and who didn't dare look up. When the outside was completed the interior was furnished in her characteristic haphazard style. She prevailed upon a few artist friends to decorate the foyer and dining-room walls and her bedroom ceiling. Louise Abbéma painted one mural which must have looked like an enlargement of a colored postcard. Charles-Emmanuel Jadin, who specialized in immense historical scenes, painted another. Georges Clairin, her "dear Jojotte," did some further decoration which must have been in better taste than the others. Clairin had executed some murals for the Paris Opera House which, of their flamboyant kind, were considered fine work. Here she installed her rue de Rome furnishings and added new acquisitions of hit-or-miss worth — the hits being somewhat outnumbered by the misses. This house was her first extravagant "folly" and the outlay in money was tremendous. How she paid for it all remains a mystery, which perhaps is just as well. She claims, as does her granddaughter Lysiane, that she had come into a handsome inheritance of 100,000 francs from an elderly relative in Holland, which is as good an explanation as any. The "folly" cost at least 500,000 francs and for this she drew credit without a worry as to how she would meet the eventual debt. Moreover, she continued to live in her usual style, which was hardly economical — she kept a staff of eight servants, she owned two carriages and she entertained lavishly.

She continued to hold her 5 P.M. "at homes" for the intimates who made up her "Court." Furthermore, on days when she was not booked to appear at the Français, she gave luncheons and dinner parties for large numbers of guests. These gatherings were always entertaining, often brilliant. This woman, who literally panicked at public functions or formal affairs, who if she were bored went into a fainting spell, had to have people around her, but the people must be those she knew or persons who amused her. She could never endure to be alone except when she was studying a part. If during any of her waking hours she were left to herself, she'd ring for *mon p'tit dame* or her secretary or even her maid Félicie, and in the tones of a petulant child demand, "Isn't anybody going to think of me?" It was nothing for her to give a two-hour-long luncheon party, receive her five o'clock intimates, then entertain ten to fourteen guests at a dinner party. The faithful Emile, her butler for forty years, was then a houseboy of eighteen and kept at that time a list of the distinguished persons his mistress received. In addition to her good friends Victor Hugo, Emile Zola, Alexandre Dumas *fils*, Gambetta, Coquelin and Victorien Sardou, there appear the names of Gustave Flaubert, Louis Pasteur, Ernest Renan, Charles Gounod, Jules Lemaître, Ferdinand de Lesseps, Henry Irving, d'Annunzio and Oscar Wilde, to mention only a few.

More than once in Emile's list there appears the entry "His Royal Highness the Prince of Wales." The Prince visited Paris frequently, for he loved that city "gaily and seriously." He was an enthusiastic theatre-goer and, as the world knows, fond of pretty actresses. In the company of friends from the Jockey Club it amused him to pay unannounced dressing-room calls on these lovelies. André Maurois describes the backstage rounds of these gay blades with their "wavy whiskers and curly hair, square monocles set in the eye, towering stove-pipe hats on their heads, the fast young men of the day drifted along the passages to knock at the little iron door which gave access to the wings of the stage." The genial monarch-to-be must have felt quite at home wherever Bernhardt was acting. When in 1882 she was playing Sardou's *Fédora*, as a lark the Prince doubled for the corpse in the scene in which the heroine weeps over the pall-covered body of her murdered lover. Parisian society was delighted. It was not only backstage that he saw Sarah Bernhardt. He called often at the avenue de Villiers and was a frequent dinner guest. News of this spread across the Channel, infuriating the London hostesses who struggled, with less success, to entice the heir to the throne to their far less amusing receptions. There was, there still is, speculation regarding the relationship between Bernhardt and that royal personage. Sir Philip Magnus in his recent book about the pleasure-loving monarch says that toward the end of the 1870's he was "fascinated by the actress Sarah Bernhardt of the Comédie Française" and that some twenty years later when he was crowned Edward VII, she was especially invited to the Abbey, to take a place along with Mrs. Keppel and other of the king's beautiful lady friends in a particular box to which the Mayfair wags later referred as "the king's Loose Box." When the present author questioned the actress' granddaughter about her grandmother and Edward VII, Lysiane Bernhardt merely replied, "They were the best of friends."

As a hostess, Sarah Bernhardt was hospitable beyond measure, a good listener and a witty conversationalist. She carried it all off in the grand style. When it came to her "Court," her family or her domestics she was less controlled but these intimates never took her rages too seriously because they knew that they passed as suddenly as they came on and that after the storm there never remained any rancor. Maurice Rostand, son of the poet-playwright, said that she "could be unjust, angry, capricious, unbearable, contradictory, provocative, rebellious, intransigeant; there was only one thing she could not be: petty!" She was also incapable of bearing a grudge. An example of this was her gracious gesture toward Madame Nathalie at the time of that formidable lady's *bénéfice de retraite*. Every *sociétaire* was entitled to a benefit performance given in his or her honor upon retirement from the Français, the proceeds of which were a farewell gift. The participants in the benefit volunteered their talents as an expression of their friendship. Nathalie and Bernhardt had long since buried the hatchet, or rather the Slap, and when the fat old actress' retirement was announced, Sarah was one of the first to sign up as a tribute payer.

In her Memoirs, Bernhardt modestly states that in 1878 all the

famous, great or royal visitors who came to Paris for the Exposition
were callers at her house. And the statement may very well be true.
The Exposition Universelle, like most World's Fairs, lost thousands
of francs for its promoters and at the same time brought thousands
of visitors to the city. The big attraction was Monsieur Eiffel's iron
tower, whose giant feet straddled the Champ de Mars and whose
point appeared to pierce the sky. Although most visitors to the
Fair looked upon the Tour Eiffel as an eighth wonder of the world,
many aesthetic-minded Parisians considered it a monstrosity, and
when the authorities announced that it was to remain as a permanent
fixture of the town countless letters of protest were written to the
papers about it.

Another attraction of the season, and a completley uncontro-
versial one, was a captive balloon anchored in the Tuileries Gardens
and operated by Pierre Giffard, a daring aeronaut who for a
nominal price would take customers in the hanging basket up to
500 meters, from which giddy height they could gaze out trem-
ulously over the fair grounds, the city and environs. Sarah, watching Giffard make several of his leisurely ascents, was entranced.
Suddenly she became fired with the desire to go ballooning herself,
not in any safely tethered contraption but in a free sailing one. She
discussed this latest whim with a balloonist she knew named Louis
Godard and he obligingly passed along the information to Giffard.
The two men rigged up a special and charming little aircraft. The
bag was gay with white and orange stripes and on the side of the
basket in golden letters was its name, the *Doña Sol*. Sarah was enchanted.

She had kept her project secret, partly because she didn't want
to upset her beloved and pampered Maurice who, she knew, would
want to be taken along, and partly because she didn't want any un-
due publicity attending this outing. Godard was to handle the
flight and she had invited Georges Clairin to be the other passenger
with her. Prince Napoleon, the now corpulent "Plon-Plon," had
expressed a wish to join the expedition, but Godard took one look

at his excessive weight and said he'd be too much of a risk. Clairin helped Bernhardt into the basket, Godard freed the anchor, vaulted aboard, tossed a few sandbags over the side and the *Doña Sol* rose above the mansards of the Louvre and headed out into the blue, cloud-flecked Paris sky.

For the actress ever to have imagined that this trip could have been kept secret is an example of her occasional moments of childish naïveté. Not only was the name of her latest hit role gleamingly announced on the side of the low-flying craft, but there in the swaying basket stood the unmistakable figure of the one and only Sarah in her inevitable white attire with characteristic yardages of scarves and veils streaming out behind her and semaphoring to the passing world directly below. The *Doña Sol,* propelled by the gusts of a summer breeze, soared prettily over the Pont-des-Arts at the inauspicious moment when Perrin happened to be crossing it. Also, inauspiciously, there happened to be crossing from the opposite direction that Narcissus of a dandy, Count Robert de Montesquiou. The two men met. Montesquiou, pointing skyward with his turquoise-handled cane, remarked languidly, "I see, Perrin, your star has turned into a shooting one!" Perrin looked up and became livid with rage. The rest of Paris looked up and became transfixed with delight. Swifter than the flight of any balloon, the story spread all over town. The scandalmongers got busy and one of their more preposterous inventions was that Sarah's latest escapade was to take her lover aloft for the novel experience of having an amorous interlude in the skies. Just where Louis Godard was expected to be looking while she and Clairin were enjoying a bit of dalliance was not made clear.

The breeze freshened and the three balloonists became cold. Sitting on small chairs in the shelter of the basket sides, they consumed a delicious *déjeuner en l'air* of foie gras, bread, oranges and champagne. They had, by now, been wafted well beyond the confines of the city. Gradually the breeze turned into a strong wind and the *Doña Sol* was violently buffeted about. Godard struggled

to steady the basket, Clairin struggled to keep down the foie gras
and Sarah suffered a severe nose bleed. Threatening clouds blan-
keted the setting sun, suddenly night was upon them and they had
no idea where they were. Barely visible in the darkness below,
they could make out a small building beside a railroad track.
Godard opened a gas valve, blew a blast on a brass horn, threw out
a guide rope to an astonished station master and they came to
ground in a whistle stop called Emerainville.

After catching a slow train back to Paris, Bernhardt hurried to
the avenue de Villiers to find a line-up of carriages outside her
house, a bevy of reporters waiting in the foyer, Madame Guérard in
tears and Maurice in a fit of black sulks because Maman had not
included him on the expedition. It took twenty-four hours and the
promise of a new pony and cart before the pampered fourteen-year-
old would speak to her again.

Next day, Sarah was summoned to appear before Perrin in his
office. From the moment she walked through the door, the administrator started raking "Mademoiselle Révolte" over the coals.
But she, in the asbestos of her egotism, was impervious to the coals.
Perrin pointed out the strict and well-known Comédie Française
ruling that no member of the troupe could at any time leave Paris
without special permission from the Administration. "Mademoiselle
Révolte" retorted that she had had no intention of leaving Paris.
Was she to blame if the winds and the elements had carried her out
of bounds? The ruling was, to her way of thinking, ridiculous to
begin with. Perrin fumed and said he'd fine her a thousand francs,
that her outrageous antics were becoming a disgrace to the great
and glorious name of France's National Theatre. Sarah shrilled
back that her non-professional life was nobody's business but her
own. As for his great and glorious theatre, she was bringing in more
money at the box office than any other actress in its history had
done with the possible and inconsequential exception of Rachel.
She was getting sick of the place with all its pompous traditions
and regulations, she yelled, and added that the limitation of weekly

appearances for an actress was frustration itself. As for the thousand franc fine, sooner than pay it, she'd hand in her resignation and she stormed out of the place, fully intending to do just that.

Her threat frightened the wits out of Perrin. He was as much aware as she of her box-office value. Next day, her resignation was brought to him. In a panic, Perrin sought out the intercession of Edmond Turquet, Minister of Fine Arts, who was able to effect a compromise. Bernhardt said she would withdraw her resignation provided she be immediately made a *sociétaire*. Such a decision had to be passed by the entire Comédie Française committee. It was, of course, a flagrant hold-up and most members resented it, but they realized that they were on the spot. For the first time in its history, the House of Molière was about to visit a foreign land. The London impresario John Hollingshead had made them an attractive offer for a season at the Gaiety Theatre. The main drawing card would be their controversial fellow-actress, and if she were not included in the company Hollingshead would cancel his contract. There was even suggested the horrid possibility that Hollingshead might go so far as to sign a separate contract with her and another company. Sarah Bernhardt was made a *sociétaire* of the Comédie Française. As a sop to Perrin and their own conscience, the committee also elected Sophie Croizette to a similar promotion.

6.

~~~~~~~~~~~~~~~~~~~~~~~~~~~

THE ROAD WESTWARD

IN JUNE, 1879, London was keenly awaiting the arrival of the
famous company. When it came to the company's most famous
member, her extraordinary art had long been talked about.
Advance rumors of her eccentricities and unconventional morals
had floated across the Channel and the public at large could hardly
wait to see her.

One person, a man of striking appearance and powerful build,
didn't wait but journeyed to Paris several weeks prior to the
British engagement. Driving straight from the station to her house
and brushing aside the butler and footman who tried to bar his
way, he strode unannounced into the main salon, where the lady
was curled up on her divan reading a script. He bowed, handed
her his card and without further formality asked if, during her six
weeks in England, she'd like to make a considerable amount of
extra money. Taken aback she looked at the card and read the
name of Edward Jarrett, which she recognized as that of a celebrated entrepreneur, the Sol Hurok of his day, with offices in
London, New York and Paris. Jarrett had connections in the
theatre and music field the world over and was known as the "Bismarck of managers." If at first Sarah was outraged by the gentleman's unceremonious entrance, she was soon taken by his manner,
which was one of brusque frankness and a certain rugged charm.
She was even more taken by his question about her liking to make
some extra money. Bernhardt not only liked extra money, it was an
ever present necessity for her. Her pleasure in making it was
equaled only by her pleasure in spending it and she was chronically

in debt. She told Jarrett that he might sit down, which he'd already done. His proposition was to book her for private recitals in the houses of rich Londoners, each recital to be for a fee higher than her monthly salary from the Français. Being a man of direct action he had come armed with a contract and she, a woman of quick decision, signed it then and there.

Jarrett, who knew that Sarah Bernhardt's every activity was hot news, lost no time in wiring the information to the British press and the French press lost little further time in republishing the tidings. Perrin sent for "Mademoiselle Révolte" and, white with anger, confronted her with a newspaper on which was pencil-marked an item. It was an announcement of her availability in London to present "her well-known drawing-room repertoire of one-act plays, monologues and proverbs [whatever that meant] all highly adaptable for matinees and soirées of the best society. For further information please communicate with Mr. E. Jarrett, Mlle. Bernhardt's secretary, at Her Majesty's Theatre." Perrin shook with cold fury. How dared she, he said through clenched teeth, how dared she appear professionally anywhere but with the Comédie Française? Sarah cooly replied why not, and asked what right he had to interfere with her augmenting the miserable salary she was receiving from his sacred theatre. Perrin reminded her that it wasn't his sacred theatre but that of its governing body of *sociétaires*, none of whom would even consider any offer to perform on the side. At that she serenely handed him a note that had been sent to her by one of the very same *sociétaires*. It had come from Louis Delaunay, a brilliantly elegant actor who for years even well into middle age was the Comédie's most popular *jeune premier*. Delaunay had written:

Would you care to play *La Nuit d'Octobre* at Lady Dudley's on Thursday June 5th? They will give us each 5,000 francs.

Perrin realized he'd lost this round but said he'd leave the matter up to the governing committee. A special meeting of that august body was held in the *foyer des artistes,* their stately Green Room. The majority were highly resentful of Bernhardt's violation of tradition and although she'd had no hand in Delaunay's defection, they blamed her for that too. The ultimate grudging decision was to allow members of their corps to accept recital engagements during the London run provided they performed no scenes from the current repertory. The committee's resentment heightened to outrage when they were informed that the Gaiety Theatre management was demanding Sarah Bernhardt's appearance in the first night's bill. They had planned as a fitting opening to present two traditional comedies, *Le Misanthrope* and *Les Précieuses Ridicules,* with casts composed of members who had been longest in the House of Molière. As far as seniority went, Bernhardt ranked tenth or eleventh. Perrin wired the situation to Hollingshead and his partner Meyer who, in the interests of their box office, were not concerned with French theatre traditions. They wired back that either Mademoiselle Bernhardt played on the opening night or the Français engagement would be canceled. With baleful reluctance, Perrin and the committee gave way to the extent of saying that between the two comedies, Mademoiselle Bernhardt would go on in the second act of *Phèdre.* The announcement caused an uproar of protest from Parisian theatre-goers. To present an excerpt from a five-act play purely as a showcase for one particular actress was blatantly making a star of her, and for over two hundred years the proud old house had permitted no star system.

The perpetrator of the ruckus was anything but chastened. Elated by a sense of power, she now realized that not only could she write her own ticket at the Comédie Française, she might eventually break away from it. She was getting fed up with its stultifying conformities. She was fast losing what Henry James has called "the serious, the religious view of that establishment . . . the view of Monsieur Sarcey and of the unregenerate provincial mind." She was training her sights on a more distant view: that of herself as a bright new star sailing forth to conquer the world. Meanwhile she might as well conquer London.

Among the multiple distinctions of the French is their tendency to be determined non-travelers. Sarah Bernhardt as the venturesome exception to the insular rule was to spend the greater part of the next forty years in travel. This, however, was her first touring trip to a foreign land and her devoted coterie regarded it as a journey to the ends of the earth. She was showered with bon-voyage presents of a precautionary nature against the hazards of the English Channel: seasick pills, headache capsules, panaceas in case of vertigo. A friend sent her a yard of Japanese silk paper to place about her shoulders before dressing as a windbreak, another sent some herb-filled poultices to plaster across her diaphragm to counteract the effects of the ship's motion, someone else contributed a pair of cork soles to clip onto the bottoms of her shoes before stepping onto the wet deck. "Our Sarah," they declared, must not catch a chill.

There was little danger of Their Sarah catching a chill, for the weather was cloudless and balmy. On the Calais dock a large group of well-wishers had gathered to wave God-speed to the nation's famous *comédiens*. Just before the final hoot of the boat whistle, a wild-looking young man leapt on board to present Mademoiselle Bernhardt with an offering of his own contrivance. This was a belt to fasten about her waist in case of shipwreck, an eventuality he seemed to regard as a foregone conclusion. It was equipped with some dozen small inflated bladders which he claimed would hold her upright and well out of the water, rather, one would surmise, on the order of a nun buoy. Each bladder, he explained, contained a lump of sugar, and it was a well-established fact that sugar was a source of energy. All she had to do was remove a pin from a little cushion also attached to the belt, pierce the bladder and extract the sugar. One bladder which was especially marked contained a phial of cognac to be used as a last resort in case, as she bobbed about in the icy water, rescue did not come for several hours. Sarah thanked the donor, gravely accepted his life-saving device and as soon as the packet boat cleared the harbor, handed it to Madame Guérard to jettison in mid-Channel where, kept afloat by its bladders, the currents doubtless carried it out to astonish the fishing fleet.

A crowd was waiting on the Folkestone quay to welcome the distinguished French troupe. In her Memoirs Sarah states that it was a thousand strong and that as she in person descended the gangplank there were cries of "Hip, hip hooray!" which may or may not have been the case. Certainly the crowd was sizable and it was headed by the mayor of Folkestone resplendent in robes and chain of office. A bouquet was handed to each of the actresses, but when it came to Sarah (and again according to her own account) she was fairly deluged with additional floral tributes. A slim, handsome young man stepped shyly forward to hand her a modest bunch of violets. He was a twenty-six-year-old actor not yet come into his own and his sensitive, poetic face struck her as being the ideal of Hamlet. It was a prophetic observation, for the young actor was to become one of the unforgettable Hamlets of all time and his name was Johnston Forbes-Robertson.

Another young man also stepped forward, larger, taller and far less self-effacing. It was Oscar Wilde, then glorying in his "Aesthetic Period" of the "Transcendental and the Utterly-Utter." He bore an armful of white lilies (among his many epithets Wilde was sometimes known as "The Apostle of the Lily"). These he spread on the ground for "The Incomparable One" to walk upon, a prospect which "The Incomparable One" didn't much relish. She had a true and tender passion for flowers and to trample a dozen or more exquisite lilies seemed a misdemeanor of wanton vandalism. Reluctantly she complied and as she stepped gingerly along, her flamboyant admirer shouted at the top of his powerful lungs, "Vive Sarah Bernhardt!" a cry he led the crowd into repeating until the actress had boarded the train.

Oscar Wilde and Sarah Bernhardt were already friends. They had met in Paris and in his extravagant fashion he adored her both as a consummate artist and as the irresistible woman she could be when she chose. It pleased her no end when he composed a sonnet to her. The fact that knowing no English she could not have understood a word of it didn't at all lessen the pleasure. For years whenever their paths crossed they protested warm, almost emotional friendship. As in every relationship Sarah Bernhardt was unpredictable. Sometimes she would be loyal to a friend through thick and thin, sometimes she would become callously indifferent. Twelve years later Oscar Wilde was to write *Salomé*. He wrote it in French expressly for Sarah Bernhardt, and when he read the script aloud to her she was madly enthusiastic and all for putting it on the following season in London. They engaged Graham Robertson to execute the scenery and costumes. The players, they decided, must all be in yellow against a deep violet sky. They also hit upon the ultra-ultra idea of placing great braziers on stage in which would burn a variety of perfumes. Plans were going swimmingly when the Lord Chamberlain's office suddenly banned the play on the grounds that it was against the law for any Biblical character to appear on the British stage. That law, it turned out, went back to the Protestant sixteenth century, its purpose having been to suppress the Catholic Mystery plays. Nobody stepped forward to champion Wilde or Bernhardt except the fine Scottish critic William Archer, who wrote indignant articles to the *Pall Mall Gazette* loudly denouncing the censor as "The Great Irresponsible." But Archer's was a voice crying in the wilderness and the project had to be abandoned. Not long after came the trial and the scandal which rocked the respectable world and made a broken man of Wilde. While languishing in Reading Gaol Wilde was sorely in need of funds. He wrote Robert Sherard, who was then in Paris, asking him to persuade Sarah to purchase the rights of *Salome* for £400 and produce it at her theatre. Sherard called and Sarah was all dramatic concern over the cruel plight of her *cher Oscar*. She wept and said that although she was unable to produce the play, she'd give Sherard the money to take to their unfortunate friend and told him to call the following day. Sherard turned up at the appointed time only to be informed that Madame was out and had left no message. Next day he called again and the same thing happened. He made two further attempts but with no better results.

And yet Wilde continued to worship her. Their ensuing meetings were always charged with emotion. In 1899 after a performance of *Tosca* in Nice Wilde was to write Robert Ross, "I went round to see Sarah and she embraced me and wept, and I wept, and the whole evening was wonderful." To Wilde she was ever magically young. "What has age to do with acting?" he wrote. "The only person in the world who could act Salomé is Sarah Bernhardt, that 'Serpent of Old Nile' older than the pyramids." Shortly before he died he told a friend that "the three women I have most admired in my life are Sarah Bernhardt, Lily Langtry and Queen Victoria. I would have married any one of them with pleasure." It would seem an interesting choice.

The company's arrival in London was in chilly contrast to its warm reception in Folkestone. There was, to be sure, a red carpet spread along the platform, but no welcoming crowd was waiting on it. Charing Cross Station was dingy, draughty and half deserted. The only persons to meet them were three or four employees of the Gaiety Theatre sent to direct them to their respective lodgings. A special courier had been delegated to take care of Bernhardt. "Why the red carpet and where is the crowd?" she asked him. The carpet, he said, had been put down for the departure of the Prince and Princess of Wales, who had just left for a visit to a country estate. The crowd which waved them good-by had already dispersed. The actress was not a little put out. She had pictured being met by a delegation of dignitaries dispatched very possibly by H.R.H. himself. "Then he won't be at my opening!" she exclaimed. The courier admitted that such unfortunately was the case but that the Prince had engaged a box for each of Miss Bernhardt's opening performances in her different rôles. In the event of His Royal Highness' absence from town, the box would be occupied by his brother the Duke of Connaught. Sarah, who had never set eyes on the Duke of Connaught, thought him a dismal substitute.

As a matter of fact, she was finding everything about London dismal. The courier had a brougham waiting to take her to her residence in Belgravia. As she looked through the window at the wet pavements, the soot-blackened official buildings, the formidable private mansions, the fog-veiled street lamps, she sank into a well of deep depression from which she emerged with the alacrity of a salmon leaping upstream when she stepped into the charming house and garden at 77 Chester Square that had been rented for her six weeks' occupancy. The house was delightfully furnished, her trunks which had been sent on ahead were already unpacked, a domestic staff was in attendance and behind the gleaming bars of a brass grate, a glowing coal fire took off the chill of an English June.

The hall and sitting room were banked with enough flowers to start a horticultural show. Her footman handed her the cards. Most of them had been sent by friends in Paris but many came from British well-wishers whom she had yet to meet. One magnificent spray of Marshal Niel roses bore the simple message "Welcome! Henry Irving." There was a pile of correspondence waiting for her: requests for autographs, notes of welcome, invitations to luncheons, teas, dinners, garden parties and charity bazaars. She ran quickly through them, then cheerfully dropped them all on the floor to be retrieved by *mon p'tit dame*.

She was rather mystified that some of the invitations should have come from titled individuals. In France at that time no theatre people were socially accepted by the Upper Crust. The English attitude was becoming less strict but conservative aristocracy still regarded players as "rogues and vagabonds," and now to find the doors of London's elite opening out for an actress, and a French one at that, struck her as pleasant but odd until she found out the reason. Her old friend Marshal Canrobert, who as a former diplomat knew much of the international *beau mônde*, had written to

Lord Dudley asking him and his wife to look out for the young artist. More powerful influence came from the Heir Apparent, who asked the Rothschilds to extend their hospitality and see that she met amusing people. Word had got about that Sarah Bernhardt was to be received by Society, and Mayfair was agog.

Hardly had she caught her breath before Edward Jarrett came in with a list of the private recitals he'd booked. He spearheaded a bunch of reporters who bombarded their questions. How did she like London, what did she think of English women, what was wrong with British food. They departed and the callers started arriving. The first was a friend named Hortense Damian, a woman much in the social whirl and dedicated to everything that was chic. The word had just come into smart vocabulary. Miss Damian brought along what she called "The Chic Commandments," a jingle she'd composed which listed what the actress must do while in London, how she must ride in Rotten Row, visit Parliament, attend garden parties, pay return calls on hostesses, answer invitations in her own hand and further momentous directives which Sarah had no intentions of following.

A countess dropped in. She was followed by Lady Dudley, a charming creature and ravishing to behold. This was the era of the velvet-bound album on the parlor table containing *carte-de-visite* likenesses of theatre celebrities, royalty and popular hostesses. Lady Dudley was one of the much photographed whose pictures were on sale in the stationers' shops. Along with Lady Randolph Churchill, Lady Helen Vincent and Mrs. Cornwallis-West she was known as one of "The Professional Beauties." Lady Dudley was lively and witty and she considered it rather a lark to introduce Miss Bernhardt into the Prince of Wales set. That evening Sarah dined at the house of a baroness, where she found the food excellent and the guests delightful. She sat next the pre-Raphaelite painter John Millais, whose storytelling pictures were right up her artistic alley. She had seen his mawkish canvas "The Princes in the Tower" and as she told him how it had moved her, she tactfully wiped a tear from one eye. Millais, of course, thought her most perceptive. Next morning she rode in Hyde Park with Lord Dudley, who mounted her on a beautiful little saddle horse. As they cantered down the Ladies' Mile, the sun came out between Constable-like clouds to sparkle on rain-washed boughs, to gleam on white swan necks and the starched aprons of nannies, to flash on whirling wheel spokes and the rumps of high-stepping ponies, and Sarah Bernhardt fell in love with London. It was a love to which she was to be faithful throughout the next forty years.

She may have fallen in love with London, but her immediate concern was whether or not London was going to fall in love with her. For all the warmth with which she had been welcomed by high society, she had yet to prove herself with the British theatre-going public, and her trial by fire was to be the next day.

They opened at the Gaiety on June 4, and she suffered the worst attack of stage fright she'd had to date. This crippling *trac* always hit her when she didn't go on early in a play. Moreover she knew in advance that the house was going to be friendly. This opening was sheer torture. Here a friendly audience which had come expressly to see her had to sit through the whole of Molière's *Misanthrope* before she put in an appearance. She had to sit through it too — only she didn't do much sitting. She paced the dressing-room floor, three times she took off her make-up and put it back on again. She kept going over her lines and kept muffing them. She had never before performed a scene out of context from the rest of the play. In *Phèdre*, the first act was a spring board to launch her into the fury and passion of the second. To spring unaided was pulling herself up by the bootstraps. The call boy knocked at her door for places and she could hardly make it to the wings. The curtain rose and Mounet-Sully as Hippolyte strode on for his opening speech, which was brief. Then came her cue and she stood stock still as though paralyzed. The stage manager gave her a shove and she made her London entrance.

She states that right from the start, she pitched her voice too high and was unable to lower it. If she did, it didn't mar her performance of that tremendous scene in which Phèdre tells Hippolyte, her stepson, of the devouring love and lust she feels for him. As she uttered the long and terrible confession, she was *Phèdre en toute as fureur*. Her cry to the gods, those gods "who have lit the fatal fire in the blood of my loins," was horrifyingly wonderful. If the majority of the audience failed to understand Racine's words, Bernhardt's gestures, her craving tones carried the meaning. Sir George Arthur, who was present, said that she "set every nerve and fibre in their bodies throbbing and held them spellbound." It was one of the woman's most glorious performances — one of those magical nights when, in her own phrase, "the god was there." At the finish of the scene, she made a blazing exit and fainted. It was a genuine faint and she had to be quickly revived then dragged back, half-conscious and supported by Mounet-Sully, to receive an ovation that was unprecedented in the British theatre. The critics tossed aside native reserve and next day the papers were ecstatic.

Sarah Bernhardt's style of acting was something new to the London public. For that matter, it was new to the public everywhere. People generally were unprepared for such a combination of delicate lyricism and startling boldness. One reviewer spoke of her "orchidaceous air." Matthew Arnold wrote of her hollow eyes and consumptive looks, calling her "a fugitive vision of delicate features under a shower of hair and a cloud of lace." Ellen Terry in her own memoirs said, "She was as transparent as an azalea only more so; like a cloud only not so thick; smoke from a burning paper describes her more nearly."

Ellen Terry and Sarah Bernhardt were to become lasting friends. The enchanting actress with her joyous art and irresistible charm was the darling of England. No two players were ever less alike off stage, Bernhardt all artifice and fascinating pose, Terry all engaging simplicity and as fresh as an English garden. Terry admired Bernhardt as an actress and, probing behind the pose, loved her as a person. She called her by the unlikely pet name of "Sally B." Graham Robertson tells of a later time when Sarah was again in

London and he had gone to a matinee of *l'Aiglon*. The theatre was stiflingly hot and during one of the interminable scenes of Rostand's patriotic masterpiece, Robertson stepped outside to get a breath of air when Ellen Terry happened to come along the street. She'd been to market and, like any country woman, was carrying home a basket of eggs. She paused to greet Robertson, whom she knew well, glanced at the billboard to see which play was being done, and asked, "Is Sally B. dead yet?" Robertson told her that scene was about to go on. "Then," said Terry, "let's slip into the pit and watch Sally B. die!" At the finish they went around to the flower-banked overheated dressing room to congratulate "Sally B.," who welcomed them effusively and asked what part of the house they'd been sitting in. When they told her the pit, she was horrified. She was even more horrified when as they left she offered them the use of her private carriage and Ellen Terry said cheerily, "No, thanks. I left my basket of eggs in the pit. I must pick it up and it's such a lovely day, I'm walking home."

The artist W. Graham Robertson, whose writing is so much better than his painting, has left us many amusing glimpses of Sarah. He was often invited to her lunches and dinners in London and Paris. He recalls a time when the conversation turned to the roles each would have liked to play in life and Sarah immediately announced that she would like to have been a queen. Madame Guérard protested that no people would have ever put up with her and that her head would have been off within a week. Sarah solemnly agreed, then brightening up said, "But think how many other heads I should have had off during that week!"

Robertson never ceased to be amazed at her continual drive, her compulsion for work. "The two most vital people I have ever known," he wrote, "were Whistler and Sarah Bernhardt. Life was to them an art and a cult. They lived each moment consciously and passionately . . . I have seen the actress after a hard evening's work, come to a momentary halt from physical exhaustion, yet it was as the halt of an engine at a station. The imprisoned energy still throbbed and panted to be off again."

Another lasting friendship in the elite of the English theatre was with Ellen Terry's famous partner, Henry Irving (Terry always referred to him as "His Nibs"). It was not for some twenty years that he was to receive his knighthood — the first ever bestowed on an actor — but it is difficult to think of that elegant and scholarly gentleman as anyone but Sir Henry. He and Terry had launched their highly successful co-starring career at the Lyceum, which under the brilliant Irving management had become the most fashionable playhouse in London. It was due to Henry Irving that the social status of stage people had risen. He was an ornament to any gathering as was his beguiling partner, and daring hostesses were venturing to invite other "acceptable" actors and actresses into their drawing rooms.

Henry Irving had given a welcoming supper party for the Comédie Française company shortly after their opening, but it was later at a charity reception that he and Bernhardt got better acquainted. Like most of these ghastly functions it was torturously boring and the place was hot and overcrowded. The two celebrity victims were exhibited side by side on a raised platform while a perspiring public filed past to stare and shake hands. Irving had as stubborn a resistance to the French language as Bernhardt had to the English but the two got along famously. Most of the persons there were frumpy, middle-aged ladies, fat, red-faced and wearing overelaborate dresses and ludicrous hats. As the line of them came beaming up to be introduced, they began to strike the two guests of honor as unbearably funny. They got into a joint fit of giggles which neither could control and eventually had to make an unceremonious dash from the hall. Once outside, they fell into each other's arms in paroxysms of laughter, and after this they were fast friends until Irving's death in 1905. The language barrier being no problem, they communicated in their own esperanto and always enjoyed themselves perfectly.

During Bernhardt's subsequent visits to London, Sir Henry always gave her a dinner in his famous Beefsteak Room of the

Lyceum Theatre. As some writer put it, the Queen of the French Theatre was entertained by the reigning monarch of the English. Sir Henry's Beefsteak Room was an impressive Gothic hall hung with banners and decorated with theatrical armor. On the walls were portraits of Garrick, Kean, Irving himself and later Sargent's magnificent canvas of Terry as Lady Macbeth. Here the great actor had received such notables as Liszt, Tennyson and Kipling. Martin Harvey wrote of Irving, "seated at the head of a long table lighted with candles and loaded with good things . . . a great fire crackling in the broad, Baronial hearth, his clear-cut alabaster profile outlined against the sombre oaken panelling." On one of the occasions of Bernhardt's visits, Irving remarked in a tone of philosophical resignation that old age comes to us all. At this gloomy prediction, Sarah leaned across to Ellen Terry and said, "My darling Nell, there are two people who shall never grow old . . . you and I."

Her triumph at the Gaiety made Sarah Bernhardt more in demand than ever. The invitations continued to pour in. Many she ignored; others she accepted, or rather she'd instruct Madame Guérard to accept for her, then, at the last minute, she'd decide not to attend whatever the occasion was or she'd arrive outrageously late. Such behavior was not an act on her part. It was simply that the social amenities seemed to her a waste of time. She was equally cavalier in regard to the private recitals Jarrett had arranged, and kept a sizable audience at Lady Combermere's waiting on gold chairs for one hour before she put in an appearance. She, who in the theatre was punctuality itself, regarded these "non-pro" obligations as being of little importance except for the extra money they afforded. She seldom wrote a note of thanks for gifts or courtesies received. If she did, the note was almost undecipherable. She said of her own careless handwriting, "*Que voulez-vous?* I am too busy living to finish my words." She didn't care what she said or to whom she said it. One of her often quoted replies was to a dowager countess, who hearing her mention her son said, "I didn't know you were married." "I am not, Madame la Comtesse," she answered sweetly, "my son was *un petit accident d'amour*." Smart society forgave her because she was the sensation of the current season. Ultra-conservative aristocracy failed to share the enthusiasm. Lady Frederick Cavendish wrote to a friend:

> London has gone mad over the principal actress in the Comédie Française who are here; Sarah Bernhardt, a woman of notorious character. Not content with being run after on the stage, this woman is asked to respectable people's houses to act, and even to luncheon and dinner and all the world goes. It is an outrageous scandal!

There is little doubt that Sarah enjoyed this popular uproar. Society *per se* meant nothing to her. Even the attentions of royalty were like so many good press notices, no more. If it had not been for the reminder from a friend, she would have forgotten completely to go to a party to which she had been invited in honor of the Heir Presumptive. Large functions bored her. What counted with her were the invitations, the tangible proof of having brought herself to this degree of importance. This complex woman, for all of her success, all her eccentricity, all her *je m'en-fichisme*,* needed constant bolstering of her ego.

Her popularity was not confined to the smart set. In literary and artistic circles she was sought after as "the shibboleth of the intellectuals" and the darling of bohemian London. Oscar Wilde gave her supper parties in his Salisbury Street flat, where she wrote her name on the wall of his "White Room" along with the other signatures of the brilliant and famous. The painter Burne-Jones, who had worshipped her in Paris, continued his worship in England, and was to do so for the remainder of his life. Some years later he entrusted Graham Robertson with a note to deliver to the lady saying, "Will you give the enclosed to the Supreme and Glorious One, kneeling as you give it?"

Jarrett had arranged for an exhibition of Bernhardt's sculptures

---

* Tr.: approximately "Don't-give-a-damn-ism."

and paintings in a fashionable Piccadilly art gallery. The opening was spectacular. One hundred invitations had been sent out and four times that many persons turned up. The event was under the genial patronage of the Prince of Wales, who brought with him his beautiful Princess. Gladstone also attended. The grand, vital old statesman had a love of France and things French. He and Mademoiselle Bernhardt held an agreeable ten-minute conversation mainly exchanging views on capital punishment, of which they both disapproved. The president of the Royal Academy, Sir Frederick Leighton, complimented the artist on her "Palm Sunday," a canvas of a saccharine little girl piously holding a palm leaf in folded hands. This masterpiece was also admired by the Heir Apparent and later purchased by his brother Prince Leopold, which gives one an idea of the sense of art values both of the Royal Academy and of the sons of Queen Victoria. Ten pictures were sold and six pieces of sculpture including a bronze casting of her "Après la Tempête" (the old Breton woman with her drowned grandson), for which some misguided titled lady paid four hundred pounds. The artist, the Piccadilly gallery and Jarrett made a nice little profit.

The exhibition was enthusiastically written up in the papers, but only in the society pages. What genuine art critics thought of it has, perhaps mercifully, not come down to us. To do her justice, Bernhardt never took herself too seriously as either a painter or a sculptress. She knew she had a certain facility in these pursuits. They served as outlets for her boundless energy. Also she was finding in them a source of additional income; but she was honest enough to realize that her works sold chiefly because of her signature on the bottom of each.

The Sarah Bernhardt craze would not have kept up in London if her art as an actress had also not kept up to public expectation. In each performance of the varied repertory, *Hernani*, *Zaïre*, *l'Etrangère* and the rest, always she acted with the same magic, always that incandescent glow seemed to emanate from her and always the reviews were raves. Every time she was billed to appear, the box office took in a hundred and fifty pounds more than on other nights. She found this very satisfactory. Another well-satisfied person was the shrewd manager who had booked her private recitals. He sensed what the future might hold for Sarah Bernhardt and also for Edward Jarrett.

One day he called on her and asked her point-blank if she'd like to make a fortune. Never averse to such a possibility, she enquired how and he proposed a six months' tour of the United States. Sarah gasped and said that the Comédie would never grant her so long a leave. Besides she could act only in French. Jarrett said that leave from the Comédie might be arranged, as for the language problem, he assured her she could act in Chinese and the Americans would turn out in droves to see her. Sarah laughed and graciously dismissed him, though she didn't altogether dismiss the idea. She had conquered the civilized English, it might be an interesting challenge to find out if she could conquer the barbaric Americans. Why should she have to toady to the Français for permission? She put the idea aside for further deliberation and turned to other projects.

Zest for her work in the theatre never palled, but all the extra-curricular social whirl was becoming a bore. She was fed up with meeting so many people. She had always found animals more interesting. For some months she had hankered to own a young pet lion. Someone told her of a man named Cross who ran a zoo in Liverpool and who had two lion cubs, and she made up her mind then and there to acquire them both. Since coming to London she had already collected a small menagerie: three dogs, Miniccio, Bull and Fly, a parrot called Bizibouzou and a monkey she christened with the inspired name of Darwin. Profiting by some free time when she was out of the bill at the Gaiety, she and some friends hopped a train for Liverpool and drove to the Cross Zoo. She looked up the owner, introduced herself and said she wanted to buy his lion cubs. Mr. Cross without further communication led her to a large cage where she confronted the former cubs who had grown to dimensions comparable it would seem to those of the majestic beasts guarding Nelson's Column in Trafalgar Square. She had to admit that as potential pets they were a bit oversize. She hesitated before the elephants. She adored elephants and longed, she said, to own one. But again the size problem arose. After feeding one a full bag of peanuts and lovingly caressing its trunk, she went on to inspect the rest of the collection. She eventually settled for a young and playful cheetah which, Mr. Cross said, could be trained to hunt antelope, a useful attribute for a house pet. She also purchased a gigantic wolfhound with bristling coat and sharp-pointed fangs which proved as docile as a spaniel. By way of a dividend, Mr. Cross presented his distinguished customer with six chameleons of the ordinary variety as well as a rare specimen of the same reptile that had the body of a miniature prehistoric monster and the protruding eyes of a lobster. Each eye focused independently of the other, much of the time they were crossed and by way of tribute to the donor, Sarah named it "Cross-ci Cross-ça." She thought the grotesque beastie completely charming and insisted upon going to a jeweler to have a tiny gold chain fastened about its neck — a job the jeweler could hardly have relished. Then she pinned the end of the chain to the lapel of her jacket as an ornament to wear, she said, when she was in a reptilian mood.

It was still light when they arrived back at Sarah's house. The evening was balmy and the customary gathering of friends were waiting for her in the garden. In addition to the ever present Madame Guérard there were Louise Abbéma and Georges Clairin, who were house guests. Gustave Doré had dropped by. Doré was very much "the thing" in London and, according to E. F. Benson, was "fairly crawling with popularity" and ran his own Doré Gallery in Bond Street. With him was an Italian portrait painter named Giuseppe de Nittis and a young composer whose name is of no importance. The hour was serene. Miniccio, Bull and Fly were dozing on the grass beside the guests, Bizibouzou was peacefully observing the sunset from the top of his cage and Darwin, on the end of a long rope, searched himself for fleas with the sad expression of an ancient philosopher. The returning hunters went directly into the garden and let loose their live trophies. The cheetah made a joyful bound for the three small dogs, who shot for some bushes under which they cowered yelping while the cheetah, delighted with its success, growled triumphantly. The wolfhound, apparently mistaking Darwin for a wolf, streaked after the poor simian, who fled up a tree chittering in terror. The parrot flew about squawking and letting out droppings and the chameleons did nothing of note. Madame Guérard screamed and crossed herself, the butler dropped a tea tray, de Nittis kept flailing the air with his cane, Doré walked with stately alacrity into the house and everyone else, including Sarah, burst into maniacal gales of laughter. Passers-by peered in amazement over the garden wall and scores of faces appeared at windows in the dignified houses surrounding Chester Square.

It was generally known that No. 77 had been leased to the questionable celebrity and rumors concerning fantastic goings-on in the place began to spread. It was said that Sarah Bernhardt had a menagerie of carniverous wild animals running loose in her garden, that inside the house on certain nights she held a Witches' Sabbath, that every morning she stood on her balcony smoking cigars, that she practiced pistol-shooting in her back yard, that she was taking boxing lessons and had broken four of her instructor's teeth and that for the price of one guinea she would exhibit herself dressed in man's attire. A gullible portion of the public believed these idiocies. Two boxing and fencing masters sent her their cards. A tailor offered to make her a gentleman's dress suit not only gratis, he'd pay her a hundred pounds if she'd pose in it for an autographed picture to be placed in his window. And she received several boxes of cigars from unknown admirers.

These reports in the London scandal sheets leapt with lightning speed across the Channel and the Paris press gobbled them up. Even a paper of as high a standard as the *Figaro* came out with an account of the alleged Bernhardt capers. The article, by Albert Wolff, a staff writer, upbraided the wayward actress for behavior unworthy a member of the House of Molière. This was too much for the wayward actress. She dispatched a long and costly telegram to Wolff categorically denying the reports. She defended her art exhibition of which, for some reason, Wolff disapproved, by stating that as one of the most poorly paid members of the Français, she had a right to make up the difference. Her wire concluded:

> As to the respect due the House of Molière, dear M. Wolff, I lay claim to keeping that in mind more than anyone else . . . And now, if the stupidities invented about me have annoyed the Parisians and if they have decided to receive me ungraciously on my return, I do not wish anyone to be guilty of such baseness on my account, so I will submit my resignation to the Comédie Française.
>
> I am sending you this letter by wire, as the consideration I have for public opinion gives me the right to commit such folly, and I beg you, dear M. Wolff, to accord my letter the same honor you did the calumnies of my enemies.

Wolff obediently afforded the letter that honor. The announcement came as a bombshell which resounded throughout Paris and rocked the corps at the Gaiety. A delegation called on their rebel member. It was headed by the grand old comedian Edmond Got, the *doyen* or dean of the Français. Got pontificated about sacred traditions and glorious hierarchy. Sophie Croizette took her friend to her bonny bosom and protested that the committee would never accept her resignation. Coquelin affectionately patted her hand and told her not to be a rash child — that once in the Français one was there for life (Coquelin himself was to leave the institution some seven years later). Mounet-Sully put in his plea in his usual voice which Sacha Guitry said sounded as though he were addressing one at distance of fifty yards and separated by a river. His affair with Sarah had ended by then but they had remained good friends. He thundered on about probity and moral obligation. Mounet came from a long line of Huguenot pastors and Sarah wrote that "his whole speech savored of Protestantism." The person who had most influence was the fine actor with the unfortunate name, Worms, a warm and direct man who merely asked her where she thought she'd find herself better off, and when a telegram arrived from Perrin with assurances of devotion and admiration, she decided to postpone her decision.

During her years at the Comédie, Sarah Bernhardt's health had never been consistently good. In London it was no better. She still had genuine fainting spells, still occasionally bled at the mouth. Toward the finish of the Gaiety run, she was booked for two appearances on the same day: a matinee of Dumas *fils' l'Etrangère* followed by an evening performance of *Hernani*. She had caught a severe cold and was in a state of utter depletion with a racking cough and a high temperature. In her dressing room prior to the matinee, she went into such a violent chill she couldn't put on her make-up. Twice she fainted. The prospect of getting through the matinee seemed insurpassable, let alone *Hernani* that night. Of the two, Doña Sol was a far more difficult but far more important role than that of Mrs. Clarkson, the heroine of *l'Etrangère*. Fifteen minutes before curtain time she sent word to the management that she'd not be able to go on for the matinee. There was, of course, a backstage *crise* but she remained adamant and a change of bill had hectically to be slapped together. When it was announced that due to the sudden indisposition of Mademoiselle Bernhardt, the play for that afternoon would be *Tartuffe*, three quarters of the audience got up and demanded back their money at the box office. That evening she managed with heroic effort to get through *Hernani* and the house was a sell-out. Next day, however, the papers were full of indignation over her cutting the afternoon performance.

The Paris press was even more indignant. She was accused of putting on an act, of deliberately shirking her duty. Sarcey wrote testily that "the time comes when troublesome children must be put to bed." The outcry was unjustified. Whatever her off-stage behavior, in the theatre Sarah Bernhardt was a conscientious professional. Never during her long career did she cancel a performance unless it was physically impossible for her to go on and often she played in a state of illness that would have defeated any other actress. This was a great and serious artist, dedicated to her work.

London forgave her. The engagement ended in clouds of glory and the company returned to France, the home journey being considerably enlivened by the added impedimenta of the Bernhardt livestock, of which the cheetah caused a near mutiny on the Channel boat. Paris welcomed back her beloved *Comédiens* although there was marked public antagonism toward the leading actress. The season was to open with the annual tribute to Molière, that *Cérémonie* at which, seventeen years earlier, Sarah had distinguished herself by whacking Madame Nathalie in the face. There was much speculation as to whether or not she would risk taking part in this year's function. She received anonymous letters warning her not to. Some were even written to the papers, one of which read:

My poor Skeleton, you will do well not to show your horrible Jewish nose at the Opening Ceremony day after tomorrow. I fear it would serve as a target for all the potatoes that are now being cooked especially for you in your kind city of Paris. Have a paragraph put in the papers to the effect that you have been spitting blood and remain in bed and think over the consequences of excessive publicity.

A Subscriber

Perrin summoned her to his office and suggested that it would be the better part of valor for her not to take part in the *Cérémonie*, that she was certain to be met by hisses and catcalls from a hostile public. The prospect of facing a hostile public was as the smell of gunpowder to a war horse for "Mademoiselle Révolte." In a quiet, even voice she announced, "I shall take part in the *Cérémonie*, Monsieur," and swept out of his office.

The performance was the traditional one: the bust of Molière on its pedestal placed stage center, the players coming on in pairs to bow and pay homage with a short scene from one of the Master's works. Sarah chose to go on alone; her reason, she said, was that she did not wish any escorting actor to have to share whatever demonstration might be in store for her. Her turn came and she made her entrance. Sarah Bernhardt's entrances were usually electrifying spectacles in themselves, but now she walked on with simple dignity and head erect. The audience, which had greeted each of the other participants with a dutiful hand, watched her in stony silence. She came directly down to the footlights and faced her potential firing squad. She didn't bow, she hadn't paused to bow to Molière, she merely stood stock still. Her expression was neither ingratiating nor defiant. It was one which merely implied, "Well, here I am, what are you going to do about it?" What the audience did was wait for a number of breathless seconds then, of a sudden, break into spontaneous and thundering applause. There were even a few cries of "Welcome home, Our Sarah!" Paris had forgiven her prodigal *enfant terrible* as Paris was to do time and again.

During the ensuing months, Bernhardt continued to ponder an eventual break with the Français. She realized the prestige of being with France's leading National Theatre. The grand old house itself she regarded with admiration — actually with reverence. Even after she had left it, her veneration remained steadfast. One evening when she happened to be there as a spectator, standing in the foyer between acts, she spied a certain visiting European king who was still casually wearing his top hat. Leaving her party, she sailed across to the sovereign, bobbed him a perfunctory curtsey and said, "Monseigneur, in this shrine of art, one does not remove one's crown, but one removes one's hat." But at the present time she was tired of serving as a priestess in that shrine.

What finally brought about her rift was when Perrin insisted upon casting her in the part of Doña Clorinde in Emile Augier's

L'Aventurière. She loathed the part and loathed the play, which is indeed an insipid affair all about moral honor and the triumph of virtue, without any good dramatic bite. Like much of that author's work, it is written in mediocre verse. As Tristan Bernard, the *boulevardier* of the '90's, was to say, "I have great admiration for Emile Augier. I doubt if it would last through a first reading." During rehearsals, Sarah, being ill, was absent several times. She studied her part half-heartedly and kept forgetting her words. One day when Augier himself remonstrated with her she snapped back, "What do you want me to do? I know I'm bad, but not as bad as your lines!" She was too tired to bother with fittings for her costume, and the day before the première she developed a racking sore throat and laryngitis. She went to Perrin and entreated him to postpone the opening for one more week. Perrin refused, declaring he was fed up with kowtowing to her whims. She went through with the performance and it was the biggest flop of her career. She played with shocking carelessness, frequently going up in her lines. Her voice, due to the laryngitis, was a rasping foghorn, and her costume was not only hideous but miles too large. She said herself that she looked like an English teapot. The audience was disgusted and her notices were deservedly bad.

After reading every one, she sat down and wrote the following letter to Perrin:

Monsieur l'Administrateur. You forced me to play when I was not ready . . . what I foresaw came to pass. The result of the performance exceeded my expectations . . . This is my first failure at the Comédie and it shall be my last. I warned you on the day of the dress rehearsal and you ignored my warning. I keep my word. When you receive this letter I shall have left Paris. Be so kind, Monsieur l'Administrateur, as to accept my immediate resignation, and believe me yours faithfully . . .

She made two copies of this letter and had each sent by hand to the editors of the *Figaro* and the *Gaulois* respectively. The original intended for Perrin she casually dropped in a mail box, then hurried out of the city to remain for a few days of anonymity in a hotel at Havre. Perrin had the shock of reading the newspaper announcement of his prize star's flight from home orbit before her letter of resignation reached him. No need to dwell on his reaction nor on that of the governing body. They filed a breach of contract suit against her for the sum of 300,000 francs, which was later reduced to 100,000. As a sidelight on Bernhardt's sense of financial obligation it might be mentioned that she never paid these damages. The suit was delayed in litigation for twenty years. Finally in 1900 she settled by letting the Comédie Française, whose building had been nearly destroyed by their fire of March 8, move into her theatre for ten months while she went on tour. At the time of her departure she did have to forfeit 40,000 francs of her "benefit money" which had automatically been deposited in trust at the Français. One of the rulings of that organization is to retain a portion of the salary of every *sociétaire*, the accumulated sum of which is returned at the time of departure provided the member departs in the good graces of the Administration and Governing Body. It may be imagined in what sort of graces Sarah Bernhardt departed.

She must have realized the rashness of this step, but if the future was uncertain, she faced it boldly and with a sense of liberation. Sir George Arthur said that she was as well adapted to the official atmosphere of the Comédie Française as Whistler might have been to the standards of the Royal Academy. Paris, of course, denounced her as a renegade and deserter but she didn't care. Years later when Lysiane Bernhardt dared question her grandmother about the ethics of her action, Sarah answered with one of her characteristic speeches, which might have come right out of *l'Aiglon*: "The Théâtre Français is and always will be the ensign of our country's dramatic art. It is true that I refused to serve in its ranks. Am I therefore a deserter? No! My role was to unfurl that flag to the winds of other nations . . . to make it known beyond other frontiers. The future alone will judge whether or not I have accomplished my mission."

The first winds to flutter that flag were the breezes of England. Hardly had news of her final break reached London than Hollingshead and Meyer made her a handsome offer for a return engagement at the Gaiety, she to head a company of her own in whatever repertory she chose. She accepted with alacrity and immediately assembled a first-rate cast which she herself directed in a repertory. With her infallible instinct for theatre, she made sure her choice of plays would go with the public: one or two of the classics that offered her more spectacular roles plus Scribe's *Adrienne Lecouvreur* and the Meilhac-Halévy drawing-room comedy of pathos *Froufrou* — less classic but better box office. It was her first plunge into the career she was to follow from now on, that of an actress-manager.

London welcomed her back rapturously that season of 1880. Theirs was a happy frenzy that was to renew itself throughout the years on each of her recurrent visits. No wonder she adored the British capital. Her houses were sell-outs and the press unanimous in praise. A few Paris critics came over to inspect her acting, half hoping it would be inferior to that of her Français performances, but even they had to admit that in her new independence Sarah was better than ever. Sarcey wrote in *le Temps*, "Nothing, nothing at the Comédie Française will ever replace for us this last act of *Adrienne Lecouvreur*," and the *Figaro*'s usually acid reviewer, Vitu, said that Sarah Bernhardt had risen "to a height of dramatic power which could never be surpassed."

When she returned to Paris, the dignitaries of the Français again called on her and implored her to return to the fold. All would be forgiven, they promised her, and the 100,000-franc fine would be canceled. She merely smiled and showed them her London box-office statements with grosses half again higher than those taken in by the House of Molière. She thanked and embraced them all, then skipped off to Brussels, where at the Théâtre de la

Monnaie she played *Adrienne Lecouvreur* and *Froufrou* to cheering
audiences. Her next stop was a week at the Royal Theatre in
Copenhagen. The King and Queen attended her opening night.
With them in the box were the King and Queen of the Hellenes
and the Princess of Wales. Of the latter Bernhardt wrote that
the Princess' beauty blinded her to anyone else present. She and the
future Queen Alexandra formed a real friendship that lasted for
many years. At the finish of the play, the royal ladies tossed their
bouquets onto the stage, the leading man gathered them up and
Sarah clutched them to her heart with fitting gestures of ecstasy,
while the house gave her a standing ovation. The audience went
equally wild over *Froufrou*, and Sarah Bernhardt was the toast of
Denmark. The King presented her with the Danish Order of
Merit, which, adorned as it was with diamonds, Sarah found to be
very pretty. The royal yacht was put at her disposal to take her and
her company out to Elsinore for a visit to the castle and Hamlet's
tomb. They returned at sundown. Preceding the yacht was a
smaller craft manned by students who, as they sailed along, sang
ancient Norse folksongs and scattered roses on the water.

"And all that was for me," she wrote in her Memoirs, "all those
roses, all that love, all that musical poetry!" Then she winds up
modestly, "And the setting sun . . . it was also for me. I felt very
near to God."

There was one jarring incident which might have ruined the
success of her Copenhagen stay. At a supper in her honor after
the final performance, the German ambassador, a Baron Magnus,
rose and glass in hand proposed a toast, "To the country that has
given us such great art. To France!" Sarah, who was a fanatic
patriot and like many of the French remembered 1870 and still
smarted under the loss of Alsace and Lorraine, sprang to her feet,
raised her glass and cried in ringing tones, "Yes, to France, Mr.
Prussian Ambassador, but to France in her entirety!" And at that,
the orchestra spontaneously struck up the *Marseillaise*. The gesture,
colorful as it was, caused a diplomatic crisis. Baron Magnus was a

delightful and popular man and for him to be openly snubbed at a public function was considered a slur on Danish hospitality. The next morning at an early hour the French ambassador called on his imprudent countrywoman and persuaded her to write a note of apology to the baron, which she did in her most disarming manner and the incident was closed.

After these triumphs she returned to Paris. Her old friend and former Odéon manager, Duquesnel, came to her with the suggestion that since the French public had not yet seen her superb new performances, *Froufrou* and *Adrienne Lecouvreur*, he book her for a brief whirlwind tour of the larger provincial towns of France. He was cautious enough not to risk any Paris appearances. It was a joint venture and a profitable one.

Sarah was elated and invigorated. The Road, that adventure-filled highway whose joys so few of today's actors have dared to explore, was opening out before her, leading to further horizons. For the immediate future, that road led Westward across the Atlantic, and she had already settled her plans to follow it.

7.

"THE" BERNHARDT IN AMERICA

AFTER HER TREMENDOUS personal success with the Français troupe in London, the wily Jarrett had bided his time. He knew that once she had freed herself from the distinguished shackles of the House of Molière she could, if properly handled, prove to be a gold mine for herself and for him. The news of Sarah's "Great Break" was carried in all the London papers and as soon as he'd read it, Jarrett was on the next Channel train for Dover and Paris, a contract in his pocket. His proposition was to send her on an extensive tour of the United States in a repertory of eight plays of her own selection, with a company which she herself would assemble and direct. The financial terms were enticing. When one considers the buying power of the dollar in 1880 compared with what it is today, they were downright staggering. He guaranteed her one hundred engagements over a period of four months at $1000 a performance, plus 50 per cent of the gross if the night's receipts went over $4000. She would receive an additional $200 weekly for hotel expenses. The company would play the leading Eastern and Southern cities, traveling via special train on which Madame would have her own private car and her personal entourage, two maids, two cooks, a waiter, her *maître d'hotel* and Madame Guérard, her dear *mon p'tit dame*, who would act as companion and secretary — all of their salaries to be paid by the management.

She was to furnish her own theatre wardrobe. And that was no mean stipulation. If her off-stage attire was an eccentric abandonment of white scarves, trailing veils and dresses which might have doubled as nightgowns, Sarah Bernhardt's professional clothes were veritable works of art. She had a scholar's familiarity with period dress acquired through an insatiable study of paintings, prints and books on historic costuming. She designed all her theatrical wardrobe herself with authenticity, exquisite attention to detail and a lunatic disregard of cost. Her silks were woven to order in Lyon, her velvets were imported from Italy, her furs from Russia. Every item of trimming or embroidery was lavish, from Doña Sol's high-standing collar of genuine Alençon lace in *Hernani* to the tiny hand-made satin tea roses that covered the panier skirt of Adrienne Lecouvreur. As Froufrou she wore one outfit of swirling taffeta encrusted with beads of real crystal and inserts of mother-of-pearl, and Marguerite Gauthier's ballgown cost the interpreter of that *Lady of the Camellias* 10,000 francs. Plays, in those more leisurely days, were often five-acters, and as a star had sometimes as many costume changes in one performance, the outlay for a big repertory was fairly astronomical.

In addition to facing these prospective expenses, Bernhardt had other debts: to art dealers and decorators, to tradesmen and *couturières*, to her large staff of domestics who, through some inexplicable loyalty, stayed on in her service in spite of being often unpaid or having occasionally to dodge a flying paperweight which their mistress in one of her sudden rages might hurl at their heads. For all the success of her recent English and European tours, the lady's funds were in their not infrequent state of low ebb. In fact, they had just about ebbed. She was earning 20,000 francs a year and spending 50,000. She signed with Jarrett.

After that, she set about selecting her repertory of plays. Of the eight she chose, only two — Racine's *Phèdre* and Victor Hugo's *Hernani* — were classical drama. The rest were mediocre affairs which, however, offered opportunities for arresting effects. Sarah Bernhardt chose her material with the unerring instinct of a clever showman, always looking for good theatre in a script, not literature. New movements in the theatre, new trends, meant nothing to her. Hugo's "Romanticism," Zola's "Naturalism," Maeterlinck's "Symbolism," the startling innovations performed in Antoine's *Théâtre Libre* impressed her not at all. When she read a script, the only question in her mind was, "Does it act?" or, more specifically, "Does it give *me* a chance to act?" Her art or, to be accurate, her showmanship, made a bad script seem good. She could interpret a scene of violence with such frightening control, such smouldering fire, the rankest melodrama seemed believable. And, of course, no actress ever died with such glorious heartbreak, such touching pathos whether from poison, the dagger or tuberculosis. In only one production of her American repertory, *l'Etrangère* of Dumas *fils*, did she survive the final curtain. Thousands of playgoers traveled thousands of miles to sob audibly over Marguerite Gauthier's departure from life — which, according to those who saw it, was a mere exhalation of breath — in that hardy perennial whose actual title is *La Dame aux Camélias* but which Anglo-Saxons persist in calling *Camille*. When one realizes that there is no character who goes by any such name in the play it does seem quite idiotic that Americans can't be bothered to say *The Lady of the Camellias*. The first time Bernhardt saw the billing outside a theatre she rushed to Jarrett and demanded indignantly, "What is this *Camille*? I know no such play!" When it was explained to her, the misnomer struck her as unbearably funny and whenever she saw the announcements in print, she'd go into gales of laughter. Over the years, critics have panned this opus as sentimental trash, more a libretto than a play. Yet for all the jeering of the intellectuals, *La Dame* was to be the Bernhardt box-office standby for nearly forty-five years. Whenever the financial till was empty, she'd recoup some of her losses with a revival performance of Dumas' frail heroine, which she played over three thousand times.

On October 15, 1880, Madame Sarah Bernhardt's troupe, shepherded by Jarrett, set out for the New World; the star with exuberant elation, her fellow players with apprehension and a Gallic distrust of any country beyond the borders of France. Their vessel was a battered old tub, part steam, part sail, called the "America," which bore the unfortunate reputation of being a ship of ill-fortune. On one voyage during a storm, she had lost half the life-boats, of which she had an insufficient supply to begin with. On another, her pumps started working madly in reverse and sea water flooded the coal bins. The machinery was ancient and ominous sounds of coughing explosions and shrill wheezings issued periodically from the engine room. Her paint was chipped and her hull looked as forlorn as a scrofulous sycamore.

A crowd of unknown "Sar-adorers" stood waving at their idol from the Havre docks. Clairin, Louise Abbéma and a few other members of the Bernhardt "Court" had come down from Paris to bid their queen good-by. Maurice, then a lad of sixteen, was there too, of course. He kept going dolefully ashore, then rushing frantically back up the gangplank to hug and kiss his mother, who returned his embraces with passionate ardor. Both of them cried a great deal. Eventually a sailor was able to shoo Maurice permanently onto the quay, the gangplank was lifted, the whistle sounded, the crowds waved and Sarah, swathed in an extra number of white scarves, a ship's officer in attendance, stood at the rail in an intrepidly nautical pose. The pose lasted until the "America," her ancient engine chugging, her steadying sail set, headed out into the choppy waters of the lower Channel. In a few minutes Sarah's face took on an interesting shade of green and when the ship went into its first wallow, she bade a hasty adieu to the officer and barely made it to her cabin. There she remained for three days amid such a profusion of flowers all that appeared to be lacking was her famous coffin. Beyond this temporary resemblance to a mortuary chapel, the cabin was lavishly appointed. Her sable bed-throw covered the berth. The linen was her own, the sheets and the cases for the five pillows on which she habitually slept bearing her crest, a large S.B. surmounted by a small but defiant *Quand Même*. The dressing table gleamed with her gold toilet set and on every available surface stood silver-framed photographs of Maurice.

On the fourth day Madame Sarah emerged and went up to the main lounge to hold public court with Jarrett and the more important members of her company. Doubtless she held occasional private court in her cabin with a handsome actor named Angelo who, on this first United States tour, was her leading man and *pro tem* lover.

Even at sea her thoughts were on the theatre and her work, and with her indefatigable zeal she called daily rehearsals although often the weather barely permitted. It was a rough and eventful crossing. The events were subsequently highly dramatized in Sarah's own Memoirs, which would have us believe that the ship weathered a hurricane during which it twice almost capsized, that this tempest was followed by a snowstorm worthy the Ancient Mariner, that the lives of the first-class passengers were threatened by some ruffians from the steerage and that, late one night, she prevented an emigrant girl from jumping over the stern railing and later officiated at the delivery of the poor creature's illegitimate child. (Sarah was named the baby's godmother, but we do not read of her going to any further lengths of godmotherly duty.)

One incident, retold by most of the biographers, does seem to have the ring of truth. Among the passengers was a dumpy little American woman who spoke to nobody and was conspicuous only because of her heavy mourning and dismal expression. One evening when the waves outside were particularly mountainous, she and Sarah happened to meet at the top of the main companionway. The ship gave a sudden lurch, the woman lost her balance and Sarah grabbed her just in time to prevent her from lunging headlong down the stairs. Once back on her feet, the woman muttered her thanks in a rather dazed manner and added something to the effect that perhaps God had not wanted her to die just yet. Then politely she asked to know her rescuer's identity. Bernhardt, in the magnanimous manner of royalty bestowing further beneficence, announced her name, expecting the woman to be happily stunned.

It was Bernhardt who was stunned, and not too happily. The woman recoiled, fixed the actress with a look of accusing hatred, and in a tone of venom hissed the words, "I am the widow of Abraham Lincoln!" Sarah's reaction to this moment of melodrama was fairly good theatre too — if indeed she reacted the way her autobiography reads:

> I too recoiled [she wrote], and a great sorrow overcame my entire being, for I had rendered this unhappy woman the one service she didn't want . . . that of saving her from death. Her husband, President Lincoln, had been assassinated by an actor, and it was an actress who prevented her from rejoining him.
>
> I returned to my cabin and stayed there for two days, for I hadn't the courage to encounter this touching soul to whom I would never dared have spoken.

It would perhaps be uncharitable to suggest that Madame Sarah's self-imposed two-day exile in her cabin was due more to rough weather than to compunctions about the sensibilities of Mary Todd Lincoln.

A considerably gayer episode occurred three days out of New York. On the morning of October 23, her birthday, *mon p'tit dame* waked her with a present Maurice had entrusted to her care, and at sight of her son's writing on the card, Sarah burst into happy tears. Madame Guérard was followed by Sarah's personal entourage and the members of her company, each with a little gift. Her "godson," the new-born steerage baby, cradled in a basket of oranges and apples, a gold paper star on its tiny forehead, was briefly presented and fortuitously whisked away before doing any appreciable damage to the oranges and apples. Then came a delegation from the crew with a gigantic bouquet of what looked to be genuine flowers but proved to be raw vegetables some genius of the kitchens had carved in a sort of *bouquet consommé Julienne*. One of the sailors made an awkwardly endearing speech and from Madame Guérard's adjoining cabin came strains of music, two violins and a flute played by members of the ship's orchestra. The account of her reactions is in the Grande Sarah style:

> I was lulled and transported back to my loved ones in my drawing-room so far away. That music evoked the one tender and restful corner of my life. I wept because I was touched, tired, unnerved, weary and in great need of repose. I fell asleep amid my tears, my bosom rising and falling with sighs and sobs.

It must have been an affecting picture.

As the ship got closer and closer to American shores, the habitually taciturn Jarrett grew more and more elated. "Nobody," he announced with hand-rubbing satisfaction, "nobody knows better that I how to stage the arrival of a European star in this country!" He was quite right. His brilliant promotional campaign had been going on for months and *les Yankees* were agog to find out at first-hand more about "The Bernhardt." That is what she was called by the American public throughout all nine of her United States tours, although the sophisticates, proving their superior familiarity with the French language, occasionally spoke of her as "La Bernhardt."

On October 27, after a twelve-day crossing, the "America" dropped anchor in New York harbor. It was six-thirty in the morning, freezing cold, and the river was clogged with ice. A tugboat came alongside bearing a thoroughly chilled but intrepid welcoming committee of officials, consular delegates and important citizens. Close in its wake steamed a tender weighted down with a vast flock of newspapermen and a brass band which struck up a rendering of the *Marseillaise* that would have sounded more stirring if the lips of the players hadn't been numb with cold. This overwhelming boarding party invaded the ship, and the French theatre troupe watched with alarm. To them the invaders might have had cutlasses in their teeth instead of pencils and pads in their hands, as they swarmed along the decks and through the lounge rooms demanding, in harsh American accents, to see "The Bernhardt."

Meanwhile, "The Bernhardt" had locked herself in her cabin and refused to budge from it. Jarrett pounded on the door and firmly informed her that she must come forth and meet her welcomers. In tones of a faulty siren, she wailed that she couldn't, that she was ill, that to face such a mob would kill her. Jarrett calmly called her bluff. He was the only business associate in her long career who remained totally unimpressed by Sarah Bernhardt's trumped-up acts and impervious to her tantrums. And consequently he was the only manager who had the complete respect and confidence of his tempestuous star. She may even have been a little afraid of him, for he was a formidable man who seldom smiled. Sarah's pet name for him was "The Terrible Mr. Jarrett" and occasionally "The Ferocious Gentleman." He was then in his mid-sixties, a big handsome Englishman with the proud head of an Agamemnon. He would say to the person with whom he had any business dealings, "I have made my way in life by the aid of two weapons: honesty and a revolver." A scar under his pale-blue right eye was testimony to his use of the latter. Once, during an argument over a contract for Jenny Lind with an agent who was an out-and-out crook, he had said, "Take a look at this eye, my man, it sees clear through you!" The agent snarled, "There's one thing it hasn't foreseen!" pulled out a pistol and fired a shot whose bullet merely skimmed Jarrett's cheekbone. Jarrett replied, "Sir, this is the way to close an eye for good!" whipped out his own gun and shot the man dead.

Jarrett, pounding with authority on Sarah's locked door, pointed out the fact that she was no longer in France where she was a national figure, nor in England where she had built up a devoted public, but was arriving in a new world and about to come up against a new public which was waiting for her with more curiosity than admiration. Sarah said she didn't care. She stormed, she threatened, she wept with rage. The "Ferocious Gentleman" remained coldly adamant. He reminded her that he had engaged her for two reasons. First and foremost she was a great artist and one who could make a pot of money both for herself and for him.

Secondly, although he knew she was a fiery-tempered woman, he
knew also that she was fundamentally a loyal one. He had staked
not only his entire fortune but also his reputation in this joint
venture. It was the right psychological approach and Sarah un-
locked her door. Swathed in scarves, furs and an extra coating of
the white "Oriza" face powder made especially for her by the
perfumer le Grand, she tottered forth as if to go into the infinite
throes of one of her better death scenes.

Clinging to Jarrett's arm, she climbed the stairs to the main
salon and faced the waiting mob. The band which had come on
board, their lips now defrosted, again struck up the *Marseillaise*.
At the opening "Allons enfants," Sarah's attitude of not-long-for-
this-world frailty turned into one of passionate patriotism. Raising
high her splendid head, she stood as though the tricolor had suddenly unfurled itself behind her and the French Republic were
saluting the American one. The act, as was to be expected, electrified the gathering. After which, the French Consul-General presented her with flowers, a spokesman for the Franco-American
colony handed her a parchment scroll, the editor of the *Courrier
des Etats Unis* made a speech and a line of important New Yorkers
filed past to shake hands and babble a word or two in what they
hoped was French. Then the reporters were let loose like hounds
released for the kill. They mobbed their prey, shouting, plucking at
her sleeve, hurling questions to which Jarrett called out translations and to which Bernhardt croaked replies in her best martyr
voice and her well-known eyes-raised-to-heaven expression. Halfway up the harbor, she could bear no more and let out a cry of
anguish that would have done justice to Adrienne Lecouvreur's
poison scene. The hubbub ceased and in the silence, Sarah put on
such an effective act of fainting that even Jarrett was fooled. After
hastily informing the gentlemen of the press that they could continue their interviews later in Madame's hotel suite, he lifted his
swooned star up over his shoulder and carried her back to her
cabin, where she instantly recovered, went into shrieks of laughter

and, grabbing Jarrett by both hands, whirled him about in a mad waltz.

A crowd of inquisitive onlookers were jamming the French Line pier craning their necks to get a close view of "The Bernhardt." Jarrett's advance publicity had been augmented by the usual absurd rumors and scandalous exaggerations that seem always to have preceded the arrival of Sarah Bernhardt in any new territory. Stories of her love affairs, grossly distorted, had been circulated in dirty little under-the-counter penny-dreadfuls. One brochure bearing the title of "The Loves of Sarah Bernhardt" accused her of having seduced all the crowned heads of Europe including the Pope — if the Tiara may be counted among the crowns. Another pamphlet stated, "on incontestable authority," that she had given birth to four illegitimate sons, one by a hairdresser, one by the Emperor Louis Napoleon, one by the Tsar of Russia and the fourth by a man condemned to the guillotine for murdering his father. Preachers from their pulpits hurled anathema at her — which rather suggests that they too may have been taking a few surreptitious glances at those penny-dreadfuls. A group of high-minded American mothers in Orange, New Jersey, held a meeting on "The Bernhardt Question" and "how to defend our country against this European *courtisane* who is coming over to corrupt our sons." One little woman at the meeting who meekly suggested that if the public were obliged to investigate the private morals of actors and actresses before attending their performances, the theatres might as well close down, was ostracized by the Orange community. *The Methodist*, a church periodical with a circulation of 200,000, published a diatribe against "the decadent London society who, without scruple, opened the doors of their virtuous homes to this unwed mother." No wonder the box office had been sold out ahead of time. "The Bernhardt," when informed of this advance sale, shrugged and said, "*Mais naturellement!* They'd turn out in the same way to see Le Général Tom Pouce [General Tom Thumb] or any of the rest of Monsieur Barnum's freaks!"

Henry Abbey, Jarrett's American partner and the most important producer in New York, had come aboard with the welcoming party. Abbey was to go along on much of the ensuing tour. Bernhardt liked him and immediately gave him the name of "Monsieur l'Abbé" somewhat to Abbey's embarrassment. After the ship docked, he and Jarrett with the help of a powerful Pinkerton detective managed to get their terrified star down the gangplank and out through a crowd of ill-mannered onlookers without the poor lady having her clothes torn off. Three of "New York's finest" guarded her way to a closed cab and she was rushed off to her hotel. This was the Albemarle, a swank hostelry situated on Fifth Avenue in the lower 20's, which was considered fashionably uptown. On the ensuing blocks stood the majestic mansions of the dollar aristocracy, that of Mrs. William Astor being 'way up at 34th Street, which was practically suburbia. Fifth Avenue ended at 59th Street, beyond which were squatter settlements, pig farms and truck gardens.

Abbey had engaged for Madame a luxurious second-floor suite with a balcony strategically overlooking the main hotel entrance in the event that she might at some time be called forth like royalty to respond to the acclaim of an eager public. She was proudly informed that the last occupant of these elegant quarters had been General Grant — a bit of information to which she seems not to have responded with any marked stupefaction. What did impress her was the suite itself. The parlor had been especially refurbished to remind her of her drawing room in Paris, which meant that it was a horrendous clutter of heavy draperies, bear-skin rugs, carved teakwood furniture, a grand piano draped with a Spanish shawl, Turkish ottomans, Moorish lamps, potted palms and ponderous vases jammed with ponderous floral arrangements. A huge couch piled with satin-covered cushions and canopied with Persian hangings was practically a replica of the famous avenue de Villiers "cozy corner" on which she had posed for Clairin and other painters, sprawled out luxuriously like a voluptuous cat.

Sarah thought it was all just lovely. By way of special tribute Mr. Knoedler of the art gallery had sent over three busts on marble shafts: one of Molière, the others of Racine and Victor Hugo. With a joyous cry of "Ah! My dear old friend!" she kissed the bronze cheek of Hugo, shook hands effusively with kind Mr. Knoedler (he was to become a life-long friend). Then she announced that she was mortally exhausted by the strains and pressures of her arrival and *must* have an hour's sleep. On the heels of this announcement, three of the newspapermen made their appearance. At sight of them, she let out one of her death scene cries and flung herself onto the carpet, full-length, face down and arms out at the sides. The men fled, only to return immediately with four more reporters. Sarah, her face smothered in the carpet pile, moaned and asked Jarrett how many more of these tormentors were due to arrive. He coolly informed her that he was expecting some fifty. With the yowl of an enraged lynx, she leapt to her feet, dashed into the bedroom, locked each door except one which had no key and pulled a heavy bureau in front of that. Then she again hurled herself down spread-eagle on the floor. Jarrett, speaking in French through the keyhole, again reminded her that this was her first visit in a country that was intrinsically wary of foreigners and she'd better not start out by antagonizing the press. She replied that unless she got an hour's sleep, her antagonization would be Homeric. *Mon p'tit dame* placed a gentle hand on Jarrett's shoulder and warned him that if he tried to force the barricaded door, Madame was quite capable of leaping out of the window. "The Ferocious Gentleman" agreed to let her have a short rest and Sarah compromised on forty minutes.

For all the chatter and bustle that came from the adjoining sitting room, she fell instantly to sleep, woke on the dot of the stipulated time, called for her maid and Madame Guérard, who helped her into a gossamer white robe held at the waist by the well-known turquoise and hammered gold belt, and pale but brave as an accused martyr, she emerged to face her inquisitors. Her witness stand was the Oriental cozy corner, onto whose cushions she sank and pulled a sable bed throw over her lap. There were now more than sixty reporters jamming the room and the small entrance hall, and at the sight of them, Bernhardt held her tiny hands up over her eyes and gave forth a pitiful moan. Jarrett assured her such mass conferences would not be held in other cities. These were representatives of a nation-wide press whose stories would be telegraphed to their home newspapers. The reporters started firing their questions, Jarrett interpreted and "The Bernhardt" answered. Most of her answers were in an indignant negative as most of the questions were absurd. No, she did not always sleep in a coffin. No, she did not feed live quails to her pet lion. No, she did not sometimes dress in man's clothing and smoke cigars. Certainly not, her dressmaker did not keep a skeleton in her workshop on which to fit the creations she made her. When one man wanted her to state the value of her jewelry she told him that was none of his business. When another asked what her favorite food was, she answered in exasperation, "*Des moules*," and the next day most of America read with shuddering fascination that France's greatest actress ate nothing but mussels for all three daily meals. After this, Jarrett took it upon himself to answer the questions while his star sank back amid her cushions and serenely went to sleep. She woke as the last inquisitor, a cartoonist, was about to depart. He'd been making a sketch of her and she demanded to see it. He had drawn her in the pose in which she'd been lolling. The body was a series of jointed water pipes and the head, a skull topped by a wig of writhing snakes. In justifiable fury Madame tore the nasty page in half and flung it at the man's feet. He picked it up, put it in his portfolio, and later that day every New York and Brooklyn paper printed the cruel caricature.

This was only the first of endless cartoons to be published during the Bernhardt tour. Hardly an issue of *Puck*, the humorous periodical, or of a shoddy little weekly called *Chic* appeared without one of these offensive jibes. She was presented as a cane with a sponge on the end of it, as a narrow factory chimney crowned with an eagle's nest. They parodied her slim gracefulness by representing her as a seductive boa constrictor, and one really funny drawing showed her as an animated rope which, in the frenzy of a highly emotional scene, has tied itself into a series of knots.

If, after the ordeals of her first day in the United States, Sarah Bernhardt had planned to spend a quiet evening at her hotel suite in the restful company of Madame Guérard or perhaps some distracting hours of dalliance with Angelo, Jarrett and Abbey had other plans for her. They were the joint owners of the Park Theatre, where one of their leading American stars, Clara Morris, was appearing in a play called *Alixe*.

As a person, Miss Morris was the antithesis of Madame Bernhardt. She was modest, self-effacing and so hated publicity that she maintained a private path from her lodgings in Park Street to the Park Theatre to avoid reporters or any staring public. As an actress, Miss Morris was also the antithesis of Madame Bernhardt. She had neither elegance nor finesse, her acting was crude at times and at other times startlingly realistic, her voice was nasal and her accent blatantly American. Her admirers claimed she was a brilliant example of the "Natural School" and forgave the fact that she pronounced the French capital as "Parus." But she had a compelling personality, a gift for simple pathos and an extraordinary ability to wring buckets of tears from her audiences. In those days, the theatre-going public liked nothing so much as a good cry, and in *Alixe* Clara Morris had an agreeable number of tear-jerking moments. The play was a hit.

Abbey and Jarrett decided that a good publicity stunt would be for France's great tragedienne to pay a gesture of tribute to America's current Muse of Tragedy, of whom needless to say Bernhardt had never remotely heard. The act was well staged even though it might not have been in keeping with the rules of play-going etiquette. Timing their arrival at the theatre a good ten minutes after the curtain was up, Sarah, flanked

by her two managers, was ushered down the aisle a few seconds before Clara was to make her first entrance. In case anyone in the
audience might fail to notice these latecomers, a sputtering calcium
light followed their progress. As they neared their first-row seats,
the American star came on stage, a large bouquet in her hand. The
orchestra brought the audience to their feet with the *Marseillaise*.
What happened to the development of the plot of the play at this
moment has not been reported. Maybe *Alixe* was the sort of drama
which could survive interruption. At the finish of Rouget de
Lisle's stirring anthem, Miss Morris, who was a powerful lady,
hurled her bouquet, all but hitting Madame Bernhardt in the head
with it, and blew a hearty kiss across the footlights. In a telling
gesture of ecstasy, Sarah clutched the bouquet to her heart, then
took from Abbey a sheaf of roses, gracefully tossed them to fall at
Clara's feet, blew back a kiss with the outstretched arms of a
Delphic priestess and the house went wild. Then they settled back
to get their admission's worth out of *Alixe* while "The Bernhardt"
composed herself into an attitude of following with rapt attention
a performance not one line of which she could possibly have understood.

On her first day ashore, she'd gone through the ordeal of the
gentlemen of the press, on the next she was put through a second
ordeal, that of facing those less gentlemanly functionaries, scarcely
noted for their sensibilities, the U.S. Customs inspectors. In the
morning Jarrett came by to take her over to Booth's Theatre on
6th Avenue and 23rd Street, where she was booked to play and
where her costume trunks of which there were over a hundred
had been sent in bond. When she arrived backstage, she was horrified to see that they'd been opened and were being ransacked by
twenty filthy-handed, cigar-smoking inspectors and two shrill
harpies who turned out to be dressmakers summoned to evaluate
the wardrobe. As each exquisite gown was hauled ruthlessly forth,
the harpies pounced upon it to go over every seam, every bit of embroidery, every flounce of lace, less for purposes of evaluation than

to take mental notes and even draw sketches for future copies of the smart models they hoped to duplicate. Sarah, with a cry of anguish, rushed into the mêlée of vandals as though to save loved ones from slaughter, called for her maid and theatre dresser to handle the unpacking, sent out for five hundred yards of muslin to spread on the stage and cover the heaped-up pile of costumes and left her *maître d'hotel* armed with a revolver to keep guard overnight.

To soothe her ruffled spirits, she went for a carriage drive with a New York friend who took her for a brief trot through a portion of the city. The rushing traffic elated her and she squealed with pleasurable terror at the overhead roar of the "Rapid Transit Elevated Railroad" as its coal-burning engines spewed forth live ashes which showered down onto the avenues below. The tall buildings excited her still further and in an ensuing interview she told one reporter that her newest ambition was to become an architect so as to design a few skyscrapers. Her friend drove her to the East River for a view of the "Miracle of Manhattan," the partially completed Brooklyn Bridge. The gigantic steel span with its network of web-like cables filled her with wonder and an effective moment of dizziness and she cried out with rapture at the sight of the city silhouetted against a clear winter sky. "I returned to my hotel," she wrote, "reconciled to these great people."

She must have been yet more reconciled after her opening at Booth's "Temple of Dramatic Art" on November 8. The play was Scribe and Legouvé's *Adrienne Lecouvreur*. The house was packed with New York's smartest and richest (the top price for a single ticket was $40), the majority of whom had come mainly out of curiosity. It was less the artist of distinction than the woman of scandalous reputation they were waiting to see. They had to wait until the second act, for the starring role of Adrienne does not appear in the first, a violation of dramatic convention which so outraged one spectator, he stamped off to the box office and at the top of his lungs demanded his money back. The demand was refused and the man stamped back to his seat in a fury that changed into emotions of wonder and fascination when the curtain rose on the second act and that frail, intoxicating woman glided onto the stage. Her very appearance came as a shock to the public. They were unprepared for this miracle of delicacy, for her feline grace, for the effect of an incandescent, shimmering aura she gave forth as though she were creating her own eerie limelight. Most American theatre-goers had a preconceived idea that Bernhardt was going to be another Rachel, the French tragedienne who had come to their country twenty-five years earlier and had not been a success. The very term *tragédienne* implied an Old-School player-queen of heroic build and thundering voice. As one reviewer expressed it, "We were expecting Corneille. What we got was de Musset." The house sat hushed and transfixed. A knowledge of French was not needed. When Rachel had played New York, she complained of the distracting sound made by the audience turning the pages of their translation brochures in unison. If translation brochures were sold for the Bernhardt performances, nobody referred to them as long as she was on the stage. One watched nothing but that enchanting wraith, heard nothing but that voice which had in it "the cooing of doves, the running of streams, the falling of spring rains." They shivered as though with ice on their spines when that voice clarioned in rage or anguish and her acting became the flash of forked lightning. It was only after her final scene in which, of course, she died and, as Adrienne, most effectively from poisoning, that the hush of the spectators broke into roaring applause and shouts of enthusiasm which didn't quiet down until she had taken twenty-seven curtain calls.

Sarah Bernhardt's curtain calls were an act in themselves. Instead of bowing, she would stand stock still, her hands either clasped under her chin or with a palm placed on either cheek, then she'd stretch her arms straight out before her in spectacular recognition of the public. Occasionally she'd break the pose to give her hair a quick, nervous ruffle and always she'd pant as though having given her all — she was spent but still gallantly game to the finish.

It was part of the Bernhardt protocol that for her curtain calls, her leading man should stand close by in the wings to lend his support in case she needed it. After each bow, the great lady would sail off stage, suddenly totter as if about to swoon, clutch onto the gentleman's arm for a reeling moment of recovery, then sail back on for another ovation. One leading man told a reporter that he greatly enjoyed rendering this service, particularly as the star's aphrodisiac perfume was so strong, his coat sleeve would reek pleasurably for hours afterward.

During the opening-night ovation, bouquets were hurled at the great artist's feet, ushers staggered down the aisles with monumental flower baskets and the stage manager stepped out from the wings with a large wreath trimmed with a tricolored ribbon on which were pasted gold letters reading, "For our Sarah from the painters and sculptors of Paris." Sarah kissed the ribbon and wept becomingly.

People so jammed the alley to the stage entrance, Abbey and Jarrett had to escape with their star through a side fire escape. A crowd ran after her carriage back to the Albemarle Hotel, where they stood on the street below her windows applauding, cheering and whistling. The whistles frightened the daylights out of Madame until Jarrett explained that they signified appreciation in this country, not derision as they do in Europe. As Abbey had foreseen, she was called out like royalty onto that balcony time after time to wave and blow kisses and, in spite of the freezing cold, was obliged to stand bravely at attention while a German band slaughtered the *Marseillaise*. Her national anthem was to become practically a theme song throughout her United States tour. Whenever she arrived in a new city, whenever she made a public appearance, if a band was handy, it struck up the glorious tune. Not always gloriously, however, and there must have been many times when Sarah Bernhardt winced visibly and Rouget de Lisle whirled in his grave.

Overnight "The Bernhardt" became "*The* Thing." Her every

move was reported in the papers, the women's pages published daily accounts and sketches of her gowns, furs and jewelry. Merchants and manufacturers took advantage of the fad and Sarah Bernhardt perfume, Sarah Bernhardt candy, Sarah Bernhardt cigars, and even Sarah Bernhardt eyeglasses appeared on the market. A brewing company brought out large billboard posters in lurid colors showing two likenesses of her, one an exaggeration of her thinness, the other a quaint fantasy of her fattened out into stylish curving hips and billowy bosom. The caption read, "Sarah Bernhardt before and after six months of drinking our bitter." Dumont's Minstrel Burlesque put on a specialty act called, "The Cannibals of Barren Island," in which their leading comic in blackface, calling himself "Sarah Heartburn," writhed about the stage in frenzied emotion and fell dead a number of times.

For all the furore she made in the theatre, she was anything but a success in high society. Although the members of London's elite may have opened wide their aristocratic doors for the entertainment of Madame Sarah, New York's Four Hundred kept their somewhat less aristocratic doors prudishly closed to her. The scandalous rumors had been whispered over cups of tea into the titillated ears of the town's leading hostesses who, being righteous and pure-minded, had believed every word of them. In 1880 the pillars of Manhattan society, Mrs. Jay, Mrs. Van Rensselaer or Mrs. Stuyvesant Fish, would no more have held a soirée in honor of Sarah Bernhardt than a Southern hostess in 1930 would have given a tea for Josephine Baker.

Even the well-known gentlemen hosts of the metropolis, the cotillion leaders such as Ward McAllister, balked at receiving "The Bernhardt" within their restricted circle. If any one of them should have put himself out for her it was the multi-millionaire James Stebbins, an art collector and prominent member of the international set. When previously he had been living in Paris he had gone to elaborate lengths to be presented to Madame Sarah and after he finally succeeded, he had written her more than ten imploring letters begging her to honor his house on the Champs Elysées with her presence before she deigned to accept. After which social triumph, he had showered her with flowers, notes of gratitude and an enamel box from Fabergé. The great artist arrived in his home town and Mr. Stebbins kept conspicuously silent. When Jarrett approached him on the idea of having Madame recite at one of his soirées, the gentleman drew himself up to his pompous height and said, "Sir, we are no longer in Paris; this is New York!"

The only person daring enough to entertain Madame Sarah was James Gorden Bennett, who had known her when he was managing his Paris edition of the *New York Herald*. Even Bennett didn't risk being turned down by Gotham's society ladies. He settled for an aftertheatre supper party in a private room at Delmonico's, which Sarah defined in her Memoirs as being "le Café Anglais de New York." With the exception of the guest-of-honor, the diners were all men, distinguished members of the financial, diplomatic and literary worlds. The evening was an unqualified success — the food and wines excellent, the conversation brilliant and everyone's behavior beyond reproach. However, word came out in the gossip columns (not, let us trust, in Mr. Bennett's own *Herald*) that "The Bernhardt" had been the toast of an orgy held behind the locked doors of a private room in Delmonico's. In an attempt to rectify the erroneous impression James Gordon Bennett's supper had made, Jarrett and Abbey arranged an exhibition of Madame Bernhardt's sculpture to be held within the eminently respectable walls of the Union League Club. Invitations were dispatched to the Four Hundred and about half that number showed up. It was the masculine half which jammed the halls and foyer that afternoon: stockbrokers, sportsmen and a few young bloods known at the time as "howling swells." Amid the milling mob of city coats, Prince Alberts and pin-striped trousers. Sarah looked vainly about for a single woman other than the female members of her own company.

In addition to the stories about the actress' morals, word had gotten about that the plays in her repertoire were "Frenchy," meaning naughty, and of course the ladies who wouldn't have dreamt of receiving her off stage couldn't wait to go see each and every one of her on-stage appearances. They identified the star with certain of her glamorous but sinful roles: Marguerite Gauthier ("Camille" to them), who had been a professional *courtisane*, and Adrienne Lecouvreur, who was openly the mistress of Marshal de Saxe. Although they rushed to be shocked by such drama, they forbade their daughters to attend any with the exception of *Phèdre*. The fact that Racine's sultry heroine is aflame with an incestuous lust for her stepson must have been mitigated by the more cultural fact that the piece is a classic.

If she was snubbed by Gotham high society, Sarah could not have cared less. She was probably quite relieved as she hated formal functions. She had a number of good friends in New York, Americans she'd known in Paris or London, not socially registered to be sure, but intelligent, amusing persons, writers, artists, singers. Her real friends were always devoted to her. During the day, she kept herself busy, receiving callers, sight-seeing, visiting museums and shopping on the "Ladies' Mile" of Broadway. When Sarah Bernhardt shopped, she was not like other women. As they would purchase gloves, handkerchiefs or perfume, she'd buy furs, live pets and costly materials by the yard. The latter she'd order in vast quantities with the intention of having them all eventually made up into hangings or costumes, but never getting around to it. There were bolts of uncut satins, velvets and brocades lying idle in her storage rooms for years.

The box office at Booth's Theatre did a thriving business. And, of course, when *La Dame aux Camélias* was on the bill, the line of ticket buyers and standees stretched clear around the block. Many actresses have played the role of Dumas *fils'* lovely and repentant sinner and most actresses have over-emoted. The secret of Bernhardt's success was in the disarming simplicity of her approach. She played Marguerite Gauthier with an exquisite frailty, a poetic pathos that was almost unbearable. All the heartbreak of Verdi's music at its most touchingly sentimental was in her interpretation, and after her death scene the audience sobbed audibly. Commodore Vanderbilt came to every one of her performances, sat conspicuously alone in a box and wept shamelessly into an enormous white handkerchief. When Sarah was about to leave for France, the Commodore called to pay his respects and ask her if there were not some souvenir of her American visit he could give her. Sarah, in a brilliant flash of diplomacy, asked to be given his handkerchief.

During Bernhardt's subsequent visits to America, at least five of which were announced as "Farewell Tours," the play most in demand was *Camille*. As late as 1912, the *New York Globe* carried a jingle about it entitled "Boo-Hoo":

> Who's done Camille in ev'ry clime
> From here to Zanzibar,
> And trickled briny tears enough
> To float a man-o'-war?
> Who did it when our grandma was
> A lassie blithe and gay?
> Who'll still be doing it no doubt
> When Baby Doll is gray?
> Who needs but pack her gladsome rags
> And hit the farewell trail
> Whene'er the treasurer reports
> She's running out of kale?
> Who slips it o'er in perfect French,
> Assures US that it's art,
> And hauls our Yankee shekels
> From the show-shop in a cart?
> Who makes us say "How wonderful!"
> And "Mabel, ain't it fine!"
> And wonder what it's all about?
> Why Bernhardt the Divine!

"La Bernhardt's" final New York performance was a matinee of *La Dame*. The audience was more rapturous than ever. There

were seventeen curtain calls after the third act and twenty-nine at
the finish. The play ran an hour overtime due to constant inter-
ruptions of lengthy applause. This last bit of information is taken
from the star's own autobiography, with or without whatever pinch
of salt the reader cares to apply.

Upon her attempted exit from the theatre, she was literally
mobbed and chiefly by hysterical women trying to speak to her,
to shake her hand, to touch her. One tore off her own gold brooch
and pinned it on Sarah's coat. Another brandished a pair of scissors with which to snip off a lock of Madame's hair, and instead
came away with the end of an ostrich plume from her hat. One
overwrought girl held out an autograph book and when she realized
she'd brought no ink, bit into her own wrist and dipped the pen
in blood. Much as she basked in adulation, this was a little too much
for Sarah, who fled back into the theatre. As was to be expected,
Jarrett and Abbey came to the rescue. They hit on the ruse of
having Jeanne Bernhardt exchange her hat for Sarah's, which was
heavily veiled. Jeanne also swathed herself in her sister's all-en-
veloping chinchilla cloak. While the star and her managers escaped through a fire exit, Jeanne found it a lark to brave the mob
and sign her sister's name.

That evening they set out for Boston, stopping off on the way at
Menlo Park to call on Thomas Edison, it being a publicity stunt of
the management that "the most famous man of America should
have the pleasure of meeting the most famous woman of France."
How Mr. Edison, and more particularly how Mrs. Edison and her
domestic staff, felt about the pleasure is matter for conjecture, for
the call was made well after midnight. The visitors were driven
from the station into what seemed an endless and pitch black night
which suddenly burst into a fairyland of light, coming from hundreds of electric bulbs strung on the trees in garlands of welcome.
Sarah was entranced and the first question she asked Edison was,
"Will we ever have electricity in the theatre?"

Thomas Edison, unimpressed by the theatre in general and wary

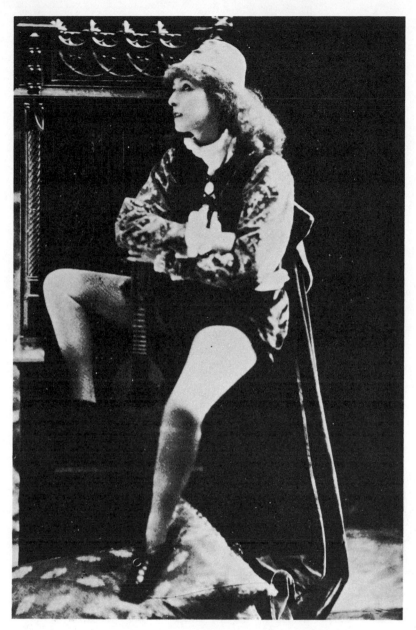

Sarah Bernhardt as Zanetto, the strolling boy troubadour
in Coppée's *Le Passant*

(Harvard Theatre Collection)

The Queen in Hugo's *Ruy Blas*
(Hoblitzelle Theatre Arts Library, The University of Texas)

Doña Sol in Hugo's *Hernani*
(Harvard Theatre Collection)

In *Froufrou* by Dumas, *fils*
(Hoblitzelle Theatre Arts Library, The University of Texas)

In Sardou's early success *Théodora*
(Harvard Theatre Collection)

The Duc de Reichstadt in Rostand's *L'Aiglon*
(Harvard Theatre Collection)

Péléas to Mrs. Patrick Campbell's Mélisande in Maeterlinck's hit
(The Bettmann Archive)

One of her finest roles, Phèdre in Racine's classic
(Theatre Collection, New York Public Library)

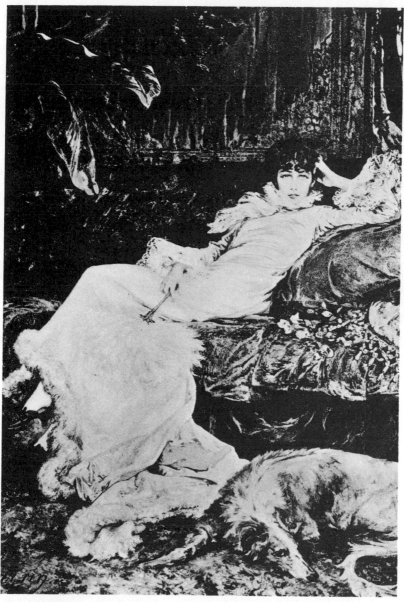

Georges Clairin's portrait of Sarah caused such a stir at the
1876 *Salon* that many Parisian women soon began copying the pose
when receiving their clandestine afternoon visitors

(Harvard Theatre Collection)

Four great co-stars
and leading men:
Jean Mounet-Sully
(The Bettmann Archive)

Constant Coquelin
(Harvard Theatre Collection)

Edouard de Max
(Theatre Collection, New York
Public Library)

Lucien Guitry
(*Cent Ans de Théâtre*,
Editions L'Image, Paris)

Sarah the sculptress
(Harvard Theatre Collection)

Sarah's arrival in New York in 1913
(on right is her producer, Martin Beck)

(Courtesy of Mrs. Martin Beck)

Her private car aboard the "Sarah Bernhardt Special"
(Theatre Collection, New York Public Library)

On tour in Texas
(Theatre Collection, New York Public Library)

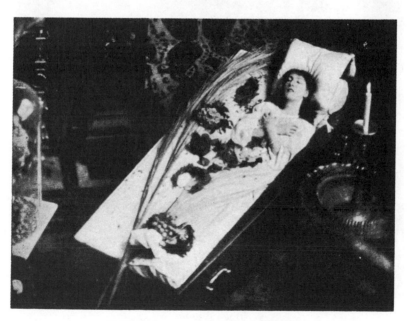

Sarah in her much publicized coffin
(The Bettmann Archive)

In late bloom
(Hoblitzelle Theatre Arts Library, The University of Texas)

Lou Tellegen, Sarah's last leading man
(Brown Brothers)

Belle Isle
(The Bettmann Archive)

With Houdini
(Hoblitzelle Theatre Arts Library, The University of Texas)

Madame Sarah on her final American tour
(Theatre Collection, New York Public Library)

of the very title "French actress," received his guest with guarded politeness. But in no time at all she managed to captivate him. At least so she modestly claims in her Memoirs:

> His marvellous blue eyes, more luminous than his incandescent lamps, permitted me to read all his thoughts. I realized that I must conquer him and my combative spirit summoned forth all my seductive forces to win over this shy and delightful scholar . . . A half hour later, we were the best of friends in the world.

She declared that she was charmed by his "timid and courteous grace and by his profound love of Shakespeare."

The great inventor and the great actress apparently took warmly to one another. A pleasant supper was served, after which Madame was taken into a library where was a strange device known as a telephone over which she spoke with one of Edison's aides who was all of a mile away. As she spoke no English and the aide not a word of French, the conversation could not have been a lengthy one. She was then escorted on an inspection tour through the laboratory where, according to her Memoirs, the noise of the machines, the turning of wheels, the flashing of lights so overwhelmed her, she lost consciousness. Whether she completely lost it or not, it was an effective reaction as she wilted gracefully onto the chest of the Wizard of Electricity, who carried her into another workshop where she recovered and was introduced to the latest wonder of invention, the phonograph. A recording was made on a cylinder. Two apprentices sang "John Brown's Body" which was translated as "Le Cadavre de John Brown," the Golden Voice spoke some lines from *Phèdre* and Mr. Edison himself sang "Yankee Doodle" off-key. When the result was transmitted through the horn of the playing machine, it sounded like the squawks of a Punch and Judy show. Sarah went into fits of uncontrollable giggles for which she made up when she said good-by and told her host that he had much in common with Napoleon. It is to be hoped that the eminent genius took this as deserving appreciation. The theatrical party hurried to the station and took a 3 A.M. train for Boston, and it is to be assumed that Mr. and Mrs. Edison hurried upstairs and took to their beds.

8.

THE SARAH BERNHARDT SPECIAL

In the Massachusetts capital Sarah Bernhardt stayed in the Hotel Vendome, "which," according to her Memoirs, "is situated in the Faubourg Saint Germain of the town." And it still is, if likening Commonwealth Avenue to Paris' bastion of royalist aristocracy may be of satisfaction to present-day Bostonians. Her suite was a delight to behold. In her bedroom, the dismal hotel draperies had been removed from the windows and replaced by billowing white muslin curtains festooned with blue taffeta ribbon. The bedspread was of quilted white satin and crested with a "Quand Même" of gold embroidery. The sitting room was a mass of art treasures in the way of Persian rugs, oil paintings, statuettes and fine vases sent on loan from unknown local admirers. When she protested that with such a valuable collection amassed in one place, there might be danger of theft, a greeting spokesman assured her that the objects were all insured and that "Our citizens want Madame to realize that Boston is a city of culture." The place was a veritable hothouse of banked flowers, and a silver tray on a vestibule table was snowed under with calling cards and invitations.

In contrast to Gotham's attitude of social ostracism, this Athens of America, this stronghold of Puritanism received France's actress with the Back Bay equivalent of open arms. If the inevitable scandalous gossip had reached their well-bred ears, the Proper Bostonians were neither shocked nor outraged. Their interest was in her artistry, not her reputation. In Boston, the city of cautious scholarship, the critics went overboard. "Before such perfection," one of them wrote, "analysis is impossible." Every evening the Globe Theatre was jammed with the flower of New England and even the teen-age *jeunesse* of Beacon Hill were taken to matinees of the so-called shockers: *Adrienne Lecouvreur, Phèdre, Froufrou* and that drama of heartbreak and misnomer which for once was called by its correct title *The Lady of the Camellias*.

The doors of the exclusive houses on Beacon Hill were opened wide to Madame Bernhardt and she in response opened wide her heart to the civilized old city and its kindly people. She was especially intrigued by the Boston ladies. She found these votaries of culture and extraordinary hats charming with their good manners, their quiet voices and their determined *bas-bleuisme* (the French sounds less harsh than "blue-stockingness"). She was amused by their serene supremacy over their men and delighted in the legend that it was a woman who, leaping from one of the landing boats of the *Mayflower*, insisted that a female be the first to set foot on New England soil. In her Memoirs she summed them up as "Puritans with intelligence, independence and grace." The leading hostesses welcomed her into their formal parlors and generous dining rooms and, as most of them spoke French, albeit in a staunchly Yankee accent, the star enjoyed herself immensely.

She was serenaded by Harvard students and a delegation escorted her on a visit to their campus. In the library she stood for a minute of respectful silence before the autographs of Milton and Shakespeare. Then she spied a bulletin board onto which students pinned questions relative to their courses with a blank sheet below for whoever could furnish the answers. On being told that one of the questions was "What are the principal works of the French dramatist Victorien Sardou?" Madame grabbed a pencil and obligingly wrote out a list. In the next ensuing years how she could have augmented that list with the titles of the plays she was to immortalize for Sardou! — *Fédora, Théodora, Tosca, Cléopâtre, Gismonda, Spiritisme* and *La Sorcière*.

One of her best Boston friends was a diplomat's wife, a lady who

not only moved in social circles but was equally at home amid the
Brook Farm and "Brahmin" intelligentsia. How Bernhardt ever
came to profess an admiration for the writings of Henry Wadsworth Longfellow, how she had ever even heard of him, is as impossible to figure out as are the sources of any other of her wildly
divergent enthusiasms. As part of her vast travel paraphernalia, she
had brought along her sculptor's tools and equipment and she told
the diplomat's wife that the ambition of her life was to model a bust
of the poet, and would her friend kindly arrange for some sittings.
The diplomat's wife conveyed the message to the creator of
Evangeline, whose reaction was one of immediate alarm.

"Tell Madame Bernhardt," he said, "that I am about to leave for
my country house near Portland, Maine. However, within the next
few days I'd be delighted to receive her here in my Cambridge
home for tea." Then he added with hasty caution, "But be sure to
come along with her as I'll need a chaperone." Longfellow was
then seventy-three. He safeguarded himself with a second chaperone in the person of Mrs. William Dean Howells, as well as with
the additional presence of Dr. Oliver Wendell Holmes. Longfellow spoke excellent French and the little gathering went off
swimmingly. At one point, Sarah, raising her eyes in her best
ecstasy expression, rapturously announced that of all the poems she
had ever read, not excepting those of her beloved Victor Hugo,
her favorite was *Hiawatha*, which she called in caressing tones
"Ee-ah-vah-tah." It would have been interesting to have heard the
Golden Voice reciting those lines about the "Shores of Gitchie
Goomie." France's eminent tragedienne was delighted with America's venerable bard, who was pleased by her flattering protestations
of admiration. His sense of pleasure changed into one of acute discomfort when, as he was seeing her to her carriage, she suddenly
stopped to cry out in tones that re-echoed down the quiet Cambridge street, "*Ah que je vous admire!*", flung her arms about his
neck and kissed him resoundingly on both blushing cheeks.

For all Sarah's enjoyment of Boston and the Bostonians, it was in this city that she was subjected to the first of a series of infuriating and repetitive experiences. It started immediately after the company's early morning arrival in town, when she was setting out for her hotel with Jarrett. Hardly had their cab left South Station than a wild-eyed reporter jumped onto the carriage step, yelled at the cabbie to halt his horse and demanded in broken French when the famous actress was expecting to visit the famous whale. Sarah, thinking him demented, cowered back against Jarrett, who was about to hurl the man bodily off into the street. But the reporter, who was persistent and eloquent, hailed over from the sidewalk an innocuous-looking person whom he introduced as a Mr. Henry Smith. Mr. Smith, it seemed, was the owner of a cod-fishing fleet. One of his crews had recently encountered a mammoth whale with two harpoons in its sides, weakened but still alive. They had captured the monster, brought it back into harbor, and at the moment it was moored to a dock in the Charles River, to all intents and purposes awaiting "The Bernhardt's" visit in order to expire in peace. It was a unique spectacle, he said, one she was not likely to see again, and when would Mr. Smith have the honor of showing it to Madame. Always intrigued by any prospect of the bizarre, Madame asked Jarrett if he didn't think it would be a lark to accept the invitation. The "Ferocious Gentleman," who anticipated nothing particularly lark-like in the expedition, grudgingly accepted, thinking that in any case this might offer the chance for a publicity angle — little foreseeing the dimensions of that angle. He told the reporter and Mr. Smith that Madame would view their marine exhibit the following day and subsequently arranged with a Mr. Gordon, a Bostonian of social prominence, to escort Madame on this unconventional outing.

Mr. Gordon, driving his own coach-and-four, arrived at the Vendome the next morning. The day was bitter cold and Sarah, swathed to her nose in several layers of fur, climbed up the coach ladder, and dramatically taking her place beside Mr. Gordon on the driver's seat, struck the proud attitude of the Russian princess she was eventually to play in Sardou's *Fédora*. Mr. Gordon cracked his whip and his foursome made it in smart time to the dock where Henry Smith and a group of reporters were waiting. Beside them, coated in ice, the whale bobbed dolefully in the ripples of the Charles. Smith insisted that the wretched beast was still alive and that its rising and falling motion was the effect of its final gasps. After which melancholy announcement, he escorted Madame over a temporary gangplank leading onto the helpless captive's back and with outstretched hand, offered her the novel experience of walking on the back of a whale. To Sarah the experience, if novel, seemed peculiarly uninviting, but she noted the increasing number of onlookers and, being a woman never to turn down a challenge, she grabbed Smith's forearm and ventured out onto the mammal's dorsal surface, on which the two of them slipped, slid and lurched about for a number of merry moments. Then Smith made the appetizing suggestion that she pull out one of the creature's bones. Sarah, with ill-concealed aversion, reached down and drew forth a small, osseous sliver which had obviously been planted in a freshly cut hole. After which curious ceremony, she skidded back onto the dock and made a dash for sanctuary beside Mr. Gordon on his coach top. The gentleman-driver cracked his whip and the horses started off at a smart trot. "The Bernhardt" was in a state of boiling agitation, and Mr. Gordon, thinking she'd appreciate a means of letting off steam, offered to let her take the reins. Sarah, who had never taken the reins of so much as a Shetland pony, undauntedly seized the stout straps with results that nearly ended in disaster. The four animals, sensing a new and inexperienced hand at the controls, broke from their smart trot into a wild gallop. The top-heavy vehicle careened around a corner at an angle that would have capsized a sailing vessel, and it was only Gordon's timely grabbing of the reins that prevented horses and coach from crashing through the plate-glass windows of a florist's shop.

Back in her hotel suite before a blazing fire, Madame B. with a sigh of relief shed her voluminous furs. If she thought she had also shed the embarrassment of Smith and his wretched whale, she was to be brutally disenchanted. During the early '80's the newspaper photographer may happily not have been in existence but all American journals had their numbers of quick-sketch artists who at a moment's notice could be despatched to every corner of a city to cover the more unusual events of a day. That evening and the following morning every paper in Boston and its environs carried a reproduced drawing of France's great actress savagely ripping a massive bone from the gashed side of a whale. The caption read, "How Sarah Bernhardt gets the whalebone for her corsets." As if the newspaper publicity were not sufficient offense, Henry Smith turned his pitiable behemoth into a sort of tent show, admission to which was twenty-five cents. He commandeered some jobless derelicts as sandwich men to tramp the pavements bearing signs which read, "The phenomenon of France visits the phenomenon of the sea." And as further bally-hoo for his exhibit he acquired a horse-drawn calliope which blared through the streets displaying a billboard in horrendous colors, again showing the actress in a de-boning act and the caption, "Come see the gigantic whale killed by Sarah Bernhardt to furnish bones for her corsets which are made exclusively by Mme. Lily Noah of New York." How much Mme. Lily Noah paid Mr. Henry Smith for the ad is not a matter of record. The fact that never in all her life did Sarah Bernhardt wear a corset seems not to have concerned either of them.

After Boston the company played New Haven, Hartford and Springfield, in each of which towns the first thing to greet the star's horrified eye and ear was Henry Smith's blaring calliope. By now the billboard announced the added attraction that the giant cadaver was being kept in a state of perfect preservation by the daily administration into its stomach of two tons of salt at $100 per ton. At New Haven, Smith was waiting in the lobby of Madame Sarah's hotel and upon her entrance bowed obsequiously. Madame's response to his greeting was in the form of a couple of violent and well-aimed whacks on his beaming face. Smith, his face continuing to beam, bowed again, this time almost to the ground, muttered some words of gratitude and a few minutes later sent up to her suite an immense bouquet of roses which Madame with a yowl of fury hurled out of the nearest window. In Hartford a similar bouquet met a similar fate. Here she vented her wrath by purchasing a couple of Colt revolvers. Sarah was an excellent shot and in making the purchase she was probably settling on Smith as the perfect target for her marksmanship. In Springfield, after she had again hurled another bouquet out of her window, she was taken to visit the Remington firearms factory, where she had the gratifying privilege of firing one of their cannons, doubtless imagining Smith as being tied to its mouth.

In spite of its daily tons of salt, Smith's sideshow was becoming rather high, but in spite of the smell, it continued to attract the crowds and the persistent promoter was making a fortune. What eventually held him up was the Canadian border, across which dead whales were not welcome. Henry Smith and his mammoth were left behind in upper New York State while Sarah Bernhardt and her troupe continued on to Montreal.

They arrived in the pitch dark of a sub-zero pre-dawn and were met not by any whale but by what looked to be hundreds of bears each carrying a lantern. This proved to be a vast delegation of officials and French-Canadian citizens wearing heavy fur coats and astrakhan hats. The flickering lantern lights played eerily on their ruddy faces and on the steaming breath that came from their cheering throats.

The Montreal engagement was a huge success due partly to some excellent publicity furnished by the Catholic archbishop who for several weeks had fulminated from his pulpit against the arrival in their pious city of this theatrical whore of Babylon. Time and again he had forbidden his flock to attend any of her performances and, of course, the flock couldn't wait to attend every one of them. The particular play over which as a contaminating influence the holy man seems most to have worked himself up was Scribe and

Legouvé's *Adrienne Lecouvreur*, whose plot deals with the fatal rivalry between the actress Adrienne, an admitted courtesan, and the Duchesse de Bouillon, a woman of shameless morals, each of them the mistress of Marshal de Saxe — a subject he considered to be so evil, the archbishop recommended the immediate excommunication of both Sarah Bernhardt and Eugene Scribe. (Legouvé, the second co-author, seems to have been let off the indictment.) As Scribe had already been dead some twenty years, to excommunicate him would have offered complications.

The Montreal première was spectacular. The evening, as was to be expected, opened with the *Marseillaise*, but this time not routinely sawed and tooted out on the strings and wind instruments of a theatre orchestra. Instead, it burst spontaneously and *a capella* from the young throats of over two hundred French-Canadian students jamming the top gallery who suddenly remembered that their sweet old city and picturesque province had first belonged to France and that they were the sons of Britanny and Normandy. That night at least they were all dedicated patriots of the original Mother Country. Her Majesty's representative, Governor of the Province of Quebec, the Marquis of Lorne, son-in-law of Victoria, conspicuous in an official box, stood uneasily at polite attention during the rendering of France's stirring anthem, at the finish of which he signaled the orchestra leader who dutifully obliged with a staidly proper and sternly remindful playing of *God Save the Queen*. The play went on. The star's first entrance and every subsequent appearance was met with shouts and thunderous applause. As she took her final curtain calls, she was all but knocked flat by the bouquets hurled by the audience, while from the gallery the students released a number of white doves to whose necks were loosely attached sonnets and love poems which were supposed to flutter down at Sarah's feet as the gentle birds circled gracefully over her head. It was a pretty idea which hardly worked out. The doves, terrified by the lights and the noise, circled wildly not over Sarah's head but over those of the audience, and what came down was not a collection of love poems, and it didn't flutter so much as plop.

For all the unfortunate behavior of the doves, nobody objected unless possibly one or two victims of the plops. The house continued wild with enthusiasm. People shouted in French, calling for "Notre Sarah." That night and after every subsequent performance of the Montreal engagement, students waited in the bitter cold outside the stage door to carry "La Divine" on their shoulders to her waiting sleigh from which they'd unharness the horses and, lining up in the shafts, run her back up the hill to the Windsor Hotel. Doubtless the horses and coachman were grateful for the relief.

Montreal aroused in Sarah Bernhardt the sense of adventure. Setting aside her habitual abhorrence for fresh air, she took daily sleigh rides glorying in the severe, sparkling cold. There was always an overheated hotel suite or her tropically temperatured dressing room to return to. She dismayed her ever-present retinue and astonished any onlookers by suddenly giving way to crazy impulses. One sharply clear afternoon, while going at a fast clip past a bank of fresh snow, she jumped from the sleigh, flung herself backward into the drift and, waving her arms up and down at their sides, created one of those imprints which children call "making an angel." Another time she frightened the daylights out of Jarrett by again jumping from her sleigh and, calling to her sister Jeanne to follow her, ran down a slope to the river, where the two of them played a hair-raising game of leaping from ice floe to ice floe on the semi-frozen surface of the St. Lawrence. Jarrett, standing on the shore, yelled for them to come back instantly. When, after quite a few moments, they finally did, "The Ferocious Gentleman" was livid with rage. Sarah, flushed from her hazardous exertions, merely laughed and called him the current equivalent of a stuffed shirt. Jarrett, still livid, reminded her that he had staked his entire fortune on her and the success of the tour, that thus far he had recouped only 10 per cent of the outlay and that her silly actions might have resulted not just in her demise but in his loss of the remainder of his finances. It was a sobering thought and one which Jarrett knew would appeal to Sarah's business sense. She patted his cold cheek and promised in future to be good.

That Sarah had brought Jeanne along on the tour was an example of the actress' obstinate family loyalty, due perhaps to her Jewish heritage. It was unfortunate that Jeanne Bernhardt went along on this first United States tour. Actually she didn't start out with the company, being ill at the time of their departure. She was left behind in Paris with the understanding that after her recovery, she would take a later ship and join up with the troupe in New York or Boston. Meanwhile, Sarah engaged an actress named Marie Colombier to play the feminine roles second in importance to her own.

Marie Colombier was an attractive wench of scanty talent and much scantier virtue whose chief claim to fame is that Manet painted a deliciously saucy portrait of her. Marie had been a casual friend of Sarah's ever since their contemporary days at the Conservatoire. She was a gay and vivacious creature with biting wit and a wicked tongue, and Sarah found her amusing. As far as Mademoiselle Colombier's acting was concerned, Madame could afford to be indulgent knowing the young woman could never steal a scene from her.

It was one of the great artist's weaknesses that her magnificent sense of showmanship was focused chiefly upon herself. She was the high-handed exception to the intelligent actor-manager's rule that the ultimate value of a play depends upon the excellence of each and every member of its cast. This actress-manager knew that almost any adequately constructed play in which she had her particular "Bernhardt specialty" type of part would be a sell-out in spite of the possible mediocrity of the other performers. Furthermore it was Madame's pleasure that they remain mediocre. What professional jealousy she had was reserved for the second-rate actress who started to show alarming signs of becoming first-rate. For the artist who had already achieved greatness, she felt not the slightest rivalry. When she co-starred with Mounet-Sully and Coquelin and later with Lucien Guitry, it was with a joyous sense of mutual stimulation. But then, to be sure, they were men whose great virility went to emphasize her feline femininity. Her attitude toward the contemporary leading actresses was affability itself. She dearly loved the delicious comedienne Gabrielle Réjane, adored Ellen Terry and expressed her esteem for Mrs. Patrick Campbell by playing Pélléas to Mrs. Pat's Mélisande in what must have been a rather curious performance of Maeterlinck's moon-struck drama. She professed nothing but worshipful admiration for Eleonora Duse, although in later years after Italy's exquisite tragedienne had fallen upon hard times, hearing her name mentioned one day, Sarah in child-like innocence asked, "What ever became of that old lady?" (Duse was fifteen years younger than she.)

When Madame Bernhardt engaged Mademoiselle Colombier, she probably had every intention of having her play the specified supporting leads. In fact when Marie questioned her about the possibilities of Jeanne's returning to the cast, Sarah in tones solemnly reproachful swore "on her sacred word of honor" that no actress but Marie Colombier would be entrusted with such significant roles. She sounded convincing, and Colombier told as much to an admirer who came to see her off on the boat train at the Gare Saint Lazare. The gentleman snorted, "Her sacred word of honor! I wouldn't trust it as far as Asnières!" Sarah's "sacred word of honor" went according to her own code which even she, in one of her flashes of disarming honesty, might have been the first to admit was as subject to change as her moods. One of its rules was that devotion to family came before obligations to employees or friends, and when Jeanne Bernhardt stepped off the ship in New York, Sarah, by way of sisterly welcome, informed her she was to play three of the second rôles and conveniently forgot all previous commitments to Colombier.

Marie Colombier didn't forget, nor did she ever forgive. However, she disguised her sense of outrage behind a carefree manner of bright good humor and bided her time. What's more, she put that time to good account. Back in Paris, after agreeing to go on the Bernhardt tour, she had made a further little agreement on her own with the newspaper *l'Evénement* to write and mail in every few weeks a series of humorous articles reporting the highlights of Madame Sarah's invasion of America. Colombier had a pen as sharp as her tongue and when her maliciously exaggerated yet highly amusing pieces began to appear in the racy pages of the *Evénements*, they fanned the resentment that was smouldering amid the French public against their national actress. That *monstre bien aimé* had resented her departure from the Comédie Française, had resented her whirlwind tour of Europe and England (probably because it had been so successful) and now resented her wasting French acting and drama on the desert air of a country Baudelaire had dismissed as "a land of barbarians illuminated by gas."

The next stop after Montreal was Philadelphia, which City of Brotherly Love "The Bernhardt" found dull in the extreme. The one interruption to the tedium was a highly successful exhibition of her sculpture which Jarrett and Abbey arranged — again in the mausoleum-like confines of a Union League Club. If her theatre managers may have lacked a sensitive approach to the plastic arts, they had an unerring sense of the proper setting for their star's mortuary type of statuary. A number of marbles were purchased. This flattered the sculptress and brought a certain amount of relief to the stage crew in charge of baggage whose duty it had been to haul along such marmoreal overweight in the scenery cars.

The first stop after Philadelphia was Chicago. Jarrett had written the mayor in advance asking for a bodyguard of extra police to be on hand in the station, a request the mayor, who had never heard of "The Bernhardt," considered absurd. He heard plenty later when he was told that, upon arrival, the lady was all but annihilated by mobs of hysterical greeters, separated from her protecting retinue and eventually rescued by an unknown ruffian who lifted

her up on his shoulders, bore her safely to a cab and deposited her
at the Palmer House. According to her own story as told to
Lysiane, the fellow was a penitentiary escapee wanted for the
murder of his sweetheart and this knight-errant act in saving Sarah
from the crowd resulted in his recapture by the police. She went
on to tell Lysiane that some days later, she made a special journey
out to the Joliet penitentiary to perform before the prisoners and to
exchange a few words of gratitude and compassion with her rescuer
who, the warden informed her, was to be hanged the following
morning — the thought of which so unnerved her, she could barely
stagger through her performances for three nights running.

Those performances were all sell-outs due, as usual, to the vast
amount of advance publicity, much of which was, as usual, unsolicited. Again as usual, the clergy helped out, representing "The
Bernhardt" as being on a par of bestiality with one of the creatures
of the Apocalypse (and who wouldn't rush to see a leopard with
seven heads and six horns!). Here it was the Anglican cloth that
did the groundwork, the Episcopal Bishop of Chicago in two
sermons denouncing her so eloquently, Abbey wrote him a letter,
which the manager saw was reprinted in all newspapers:

> Your Excellency:
> I am accustomed when I bring an attraction to your town, to
> spend $400 on advertising. As you have done half the advertising
> for me, I herewith enclose $200 for the poor of your parish.

The press continued to come out with the usual exaggerations and
reporters to ask the usual impertinent questions. "Is it true," one
inquired, "that you have had four children and never any husband?"
to which she snorted back, "Certainly not! But at least that would
be better than the case of some of your American women who have
had four husbands and never any children."

Bernhardt enjoyed Chicago. Her quarters at the Palmer House
roused in her continual and gleeful mirth, for she occupied the

"honeymoon suite," an elaborate nightmare in Egyptian style with sofas like Cleopatra's barge, lamps whose bases were bronze sphynxes and clocks imbedded in black marble pyramids. Sarah found excitement in the raw newness and bustle of the great prairie city which Marie Colombier described at that date to be "America as it is imagined in Paris, a city of iron with locomotives smoking in the streets . . . telegraph wires so numerous they hide the sky, banks the size of the Louvre, insurance houses like the Palace of Versailles. All this, swarming with 600,000 inhabitants who come and go, frantically running after the Almighty Dollar."

From here the troupe was launched into its backbreaking tour. They traveled via the "Sarah Bernhardt Special," an up-to-the-minute conveyance consisting of three Pullmans for the personnel and her own private car, known as a "Palace Car," for Madame Sarah. The scenery, costumes and heavy luggage went on ahead in a freight express, also special, and for the passage of both trains, all tracks were cleared.

The schedule was brutal. There were any number of one-night stands. Often the corps would arrive in a place as late as 6 P.M., give the show at 8:30, then return to the sleepers for a midnight departure. All next day they might travel until another late arrival in the next town and likely as not be put through a repetition of the same hurried routine. It was tough for the actors. During the '80's trains were not of the cleanest and what with no time for a bath at a hotel between arrival in town and the hour for showing up at the theatre, they had to wash off the soot as best they could in the cold water and cracked basin of a dressing-room washstand. Food was a problem (not that American food hasn't always been a problem for any Frenchman). The average table d'hôte dinner on the road was for them merely a bare and somewhat revolting necessity for the preservation of life. The "Sarah Bernhardt Special" carried no diner and made no station stops where a Fred Harvey lunch-counter lady clanged a brass bell and whooped out to passengers to "come an' git it!" There were many days when the players dolefully subsisted upon crackers, sardines, fruit and Apollinaris water. There were other, and rarer, days when their star, overcome by a sudden pang of concern for her flock, would dispatch Claude, her *valet-de-chambre*, forward to their cars with platters of cold meats, salads and wine.

Madame Sarah always had plenty of provender to spare, living as she was in her "Palace Car," the *dernier cri*, the *ne plus ultra* in travel luxury. Its walls were of inlay wood, its overhead gas lamps of gleaming brass. Bright Turkey carpeting and zebra rugs covered the floor, draperies of velours trimmed in chenille hung on either side of the doors and the window tops were decorated with panes of colored glass. The lounge area contained comfortable sofas and easy chairs elegant with lace antimacassars, a reading table covered with magazines, a writing desk, an upright piano, card tables and a number of rubber plants and potted palms. Before the tour was finished, it contained a lot more in the way of souvenirs and acquired junk. Careless as she was about possessions, Sarah could never deliberately throw anything away. Admirers were continually bringing her presents. They brought them to the stage door, to her hotel suites, they even waited on station platforms with tributes of vases, paintings, statuettes, music boxes, ornamental bronzes and further well-intentioned horrors. Always the place was a profusion of flowers and always suffocatingly overheated by a coal-burning stove whose fire, even in the warmer climates, was never permitted to go out. Next to this main salon was a dining room with a table seating ten, gleaming with embroidered linen and the lady's own crested china, glassware and flat silver. Off this was a kitchen where two Negro cooks strove with perspiring valor to add French flavor to Southern cooking. The star's sleeping quarter was equipped with an immense brass bed, a carved mahogany dressing table, a gilt-framed cheval glass and a ribbon-trimmed basket for her dog, a highly unpleasant Belgian griffon named Hamlet the Third. Next door was a smaller bedroom for Madame Guérard and down the corridor a double

compartment which Jarrett shared with Abbey when the latter
joined up with the tour.

At the far end of the car was a commodious observation platform
equipped with comfortable wicker chairs. Here "La Bernhardt"
swathed to her eyes in furs and scarves would sit from time to time
and watch the passing countryside. On all her countless tours, she
never traveled without a pair of powerful field glasses. This contradictory woman of frailty yet self-renewing energy had a zestful
interest in new places, an alert curiosity to see how people lived, to
compare one region with another. She responded with exhilaration
to beautiful scenery, she thrilled to watch a sunset or a moonrise.

She wasn't able to watch many moons rise from her observation
platform after an attempt had been made by a holdup man who was
caught one night riding the rods underneath her car in an attempt
to detach it from the rest of the train at a lonely point along the
line where a gang of bandits was waiting to leap on board and
make off with Madame's over-publicized jewels. After this bit of
thwarted Western melodrama, the "Palace Car" was shunted
nightly to a position of security between two of the Pullmans. The
incident caused alarm among the more apprehensive members of
the troupe who with Gallic concern, less for their lives than for
their salaries, placed the latter in their socks and slept with their
shoes on, tightly laced. Madame Sarah herself reposed with her
own lethal weapon strategically placed under her five pillows. This
was a small, pearl-handled pistol which she herself admitted was
incapable of being fired but whose presence was apparently a
comfort.

In the morning, the "Palace Car" would be shunted back to its
position of regal importance at the end of the train. The car was
aptly named, for its stellar occupant lived in it like a sovereign and
her touring routine took on the quality of a Royal Progress. Before the start of any trip, she would summon the engineer to her
presence, shake hands with him and, through the handiest interpreter, find out how long the man had been in service, if he were

married and if so how many children he had. If his answers assured her of his reliability as an engineer, she would graciously dismiss him, and at the journey's finish send him up a tip. Occasionally she'd send along a souvenir for his wife. How the average American engineer's wife reacted to her husband's bringing home a souvenir from a French actress is another story.

Inside her rolling palace, Queen Sarah held continual court as she did in her more stationary one back in Paris. She would invite particular members of her company in for meals which were as sumptuous as the two colored cooks could dish up. Afternoons, as the train raced along over rough roadbeds, she would receive for tea, delicately attired in a flowing housegown and handling the jiggling cups and saucers with the ease of a dowager duchesse in the ancient stability of a Faubourg Saint Germain mansion. Sometimes she would hold gatherings of informal entertainment when someone would perform on the upright piano and someone else would sing or go into a Music Hall turn. Sometimes they'd act out charades or play dominoes. Sometimes there would be a card game, and at that pastime sometimes Sarah cheated a little.

Every now and then, she jotted down notes for the Memoirs she was to write the following year. These contain a few interesting statements regarding her private philosophy.

> Little bothers me [she wrote]. You should live for those who know and appreciate you, who judge and absolve you and for whom you have love and indulgence. The rest is merely *the crowd* . . . from whom one can expect only fleeting emotions, good or bad, which leave no trace.
>
> One should hate very little, because it's extremely fatiguing. One should despise much, forgive often and never forget. Pardon does not bring with it forgetfulness; at least not for me.

Sarah Bernhardt never forgot that she was first and foremost an actress. She possessed the conscientiousness of the dedicated musician who whether at home or on tour would never dream of letting a day go by without a certain number of practice hours. She was continually calling in members of her cast to restage a scene or run through a line rehearsal. She might hold a reading of a play which had struck her as a possible addition to her large repertory and if she liked it, she'd assign the parts and start rehearsing it then and there above the clacking of the wheels, the whooping of the whistle and the billowing clouds of choking soot from a tunnel passage.

Such was to be Sarah Bernhardt's touring routine during the next forty years of her career. As late as 1915 when she was seventy-one her American manager wrote: "Her energy and enthusiasm are endless. I never saw her show the slightest fatigue; I never saw her bored, I never saw her miss a beautiful bit of scenery from the car window or fail to appreciate a good joke."

The steady members of the "Palace Car Court" who were invited in for daily attendance, in addition to the ever-present Madame Guérard, were Jarrett and Abbey, Jeanne Bernhardt, Marie Colombier and the actor Angelo. Angelo was the favorite courtier, being both leading man and official lover. He was handsome and ingratiating — as an actor not overly gifted — as a lover, who knows? Who, for that matter knows how gifted as such were the rest of her lovers or what any of them meant to her? When Madame Sarah went on tour, she carried along a secretary, a lady's maid, two theatre dressers, her *maître d'hotel* and occasionally her chef. She sometimes carried along an attractive young actor as leading man to double in brass as lover for the duration of the tour. On this, her first United States venture, Angelo seems successfully to have fulfilled both duties. On her seventh and third from final American visit in 1910, the actor cast for the double bill was the absurd and overly beautiful Lou Tellegen, who shortly afterward married Geraldine Farrar. Madame Bernhardt was by then sixty-six and Mr. Tellegen some thirty-five years her junior.

Angelo must have found his off-stage role interesting if not at times hair-raising. His mistress' passion for collecting exotic live pets found outlet as their route carried them South. At one stop she brought on board two large black snakes which seemed harmless enough until they started a wriggling journey through the other cars, and when one of them writhed cozily up onto the seat beside the company's wig dresser, the ensuing hysteria was such that the "Terrible Mr. Jarrett" had the creatures hurled off the train. In Louisiana, Sarah purchased a small alligator whom she named Ali-Gaga. It was a friendly little reptile which manifested a devotion to its owner, following her about in her dressing rooms, her hotel suites, her private car. During meals, it lay docilely at her feet and at night it had a cozy habit of crawling under the covers of her bed. Writing about this last locale, André Castelot remarks, "We do not know the reactions of Angelo." Ali-Gaga's days were cut short by an early demise due, according to Marie Colombier, to a surfeit of champagne.

Ali-Gaga was not the only Louisiana alligator Sarah Bernhardt was to acquire. During a subsequent tour some twenty years later, there was staged for her the much publicized "Crocodile Hunt" when she was the guest of Mr. Charles Bell, a millionaire who owned a vast plantation outside of Lake Charles. The place boasted a number of lakes, a river and some rare bird and animal specimens. Sarah insisted that in such terrain there must be crocodiles (she was unaware that in this country they were alligators) and she requested that a crocodile hunt be organized. As there wasn't a trace of either crocodile or alligator on the estate, the obliging Mr. Bell sent off telegrams in all directions and managed to get hold of a baby 'gator, which was dumped into one of the lakes. The next morning was chilly and Madame Sarah emerged in a sealskin coat carrying a vast muff. After a bit she tossed coat and muff aside to reveal herself dressed as for an operetta safari with high-heeled shooting boots and a white suede jacket on the lapel of which was pinned a wilting hibiscus blossom. Brandishing a wide-brimmed hat trimmed with pheasant feathers, she shouted dramatically for the "beaters" to bring forth the "pirogues." There being neither "beaters" nor "pirogues," the hunting party had to make do with Mr. Bell, a gardener and a motorboat. They set forth but could track down no prey. Finally the gardener located the baby 'gator, tied its foot to a line, handed the other end to Madame, and she hauled in her trophy only to find out that the beastie was in a state of hibernation. On being informed that it would in all likelihood sleep for three months, she had it shipped via freighter to her country house at Belle-Isle while she took a fast steamer back to France. When the creature arrived, as it was still in its torpor, Sarah uncrated it herself. The tiny Manchester terrier she then had, excited by the strange reptilian, barked madly and started snapping at its nose. The alligator, alas, came suddenly out of its long winter's sleep and snapped back and the small dog disappeared down the tooth-lined maw. Madame's secretary, Pitou, grabbed a gun and shot the monster and Sarah, grief-stricken over the loss of her terrier, had the 'gator's head dissevered, mounted and hung in her hall. She would point it out to her guests and say mournfully, "My beloved little dog — his tomb!"

It was during this first United States tour that Sarah Bernhardt came near to being lost to the world and the rest of her company along with her through the collapse of a railroad bridge during the heavy spring floods. The bridge spanned the Bay Saint Louis outside of New Orleans. I say it did because in her own memoirs Madame Sarah says it did, as does Marie Colombier, and Castelot locates it in that general vicinity. But then the inevitable contradictions arise with Bernhardt herself giving her granddaughter another site, and Lysiane writes that the disaster was missed by seconds while crossing the Ohio River. As the French are not noted for their accuracy in regard to American geography, we can dismiss the exact locale as being of little interest.

What happened was that as the "Sarah Bernhardt Special" was going along at its customary clip, the brakes suddenly went on and the train came to a full stop at a small station located near a river which was overflowing its banks. In a few minutes Sarah, looking out her window, could see Jarrett in frenziedly animated conversation with a man in dungarees who was standing quite still, stubbornly shaking his head. After a time, they walked over to the train and entered Madame Bernhardt's lounge. Jarrett introduced the man as the engineer and added the chilling information that turbulent waters had weakened the supports of a bridge lying shortly ahead of them and the engineer was afraid to risk a crossing. There was no other way of getting around the five-state flood unless they retracked back halfway to Cincinnati. This would mean a two-day delay in reaching their next show town, New Orleans, where, she was informed, the box office had been completely sold out. However, the powerful impresario had brought some of the persuasive Jarrett pressure to bear and the engineer had finally agreed to try for a dash across the weakened bridge provided they would give him $2500 in advance to buy a money order made out in his wife's name which he would entrust to the local station master. If the venture turned out successfully, the engineer would refund the money. Jarrett fixed Madame with his cold blue eye and asked how she felt about taking a chance. "Madame Quand-Même's" love of a challenge plus the prospect of that sold-out box office in New Orleans immediately prompted her to exclaim that of course she'd take the chance, and she called to *mon p'tit dame* to bring forth her money bag.

One of the more imponderable eccentricities of Sarah Bernhardt was her refusal throughout her long life, throughout the thick and thin of her vast fortunes gained and squandered, ever to have a checking account in any bank. She insisted upon being paid in gold coins which she carried with her or entrusted to Madame Guérard in a horrifyingly battered old chamois bag. Out of this she paid her company, her servants, her creditors, doling out the coins with sensitive and seemingly reluctant fingers. There was something curiously remindful of the medieval miser in the gesture. For extravagant as she was and given to occasional impulsive acts of exaggerated generosity, she hated the physical parting with a single gleaming piece. When her fortunes were at high peak and the profits too cumbersome for the chamois bag, she put the golden overflow in a metal-bound chest which she kept under her bed.

Guérard produced the bag which Sarah handed over to Jarrett telling him to take out $2500 in coins. Then suddenly she hesitated. Hadn't they better, she asked, inform the rest of the troupe about the bridge and give them a choice of staying on the train or getting off at this station? She summoned the entire company before her. Addressing them as *"mes chers et braves enfants,"* she told them of the peril lying ahead and delivered such an eloquent eve-of-battle speech, every one of them, with the exception of an eighteen-year-old ingénue and an assistant treasurer, declared to stay. The company returned to their Pullmans, the engineer returned to his iron horse and the train started. The occupants of the "Palace Car" sat rigid but intrepid. Jarrett furiously puffed a cigar in defiance of Madame's ruling that no tobacco could ever be smoked in her presence. Angelo looked handsomely brave but ashen. Marie Colombier took Hamlet the Third onto her lap and started brushing him. Piron, the character actor, hummed a tune somewhat off-key. Madame Guérard sporadically blessed herself. Sarah sat with a protective arm around Jeanne, who found a ghoulish pleasure in reminding her sister that her hotel room the previous night had been number thirteen and that a stage-door fan had tossed a sprig of heather at her. Sarah, who harbored numerous obsessive superstitions, had a horror of the number thirteen and regarded the least brush of a sprig of heather as baneful as the evil eye, and would under less tense circumstances have slapped Jeanne in the face. Instead, she silently addressed her convent superior, Mère Sainte-Sophie, who she felt must surely be in heaven, suggesting that the saintly soul use her influence with the Holy Powers to have them sustain the bridge. By now the engineer had worked up full steam and the train was going at mad top speed. It careened around corners at hair-raising angles, swayed, rocked, jounced and hurtled a couple of passengers from their seats. All at once they knew they were on the bridge. Sarah glanced down at the roiling flood waters,

then hastily cast her eyes heavenward in further communication
with Mother Sainte-Sophie. Jarrett's cigar took on the aspect of a
volcano about to erupt and Madame Guérard looked more as
though she were doing some sort of sitting-down exercise than repeatedly crossing herself. Piron's tune ended in a series of gulping
sounds and Marie Colombier brushed Hamlet the Third so violently he bit her. The train rocked more crazily than ever, wild
groaning noises issued from the tracks and Jeanne, in manic gaiety,
called out, "Here we go downing, sister!" Then gradually the
wheels began turning more regularly. The roadbed below them
felt firm. The engine panting like a pursued animal finding shelter
slowed down and came to a halt. People in the other cars shouted,
"We're across!" And at that, there arose from behind them a
sound of thunder. Bernhardt, rushing to the observation platform,
arrived in time to see a column of water rising like a majestic geyser
which when it fell back revealed the two broken halves of the
bridge, their ends plunged into the water.

The entire troupe, relieved and jubilant, piled into the Palace
Car to hug and congratulate their leader as though she were Joan
of Arc who had just successfully raised the siege of Orléans. She
embraced them all and ordered rounds of champagne. She also
sent up word to the engineer telling him that he and his wife might
keep the $2500. However, as she looked about at her trusting
flock, her conscience, which like her "sacred word of honor" was
unpredictable, began to bother her. She blamed herself for risking
these persons' lives in her impulsive and ego-prompted act. In her
Memoirs she wrote:

> For a long time my nights were troubled by frightful nightmares.
> When any player spoke to me of a baby, a mother, a spouse back
> home, I'd turn pale and a profound emotion would agonize me.
> I felt a contemptuous pity for the *I* that I was.

The *I* Sarah Bernhardt was continued its eventful journey. In
New Orleans she met with harsh public criticism because, for some
uncharacteristic whim, she refused to give a charity performance

for the French-speaking flood victims. They played a one-night stand in Mobile, where the stage was so small, the sets didn't fit and the actors had to make their entrances at such grotesque angles, their star went into fits of hysterical giggling, fled from the stage and Jarrett had to refund the money at the box office.

This was not the only occasion during the tour that "The Ferocious Gentleman" had to go to such painful measures. Madame Bernhardt, conditioned to sell-out audiences, could never endure the sight of empty seats and on the occasions, which happily were few, when the houses were poor, she'd go conveniently into a *crise de nerfs* from which Jarrett knew there'd be no rousing her until he had canceled the performance. He could afford to be philosophical about such exigencies. The losses of a night or two were far outbalanced by the profits he was making.

In Georgia, as the "Sarah Bernhardt Special" stopped for engine water at a country siding, its leading passenger, beholding through her window a flock of crows, ordered the engineer to hold the train there for a half hour while she and the sports-minded members of the company got out to enjoy a little bird shooting. Hardly had the first gun sounded than a sheriff appeared, arrested the hunters, loaded them into a buckboard and drove them to his house. His ground for arrest was not the shooting of crows, which heaven knew was of benefit to the local farmers, but because it was Sunday and these foreigners were breaking the Sabbath law. Once arrived at his house, the sheriff locked his captives in the parlor while he went into an adjoining bedroom to pray and consult the Bible. After due and pious consultation he emerged, fined the culprits an over-all sum of $1.50 and released them to run back across the fields to their train.

In Toledo some newspapermen, in a mistaken gesture of tribute, serenaded the great actress under her window at eight in the morning and, for their efforts, received the contents of a pitcher of water dumped onto their upraised faces. In transit one night, there broke out in the car next to Bernhardt's a fight between two male members of the corps. Their star, hearing the commotion, leapt from her bed and, clad only in her nightgown, rushed to fling herself between the two belligerents who, after such heroic intervention, shamefacedly shook hands and retired each to his bed. It was April when the tour reached Buffalo for a week's stand. Madame, instead of going to a hotel, chose to live in her "Palace Car," which was backed into a wooded park beside a brook. Every evening an open carriage arrived to drive her through the soft spring air to the theatre and she declared that it was the next best thing to a trot around the lakes in the Bois de Boulogne.

When she returned to New York, she had given a hundred and fifty-seven performances in fifty-one cities. *Froufrou* forty times, *Adrienne Lecouvreur* seventeen, *Hernani* thirteen, *Le Sphynx* six, *Phèdre* six, *Princesse Georges* seven, *l'Etrangère* three and, of course, that hardy *Lady* of the perennial *Camellias* sixty-five. It was a triumphal return and the papers were full of the news. For over six months, the name of Sarah Bernhardt had been a cliché in the press. Reports of her box-office receipts had, along with all the other gossip, been grossly exaggerated and the magazine *Puck*, a blatantly anti-Semitic publication, printed a cruel cartoon showing her with an exaggerated hooked-nose, holding a tiny dog amid a shower of gold. Its title was "The Jewish Danae."

Judge, another periodical, paid her a kinder tribute: "We shall miss the tearing terror of Sarah Bernhardt. We shall miss her smile of love and her expression of trust and confidence. We shall regret the absence of that thin countenance on whose surface appeared more of the counterfeited soul than anybody has succeeded in picturing. We shall miss that magnificently cultured voice, those secluded eyes, those conspicuous teeth, that serpentine twist of the body and the tiger too. But our loss will be her gain. She takes about half a million in clear profits with her; and have we not our Clara Morris and her regular prescriptions left?"

On May 3 she gave a farewell matinee of *La Dame*. Her dressing room and the corridor leading to it were stacked with over a hun-

dred and thirty bouquets and wreaths. The audience went gratify-
ingly wild. At the final curtain the great Italian actor Tommaso
Salvini strode onto the stage to present her with a jewel box of
lapis-lazuli, and America's own Mary Anderson in the exquisite
loveliness of her dewy youth ran shyly out to give her a pin of
turquoise forget-me-nots.

A few days later, Sarah Bernhardt set sail for France. *Judge*
had somewhat overestimated her profits but the actual figure was
not to be sneezed at, for, stashed in her metal-bound chest and the
battered chamois bag, was $194,000 in gleaming gold coins.

9.

LA "DAMALA"
AUX CAMELIAS

SARAH BERNHARDT sailed for France, again on the "America." Crowds jammed the pier to cheer her off and hundreds of handkerchiefs fluttered farewell as the battered old tub backed out into the North River. Her cabin was so completely banked with flowers, the overflow had to be spread down the corridor. She was elated, eager to get home and desperate to see Maurice, who she knew would be waiting on the dock at Havre. Even her deep, obsessive mother-love had to be expressed in a production. Toward the end of the voyage, she spent sessions in her cabin rehearsing how most effectively to say, "Ah! Maurice! My son!" or "Ah! My son! Maurice!"

The young man was indeed on the end of the dock and he leapt aboard before the gangplank was secured. He was followed by Clairin, Louise Abbéma and other close friends. They all embraced, laughed and wept copiously and Clairin rushed ashore to get a tricolor. He returned happily waving a flag of Holland, but nobody cared. Then came a delegation from the Life-Saving Society of Havre. They brought with them a mammoth bouquet of flowers "grown on the sweet soil of France" as well as a request that Bernhardt stay over to give a benefit for the widows and children of their brave comrades lost at sea. She immediately agreed to do so. It never occurred to her to ask the other members of her company whether or not they resented a twenty-four-hour delay in their return to Paris. One person certainly resented it and that was Marie Colombier, who by now was resenting everything about her star. When she had set out for America, Colombier had left behind her a pile of unpaid bills amounting to many thousand francs. Her creditors had put in claims with the authorities and no sooner had she set foot on shore than bailiffs served her with writs and seized her luggage. In desperation she appealed to Sarah to intercede but that lady, distracted by the excitement of her riotous homecoming, dismissed Colombier's problems with a laugh and did nothing to help.

That night, they played *La Dame aux Camélias* to a packed and cheering house. At the end, Madame Sarah was presented with a Life Saver's certificate and medal of honor. Clutching these trophies to her heart, she cried out in the ringing tones of an intrepid captain setting forth from Finisterre in a full gale, "I shall save someone! I promise you I shall save someone! Of course, I don't know how to swim . . . but that's of no consequence . . . I shall learn!" No doubt at the moment in which she uttered this noble promise, she meant every word of it.

The citizens of Normandy may have given her a rousing welcome but she encountered no similar ovation in Paris. No public was waiting in the Gare Saint Lazare to shower her with congratulations on her American triumphs. As a matter of fact, hardly anyone knew about such triumphs. Her homecoming was met with the same sort of resentment that greeted her first return from London. She had departed from her homeland under a cloud of disapproval. Parisians could forgive neither her defection from the Français nor her unorthodox manner of announcing it. They begrudged the highly successful European jaunt she had taken prior to her American tour. As for her going to the extreme of crossing the Atlantic for the sordid purpose of extracting money out of vulgar Yankee millionaires, illiterate cowboys and, for all they knew, blanket Indians, it was an insult to the glorious names of Racine and Molière, to the prestige of the French theatre itself. Furthermore, nobody had the slightest idea that she had made any money.

During her absence, jealous enemies and vicious gossip writers had spread their venom, and it was the general consensus that Sarah Bernhardt's overseas tour had been a colossal flop — which, many persons thought, served her right. If twenty-six years previously Rachel had met with no success in the Western Hemisphere, how dared this upstart think to compete with France's greatest tragedienne of all time? Moreover nearly all the theatre-going public had been following in *l'Evénement*, Marie Colombier's serialized accounts of the trip which were very amusing. They were also definitely bitchy, exaggerated and largely untrue. They reported most of the mishaps and few of the triumphs, and a fickle public took them as evidence that Sarah Bernhardt in America had come a-cropper. It began to be said that at the age of thirty-six, she was rapidly becoming a has-been, and that her popularity was on the wane if not over. Indeed there were alarming indications that this might be true. No manager came forward with any offer, no playwright submitted any script.

After the spectacular success of her London, Brussels and Copenhagen appearances and her whirlwind tour of the leading provincial cities, she had been approached by the most popular dramatist of his day, Victorien Sardou, who declared that he could not wait to write a play especially for her, that in point of fact, he had already started it and would have it finished and ready to hand to her the very day she returned from the United States. Sardou had been seconded by Raymond Deslandes, who was then running the fashionable Vaudeville and who made them both a firm offer to put into immediate production whatever the piece might be, so long as it was written by Monsieur Sardou with Madame Bernhardt as its star.

Madame Bernhardt waited for a week or so but no script was handed her by Sardou and not a murmur was heard from Deslandes. Swallowing her pride as though it were an excessively bitter pill, she sent off a note to Deslandes informing him she was back in town — as if all Paris didn't know it — and asking what was what regarding his production plans. Deslandes sent back a reply as brutally evasive as a casting agent's "leave me your telephone number," the gist of which was that Monsieur Sardou had become so involved with other commitments, he had not been able to work on the proposed play.

Sarah was growing desperate. Her friends, her "Court," were as loyal as ever but they were of no particular help. Her way of living was as extravagant as ever and that $194,000 was being indiscriminately squandered on lavish entertainment, useless furnishings and the slightest whim of Maurice, who was cultivating more and more expensive whims. To be sure, she had no immediate need for money but she always had an immediate, a chronic need to act. To assuage the latter, she accepted a three-week return engagement from Hollingshead. Again the tricolor fluttered over the Gaiety Theatre and again the British public went wild over Sarah. The loyal Londoners turned out in droves to see her. Once back home, the disloyal Parisians continued to ignore her.

Then in July, she suddenly saw her chance and she pulled off one of her most audacious *quand même* acts. To celebrate the Glorious Fourteenth and in further celebration of the tenth anniversary since the hated Prussians had marched out of Paris, a super gala had been planned to take place at the Grand Opéra. All the notables of the Republic were to be present. The flag-trimmed box of honor would be occupied by President Grévy and the Chief-of-State Jules Ferry, while conspicuous in the front row would sit the old lion of France, Léon Gambetta. The opera scheduled for the evening was a fiftieth anniversary reprise of Meyerbeer's *Robert le Diable*. This would be followed by Mounet-Sully's reading of a patriotic poem and, as a grand finale, Madame Agar, accompanied by the full orchestra, would recite the *Marseillaise*.

Ever since their joint success in Coppée's *Passant* Bernhardt and Agar had remained excellent friends. Over the intervening years, the older actress had put on considerable weight, but she was still beautiful, still popular and still prone to love affairs. Her current passion was for a handsome Captain of Dragoons far younger than she and at that time stationed in Tours. Madame Agar had a faithful old maid named Hortense, who from the moment she first saw her at the Odéon had adored Sarah, always referring to her as "La Divine," and "La Divine" knew that if she asked her to, Hortense would go to the ends of the earth to please her. She contrived a clandestine interview with the elderly maid, took her into her strictest confidence and together they hatched a plot. Hortense, who at heart was a frustrated ham actress, fell happily in with the plan and played her part to perfection. The afternoon of the July 14 Gala, while Agar was resting prior to her "Spirit of the Marseillaise" appearance, Hortense, in a beautifully simulated state of agitation, came panting into her mistress' boudoir. She had just run into the orderly of Madame's handsome officer, she said. The captain, it seemed, had suffered a bad fall from his horse and had been taken to the hospital. He, the orderly, had been sent to Paris to rush a surgeon down to Tours. At the news, Madame Agar did some rushing of her own. She sprang from her chaise longue, dressed with quick-change speed and within fifteen minutes was racing in a hired hack to catch the first train for Tours. She told Hortense to notify the Opéra Gala directors of her unavoidable inability to appear and to notify them at once in time for them to get another actress — instructions which Hortense conveniently ignored.

That evening the Gala was going swimmingly. Meyerbeer's old *Robert le Diable* had concluded to a warm reception and Mounet-Sully, handsome as ever and still the male idol of Paris, had already gone on to recite his patriotic poem. He finished and took his customary bows to his customary applause. As he stepped off into the wings, Sarah Bernhardt, who knew her timing to the split second, stepped in through the stage door, swathed in an enveloping cloak and wearing on her flaming head the Phrygian bonnet of the Marseillaise figure. The two managers who were running the show stared as though at some evil apparition. They knew of her current unpopularity. Her mere presence backstage filled them with panic. She smiled charmingly and announced, "My good friend Madame Agar had to go off to the bedside of a dying relative. She wishes me to take her place." Then turning to her former lover she asked sweetly, "Mounet, *mon cher*, will you kindly help me off with my wrap?" The great actor removed her cloak with the stunned motions of an automaton. But his eyes kindled with quick admiration at the breathtaking sight of Sarah in the traditional robe, all dazzling white except for the tricolor streamer from her shoulder to her slender waist. The two managers looked as though they were about to bolt from the Opéra House and possibly on out of town. Sarah laid a reassuring hand on the arm of one. "Don't worry," she said, "I have far more to lose than you" — which God and she knew was only too true, and while she spoke with confidence, she was probably inwardly perishing with stage fright. The orchestra leader tapped his baton, the drummer started the thrilling rolls that herald Rouget de Lisle's spine-tingling anthem, President Grévy rose in his box, the audience rose too and Sarah Bernhardt came on like Triumph itself. At sight of her, gasps came from throughout the house and the conductor all but toppled off the podium. The tension lasted only a second, then the orchestral music started and the music of the Bernhardt voice sounded magically above it rising to the crescendo of *"Aux armes, citoyens!"* and at the finish when she unfurled and held aloft the flag of France, she was "La Gloire" incarnate.

No need to state that the house went mad. They applauded, they cheered, they rushed down the aisles to shout, "Sarah! Our Sarah!" President Grévy tossed a large sheaf of roses intended for Madame Agar at Sarah's feet, and Gambetta in the front row roared his approval like the king of beasts. It was one of those tumultuous occasions of Gallic rapture when strong men weep, strangers embrace like brothers, and ladies can find nothing more appreciative to do than faint. The reborn star was forced to repeat her recitation twice again and each time she received the same ovation. When it was finally over, so many flowers and bouquets had been hurled across the footlights, it took the full stage crew of the Opéra House to clean up the mess. "La Divine" had made her comeback. As a short but pleasant sequel to the events of that evening, it may be worth reporting that Madame Agar, when she discovered the trick that had been played on her, far from being incensed, thought it all a great joke. She had, of course, found her Captain of Dragoons in perfect health and more than ready to soothe away her worries. She returned to Paris in high spirits and forgave Hortense, while Sarah continued to remain her good friend.

Almost overnight there was an about-face change of attitude toward Bernhardt on the part not only of the public, but of the profession. The most satisfactory change must have been that of Victorien Sardou, who came to her hat in hand. The hat, in this case, was the manuscript of *Fédora*, the first of many plays he was to write exclusively for her or, as has been said, "to tailor perfectly to her measurements," the first joint venture for this author-player team which was to prove one of the most successful in the history of the theatre.

Victorien Sardou was hardly a great dramatist. The only plays of his which today might survive are *Diplomacy*, *Mme. Sans-Gêne*, *Divorçons* and, of course, *Tosca*, which is perhaps best heard in Puccini's version. But as Bernhardt was the greatest show woman of her time, Sardou was the greatest show carpenter. The British critic A. B. Walkley said, "With Sardou playwriting is not merely as much a trade as play-making. Sardou has perfected the clockwork play." He has been called "a mere set of fingers with the theatre at the tips of them," and Henri de Regnier commented to Dumas *fils*, "Ah, that Sardou! Does he know his theatre! or rather his public!" He did indeed know every trick for intriguing that public, and G. B. Shaw dismissed his brilliant bag of such tricks as "sheer Sardoudledom." In a day when Ibsen, Chekhov and the "problem" dramatists were coming into fashion, Sardou preferred to write good theatre. His only aim was "to interest, amuse, move, excite and thrill the large public that went to his plays; and being a man of genius, he did this as well as any playwright has ever done it," wrote Maurice Baring. The acerbic Edmond de Goncourt, who didn't like Sardou, as he didn't like many people, accused him of being *"un cabotin exclusivement preoccupé d'argent."* If such an accusation is true, the preoccupation was richly rewarding. Stagey, sometimes even claptrap as his plays may be, they epitomized the theatre of an epoch and, with Sarah for interpreter, they brought in fantastic grosses at the box office. After a number of joint successes, the star and her play-maker became spoken of as "The Two S's" and it was a *bon mot* of the boulevards that "There is but one Sarah and Sardou is her prophet." One wonders about the spelling of the last word.

But this profitable association was not to be started immediately. That afternoon in June when the playwright called at the Avenue de Villiers with the script of *Fédora,* he was again accompanied by the Vaudeville manager, Raymond Deslandes. Sarah received them out in her garden, which was a jungle clutter of flowers, bushes, vines, fruit trees and potted plants. It was almost impossible to move without kicking over or trampling some bit of flowering vegetation, and Sardou, who was an instinctive director, had a way, when reading aloud one of his plays, of striding up and down before his listeners, acting out every part himself. During the course of this reading he broke several shoots off a rose tree, knocked over a porcelain jardinière and decimated a herbaceous border. His hostess heard him out with unprotesting attention. Her instinct for sure-fire theatre was as unerring as Sardou's and she saw in *Fédora* not only a big box-office draw but for herself a superb part complete with spectacular death scene.

All graciousness she turned to Deslandes, who proposed an immediate production at the Vaudeville, with a salary for her of 1000 francs a performance and a guarantee of one hundred performances. This was a staggering offer for those days and Sarah knew it. However, she played with her visitors like a cat with two mice. Her pride was still rankled by their earlier brush-off after her return from America. With a quiet smile she gently accused Deslandes of joking. She was well aware, she said, that the Vaudeville when sold out could bring in a capacity gross of 7500 francs. She wouldn't dream of appearing there at less than 1500 francs a performance plus 25 per cent of the net profits. Deslandes fairly reeled at the demand, but the lady stuck to her guns and almost tearfully he gave in. Then the two men asked her how soon she could go into rehearsal and with a pretty gesture of regret she answered that alas she would not be available until 1882! She had signed up with Jarrett for an immediate extensive tour of Europe. If, she added, during her six-month absence, the gentlemen felt obliged to find another actress for the part, she could not, of course, stand in their way. The gentlemen took their leave in a state of shock. Sarah knew she was taking a gamble, but she felt certain it was one at which she would win.

The tour began in London, again at the Gaiety. On this third return engagement she appeared in *La Dame aux Camélias*, a play hitherto banned by Lord Chamberlain censorship. With some trepidation the ban had been lifted. They need not have worried, for Sarah managed to play the frail *courtisane* with such delicacy, Victoria herself some years later considered it a risk not too great for Royal ears, and Bernhardt was to give a command performance of it before the dumpy little Queen in her hotel at Nice. Ellen Terry, after watching this exquisite interpretation of Marguerite Gauthier, said, "On the stage she has always seemed to me a symbol, an ideal, an epitome rather than a *woman* . . . She is always a miracle . . . It is this extraordinary decorative and symbolic quality of Sarah's which makes her transcend all personal and individual feeling on the stage. No one plays a love-scene better, but it is a *picture* of love . . . rather than a suggestion of the ordinary human passion as felt by ordinary people." Sarcey, who had come puffing over from Paris to see the performance, wrote back that it was: "A pleasure . . . an enchanting, a delicious pleasure . . .

something perfect, with none of the correct and cold perfection which is born of negative qualities . . . but an animated and living perfection."

By now Bernhardt had built up a cult of London worshippers. The public collected her photographs, young girls kept scrapbooks of her press notices, aspiring actresses memorized her roles, the recitations of which a merciful providence spared her from having to hear. She said of herself, "I attract all the lunatics of the world." Friends told her about one old spinster who in a corner of her lonely lodgings had set up an altar consecrated solely to "The Divine One." In addition to many cabinet photographs, it bore a number of objects she had touched: a pair of gloves, a handkerchief, a hair pin. As they told her about this elderly eccentric, they laughed inordinately, but "The Divine One" silenced them saying, "Don't make fun of her! I love her very much." Then she added, "She probably drinks!"

The European tour which followed England led first through middle France and the Midi. It continued on to Northern Italy, Greece, Hungary, Switzerland, Belgium and Holland. The Bernhardt legend had permeated Europe and everywhere the public flocked to see her act whether or not they understood a word of French. Those who hadn't the price of a ticket stood for hours outside hotel entrance or stage door to watch her go in or out. In Scandinavia her train while passing through a tiny hamlet was slowed down at the petition of the villagers who wanted to tell their children and grandchildren they had seen Sarah Bernhardt waving through the window. One adoring author was to write:

Among those waiting at the stage door are the rich whose only worth is that they admire you, and there are the wretched who raise themselves up like the great ones of the earth because they will see Sarah pass by, and there is perhaps a criminal, a man abandoned by all, and who will be seized the moment you have passed. But he will say "Death does not matter now. I saw Sarah before I died."

It was the last era of Royalty, and she found herself the toast of the Austria of the Hapsburgs, the Spain of the Bourbons, the Russia of the Romanoffs. However, she purposely avoided the Germany of the Hohenzollerns. When asked why her tour did not include such cultural centers as Munich and Berlin, she snorted indignantly, "What! Defile my hands with Prussian money? The hands that Victor Hugo has kissed?" One story goes that a German impresario, one Herr Von Stirtz, once called on her to try to persuade her to play in his Fatherland. Bernhardt flatly turned down his proposal. Von Stirtz begged, flattered and cajoled, but the patriotic actress could not be budged. Finally the man rose, clicked his heels and declared: "Your price, Madame, will be ours, no matter what," and at that Sarah cried out in ringing tones, "Five thousand millions!" which was the price exacted from France by Prussia for war damages. Von Stirtz beat a hasty retreat.

Crowned heads came to see her in the theatre, and she gave command performances in their palaces. Alfonso XII presented her with a diamond brooch, Franz Joseph gave her a parure of rare cameos, while Umberto of Italy paid tribute with an exquisite eighteenth-century Venetian fan. The Archduke Frederick of Austria put his Schloss at her disposal, saying that no hotel was a fit residence for a Queen.

It was dead winter when Sarah Bernhardt invaded Russia. The one and only setback to her triumphant royal progress was in Odessa. This was a period when anti-Semitism was rampant, pogroms were frequent and because word had gotten about that Bernhardt was half Jewish, she was mobbed and might well have been stoned but for the intervention of the police. St. Petersburg was a different story. Here her success was spectacular and special trains were run from Moscow for theatre enthusiasts to join the block-long lines outside the box office. Every evening a red carpet was unrolled over the snow from the curb to the stage door and after each performance crowds ran behind her sleigh and fought to pick up the flowers she tossed to them. The French Ambassador paid official tribute with a formal dinner. When she spoke with admiration of his distinguished position and high functions, he replied, "Madame, France has only one ambassador — Sarah Bernhardt!" Twice she was invited to perform at the Winter Palace. After her first performance, Alexander III stepped forward to meet her, and as she started to make a deep reverence, the Tsar of all the Russians stopped her saying, "*Non*, Madame, it is I who must bow to you." And this he did before his entire Court. The incident caused a lot of talk among high society. But His Imperial Majesty's gesture of homage to an actress was not the only topic of gossip concerning Madame Bernhardt. For if the Russian capital was the scene of one of her great professional victories, it was also the setting for her private Waterloo.

As to how Sarah Bernhardt first met Jacques Damala, accounts differ. Some say Sardou brought him to call, others claim that he was introduced by Jeanne Bernhardt. The tragedy was that she ever met him at all. He was eleven years her junior, handsome as Adonis, insolent, vain and altogether despicable. He came from a prominent family in Athens (his actual first name was Aristides) and was stationed in Paris as an attaché to the Greek Diplomatic Corps. He had further established himself as one of the most notorious Don Juans ever to raise mayhem in the feminine world. Wherever he went women completely lost their heads over him and he treated them all with haughty indifference, boasting that no woman had ever meant anything in his life. One prominent lady of fashion killed herself over him and because of him two others were divorced — a sin considered in those days far more heinous than suicide. He was said to have gone in for all manner of vice, including an addiction to morphine, but was still youthful and strong enough to conceal the latter. The scandal columns were full of his amours and wild escapades and a titillated society summed him up as being a combination of Casanova and the Marquis de Sade. Eventually his behavior proved too outrageous even for the lenient French capital and the local authorities requested the Greek legation to move him outside the country. The "Diplomatic Apollo," as he was sometimes called, was about to depart to take up a post in St. Petersburg when he was introduced to "La Divine Sarah."

The moment she set eyes on him, Sarah's divinity deserted her and she became all too mortal. Never in the course of her many love affairs had she made a fool of herself over any man; but over this despicable rotter, she was for a time to become a complete and abject fool. When he walked suavely into her drawing room and kissed her hand with blasé casualness, she gasped. She was accustomed to men approaching her presence for the first time with courtly diffidence, even with a certain reverent awe. This arrogant devil appeared to regard the occasion as being of no more importance than going through the motions of meeting any feminine nonentity who, he took for granted, would immediately be swept off her feet by his irresistible looks and charm. Such obvious indifference was an immediate challenge.

Damala sank into an easy chair, took out a gold cigarette case and lit a match from a jeweled box. He probably knew that Madame Bernhardt never allowed anyone to smoke in her presence, but he also knew that he wasn't just anyone. They chatted for a time, he keeping his end of the conversation easy but carefully impersonal. At one point he let fall the remark that if he had ever had one ambition in life, it might have been to act. As a means of prolonging his visit Sarah suggested that just for fun he might be interested in reading over with her a scene from her forthcoming repertory. Damala with a shrug which was indicative that nothing much ever interested him said he wouldn't mind and they read a bit from *Froufrou*, he taking the leading male role of Sartorys. He proved to have a certain facility. He also had a fine speaking voice with a pronounced Greek accent which gave it extra appeal in Sarah's opinion. By now quite dazzled, she told him he had great talent and added that if ever he grew tired of diplomatic life, who knows, he might find himself in her theatrical company. He bowed courteously, kissed her hand as casually as he had before and took his leave. Within a few days he called again and then dropped by the afternoon before he left for St. Petersburg. Always his manner was the same, courteous yet distant, nonchalant yet slightly mocking. At one moment he was all graceful charm, at the next all cold arrogance. Sarah, who was rapidly losing her heart, for the first time in her life started losing her head. She turned on the full battery of the wiles which heretofore had made an adoring slave of any man she cared to conquer, but this time with no success. Damala was playing a game, and it amused him to realize that the most celebrated woman in Europe could be his at the wink of his long eyelashes. The nearest he came to any overt gesture was as he said good-by. He kissed her hand, meaningfully held it for a palpitating moment and whispered, "Come to St. Petersburg. I'll be waiting for you."

Sarah was in a delirium of infatuation, bafflement and frustration. She wanted this fascinating, this dissolute, this maddening seducer more than all her worthwhile lovers put together. Russia had not been on her itinerary but she insisted that it be included. The St. Petersburg booking was impossible to arrange before January, and during the intervening months she was in a fever of impatience. She had, as usual, a current lover and he, as not unusual, was her leading man — this time, not Angelo, who was also in the company, but a far more gifted actor named Philippe Garnier.

Damala had spent the intervening time carousing with dissolute society and raising havoc among the feminine element of the Russian smart set. Then Sarah reached St. Petersburg and the Bernhardt-Damala affair started furiously and was the talk of the town. The two were seen everywhere together and the actress would accept no invitation unless her lover were also included. This openly scandalous behavior was much resented by the aristocracy. When after one performance a certain Grand Duke sent his equerry with an invitation to supper, she answered that she'd be delighted to accept and would bring Monsieur Damala along. A few minutes later, the equerry came back with the message that His Imperial Highness had remembered a previous engagement and to his regret would have to change his plans.

Sarah didn't care. She was madly, idiotically in love. It could not have been a genuine love, but a sort of insane intoxication, a frantic obsession. There seems to have been little tenderness in this whirlwind affair. Certainly not on the part of Jacques Damala, who was incapable of such a human emotion. One person who did care, however, was Philippe Garnier. Whether or not during his own romance with Sarah he had been deeply in love himself is debatable; but his pride was hurt. Moreover, Garnier was a man of distinction and taste and it offended him to see this great artist making an utter fool of herself. Giving as an excuse a bad case of bronchitis and the severity of the Russian winter, he handed in his notice and quietly left for Paris. At that Jacques Damala handed in his resignation to the Greek legation to become an actor in the Bernhardt company. The star whose infatuation had completely warped her usually unerring judgment cast him in Garnier's role of Sartorys in *Froufrou*. She also took Armand Duval away from the unfortunate Angelo and let Damala go on regularly in *La Dame aux Camélias*. At least she had the sense not to let him play *Hernani*. He couldn't have anyway, for his mind, gradually deteriorating from the effects of brandy and morphine, was incapable of retaining the long speeches of rhymed couplets.

As an actor, Damala was rather atrocious. He had no qualifications beyond the over-assurance of an amateur. His only asset was his good looks, for he had no technique, no sense of timing and his strong Greek accent made him at times unintelligible. That irresistible charm that he exerted over women didn't come over the footlights and he let down every scene he was in. Sarah, blind to his defects as an actor, kept insisting that he had genius, that given a few months' experience he'd prove to be one of the most brilliant newcomers in the theatre.

To Damala's appalling defects of character, Sarah was also blind, or else she deliberately blindfolded herself. She must have known in her inmost heart that the man was a dissolute wastrel. She may have fooled herself into thinking she could reform him. She was not yet aware that he took morphine. He was still able to conceal the symptoms and no one in the company knew he had the habit with the exception of Jeanne Bernhardt. Jeanne would have been afraid to warn her sister for dread of what Damala might do in retaliation. Also Jeanne was able, through the Greek, to get her own daily dosage, for the young woman had by then become a hopeless addict.

Sarah had a horror of narcotics in any form. Only the previous year in London she had come upon Jeanne giving herself a shot and, seizing the horsewhip she kept for a pet puma, had beaten the wretched girl until she was senseless, then had locked her up in her hotel room for forty-eight hours to repent on bread and water, after which she assumed she'd effected a cure. Not many years later Jeanne died, a complete wreck.

From Russia, the tour had continued southward. To Bernhardt's torments of physical obsession was added the humiliation of jealousy. Damala, who could not stay faithful to any woman for more than a few weeks, was casting his handsome eye over some of the younger actresses. It lighted on a little person in the company to whom he started making advances or, to be more accurate, the little person as always was making him advances which he was showing marked willingness to accept. Like an ordinary woman nearing forty, playing a failing game with a young lover, Sarah completely lost her head. Thinking it a means of holding her vacillating man, she proposed marriage and Damala accepted. What made him do so is not hard to fathom. The idea was so preposterous, it appealed to his sardonic character; he was getting a fair amount of acclaim basking in Bernhardt's glory, and once married to her he'd be getting a fair amount of the vast financial sums she was taking in. They were in Italy when these nuptial plans were hatched.

Sarah Bernhardt was a Roman Catholic, Jacques Damala Greek Orthodox. It was impossible for them to obtain a license either in Italy or in France. Protestant England was not so particular. There was a five-day break between the last performance in Naples and the next, a one-night stand in Nice. The couple, like two giddy runaways, skipped off to London and on April 4, 1882, in St. Andrew's Church, Wells Street, Sarah Bernhardt became Madame Jacques Damala. She had fully anticipated being able to make it back to Nice in time for the performance, but the ceremony had to be delayed over an hour due to the carelessness of the bridegroom, who had left the papers at the hotel and had to go back for them. The result was that they missed the boat train to Dover and Bernhardt missed out on her professional obligation. The theatre in Nice sued her for 25,000 francs for breach of contract, a sum which, in her state of married bliss, she cheerfully paid along with some outstanding debts of the bridegroom.

She must have had an occasional inner qualm about this rash act, for she sent Sardou two telegrams. The first said she was about to die and regretted not having done his *Fédora*. The second assured him that she hadn't died, she was merely married. In a few weeks she was giving out to her friends the feeble excuse that she'd gone into this because marriage was the only thing she hadn't experienced. On her return to Paris in May, the bride's first ordeal was to confront her son.

"Maurice, *cheri*," she said, "I have news for you."

"I know, Maman," the boy said coldly, "you have married *Monsieur* Sarah Bernhardt."

Soon after this a benefit was being planned for some worthy cause and Sarah volunteered to perform gratis the complete production of *La Dame aux Camélias*. Paris had never seen Sarah Bernhardt's Marguerite Gauthier. Also they had never seen "Monsieur Sarah Bernhardt" as an actor. Later many wished they never had, as far as the latter was concerned. The house had been agog to watch his performance. When he made his first entrance there was much excitement: whispers of "It's he!" and "Sarah's husband!" Opera glasses were focused and people strained to get a better view. Whatever they were expecting, they were definitely let down. He was not good. He was also not bad, which might at least have made for a few titters. The next day the press was wildly enthusiastic over Bernhardt's performance but justly critical of her leading man. One critic called the whole thing an exhibition which did not turn out a happy one. He admitted that in the last act, the handsome young man had a few movingly sincere moments and wound up by saying, "with a great deal of work he might perhaps make a passable actor. Certainly he has with him a great teacher whose coaching should prove profitable."

Damala, who read his notices with increasing fury, found this last cut especially galling. Anything but chastened, he accused the critics of jealousy and of deliberately plotting against him. Also for some distorted reason he blamed his wife for his fiasco. She, after glancing at the notices, dismissed them with, "Bah! It means nothing. I had as bad or worse when I started out."

A few weeks later, Sarah played a short return engagement in London, taking along Damala as lead and limiting the repertory to La Dame.

The opening night, the house again went wild over the Divine Sarah. Toward the far from divine Damala they were polite, due doubtless to native sentimentality and the knowledge that the two were newlyweds. La Dame was the sensation of the theatrical season. The Prince and Princess of Wales attended a performance and afterward went back to the Green Room to congratulate her. The beautiful future Queen Alexandra put her arms about the actress and, still crying, said, "Oh, Madame, I am so happy to find you alive after that last act!" The Bernhardt cult was as ardent as ever. Fans fought for the scraps of the handkerchief which she tore up in the scene with the elder Duval — souvenirs which one of her maids was clever enough to save and sell to throngs outside the stage door. Sarcey, who seems to have trailed her travels like some international spy, again came across from Paris and wrote back, "Nothing can give an idea of the craze that Sarah Bernhardt is exciting. It's a mania. In the theatre when she's about to appear, a tremor runs through the audience; she appears and an 'Ah!' of admiration and astonishment escapes from every throat . . . Wherever you go, it's her they're discussing."

All this furore over his wife piqued Damala's colossal egotism. He began regretting this absurd marriage. He also began taking larger quantities of morphine.

Madame Sarah's next project was *Fédora*, and it was a major one. *Fédora* is an out-and-out melodrama so cleverly contrived it gives the illusion of being distinguished theatre. The plot is the love story of a Nihilist and a fascinating Russian princess. At that time, Russia was all the vogue and Nihilists were as sure-fire a theme for plays and popular novels as Westerns are on today's television. The Princess Fédora is led to believe that a Nihilist named Loris Ipanoff has murdered her husband, and plans a revenge by causing the man to fall in love with her so that she can entice him into the hands of the secret police. Instead of her scheme working out that way, Fédora falls madly in love with Loris, who turns out to be neither a Nihilist nor the murderer of her husband who, incidentally, proves to have been an unfaithful scoundrel; and rather than have her lover discover her attempted treachery the lady takes poison and ends up in one of those writhing death scenes that were the Bernhardt specialty. The whole thing is, of course, preposterous, but Sardou's brilliant craftsmanship made it seem believable. "Fédora," wrote Maurice Baring, "is no more like a Russian Princess than Jules Vern's *Michael Strogoff* is like a novel of Tolstoy. However it offers an actress a superb chance to pull out all the stops."

The role of Loris Ipanoff is also excellent, and the star was determined that her husband should play it. Sardou was equally determined that he should not. Before leaving for London, she had expressed this wish to Sardou, who had made evasive replies to the

effect that Damala was indeed a very handsome fellow who doubtless would develop into quite an actor, but he carefully refrained
from committing himself. Sarah, however, went ahead and committed herself with Damala mainly to put him in a better humor.
When she returned to Paris, she immediately brought up the subject
with Sardou, who very politely but firmly said *No*. She argued,
she implored, she threatened to give up the whole project, but
Sardou still charmingly polite was adamant. He was backed up by
Raymond Deslandes, who stated bluntly that if Damala were cast
as Ipanoff, he would not produce the play. For once Sarah lost a
battle and Pierre Berton was cast for the role. Damala was outraged. He spent his hours at home — or rather, his wife's home —
in baleful sulking broken by outbursts of childish temper. Sarah's
cajoling only served to make his mood more ugly. Finally, by way
of a somewhat expensive consolation prize, she took over a theatre
for him.

This was the Ambigu, and she signed the lease in her son's name,
making Maurice the managing producer of the house and director
of whatever plays would appear on the agenda. Maurice Bernhardt
was all of eighteen and he had the inexperience and swagger of a
completely spoiled mother's darling. Oddly enough, as a director,
he had acquired a certain sense of staging from that incomparable
directress who doubtless coached him in every move. In his dealings with actors and personnel he was affable one moment, arrogant
the next, and in business matters utterly incompetent. After acquiring the theatre for her husband, Bernhardt set about finding a
play and came up with *Les Mères Ennemies* by her good friend,
the Parnassian poet, Catulle Mendès. It opened in mid-November
of '82 and, oddly enough, Jacques Damala in the starring role was
not at all bad. The press was lenient, even kind, and the man's
resentments were momentarily assuaged.

All the work and planning that went into this enterprise Sarah
undertook at the same time that she was rehearsing *Fédora*. If
Sarah's marital turmoil was sapping her spirit, these rehearsals were

giving her a new charge of rejuvenating energy. Sardou himself
did the directing of all his plays. Known as *le roi des metteurs-en-
scène*, he was as brilliant a director as he was a playwright. Sardou
was an attractive man with wit, warmth and, when justly provoked,
sudden rages which had a certain picturesque allure. Working with
him was an exciting stimulant. To Bernhardt he stood for "The
theatre of an epoch . . . its smile, its joy, its terror and its
strength." He lifted every player's morale. For him Bernhardt
always made a special effort, was careful about her clothes and
turned on extra volts of her electrifying charm. He would arrive
at rehearsals bundled in a fur-lined coat and swathed in a voluminous muffler — for he had a neurotic fear of drafts even for a
Frenchman — and a velvet beret like Wagner's which he kept
pulling about. In those unhampered days the Stage-Hand's Union
had not enforced its frustrating regulations on the theatre and a
play was rehearsed in its finished set, complete with furnishings,
while the actors were allowed to handle the actual props. Before
starting the day's work, Sardou would test every chair, make certain every door worked, inspect every item on the prop list. After
the actors started, he'd watch each move, listen to each word from
all over the darkened house — the front row, the side boxes, the
back of the top gallery — all the while flinging off his coat and
muffler one minute then putting them back on the next. Toward
3 P.M. he'd tire of such gymnastics and knock off work for a short
respite, during which he'd have ordered cakes brought in from a
nearby *pâtisserie* which he'd share with the cast along with some of
his excellent port which had been a gift from the King of Portugal.
All during the recess he'd talk a blue streak recounting endless amusing stories and anecdotes.

Fédora opened December 12, 1882, and was a joint triumph for
both author and star. Sarah's performance was superb and her
appearance in flowing garments rich in ornamentation breathtaking.
"A secret atmosphere emanated from her, an aroma, an attraction
which was at once exotic and cerebral . . . she literally hyp-

notized her audience." Maurice Baring recalls that as Fédora she
played "with such tigerish passion and feline seduction which,
whether it be good or bad art, nobody has been able to match
since." While Jules Lemaître went overboard with:

> The electric, chimerical woman has again conquered Paris . . .
> Madame Sarah Bernhardt by her characterization, her allure and
> her kind of beauty, is eminently a Russian Princess, unless she is
> a Byzantine Empress or a Begum of Muscat; feline and impassioned,
> gentle and violent, innocent and perverse, neurotic, eccentric, enig-
> matic, woman-abyss, woman I know not what. Mme. Sarah Bern-
> hardt always seems like a very strange person returning from far
> away; she gives me the feeling of the exotic, and I thank her for
> reminding me that the world is wide, and that it cannot be con-
> tained in the shadow of our steeple, and that man is a multiple be-
> ing, and capable of everything.

After the final opening-night curtain, there had been the usual
ovation as Paris reclaimed its Sarah. The usual crowds streamed
into her dressing room, the usual bouquets piled up clear down the
corridors. Damala's show at the Ambigu had let out earlier and he
arrived backstage at the Vaudeville in time to realize that his wife
had chalked up another big triumph.

Catching sight of his baleful face glowering at the back of the
throng, Sarah abruptly stopped acknowledging the rapturous congratulations of her admirers and started babbling incoherent nonsense about why Pierre Berton was playing the lead, how everyone
had wanted her husband for the part, Sardou had wept and implored him to take it but Damala had made such a hit in *Les Mères
Ennemies* his contract would not permit it.

Damala was not in the least taken in and the ensuing days at home
were hell. The man's behavior toward his wife had been atrocious
from the start. Taking advantage of every chance to humiliate her,
he criticized her clothes, sneered at her affectations and openly
ridiculed her before her friends. A few nights after the *Fédora*
opening they had a shrill and ugly quarrel which went on into the

early morning hours. Sarah, who was obliged to foot all her husband's bills, had been charged with a few costly purchases which she realized had been gifts for other women. Quite understandably she protested, and she was a woman who didn't protest quietly. Damala raged back. He claimed that as the innocent victim of her snaring him into an unwanted marriage, he had a right to enjoy a few moments of liberation from this hideous slavery. He accused her of double-crossing him in regard to the role of Ipanoff, of trying deliberately to ruin his career by forcing him to appear in a less successful play, called her every obscene and vituperative name and stormed out of the house. Next morning without notice to anyone he departed for North Africa to enlist in a company of Algerian Spahis, and the Ambigu printed a hasty announcement that Monsieur X would replace Monsieur Jacques Damala in *Les Mères Ennemies.*

10.

~~~~~~~~~~~~~~~~

ATTACKS AND
COUNTERATTACKS

D
AMALA'S DESERTION was a cruel blow to Sarah, more to her
pride than to her heart, for she could never have had any
abiding love for the man. Also she must have realized that
through this marriage she had made herself a figure of ridicule to
her public. Her current success in *Fédora* was no solace, her spirit
was broken and for a time she lost her extraordinary zest for work.

Les Mères Ennemies closed and the Ambigu was on the rocks
due largely to Maurice Bernhardt's mismanagement. His mother
had sunk a small fortune into this expensive folly solely to placate
a worthless husband: 100,000 francs for the lease and an additional
100,000 to redecorate and get the shabby house in running order.
Feeling obliged to put on another play which with any luck might
recoup some of the losses, she signed with the poet-author Jean
Richepin to produce his new drama *La Glu*. The piece was first
rate and the cast an excellent one which included her friend
Madame Agar and Gabrielle Réjane, who was then just starting
her rise to joyous fame. In spite of good notices, the show ran for
only fifty performances and at a loss of 400,000 francs. Sarah gave
up the Ambigu. The eighteen-year-old Maurice gave up his career
as managing director and, one assumes, returned to lycée and the
completion of his education.

The money *Fédora* was bringing in was not enough to pay the
star's creditors. In desperation she was forced to sell her jewels, her
carriages and pair of beautiful chestnuts at auction in the Hotel
Drouot. The profits, though considerable, were still not enough

and she went to the drastic measure of closing *Fédora*, although it was still playing to full houses, and going off on a rapid tour of the European cities whose theatres had greater capacities for bigger box-office receipts.

Before leaving she commissioned Richepin to write her a play. She also, possibly in rebound from the tortures of her marriage, took him on as her lover. Jean Richepin was in every way the antithesis of Jacques Damala. Five years younger than Sarah, he was a magnificent specimen of healthy masculinity with broad shoulders, exuberant manner and a warm, booming voice. Castelot speaks of him as "a force of nature." The son of an army doctor stationed in Algeria, he served as a sharpshooter in the Franco-Prussian War, after which he'd been a sailor before the mast, a stevedore and a professional boxer. At one time he lived with a band of gypsies in the forest of Fontainebleau, at another, he performed as a tumbler-wrestler-weight-lifter in the Neuilly Fair. In '76 he wrote a volume of poems, *Les Chansons des Gueux*, which depicted the miseries of vagrants, tramps and the down-and-out with such bitter invective against the ruling social system, he was sentenced to a prison term plus a fine for offending public morals. All of this gave additional aura to his picaresque nature. A sort of Prince of Bohemia, he looked like an actor impersonating one of the romantic vagabonds of whom he wrote. Bearded, handsome, he often strode along the boulevards with his shirt open at the neck as though he were hiking along a country lane. He gloried in wind and sun and manly exercise. Of an early morning he could be seen bicycling around the lakes in the Bois, sporting a tight-fitting sweater which showed off his superb muscles. Goncourt speaks of "Richepin with his powerful and smiling personality like an acrobat who has just performed an astonishing feat." This man when he entered a room seemed to bring with him a bracing breath of fresh air, and Bernhardt, sick of the fetid atmosphere that fairly emanated from her husband, found her spirits lifted and her energy restored by his infectious vigor. They conducted a whirlwind affair on a whirlwind tour. In Copenhagen Georg Brandes wrote to a friend, "Sarah the Divine was here with her shadow Jean Richepin, the poet of *Les Caresses*. She was always with him, dined and slept with him." The tour wound up with a one-week stand in London during which she gave ten performances of *Fédora* to cheering houses, then she went back to Paris.

When she entered her house the domestic staff was in a state of agitation. "Monsieur," it seemed, tiring of his career as an Algerian Spahi, had returned. She found him in his room, lying on his bed, stark naked, serenely reading a novel. When she demanded what was the meaning of this, he coldly replied what was the meaning of what: wasn't this house legally his as well as hers? and went on reading his novel. Sarah, with a heavy heart, told Richepin what had happened and said that she felt it her duty to go back to her husband if only to rescue him from the drug habit. Richepin with expansive good humor said that he understood and he added that when she eventually came to her senses and booted Jacques Damala out of her house and life, he'd be waiting for her.

She leased the Porte Saint-Martin Theatre, where she played *Froufrou* and *La Dame* to good returns. Her prodigal husband spent the time lolling about "his" house in a stupor of morphine or flagrantly betraying her with other women. He made her life an utter hell. Sometimes he'd wander into the theatre during a rehearsal to strut about as though he owned the place. He took every opportunity to make sneering remarks about his wife in front of the company and more than once referred to her as "the long-nosed Jewess." He was openly carrying on an affair with a young ingénue in her troupe, and when Sarah found it out she fired the girl. After which Damala skipped off with the little creature to Monte Carlo, where he lost 80,000 francs at baccarat. He then had the gall to wire Sarah of his predicament and she had the foolishness to scrape up the amount and send it to him, along with a letter begging him to return. He did, and *with* the ingénue, who immediately put in a claim for back wages.

For a time he stayed home, his addiction growing steadily worse. He no longer tried to conceal it and even in the presence of company thought nothing of taking out a hypodermic needle and giving himself a shot right through the trouser leg. By now he had got up to eight or ten a day. Sarah did everything in her power to stop him. When he was away from the house — doubtless with one of his women — she would ransack his room and throw out all the phials of the stuff she could find. In those days there was little curb on the sale of narcotics. She looked up the pharmacist from whom Damala got his supply and when the man would not promise to refuse her husband any further sales, she broke an umbrella over his head. None of these expedients effected anything other than bitter quarels and vituperative invective between the miserable pair.

As always the press was cruelly gleeful. *L'Evénement* published a scathing article on the "clamorous and battling menage of the avenue de Villiers." Another paper ran a caricature of the Greek sprawling insolently on his wife's famous divan, the caption reading "La Damala aux Camélias." At last the actress could no longer put up with the public humiliations, the vicious marital indignities. One day after throwing Damala's drug supply down the drain, she threw the man himself out of the house. He entered a sanitarium and Sarah arranged for a legal separation. Being a Catholic, she never considered getting a divorce.

The year 1883 was a bad year. True enough Sardou approached her with another play, *Théodora*, but she had to put him off as she'd made a previous commitment to Jean Richepin. A man of his word, Richepin had waited until the banishment of Damala and had re-established himself as the current Bernhardt lover. He had also come forth with the promised play, and it was a pity that he had. The piece was *Nana-Sahib*, and it was awful. Laid in India at the time of the Sepoy Mutiny, the plot involves the rebel potenate Nana-Sahib, Djamma his beautiful mistress, a large cast of improbable characters and a mass of extras doubling as courtiers, Sepoys, beggars and British colonials. It had all the subtlety of a

Barnum circus pageant and the consensus of opinion was that it belonged not in the Porte Saint-Martin but over at the Châtelet, where preposterous spectaculars still delight audiences of the bourgeoisie. To make matters worse, the leading man after the first week fell ill and Richepin, who fancied himself as an actor, breezed confidently into the role, in which he was as awful as his play, and business plummeted to low depths.

Meanwhile Jacques Damala, temporarily cured, had been released from the sanitarium and through some fluke had been engaged by the Gymnase to star in Georges Ohnet's *Maître des Forges* in which as a rich but boorish iron-master with a heart of gold, Damala scored a personal hit.

The Gymnase did not give mid-week matinees. One Thursday afternoon when the Porte Saint-Martin box office had reached an all-time low, Damala showed up in the front row, made more conspicuous by the empty seats on either side of him. Whenever his former wife came down near the footlights, he'd turn around to look over the pitiful house shaking his head and murmuring, "Poor Sarah!" At the end of the performance Richepin, without waiting to take a curtain call, rushed out to the main exit and, as Damala emerged with a sneering smile, the playwright grabbed him by the back of the coat, whirled him about and gave him the mother and father of a beating-up.

This was not the only occasion when Jean Richepin defended his lady's honor with righteous force. In December there appeared in the bookshops that vile little volume bearing the title *The Memoirs of Sarah Barnum*. It had a sententious preface by Paul Bonnetain, who should have been ashamed of himself, for Bonnetain was a first-rate writer connected with the *Figaro* and the *Revue Nouvelle*. The author of *Sarah Barnum*, as has been mentioned, was Marie Colombier. For three years Colombier had been plotting revenge on Bernhardt for the outrages she felt she had received during the American tour. As an actress Colombier had made no name for herself but she had achieved a certain reputation as a purchasable daughter of joy. By then she must have become a bargain item, for she was spoken of on the boulevards as *le plat du jour* and Goncourt dismisses her as being little more than a prostitute. The book purports to be an account of the notorious rise and degrading fall of an actress named Sarah Barnum. It parallels Bernhardt's beginnings and career closely enough to leave no doubt in any reader's mind as to the identity of the heroine — if such a monster could be called a heroine. Nor is the identity of the other characters left to the imagination. Julie Bernhardt is "the Elder Jewess," Aunt Rosine is "Tante Rosette," Maurice is "Loris," his father "The Prince de Dygne" and so on. Even the Heir Apparent to the British throne is made yet more apparent under the title of the "Prince of Ireland." The text is a clutter of revolting pornography, scatological vituperation, anti-Semitic venom and scabrous lies. It attributes to "Sarah Barnum" the most atrocious behavior and sexual depravity that could have been invented by a filthy and malicious mind. Only a vulgar woman could have written it. As one reviewer pointed out, "No man would have hurled such excrement at a rival." A side light on the nature of the work is that in order to read it in the Paris Bibliothèque Nationale, one must apply for special permit to the "Réserve" — a department that contains works of a highly pornographic or blasphemous nature.*

It is quite possible that *The Memoirs of Sarah Barnum* might have gone unnoticed by the public if some indignant but misguided friend hadn't brought Sarah a copy. Her reactions and those of her entourage are not hard to imagine. The first person to do anything about this salacious libel was Maurice. Accompanied by two young friends whom he appointed as seconds, he dashed to the rue de Thann where Marie Colombier lived, burst wild-eyed into her flat shouting that he had come in behalf of his mother's honor and demanded that she name some gentleman-defendant whom he

---

* N.B. There is a volume available in the New York Public Library. Being in French, it may not have come under the scrutiny of the authorities. I should however advise against looking it up as the book hasn't even the merit of being occasionally amusing.

could immediately challenge to a duel. When she laughed and told him he was too young to be fighting any duels, he called her every name in his nineteen-year-old vocabulary, tore from the wall a framed sketch for the book's frontispiece, ground it to bits underfoot, then swearing vengeance departed with his callow "seconds."

Mademoiselle Colombier's next intruders were Jean Richepin and Sarah Bernhardt. The latter stormed in like vengeance personified. In one hand she flailed the air with a riding whip given her by Marshal Canrobert, in the other she brandished the dagger she used in *Nana-Sahib*. At sight of them, Colombier fled through a door concealed behind a tapestry, while her caller, one Jehan Soudan, stood guard against the assailants. The *London Morning News* of December 20, 1883, reports:

> M. Jehan Soudan was attacked by M. Richepin who wielded a large table knife and was very much excited. Mme. Bernhardt lashed up sofa cushions and hangings and broke a considerable quantity of porcelain. M. Richepin offered the maid 1,000 fcs. to tell where her mistress was, but without success. The party then rushed out.

The news item flashed across the Atlantic. The *New York Herald* gave it 6000 words and the *Police Gazette* bore on its pink cover a lurid drawing of "The Bernhardt's Attack."

The foreign reportage was infinitesimal as compared to the coverage in the Paris dailies. To add to the limelight, Octave Mirbeau wrote a lacerating review of the book and a scathing denunciation of Paul Bonnetain for having lowered himself to write its preface. Octave Mirbeau, novelist and playwright (his *Les Affaires Sont les Affaires* ran for years in this country as *Business Is Business*), wrote countless articles for the papers, most of which were diatribes against some current social injustice. Tall, redheaded, with blue eyes flashing under bushy eyebrows, he was a vociferous espouser of all new trends in the arts and champion of

Causes to the point of frenzy. His friends, who called him *Le Violent*, said that Mirbeau woke up every morning in a rage anticipating the hundred injustices he might encounter during the day. With it all he was a popular man. A *bon viveur*, fond of good food and fine wines, he lived extravagantly yet was continually starting crusades for the underdog. He took up the defense of the anarchist Ravachol, toyed with socialism and during a Noble Savage phase moved with his family to live in the country until he got fed up with the thick-headed stupidity of the average peasant. His unsolicited rushing to the defense of Bernhardt versus Colombier and Bonnetain was so execratory the latter challenged him to a duel which took place a few days later. During its brief course Bonnetain received a wound in the hand — not, unfortunately, his writing one — and Mirbeau was declared the victor.

The result of all this farcical ruckus was an immediate soaring of sales for *Sarah Barnum*, which went into many printings. It did nothing, however, to boost the sales at the Porte Saint-Martin box office and in a very short time, *Nana-Sahib* was obliged to fold.

Sarah, in her fury, had the bad taste to write a rebuttal to Marie Colombier by way of a short book she called *The Life of Marie Pigeonnier*. In it she tried to smear her enemy with comparable venom although she could never have brought herself to resort to Colombier's filth or vulgarisms. It was a childish and undignified gesture and served only to make Bernhardt look ridiculous. That "Beloved Monster," the Paris public, were not amused and the "Sarahdoteurs" began to wonder if perhaps their idol might not have feet of clay.

Judith Bernhardt died that year. Sarah described the event with characteristic romanticism: "She was found stretched out on a yellow sofa, wearing an elegant negligée, her head against a lace pillow. Her lovely hands were holding the little table-mat she'd been embroidering. She smiled coquettishly at death." The daughter was deeply grieved over the death of this mother who had shown her so little real motherhood. This was one of Sarah Bernhardt's many tunnel times and she fell into one of her worst periods of depression.

As always money was short. She had lost a lot through *Nana-Sahib*. Her household expenses continued at a ridiculously high level. Although her husband was no longer a liability, her son, "The Crown Prince," was draining the family till with his fast horses, his clubs, his tailor's bills and his gambling debts — for Maurice was an inveterate gambler. She turned to what was to be the sure expedient during financial straits from that time on, a revival of *La Dame aux Camélias*. Between 1884 and 1914 that frail lady and her unfading camellias were to be brought out of storage twenty-two times. For this revival she had to find a new actress to fill the role of Nichette, which her sister had played hitherto. Jeanne Bernhardt, who had become a pitiful wreck from drug addiction, died during the run of *La Dame*, and that didn't lighten Sarah's depression. She had never outgrown her fierce family loyalty. Contemptuous as she may have been of Jeanne's weakness, she loved her in a protective fashion, and this death too opened up ancient wounds.

In May she and the Porte Saint-Martin management put on Richepin's adaptation of *Macbeth*. This proved to be as lamentable a flop as *Nana-Sahib*. She blamed it on the hot weather and assured Richepin that in the cooler climes of London it would go like wild fire. It went with all the flare of a water-soaked log. It is not surprising that *Macbeth* failed in London, even if Richepin's version may have been adequate. Every classical work suffers from translation and perhaps the most acute sufferings are those undergone by the works of Shakespeare when transposed into French. Of all his plays, *Macbeth* would seem to be the least suitable for the Gallic tongue. One has only to read in the routine translation the scene with the Weird Sisters when the third witch — *troisième sorcière* — utters the eerie cry, "All hail Macbeth and Banquo" — "*Macbet et Banko, bon jour!*" — to realize the impossibility of transplanting Scotland's Blasted Heath onto the Paris boulevards.

The British public, loyal as ever to "The Bernhardt," were uncomfortably embarrassed by such distortion of their Bard and they breathed a sigh of relief when the theatre bill changed and they could again flock to the Gaity to sob happily over the death of Marguerite Gauthier.

There seemed to be a jinx attendant upon the Bernhardt-Richepin ventures, with *La Glu*, *Nana-Sahib* and *Macbeth* such dismal failures. Twenty-three years later in 1907 the two were finally to enjoy a joint success. This was with *The Sleeping Beauty*, Richepin's charming dramatization of Perrault's beloved fairy tale — an entertainment that was little more than a Christmas pantomime but done with imaginative scenery and an exquisite musical score. Bernhardt, aged sixty-three, played Prince Charming, and judging by all accounts she was indeed completely charming. The piece had a gratifying run and the Bernhardt-Richepin jinx was exorcised. In 1884, however, their relationships, both professional and personal, were not happy and the partnership dissolved.

That July, still in the slough of despond, Sarah returned to France. For solace she went to the Normandy coast, where at Sainte Adresse near Havre she owned a little villa overlooking the sea. Prior to World War II it was still standing and on the wall a commemorative plaque with the inscription:

> *C'est ici de Sarah la joyeuse demeure.*
> *On y chante, on y rit et parfois on y pleure.*

She returned to Paris still in her private tunnel. The pounds sterling she had accrued in London were slipping away like sands in an hourglass. There were no theatre prospects and again she was met with a cold indifference from the Paris public. Then one bleak day, the clouds parted, the sun shone and like a knight in glittering armor Victorien Sardou came galloping to the rescue. His weapon for victory was the manuscript of *Théodora*.

This is a shamelessly out-and-out melodrama dealing with the Empress Théodora, a former *courtisane* who, with her Emperor

husband Justinian, ruled sixth-century Byzantium. The action
takes place at the time of an attempted insurrection. In the first
act, Théodora, listless and bored with court formalities, slips off to
the Constantinople slums to consult a gypsy friend of her low-life
days whose suggested remedy for the imperial ennui is a love
potion — yes, really! This Byzantine hormone concoction works
beyond Théodora's most amorous dreams and she falls madly in
love with a young commoner named Andréas. Disguised and using
a fictitious name she visits him nightly and learns of a conspiracy
to kill the Emperor and Empress, but has no idea that Andréas is
in on it. She warns Justinian of the plot and he takes measures to
trap the would-be assassins, of which there are two, as they enter
the palace. There is a breathless pause when everyone waits, then
the sounds of a scuffle and the cry of "Help, Andréas!" as the first
man is apprehended. Théodora, the only one to hear the words, is
appropriately horrified. She rushes to an immense brass-studded
door, barricading it with her arm and body in an attitude immortalized by the photographer Nadar, and Andréas has time for a get-
away. The trapped conspirator is dragged before the Emperor and
questioned as to the identity of his companion. The man refuses to
talk and Justinian, after launching into a minute description of the
highly unappetizing tortures that await him if he keeps silent, goes
out leaving the terrified prisoner alone with the Empress. Théodora
in despair tells him that Andréas is her lover and adds that under
the unspeakable torture his friend won't be able to keep from naming him. The man begs her to kill him then and there. As they look
about for a suitable lethal weapon, he suggests the long ornamental
pin in her hair. She replies that being gold, it won't be strong
enough. He bares his chest and orders her to run it through to his
heart. As she hesitates, he threatens to cry out her lover's name, at
which she stifles his mouth with her left hand, drives home the pin
with her right and the man falls down dead. All of which, wrote
Sarcey, "is fantastically improbable but the effect is none the less
prodigious." The dénouement of this cheerful evening in the

theatre is that after several scenes of elaborate pageantry involving a large cast, Andréas is caught and executed though not before learning that his mistress is the Empress.

Justinian finds out about his consort's extra-marital dalliances and the curtain falls with Théodora being led away, about her neck a rope with which she is to be garroted. This was one play in which the Bernhardt death scene took place off stage.

Preposterous as the story outline may be, *Théodora* gave Sarah a chance to let off all the fireworks, a few yet untried. Sardou had written every line with her in mind and the role suited her like a tight-fitting garment. The piece was brilliant in construction and detail. Sardou was an avid student of history and in the case of every period play he wrote — and he wrote a great many — he put in months of scholarly research beforehand. He had long specialized in the Byzantine era and all his situations were founded on fact unless they impeded dramatic effect, in which case drama won out. Actually the Empress Théodora was not publicly strangled but died in 548 A.D. from what may have been cancer. He defended his tampering with history by stating that in the theatre:

"It would obviously be absurd to make Mary Stuart die of consumption, Marie Antoinette of poison, or Jeanne d'Arc in her bed. But an end so obscure as that of Théodora authorizes me, I suppose, in imagining for her a death more Byzantine than the real one."

Sardou's enthusiasm for historical authenticity was shared by his star. Weeks before ordering her costumes, she journeyed to Ravenna and stood long hours in the Church of San Vitale studying the magnificent mosaics with their startling portraits of Théodora and Justinian staring menacingly forth from barbaric gold. She made sketches of every robe, every fold, every detail of ornamentation. When she returned to Paris she had completed in detail a dressmaker's design for each outfit, as well as those for her stage jeweler, even to that death-dealing hairpin. Her wardrobe alone cost more than the average production. Her costumer figured out that toiling in her workrooms she and her assistants had sewn on by hand more than 4500 "gems." How the actress could move, and move with such grace, under the weight of these encrusted garments was one of the miracles of her magic.

Théodora, which opened the day after Christmas, 1884, was the greatest triumph for the "Two S's" partnership with the future exception of *Tosca*. As one biographer put it — and when it comes to accounts of triumphal events, the French can't resist Napoleonic analogy — "*Théodora* was Sarah Bernhardt's Austerlitz." She played the exotic Empress with tigerish abandon. Lemaître among the other cheering critics wrote of the aura about her that made one think of Salome, of Salambô, of the fantastic queens of Gustave Moreau: "a distant and chimerical creature . . . both hieratic and serpentine with a lure both mystic and sensual."

Théodora was the smash hit of 1884–1885. It ran for three hundred performances in Paris and over a hundred in London. It could have gone on well into the following year if Sarah hadn't listened to some stupid advice from her leading man, Philippe Garnier, who was giving a magnificent performance as Justinian and should have been content to keep on collecting his salary and the public acclaim he was receiving in the role. It had taken some strong persuasion to get Garnier to sign up. He still resented Damala's ousting him two years previously in Russia. But after a certain amount of stalling, he was back again as Bernhardt's leading man. He was also back as her lover. Garnier was an attractive person and a good actor though not by any measure a great one. He had much self-assurance and in his own opinion was quite an expert on theatrical matters. Whether or not Sarah's emotional involvement with him was at all profound, she let herself for a time be swayed by Garnier's judgment, which was anything but sound. His first project was for her to put on a production of Victor Hugo's *Marion Delorme*.

In late May of '85 Victor Hugo had died and the entire country reacted as though over the death of a national hero. All of Paris went into mourning. Hugo's body, in the pauper's pinewood coffin he had requested, lay in state for twenty-four hours under the Arc de Triomphe. It was then driven to its final resting place among the immortals of the Pantheon and thousands formed a voluntary cortege to walk behind the unadorned hearse. Among these was Sarah Bernhardt, who had quietly joined the silent throng in an inconspicuous place. Then a remarkable thing happened. As one by one persons in the procession recognized her, each stepped back a pace or two until by the time they crossed the river, she was walking quite alone behind Hugo's immediate family. It was a moving example of the sensitivity of the French people that *en masse* they realized the rapport between the great writer and his great interpreter and instinctively gave way to Doña Sol. This was one time when the limelight position was not of Bernhardt's devising.

After his death there was a Hugo revival. Philippe Garnier was certain that the poet's *Marion Delorme* would go with a bang. It went, all right, within a couple of weeks and without so much as a whimper.

Garnier's next project was downright preposterous. The actor had harbored a life-long ambition to play Hamlet. How he ever persuaded Sarah to produce this masterpiece with him in the greatest of all stellar roles while she appeared in the less than secondary position of the weak-witted Ophelia, no one knows, including Bernhardt herself. Garnier was not up to the part and the Paris public, disgusted that "their Sarah" would lower her status to play second fiddle so palpably in order to please a current lover, hissed and boo'd Garnier's every entrance and exit. The run was brief. It was also financially disastrous for Sarah and for Félix Duquesnel, the Porte Saint-Martin manager. Pierre Berton, anxious to act again with Sarah in a good play, wrote to Sardou suggesting that he urge his erratic star to revive *Fédora*. Sardou wrote back:

. . . Why would Sarah play *Fédora* in which Garnier has no role? . . . It's Garnier who runs everything in that madhouse of which Duquesnel fancies himself the director but in which he is more of a paying boarder than he knows.

Again Bernhardt's till had been scraped to the bottom. She wrote to Henri Cernuschi, a millionaire authority on Far Eastern art whose superb collection is still to be seen in the museum that bears his name:

> I am as poor as my ancestor Job: Will you buy my tiger for 3,000 frs. which I purchased at Bing's for 6,000? I'm writing to you because my tiger is *superb* and *Japanese!*

Whether or not Cernuschi complied is not known. He may have been skeptical about the "superb" quality of Sarah's tiger, as the lady's haphazard taste in art was of common knowledge.

This was not the first time she had tried to pawn off bric-a-brac on a friend. Shortly before the opening of *Théodora,* she'd found herself deeply in debt, and although she felt fairly certain that the play was going to be a hit, she needed immediate cash. The day of the première she wrote Alphonse de Rothschild asking if he'd buy some of her Oriental bronzes. The baron, suspecting the bronzes of being somewhat inferior, politely declined their purchase but sent her 10,000 francs, asking in exchange to be given a seat for the second night's performance. Sarah returned him 3000 saying that 7000 was all she needed and cheerfully forgot to come forth with any theatre ticket.

Now in 1886, as in all periods of serious financial pinch, she resorted to the inevitable expedient of a tour. Edward Jarrett was ever ready to book her on the road and this time the road zigzagged the length and breadth of South America in a repertory of plays with an emphasis on *Théodora.* Both Angelo and Garnier were hired as alternating male leads, which might seem a bit odd although the two lovers past and present apparently got along amicably. Wherever she appeared in the Latin-American continent, "La Bernhardt" was received with ovations and loud *olés.*

In Brazil she created such a furore, a priest accused her of witch-craft, which in no way hurt the box office. That liberal intellectual, the Emperor Dom Pedro, who for nearly half a century conducted a beneficent rule over the country, attended every one of her performances. In Rio at the finish of the first night of *Théodora*, the house went into mass hysteria. After pelting the visiting star with flowers, they started hurling fans, gloves, hats, slippers, canes and eventually garments onto the stage, which began to take on the appearance of a pawn shop set up in a Byzantine palace. After responding to nearly a hundred calls, Bernhardt was summoned to the imperial box, where Dom Pedro presented her with a gold bracelet, at which she put an end to the furore by conveniently fainting. Back in her dressing room the no-nonsense Jarrett abruptly brought her to by telling her that the Brazilians always behaved in this fashion, and had made similar demonstrations over Patti and Christine Nilsson.

In Buenos Aires, millionaires standing in attendance outside the stage door spread their handkerchiefs on the ground for her to walk on and students had to be restrained by the police from giving in to that characteristic urge to unharness the Divine One's horses and pull her carriage all over the city. The Argentinian government presented her with a grant of 13,000 acres of land — just where, she never quite ascertained — and in Peru she received the thought-ful donation of a carload of guano for fertilizing it. Also in Peru she was given what looked like a pearl necklace but proved to be a rope of human eyes petrified by the Indians in some secret process, an oddity which quite delighted her. In Uruguay she asked of a reporter, "Monsieur, couldn't you put on a little revolution for my entertainment?" a request with which the government failed to comply.

In Chile she lived on an *estancia* outside Valparaiso and spent her free time shooting game. Maurice had joined his mother for a por-tion of this tour and the two enjoyed slaughtering a satisfying quantity of duck and wild swan. As a prize trophy Sarah brought back to Paris the head of a large antelope which she claimed to have felled with a single shot. Maurice happened to have fired his gun at the same time and Lysiane Bernhardt says that whenever her grandmother boasted of her intrepid kill, "my father became silent and smiled into his little moustache."

In Panama both Garnier and Angelo came down with yellow fever, each having only a mild attack, but Sarah's personal maid died of it. One other member of the troupe failed to survive the tour. This was Edward Jarrett. The indomitable impresario went instantly one afternoon with a heart attack. Sarah was shocked and grieved by the loss of this man with whom she periodically rowed, but who in his cold way had wise control over her, and for whom she always felt respect and affection. "The Terrible Mr. Jarrett" was buried in Montevideo and his New York partner Maurice Grau took over for the final weeks.

During the homeward voyage Bernhardt had a bad fall which resulted in a severe injury to her right knee. She attributed it not to a sudden lurching of the ship but to the fact that just before she fell she had brushed against a pot of heather in the main lounge. This woman's obsessive fear of heather was an odd superstition which she must have invented in her extreme youth, for generally the modest little plant is said to bring good luck. One time outside a stage door an ardent fan had tried to pin a sprig of heather onto her coat, but Sarah knocked it from the bewildered girl's hand and savagely trampled it underfoot. The knee got worse. She sent for the ship's doctor, who recommended a popular orthopedic remedy of the day that sounds like a variant of Inquisition torture. This was called *pointes de feu* and consisted in the application to the affected parts of smouldering slivers of burning wood. Sarah didn't flinch from the *pointes de feu*, but she flinched from their being applied by the doctor, who had dirty hands and filthy fingernails. With a yowl of disgust and a hurtled hairbrush she drove him from her cabin and decided to wait and consult her doctor in Havre. That physician advised the same barbaric therapy and Bernhardt went through the ordeal without a murmur. This may well have been the start of the suffering that knee was to give her for the next thirty-odd years.

She then went for a rest at the estate she had recently bought in Brittany. This was on the tiny island of Belle-Isle, ten miles southwest of the Quiberon peninsula — a wild, rocky spot, at times wind-buffeted and lashed by Atlantic waves, but for most of the year moderate in climate. The islanders were fisherfolk, many of them speaking only the Celtic Breton dialect. Here on a lonely promontory she acquired a seventeenth-century fortress whose main entrance was approached by a small drawbridge. In its day it had served as a barracks for forty men and five officers, and with characteristic enthusiasm Bernhardt set about transforming it into a country house. Interior partitions were knocked down to make comfortable bedrooms. The long vaulted hall, a former *Salle du Corps des Gardes*, she converted into a combination dining room, salon and studio. Around its immense fireplace huge sofas were scattered indiscriminately and the walls were enlivened with large second-rate paintings.

Perhaps the most attractive feature of the structure was a half-open court protected from the wind and planted with little tamarisk trees. Of special pride was a fig tree she named Joseph, which at all times was carefully pampered. Joseph had its, or his, own chemise which was put on at night or during bad weather. It was a proud year when Joseph succeeded in bearing sixteen figs. The area, which was comfortably equipped with cushioned seats and reclining wicker chairs, became known as the "Sarahtorium." Here the hostess and her guests relaxed after the midday meal. The rule was for everyone to keep quiet. Some read, others sketched or wrote, while Sarah, swathed in white scarves, dozed on her special settee murmuring, "*Je dors, je dors.*" Then she'd wake with a bound and order everyone off to tennis or shrimp catching.

Bernhardt adored Belle-Isle and went there nearly every summer from 1886 to 1922. During those years she added other buildings and cottages until the place became a regular manor house with surrounding dependencies. At first she lived in her fort with only Maurice, Madame Guérard and a staff of local domestics which grew bigger each year as new ones were added and the older ones stayed on long after they'd outlived their usefulness. Then she built on extra bungalows, one for Louise Abbéma, the other for Georges Clairin, plus a studio for the latter, and after a time a studio for herself. After Maurice married she added a little villa for him and his bride and, as their daughters came along, domiciles for them and their nursemaids. She called these structures "The Five Portions of the World." There were the Villas Europe, Asia, Africa, America and Oceania. Eventually after her tremendous success in Rostand's heroic-sentimental play about Napoleon's tragic young son, she added the Villa l'Aiglon.

That was all to be in the future. During this holiday she lived in the comparative restriction of her large fortress. As always, she had her collection of animals: a number of joyously yapping dogs, a horse team named Vermouth and Cassis, a small donkey to drive in a tiny cart about the island. There were also a few less domesticated pets including an immense and ill-tempered hawk she'd named Alexis after the Russian Grand Duke, who had sent it to her. From South America she had brought back an Andean wildcat whose temper was little better than the hawk's, also a boa constrictor whose temper was indeterminable due to the fact that it was coiled up in deep slumber. The peon from whom she had bought the creature assured her that it had just swallowed an entire pig and would sleep for several months. When asked her reason for acquiring such a thing she answered airily, "To rest my feet on after meals."

One day the boa underwent a rude and famished awakening. Hearing her maid screaming out in the "Sarahtorium" its owner rushed there and beheld her reptilian footrest ravenously devouring the chair cushions. Her account of how she dealt with the situation is that she happened to be armed with the gun she used for bird shooting and that she put an end to the havoc with a single shot.

Maurice, who was also present, may have had his own version. Both may have been correct.

In addition to the wildcat and the cushion-eating boa, Sarah Bernhardt had returned to France with an enormous financial profit. She sank 250,000 francs of this immediately into a new Paris house at 56 boulevard Péreire, which was to be her home until she died. It was to become a Paris landmark and in later years any cabdriver presented with the address was likely to say "*Ah oui, c'est chez Sarah.*" It was a small but handsome building in the restrainedly ornate style of the Paris '80's. Over the main entrance a carved motif framed the letters S.B. The interior, like that of her avenue de Villiers *hôtel*, was a profuse clutter of the good, the picturesque and the dreadful. There were *quand mêmes* all over the place, above the fireplaces, embroidered on all her linen, blazing in gold on her fine set of china which after her death was purchased by Sacha Guitry. There also was sold after her death her library which was an excellent one plentifully supplied with rare books, fine bindings and first editions. Her main salon again con-tained the same well-known divan, again red damask-covered walls served as background for masks, Oriental weapons, Mexican hats and a hit-or-miss collection of paintings. The same animal skins complete with snarling heads made walking a hazard and the same tropical profusion of flowers vied in scent with the heavy Bernhardt perfume.

Many persons have written their impressions of this extraordinary room, among them Nellie Melba. The great soprano and the great actress were good friends. At one time Bernhardt gave Melba a bit of voluntary coaching to help rescue her Marguerite from the wooden acting of the average operatic soprano. The singer, who called often at the boulevard Péreire, after describing the antlers on the walls, the fur rugs and even a stuffed snake under glass says:

And side by side with this extraordinary menagerie were busts of Sarah herself, busts of mythological persons, easels, pieces of tapes-try, dying plants . . . I even remember that under one of the tables there was a large bowl of water in which several somewhat adipose goldfish swam round and round in their dusty, watery world.

Jules Huret, a journalist and one of the Bernhardt biographers, was more awed than Dame Nellie Melba:

> Whenever I enter what Sarah Bernhardt calls her studio, I am immediately struck by something. No doubt the sensation must arise from a combination of the perfumed atmosphere of the place . . . the muffled footfalls on the thick carpet, the twittering of birds hidden in the foliage of rare and costly plants, the intoxicating play of color on silk and velvet, the silent welcome of familiar animals, and above all, the voice and appearance of the mistress of the house when she comes in.

Here as in every one of her habitations she maintained a shifting menagerie. There was Osman, the immense wolfhound; a friendly lynx with which, holding it on a leash, she'd sometimes make a startling entrance; and a baby tigress named Minette, who was periodically allowed to walk about on the dinner table to the intense discomfort of the assembled guests. At one time she kept a caged lion in a corner of her studio, but the powerful scent of the King of Beasts got to be too much for everybody and he had to be donated to the Jardin des Plantes.

The year 1887 was a good year. She loved her new house, her "Court" was more devoted than ever, her social entertaining more brilliant, her money spending more extravagant and she was very happy.

A special source of happiness was another "Two S's" triumph, *La Tosca*, which along with *Phèdre* and *La Dame* was to become a fixture in the Bernhardt repertory and which she played as late as 1913. With *Tosca* Sardou had again created one of those tight-fitting garments for his star. And in one act her actual costume was dramatically tight-fitting. This was the dress for the supper scene. An Empire gown of sinuous lines, it had a long narrow train which she utilized to make an exit that no one could forget. After murdering the villain Scarpia (and her discovery of the knife on the table was said to have been a chilling moment) and placing the candles about his supine body and the crucifix on his chest, she slowly backed off stage, staring in horror, her hands to her cheeks. The train which had swirled about her feet trailed along like an undulating snake and even after she had backed out through the door, the train continued to follow until the curtain fell. If such an effect was trickery, what else is theatre? Clement Scott, the British critic, wrote that in this scene:

> she looked superb, pale as death with distended eyes and the fierce glare of a Judith.
> Sarah Bernhardt, knife in hand over the dying Scarpia, is the nearest thing to great tragedy that has ever been seen in modern times.

As Floria Tosca, Bernhardt was seduction itself. Pierre Loüys, then eighteen and yet to come into literary prominence, after seeing her wrote in his diary:

> Oh! Sarah! Sarah! Sarah is grace! Sarah is youth! Sarah is beauty! Sarah is divinity!
> I am mad, I am beside myself! I no longer know what I'm doing, I no longer think of anything. I saw Sarah Bernhardt last night.
> My God! What a woman! Sarah . . . Sarah . . . when shall I see you again. I weep, I tremble, I grow mad, Sarah I love you!

One evening there called at her dressing room an unexpected visitor. This was Prince Henri de Ligne. What was her reaction, or his, to this meeting after twenty-three years there is no telling. Apparently he asked after Maurice, calling him "our son," and apparently Sarah invited him to stop by her house the next morning and see for himself.

Both Louis Verneuil and Lysiane Bernhardt give a similar version of that meeting. Maurice by then was a handsome, polished young man who, like his mother, could turn on charm at will. The father he had never known was enchanted with him. He told his son that he intended to make a generous settlement on him, an offer which Maurice seems to have considered fair enough. The prince went further and said that he would like to legitimatize him, granting him a legal permit to bear the proud Belgian name of de Ligne. Maurice with thanks and quiet dignity declined this honor. He had been brought up solely by his mother, he said, and he considered her name his real one. Later that day the prince left Paris and Maurice escorted him to the Gare du Nord. The station that afternoon happened to be jammed with such an unusual crowd of travelers, the guards had ordered them all to queue up in lines. It was almost departure time for the Brussels train and de Ligne, afraid of missing it, approached one guard and asked to be let through, adding, "I am the Prince de Ligne." The guard with the indifferent shrug of the French petty official replied, "Never heard of you. Take your place in line like everyone else." Maurice then stepped forward and with an engaging smile said, "This gentleman is my relative who must make his train. I am the son of Sarah Bernhardt." At that the guard bowed deferentially and personally led the pair right out onto the platform. As his father boarded his first-class carriage his son said wryly, "You see, sir, the name of Bernhardt has its advantages."

Maurice was an attractive young man-about-town, fond of luxuries, fond of the smart life and, to his mother's distress, fond of gambling. To her greater distress he had a proclivity for dueling. Actually Bernhardt had a professed admiration for duelists and more than once remarked, "If I were a man I'd be fighting every day." But the enthusiasm did not hold when her son was involved in the dangerous game. Maurice's initial attempt at an affair of honor had been when he was sixteen and his mother was off on her first American tour. Among the many caricatures of Bernhardt that were always coming out in the press was a particularly vicious one by a cartoonist named Langlois. It had first appeared in the

Cri Parisien, and the original was subsequently exhibited in the Salon des Incohérents, where Maurice saw it to his livid indignation. He confronted Langlois in a Montparnasse café and demanded to purchase the picture in order to withdraw it from the exhibition. When Langlois refused to sell, Maurice tried to provoke him to a duel, which merely provoked the man to hearty laughter and the statement that he would not fight with a child. At that Maurice dashed a glassful of vermouth in his face and an *agent de police* had to be summoned. As he was being forcibly ejected Maurice shouted back that he would send his seconds the day he was twenty-one. And this he did. Again Sarah was off on tour. The duel, like so many, was of short duration. The weapons were swords. They usually were on these *opéra bouffe* occasions, as with pistols one of the combatants was in danger of being seriously wounded. Maurice, who was an expert fencer, after a few feints succeeded in making a slash on Langlois' flank which the doctor declared a wound and Bernhardt honor was vindicated.

A further duel, again in retribution for what Maurice took to be an insult to his mother, was with the playwright-novelist Paul Alexis, who had said some harsh things about the actress in his *Cri du Peuple* theatre column. Again Maurice drew a few drops of blood and again filial championship won out.

If Sarah Bernhardt had an obsessive love for her son, Maurice returned it with an all-time mother-complex. She was his ideal, his goddess. She was *she.* It is surprising that the young man ever married, but he did. Elizabeth Finley Thomas in her delightful books of memoirs, *Ladies, Lovers and Other People,* writes of her girlhood in Paris and of being taken to Maurice Bernhardt's wedding:

> We were barely seated when a murmur swept the church: "Voici Sarah!" A slender figure scarcely more tangible than a column of smoke was floating up the aisle. A cloak of grey velvet opened over a skirt of soft pink faille. The white heart-shaped face, blurred at the edges by the marabou of her coat, and the fluffy

masses of her extraordinary blond hair were crowned by the misty tulle of her bonnet. Over her large white teeth, her reddened lips drew back in that smile of conscious fascination, which is a part of the daily toilette of every Frenchwoman. As she passed us on the arm of her escort, I heard, for the first time, the golden voice made famous by the critics. The adoration of her son, by this woman of many loves and lovers, was well-known. To support him and his family, to pay his debts and extravagances, she was to drag an ageing and martyred body across two continents, in tours that continued almost to the day of her death.

Maurice's bride was a Polish princess named Terka Jablonowska, a lovely, delicate girl with a wistful expression. The expression must have grown more wistful as with time she realized the competitive enormity of her husband's bond with his mother. Bernhardt had rejoiced in theory over her son's marriage, but once he had left home her sense of loss was dramatically acute. However, he was never very far from home. He had promised solemnly to come see her every day and he more than kept the promise. Often he saw her twice or three times in a single day, at the boulevard Péreire or in her dressing room. Only the Bernhardt tours ever separated the two.

In 1889 Jacques Damala died at the age of thirty-four. After his brief success in *Le Maître des Forges* he had given up the theatre, or to be more accurate the theatre had given him up, for he never found another job, there or in any field. He drifted aimlessly in a daze of drugs, sinking lower and lower. News of his hopeless state had been brought to Sarah, who rushed to his bedside. He had been existing in a room that was little better than a hovel in the rue d'Antin. There were forty-eight grains of cocaine and fifteen grains of morphine littered about the filthy floor. Sarah arranged for this emaciated wreck of humanity to be sent to her house, where she nursed him and hired constant medical attendance. For a month he seemed to make a remarkable come-back and Sarah conceived the curious notion of putting on a benefit performance for him, a matinee of *La Dame* with herself as Marguerite and

Damala staggering through the role of Armand. Her Paris devotees dutifully filled the house, but the event was hard on everybody. Damala went into a complete physical collapse, and was sent to a hospital, where he died on August 18.

Sarah had his body shipped back to Greece along with a bust she had modeled of him to have placed on his tomb. In later years whenever a tour took her to Athens, she always made a pilgrimage to his grave. For several months she wore mourning and ever after signed any legal or financial documents "Sarah Bernhardt Damala, widow."

At forty-five Sarah Bernhardt was not only a widow, she was also a grandmother, as Terka, her daughter-in-law, had just given birth to her first child, Simone. Far from concealing her grandmotherhood as being at all detrimental to her career, she joyously gave out the news to the world at large. She also, as though in defiance of any nonsense about age, appeared in Jules Barbier's *Jeanne d'Arc*, a mediocre play in which, however, as the nineteen-year-old Maid of Orléans she was heartbreakingly appealing and utterly convincing.

BELLE-ISLE

A LISTING of Sarah Bernhardt's subsequent roles would be as laborious to write and as tedious to read as a timetable. There were revivals of old plays and productions of new ones. For successes were many, but she had her failures as well. Among the latter was a short drama of her own authorship entitled *l'Aveu*. It was quite lamentable and lasted twelve performances.

Another failure and deservedly so was *Léna*, a trashy dramatization by Pierre Berton of a silly English novel called *As in a Looking Glass*. The final scene — a death one, naturally — was like something out of the Grand Guignol. The heroine, Léna, mistakenly believing that her husband no longer loves her, locks herself in a room and, in a pantomime lasting a good five minutes, goes about the melancholy business of committing suicide. For a time she toys with a dagger which just happens to be in a desk drawer. Then she decides upon a bottle of poison, which also happens to be handy, pours the contents into a glass, drinks it and waits for the effects, sitting still and staring straight out at the audience. People who saw her claim that she seemed actually to turn green. Then, after a sudden convulsion, she falls forward headlong, her face hitting the floor, to all intents and purposes stone dead. She carried out this preposterous stunt with such realism that on opening night one spectator fainted while a well-known club man was seen to bolt out to the nearest gutter and be actively ill.

The critics were outraged by this great actress stooping to such rank melodrama, forgetting perhaps that only Sardou's skill disguised the fact that his plays too were pure melodrama. Jules Lemaître, then only thirty-six but a man with a sensitive perception and fine mind, whose good opinion Bernhardt valued, wondered if she were losing her ability to express normal everyday emotions, saying: "She seems to come into her splendid self only when she murders or when she dies." Her mail brought daily letters from admirers begging her to return to the classics as being the only vehicles worthy her artistry, and parents wrote the papers asking when Madame Bernhardt was going to appear in a play suitable for their daughters to attend.

She didn't return to any classics but she did appear in a play quite suitable for the most sheltered *jeune fille*, the above-mentioned *Jeanne d'Arc* by Jules Barbier. After this pious gesture to placate her highminded public, Sardou came forward with a new piece which was hardly of the calibre to please the parents of young girls. This was his dramatization of the Cleopatra story. Goncourt, who seems always to have cherished a grudge against Sardou — possibly because of the playwright's ability to make money — calls it "fine history ruined by a music-hall writer." Certainly *Cléopâtre* had less merit than the other three dramas he had written to date for Sarah. However, it gave her the chance to wear elaborately exotic costumes. It also furnished her with some juicy moments for violent acting. She must especially have enjoyed herself in the scene in which a slave brought her the news of Anthony's marriage, whereat in her jealousy and rage she stabbed the unfortunate slave and then proceeded to make a wreck of the palace, smashing goblets, tearing down hangings and creating as much havoc as the stage props permitted. The story goes of an elderly London dowager who, after witnessing this tempestuous display, remarked quite audibly to her companion, "How unlike, how very unlike the home life of our own dear Queen!"

Cléopâtre also gave Bernhardt a lovely long death scene in which she had a chance to writhe about as prettily as her asp. This was usually a live reptile, one of two garter snakes she kept in a jewel case on her dressing table. She was very fond of these wriggling pets and during intermissions would take them out and playfully wrap them about her wrists to the terror of her maid Dominga and any backstage caller.

Again she and Sardou worked jointly on the authenticity of sets, costumes and even make-up. Mrs. Patrick Campbell, who became one of Sarah's close friends, once asked her why as Egypt's Queen she painted her palms a terra-cotta red, a detail hardly noticed across the footlights. "I shall see it," Sarah explained. "If I catch sight of my hand it will be the hand of Cleopatra."

In 1891 Sarah Bernhardt went on a two-year tour which took her halfway around the world and back again. The amount of cargo carried in the way of sets and theatre equipment practically filled the hold of every ship the company sailed on and required a special freight train in every country they visited. Madame Sarah's own personal luggage consisted of forty-five costume crates and some seventy-five trunks for her off-stage dresses, coats, hats, furs and her two hundred and fifty pairs of shoes. There was a special trunk for her perfumes, cosmetics and make-up and a large chest for her table and bed linens including the five pillows on which she slept.

The itinerary for this tour is given at the end of the chapter. Travel was tough in those days and work for every member of the company and stage crew was rigorous. The repertory was made up of some fifteen productions, a few of them new ones which Bernhardt as always directed. She was continually calling rehearsals to run through a new scene or brush up on an old one that was getting stale. The Broadway actor who balks at going on the road or complains to Equity about rehearsal overtime might pause to consider the stamina of these Gallic troupers.

Through her many tours Sarah Bernhardt was gradually coming to be known as "The greatest of French ambassadors." She realized this and she knew just how to carry off the ambassadorial act to perfection. If at some banquet or official reception held in her honor, some enthusiast shouted, *"Vive la France!"* she would rise, hold out her arms as though embracing everyone in the room, and in a voice clear and vibrant reply, *Vive* whatever country she happened to be in, with such simple sincerity that the bonds between France and that nation were reaffirmed at least *pro tem.*

Her two-year tour was like a royal progress with triumphs everywhere. News of her success was cabled to Paris from each country, and Jules Lemaître wrote:

> Above any other person she will have known glory . . . concrete, intoxicating, delirious, the glory of conquerors and of Caesars. In all countries of the world she has been given a reception never accorded kings. She has had what princes of thought will never have.

She also had what princes of thought will never have either, a neat profit of 3,500,000 francs.

It was probably during this tour or a subsequent one afterwards that she suffered a second injury to her knee, and it was a decidedly severe one. At the finish of the last act of *Tosca* when Floria leaps off the parapet Castello Sant' Angelo, the thick mattress that softened her fall was not in proper place and Sarah landed on the bare boards of the stage. She was laid up during the day for several days but managed to keep acting every night in spite of multiple bruises and a swollen right knee.

In 1893 Sarah Bernhardt became fed up with being under any management other than her own. She dissolved her partnership with Raymond Deslandes, sold out her interest in the Porte Saint-Martin and took over the Théâtre de la Renaissance at an outlay of 700,000 francs. She was the sole producer and director and she ran it with the efficiency of a field marshal and the lavishness of a Croesus.

Her productions were sumptuous, often overly so, and her own theatre wardrobe is said to have rivaled that of Queen Elizabeth — the First, of course. All the scenery and costuming was done under her personal supervision, mostly in the workrooms she had installed. She was in the theatre fourteen hours a day, sometimes longer, consulting with designers, overseeing technical effects, rehearsing new plays, brushing up on old ones. It is said that she was a brilliant director not only when it came to getting what she wanted from individual players but in handling the movements and groupings of crowds, for many of her shows required large casts with lots of extras, who came a centime a dozen in those less costly days. When she got hungry, she'd knock off work for what she called a *déjeuner sur l'herbe*, the *déjeuner* being a picnic luncheon of cold meats, salad, cheese and wine, and the *herbe* being the floor of her dressing room where she and whomever she chose to invite sat sprawled on a large green carpet. After an hour of this pastoral repast, they'd get back to work. And with all this she would manage to appear herself in eight performances a week. Often she'd call a late rehearsal to restage a scene or break in a replacement, going on until the small hours of the morning, then seeing her company drooping with exhaustion she'd cry out, "My poor children! You're tired! Go off to bed and we'll work again in the morning." And next day she'd show up fresher than the youngest of them. When the actor Dorival commented on her almost terrifying vitality she shrugged and said simply, "*C'est mon métier.*"

In addition to this tireless backstage activity, she never neglected the front of the house. She went over every item on the box-office statements, saw to it that the audience accommodations were comfortable and, God bless her, she was the first theatre manager to enforce the regulation that ladies attending matinees must remove their hats! It is more than can be said for the present-day managements.

During her five-year tenure of the Renaissance, Bernhardt put on nine productions, three of them hits, others either revivals or catastrophes. She opened with *Les Rois* by Jules Lemaître, a well-written play which for some reason did not take with the public. It is rumored that she and Lemaître were lovers for a time. If this is true, their affair must have been a gentle one, based more on friendship than any more tempestuous emotion. Lemaître was a sweetly modest intellectual, a man of innate genuine goodness and one person with whom Bernhardt could never possibly have quarreled. Each felt for the other tenderness and profound respect. Lemaître admired her not only as an artist of genius but as a woman of genius.

> Nothing escapes her [he wrote]. She requires only a few minutes of attention to be up on the most abstruse subject. With an astonishing mind and clairvoyance she would have succeeded in any other art, in science or politics.

Lemaître wound up one letter in *Les Contemporains* with:

> Perhaps you have not been one of the most reasonable women of this century, but you will have lived more than multitudes of others and you will have been one of the most gracious of apparitions that ever soared for the consolation of man across the changing face of this world of phenomena.

To help make up the losses of the brief run of *Les Rois*, as though she had not already set herself a severe enough schedule, Bernhardt played extra matinees of the drama that took the greatest toll of her strength, *Phèdre*. Of her performances Sarcey wrote, "It's strange, stupefying, inexplicable but it's none the less undeniable that Mme. Sarah Bernhardt is younger and more beautiful than she's ever been. Her Phèdre is the epitome of art. Such an interpretation is almost a miracle." Every time she re-created this most difficult of all tragedienne roles the miracle was to recur. Sarah Bernhardt's *Phèdre* was to become a national institution. After attending a much later revival, Reynaldo Hahn wrote, "*Phèdre* interpreted by Sarah will always remain one of the most perfect things given to our sight or hearing on earth."

Sudermann's *Magda* enjoyed only a moderate success although she enjoyed playing it and included it in her touring repertoire. That rigorous critic Bernard Shaw saw it as late as 1895 and couldn't take her performance seriously. "But the incredibility is pardonable . . ." he wrote. "One feels when the heroine bursts on the scene, a dazzling vision of beauty, that instead of imposing on you, she adds to her own piquancy by looking you straight in the face, and saying in effect: 'Now who would ever suppose that I am a grandmother?' That, of course is irresistible; and one is not sorry to have been coaxed to relax one's notions of the dignity of art when she gets to serious business and shows how ably she does her work. The coaxing suits well with the childishly egotistical character of her acting, which is not the art of making you think more highly or feel more deeply, but the art of making you admire her, champion her, weep with her, laugh at her jokes, follow her fortunes breathlessly, and applaud her wildly when the curtain falls." Shaw was later to recall of that *Magda*, "How capitally vulgarly Sarah did that!"

The big success of 1898 was *Lorenzaccio*, Alfred de Musset's poetic and to modern ears interminable drama of intrigue, vengeance, assassination and further pastimes of Renaissance Italy. Written in 1834 it had never been presented on any stage. Bernhardt gave it a lavish production and played the title role of the Florentine youth with taste and poetic emphasis. The masculine characters she chose to play were never ones which required over-masculinity. Her male impersonations had the sexless grace of the voices of choir boys or the not quite real pathos of Pierrot. Jules de Tillet, an exacting critic whom up until this time Bernhardt had always disturbed rather than charmed, now admitted, "She has reached the sublime. I have never seen anything on the stage equal to what she has done in *Lorenzaccio*."

In her next success she was back to all femininity. This was *Gismonda*, a fifth opus hand-tailored by Sardou. *Gismonda* had a good run although certain of Sarah's public felt definitely let down because at the finale, instead of going into the customary death throes, she married and lived happily ever afterward with Lucien Guitry.

That fine actor was her greatest leading man. Coquelin, with whom she also played, was in the position of a co-star rather than leading man. Guitry had returned after nine years in the theatre at St. Petersburg to burst like a joyous discovery upon his native public. A Titan of a man, overwhelmingly attractive, expansive and vigorous, when he said, *"Bonjour!"* it was in the manner of giving one the day itself. Guitry was a man of profound humanity. Jules Renard notes in his Journal, "What a pleasure it is to place one's hand in his big one!" According to his son Sacha, Guitry seized upon life and embellished it. His manner of acting was one of naturalness and a powerful simplicity that came as a startling innovation to a period of artificiality and superfluous gesture. His magnetism was phenomenal and when he walked onto a stage one was struck by a Presence as when Chaliapin made one of his astonishing entrances. Even during scenes of intense emotion he hardly moved, conceding to gesture only when it was inevitable. He'd study a part while going about routine activity. "This morning at breakfast," he told a friend, "I worked out the big finale of the second act and all the time I was eating an egg. You see? Gestures are superfluous." This magnificent actor was all masculinity. Henri Bataille said of him, "Guitry is the first real man who has trodden the stage."

Sarah Bernhardt's friendship with Guitry and eventually with his family was to be a warm and long-standing one. In 1882 when the actor married Mademoiselle Pontjest in London, Bernhardt stood in as witness. Thirty-five years later she was again to serve as witness at the wedding of Sacha and Yvonne Printemps. Guitry fairly worshipped Madame Sarah. It was he who said that the title should be written *Ma Dame Sarah* as she was *Notre Dame du Théâtre*. Shortly after the First World War, the two were asked to play a short scene in a charity benefit. They met to read through the script. By then Bernhardt was old and minus a leg. Her face was haggard and her hands like ancient claws, but her voice was still the *voix d'or* and she still glowed with that unique incandescence when she spoke a line. She read through her first long speech, at the end of which Guitry was supposed to come in with a reply. No sound was heard from him. Bernhardt paused, then looked up. Guitry was dissolved in tears.

The antithesis of Lucien Guitry was Edouard de Max, Bernhardt's leading man for some twenty productions. He was a good actor. Some critics considered him on a par with Mounet-Sully. But he was prone to declaiming in a voice that was tonally magnificent but had a pronounced Roumanian accent, and he never stopped posturing. In appearance he was a mixture of Persian prince, boulevard dandy and gypsy. He was like something out of Baudelaire. His face, which was hauntingly pallid, had the tormented expression of the true tragedian. There was a sort of exotic allure about the man. His fingers were covered with Oriental rings and his handkerchief always reeked of exotic perfume. There was something rather satanic about him, a quality he emphasized in roles such as Nero. The actor was a combination of the superb and the ridiculous. A notorious homosexual, he became known as *Le Monsieur aux Camélias,* and Jean Cocteau summed him up as "a prince of *comme-il-ne-faut-pas.*" There are many stories about his off stage behavior and rather bizarre they are. He is said to have held levees at which he granted certain of his young men the honor of watching him lolling in the rose-strewn water of his immense Roman bath; that he kept a bronze bowl filled with gold coins with which, at the height of a bacchanalia, he'd shower his stark-naked guests; and further pastimes of a similar nature. In his fashion he was devoted to Madame Sarah and she, in turn, liked and admired him. There was a curious camaraderie between the two. De Max was the victim of periodic sulking moods and when he was in one of them he would address her as "The Widow Damala," which infuriated yet amused her. He was fond of playing somewhat satanic pranks on her as when he blackened his teeth before a final scene and persuaded two other players to do the same. During a moment when, with their backs to the audience, they faced the star, they grinned in unison and Sarah exploded with maniacal laughter as fortuitously the curtain fell.

The most famous actor to play at the Renaissance was Constant Coquelin, perhaps the greatest comedian France ever produced. He had also made a break with the Comédie Française. Coquelin and Bernhardt were to star together in a number of subsequent tours, but during this first season he was merely presented playing his famously funny roles in a series of Molière matinees in which Bernhardt did not appear.

The Italian writer d'Annunzio, then in the first flush of success and chronic height of his egotism, came to Paris to discuss with Bernhardt a production of his *Dead City*. His long liaison with Eleonora Duse was already well established and he brought his exquisite mistress with him. When d'Annunzio called upon Madame Sarah and saw her for the first time he exclaimed, "She's magnificent!" then added modestly, "She's d'Annunzienne!" Bernhardt was playing special matinees of *La Dame* at the time and d'Annunzio conceived the curious and possibly diabolical notion of putting on some performances of the same play in Italian, starring Duse. Duse's acting was striking for its poetic simplicity and naturalness. Her Marguerite lacked the brilliant showmanship of the French tragedienne's and her performance received no acclaim. D'Annunzio was incensed — not with the Paris public but with his lovely mistress. He turned upon her viciously, telling her she'd been a fool to let herself be trapped into such asinine competition and reducing her to one of the shattered states of despair she suffered so frequently throughout their tempestuous years together.

In 1896 Sarah Bernhardt was given a "Day of Glorification." Friends and admirers had long wondered why she had never received the Legion d'Honneur. The French government would doubtless have been willing to recognize the great artist but may have thought twice before presenting the coveted red ribbon to a woman of such eccentric reputation. There were many who felt that some form of public homage was long past due her. After all,

Sarah Bernhardt *was* the theatre and the theatre was Paris. She was "the official personage of Parisian life. She holds in Paris not only the first . . . the absolutely first place, but a place apart, comparable to none!" declared Jules Lemaître. He and a group of other writers which included Sardou, Coppée, Rostand, Catulle Mendès and others organized a day of tribute they heralded as *La Journée Sarah Bernhardt.*

The celebration began at twelve noon on December 10, with a banquet in the large Salle du Zodiac of the Grand Hotel. Here five hundred guests were gathered, each having paid forty francs, a modest sum when one learns that this included the meal, a theatre seat for the ensuing matinee, a commemorative medal and a copy of *The Golden Book of the Gala.* In spite of the early hour the women wore evening gowns and the men dress attire.

The Queen of the occasion arrived a half hour after they were assembled. She appeared on an overhanging balcony wearing a dazzling white dress embroidered in gold and trimmed with sable. At sight of her the five hundred guests rose in a body. As she came down the winding stairs, someone has reported:

> Her long train followed her like a graceful tame serpent. At every turn she bent over the railing and twined her arms like an ivy wreath round the velvet pillars while she acknowledged the acclamations with her disengaged hand. Her lithe and slender body scarcely seemed to touch the earth. She was wafted toward us in a halo of glory.

At a table on the raised dais she sat between the Minister of Fine Arts and a personal representative sent by the President of France. A short welcoming toast was proposed by Sardou "To the great and good Sarah," after which the orchestra and choir of the Concerts Colonne struck up an ode to her glory especially composed by Armand Sylvestre and Gabriel Pierné, then everyone turned their attention to the serious business of eating. The menu consisted of:

Huîtres d'Ostende, beurre, anchois, radis,
saucisson hors d'oeuvres

Relevé
Truites saumonnées froides, sauce verte

Entreés
Cotelettes de Pré-salé aux pommes frites
Poulardes du Mans à la Sardou
Spoon au Georges Goulet

Rôtis
Faisans flanqués de Perdreau Truffés
Paté de foie gras Grand Hôtel
Salade à la Parisienne

Entremets
Gateaux Sarah

Glace
Bombe Tosca
Desserts
Compotes de fruits, Patisseries

Vins
Sherry Golden, Chablis Montonne, Saint-Estèphe
en carafes, Chambertin 1884

Café Liqueurs

I have reprinted the menu only to marvel that after such a mid-day snack anyone was able to carry on with the subsequent celebrations of the day. But apparently the guest of honor, who always had the appetite of a bird and only toyed with her food, arose fresh as a girl to make her departure and:

As she went slowly up the winding stair, from time to time sending a smile or a wave of her hand to her admirers below, she seemed almost to be mounting in triumph to the sky.

There was indeed a Roman Triumph quality to this day. A hundred carriages in procession formation transported the celebrants from the Grand Hotel to the Renaissance. The streets were lined with onlookers and special police had to be stationed to hold back the crowds outside the theatre.

At that matinee the star performed the third act of *Phèdre* and the fourth of *Rome Vaincue*. Then was staged "The Apotheosis of Sarah Bernhardt." The curtain rose to reveal her seated under a golden canopy on a flower-strewn throne. Below her were grouped young actresses in classic robes wearing fillets of roses. Then one by one the leading contemporary poets came on stage to read the verses he had composed for the occasion: Coppée, Mendès, Haraucourt, Heredia and finally Rostand, whose sonnet was considered particularly fine. The first four lines are at least worth quoting:

> *En ce temps sans beauté, seule encore tu nous restes,*
> *Sachant descendre, pale, un grand escalier clair,*
> *Ceindre un bandeau, porter un lis, brandir un fer.*
> *Reine de l'attitude et Princesse des gestes!*

At the finish Sarah, pale and looking as though she were about to expire, stood dissolved in tears while from the overhead fly-loft showers of camellias rained down.

She was not the only one to weep. Her dressing room was jammed with "Sarahdoteurs" who paid their own lachrymose tribute. Maurice Bernhardt, most prominent of the weepers, kept repeating between sobs, "Nobody knows my mother. She's a good, a gallant woman." At one point Jules Renard, who had managed to get control of himself, echoed Maurice's "a good, a gallant woman" and they all cried some more. Wires from all over the world poured in. One from d'Annunzio read: "On this day of supreme glory, a grateful Italy sends its laurels to the unforgettable enchantress.
Ave."

Maurice's reiterated protestations of filial devotion may have sprung from mixed emotions, one of which might have been a

sense of guilt. Two years earlier the Dreyfus case had exploded
with all its ugly repercussions. The story of those tense days is
common knowledge. It was a tragic time when a great country was
divided into two warring camps, those blindly loyal to the Glorious
Army of France even when it had made a heinous blunder and
those who had the courage to come out for justice and believed that
French honor was at stake when an innocent man was made to suffer for a crime he had not committed, when friendships were shattered and families suffered rifts some of which were not mended
until the First World War.

The rift caused over *l'Affaire* in her own family brought Madame
Sarah much anguish. All her life she had hated any form of tyranny
or injustice and from the start of the famous trial she had been convinced of the complete innocence of Dreyfus. She had followed
the reports daily in the papers and had gone to witness the unhappy
captain's public degradation. After the ghastly sentence to Devil's
Island she had campaigned for his vindication. To come out openly
as a Dreyfusard took tremendous courage at that time. She went to
see Emile Zola, and it is said that it was she who persuaded him to
write his fulminating outcry for justice *J'Accuse!* Next day a paper
came out with the headline "Sarah Bernhardt has joined the Jews
against the Army." Her coterie of friends were divided into warring factions. To her great distress François Coppée and Jules
Lemaître were in the other camp, both belonging to an idiotically
prejudiced organization called La Ligue de la Patrie Française,
which, according to the *Oxford Companion to French Literature*,
"typified all that was bigoted, anti-Semitic and reactionary in public life." But Victorien Sardou protested along with her the innocence of Dreyfus and of course the fiery Octave Mirbeau was
vociferous in his demands for justice. She stuck to her stand even
when it came to open rupture with her nearest and dearest. Maurice
Bernhardt was an outspoken anti-Semite and a violent anti-Drey-
fusard, as were most members of the Parisian smart set. Mother and
son quarreled bitterly, so much so that Maurice moved with his

wife and daughter Simone to live in the South of France for well over a year, during which time there was no communication between them.

It is difficult to realize the tensions of those times. Even after Dreyfus had been exonerated and reinstated in the Army, feelings rose and continued to run high and nervous hostesses breathed sighs of relief when a meal terminated without any guest blundering into "the Subject." Lysiane tells of a luncheon at the boulevard Péreire when she was a small child a few years after the turn of the century. One of the guests casually mentioned the name of an important department store owner whose name happened to be Dreyfus — no relation to Alfred. Edouard Geoffroy, a corpulent elderly beau who danced daily attendance upon Madame Sarah and was insanely jealous of all her other "courtiers" muttered something about the misfortune of having the same name as that of "the Traitor." Georges Clairin, Sarah's Old Faithful, who had stuck by her undaunted pro-Dreyfus stand, barked at Geoffroy to shut up. Maurice shouted at Clairin to keep a civil tongue in his head, Sarah shrieked at her son to be quiet, the other guests began arguing at once and the whole tempest started up again. In his vehemence Geoffroy shot a plateful of salad onto Louise Abbéma's lap. The little girls, Simone and Lysiane, went into fits of giggles. Maurice made such a sneering comment about the treachery of all Dreyfusards that his mother reacted by smashing a plate. Maurice rose and left the room taking with him his gentle wife, who burst into tears. Sarah then smashed another plate on Geoffroy's shoulder, the butler and footman fled for cover in the pantry and the luncheon broke up. Lysiane, who was some years younger than her sister, sat on in her high chair serenely drinking up the wine with which her grandmother in her agitation had mistakenly replenished her silver mug.

In 1899 Bernhardt again put on young man's costume and did *Hamlet*. The verb is used advisedly for what she did was to interpret the title role in a manner that was very direct, very natural and very, very feminine. The translation was the joint work of Marcel Schwob and Eugène Morand, and they followed the original version with pedantic exactitude. In Paris it was considered a success although opinions regarding Bernhardt's own performance were varied and heated. Many found it superb. Others couldn't bear it. Catulle Mendès, who admired it greatly, went so far as to fight a duel with a dissenting journalist friend, the actual bone of contention being over the momentous question of the color of Hamlet's hair. Maurice Baring found it excellent and claimed that this was the first time the role had been correctly interpreted.

When this production was taken across the Channel, the public were receptive although not all the press was over-polite. *Punch* said that the one thing needed to make it a perfect *Hamlet* was the appearance of Henry Irving as Ophelia. While Max Beerbohm, who headed his review "Hamlet, Princess of Denmark," wondered if next Madame Bernhardt would play Othello to Mounet-Sully's Desdemona. Max, who professed to be a "lover of Sarah's incomparable art," found her quite unbelievable as a man. The one good quality he granted her in the role was "the poise and dignity of a person of consequence and unmistakable *thoro'bred:* Yes! the only compliment one can conscientiously pay her is that her Hamlet was, from first to last, *très grande dame.*" The French translation added to his discomfort, and when "Rest, rest perturbed spirit" came out as *"Paix, paix, âme troublé,"* he found it rather like "Lou, Lou, I love you" and had an almost overwhelming desire to laugh. The serious dedication of the Adelphi audience struck him as being equally ludicrous. No one dared so much as smile. A smile, he said, would have gone into a laugh and "one laugh in that dangerous atmosphere and the whole structure of polite solemnity would have toppled down, burying beneath its ruins the national reputation for good manners. I, therefore, like everybody else kept an iron control upon the corners of my lips. It was not until I was halfway home and well out of earshot of the Adelphi that I unsealed the accumulations of my merriment."

Word of this unorthodox *Hamlet* received a world-wide press. The *New York Herald* reported, "Madame Sarah's interpretation of the Melancholy Dane has caused two French journalists to fight a duel over it and made our Julia Arthur ambitious to play it too. Which one of these effects is the more serious remains to be seen."

Ever ambitious for greater and greater success and ever in need of more and more money, Bernhardt decided to move into a theatre that had a larger audience capacity. The Théâtre des Nations in the Place du Châtelet was available and she signed a twenty-five-year lease on it. She was fifty-five at the time and would have been eighty when the lease would expire. No doubt she was confident of renewing it at such a date, going on the theory that a bigger auditorium was kinder to an aging face. Her first move was to re-christen the place the Théâtre Sarah Bernhardt, a title that was to be changed back to its original one during the Second World War Occupation when Nazi officials learned that the actress had been half Jewish. It is running to this day, again under her name — a great barn of a house about the size of the New York Winter Garden. In this theatre from 1899 to 1915 Sarah was to appear in forty different roles, twenty-five of which were new creations.

The building when she took it over was shockingly run down and she ordered it completely renovated, needless to say at colossal expense. The results were handsome in the extreme and for that day rather startling. Hitherto traditional theatre décor had been of the red plush and gilt Cupid school. The Théâtre Sarah Bernhardt was elegant in yellow velvet hangings and brocade paneling, also yellow, contrasting with ivory white woodwork. In the spacious foyer hung life-size portraits by Clairin, Abbéma and that genius of the decorative poster, Mucha, of Bernhardt as Phèdre, Théodora, Lorenzaccio and the Princesse Lointaine.

Her personal backstage quarters consisted of a five-room suite. Up a short flight of steps, a twenty-foot-long vestibule led into a salon with yellow satin hangings. After the success of *l'Aiglon*, the décor was of the Empire period. (According to Maurice Rostand

it was "Empire augmented by Lalique.") Below an ornate marble
mantlepiece, a fire burned all winter and much of the summer.
Equally overheated was the star's dressing room, which had cupboards spacious enough to hold fifty costumes, a vast make-up table
with an eight-paneled mirror, a Directoire cheval glass and an ornamental wash basin. An adjoining bathroom contained a huge tub
which was usually filled with the overflow of the flowers she was
constantly receiving. A winding staircase led down to a dining
room. It, too, was elegantly furnished and had a table which could
accommodate twelve guests. Adjoining this was a small but fully
equipped kitchen. It was in this dining room that she would receive the crowds that swarmed behind stage after every final
curtain. Although before a performance she would allow only
special intimate friends to stop by her dressing room, between acts,
if she were not making a costume change, she'd admit a few callers
for she was always available to her public. Several times a week
and every Sunday between the matinees and evening performances
she had friends in for a meal in her private dining room.

Sacha Guitry in his enchanting book, *If Memory Serves*, recalls
how as a small boy he'd be taken before every Sunday matinee
"to kiss Mme. Sarah" in her impressive dressing room, torrid as a
hothouse and banked with masses of flowers gasping their last, as
she sat waiting for her cue. Or rather as she sat waiting for the call-
boy to knock on her door saying, "Madame, it will be eight o'clock
when it suits you." Be it to her professional integrity that she was
never late!

Edmond Rostand's son Maurice also wrote of his small boyhood
visits to the famous *loge*. The Rostands were among the privileged
few who had permission to see her prior to a performance. The
first time he was taken there by his father the star was in the
process of making up rather frantically. To his eyes she seemed, he
says, "to have no age unless that of the fairies . . . both astonishingly old and astonishingly young. She seemed to have come down
through the ages yet she'd go into childish peals of laughter. Vari-

ous maids bustled about and she'd give them impatient orders in the manner of imitating an enraged lioness. But these scenes had such a theatrical, such a harmonious and such a premeditated quality they could have frightened nobody. On the contrary, one was tempted at the end to applaud as over the dizzy act of an acrobat. One of her maids was called Dominga: she looked like a Corsair in female garb and she frightened me badly when she'd kiss me with her bristling moustache."

It was in the Théâtre Sarah Bernhardt that Edmond Rostand first read aloud the script of *l'Aiglon*. The poet-playwright had first come into the actress' life at the Renaissance when she produced his *Princesse Lointaine*, a dreamy fantasy in which she played that Far-Away Princess "crowned with silver lilies, sumptuous and sad like one of Swinburne's early poems." Rostand, only twenty-seven at the time, was by no means unknown. His inconsequential but charming little play *Les Romanesques* had already been a success at the Français. *La Princesse Lointaine* was not so lucky and Bernhardt lost 200,000 francs. But that didn't bother her. She made it all back triple-fold with a revival of *La Dame*. Moreover, through this venture she had founded a deep and tender attachment to this gifted young writer, twenty-four years her junior.

Rostand, who was born in Marseille, had all the fire and panache of the south, coupled with the elegance of a *grand seigneur*. Handsome, rapier slim, he was an impeccably tailored romantic, as well-groomed as his plays. Sacha Guitry said that "his youthful success, his delicate face, his charming voice made him as seductive as possible." And after he, with the glorious cooperation of Coquelin, immortalized *Cyrano de Bergerac* he became the popular playwright of his day. He had the right receipt for stirring his audience or reducing them to tears at just the right time and, his plays being written in graceful verse, were given more credit by the sophisticated elite than they may have deserved. Arthur Symons, who was not so enthusiastic, said that Rostand appealed to the public as a millionaire appeals to society. His morning mail brought

letters from budding poets begging advice, elderly countesses asking him to tea and dewy-eyed literary ladies protesting undying
devotion, which letters he seldom answered. He was bombarded
with social invitations, most of which he turned down. He was no
misanthrope, but abhorred wasting time with people who meant
nothing to him.

For all the adulation he remained retiringly modest, preferring
the companionship of his family and a few intimate friends. There
are the inevitable speculations as to whether or not Rostand was
at one time Bernhardt's lover. Any such supposition strikes me as
nonsensical; not because of the discrepancy in age — an inconsequential thing like that would never have bothered her — but because she considered him her special protégé, her attitude being almost motherly. She was passionately possessive about him, always
referring to him as *mon poète*. And Rostand was touchingly dependent upon her. To him she was a brightly protecting angel and
"he hung from one of her rays. He found her necessary to his life
as the earth finds the sun." Sarah was devoted to his wife and children, regarding them as part of her family. Few days passed when
they failed to exchange visits.

Two years after *La Princesse Lointaine*, came another Rostand
offering, by "Madame Sarah's poet," *La Samaritane*, an "uplift"
verse drama based on the meeting of Christ with the woman of
Samaria, for which audiences felt obliged to profess admiration although it sounds like a crashing bore. It must certainly have been
quite suitable for those sheltered young daughters. However,
Rostand himself didn't allow his young son to see it due to the fact
that the woman of Samaria had, before her conversion, been a
woman of sin, although illogically enough, he took him to see *La
Dame aux Camélias*.

Then in 1900 *l'Aiglon* burst upon the theatrical world. It was
a long time a-bursting, for rehearsals lasted six months with time
out for Sarah and Rostand to make a trip to Vienna for the purpose of studying Schönbrunn Castle and the haunts of Napoleon's

luckless son. All during this period Sarah continued to direct and act in her regular repertory.

Sacha, who knew much about the preparations for *l'Aiglon* as his magnificent father was the original Flambeau, has left an account of those rehearsals. The cast, he wrote, would be called for 1 P.M., and the minor players and extras would show up more or less on time. Lucien Guitry would stride in about 2:30 and Rostand usually arrived at 3. At 3:45, Madame Sarah made her entrance and the whole company came up to kiss her hand. As there were some fifty persons to perform this ceremony one by one, this took a bit of time. Further delay came while Madame Sarah changed her clothes, for in order to feel unhampered by her trailing skirts and scarves and free to make the moves and gestures of a twenty-year-old youth, she always rehearsed in her Lorenzaccio costume. At five, work was suspended for "Madame Sarah's cup of tea" during which formality, everyone sat watching her with patience and tender respect. It is extraordinary that the play ever got readied for opening.

Everyone knows that *l'Aiglon* deals with Napoleon's delicate son the Duc de Reichstadt, wasting away from ill health and neglect in the confines of Schönbrunn, unloved by his silly mother Marie Louise, tyrannized by the wily Chancellor of Austria Metternich, obsessed by the legend of his father and pathetic dreams of re-establishing the Bonaparte Empire with himself, the rightful heir, at its head to lead the Grande Armée on to a repetition of the old glories. A six-act verse drama, it is filled with tender scenes of pathos and sentiment plus the sort of patriotic speeches that reduce a French audience to tears and shouts of *"Bravo!"*

Sacha Guitry tells of the rehearsal of one particularly stirring moment in the act set on the plain of Wagram, in which the Eaglet, who in company with the faithful Flambeau, one of Napoleon's old *grognards*, is about to embark upon the valiant but hopeless venture of returning to France, cries out, "I grab the mane. *Alea jacta est!*" Sarah stopped the proceedings to ask Rostand the meaning of the line. The poet started to translate the Latin and she interrupted saying, "I *know* that means 'the die is cast,' but what's this mane I'm grabbing?"

"The mane of the horse," Rostand replied.

"What horse?" she demanded.

"The horse you are about to mount."

"*I'm* going to mount a *horse?*" It had been some twenty years since her days of riding side-saddle in the Bois or Hyde Park and the prospect of leaping tight-trousered astride a live steed appalled her.

She ordered the stage manager to send out for the tamest horse in Paris. A seemingly gentle animal was procured and they started the scene, but in a moment of irritation or possible boredom it stamped its hoof, and Sarah pronounced it wicked and not to be trusted. Next day a man led onto the stage a slow-lumbering nag whose head was completely swathed in what proved to be a pair of woolen underdrawers. As he unwound this curious covering the owner extolled the virtues of his horse who, he said, was afraid of nothing, yet had the virtue of a lamb, a dove and an early Christian martyr. Sarah, who was skeptical, insisted that the creature be put to a test, ran straight up to it and screamed, "Boo!" The horse looked mildly astonished, then sighed, hung its head and went into a contented sleep. She then called for someone to sound the thunder machine. A stagehand, using a large hammer, struck a deafening blow on the metal sheet. The horse slept on, looking patiently dejected. Still not reassured, Sarah ordered every person present to form a large circle then at a given signal, make a giant rush upon it, shouting in unison, "*Vive l'Empereur!*" This had the effect of waking the horse, whose sole reaction was to emit a loud trumpeting noise which did not issue from its throat. All of them, including the star, went into immediate paroxysms. Lucien Guitry suggested that the beast was a Republican expressing its opinion of Empire. Sarah declared that it was a common pig, but that as it appeared to have no nervous system, she'd hire it.

Rostand then came out with the information that there would have to be an additional horse for Guitry, an announcement which had a depressing effect on the actor. At this the owner started winding the woolen underdrawers about his equine's patient head saying sadly that in that case they would have to get two other animals. When asked why, he explained, "You see, my fine horse is afraid of only one thing in this world. He's afraid of other horses. So I must lead him through the streets blindfolded. If another horse gets near him, he goes completely to pieces."

The outcome of this was that the scene was eventually played minus any quadrupeds. Bernhardt cried out her line about grabbing the mane in a ringing voice, her arms and eyes raised on high as though she were expecting some Pegasus to charge down from the heavens, and before any such unlikely occurrence took place, the curtain fell to thundering applause.

L'Aiglon always played to thundering applause. The opening night was March 17, 1900, and *Tout Paris* attended — celebrities from the theatre, literary and high society worlds. Particularly prominent was Prince Murat and further personages of the Bonapartist aristocracy. Between acts, Sarah sent a wire to Prince Victor Napoleon in Belgium saying, "To-night I am up to my waist in Empire." The success of that night seemed like another victory of Wagram. From then on the slim figure of the young Duc de Reichstadt — the "White Hamlet" as some called it — in the tight-fitting uniform of pure white relieved by colorful medals and black stock, topped by the delicate head with its unruly gold mop of hair, established itself as an almost universal image of Sarah Bernhardt, and there is no doubt that she was superb in the role. At one moment she was a lively little boy as in the scene when she jumped onto the knees of her grandfather Franz Joseph or when she discovered that the uniforms of her wooden soldiers had been secretly repainted by Flambeau changing the colors of the Austrian army into those of the French, and her reaction was the joyous incredulity of a child discovering a Christmas tree. At other times she was a youthful hero, the embodiment of the imperial epic as, standing on the deserted battlefields of Wagram, she cried out, "Paris, I already hear your bells!" and further "smiling the boy fell dead" apostrophizings. And of her death in the final act it was said that she drew a last breath, "dying as angels would die if they were allowed to." The play ran nearly a year. That summer it served as a big show piece during the 1900 Exposition and Sarah Bernhardt and Edmond Rostand were the most talked-about personages of Paris.

Rostand, however, was not in town to bask in his glory. Never a physically robust man, he had contracted pneumonia the night of the opening and spent the spring convalescing in Montmorency with his family. Every day, Madame Sarah would drive out in her two-horse landau swathed even in hot weather, in that much photographed chinchilla wrap which James Agate said recalled to him the breasts of seabirds, to pay "her poet" a visit, always bringing him a bunch of Napoleon violets. The devotion of Rostand and Bernhardt continued until the poet's premature death from Spanish influenza in 1918. The day he was made a member of the Academy, Sarah in the company of Maurice and Rostand's son, another Maurice, sat in the visitor's gallery. For the three it was a day of considerable emotion. Sarah cried, both Maurices cried and they all had a lovely time.

L'Aiglon did not create the furore in London that it had in Paris. After all the British hardly shared with the French their sentimental veneration of Napoleon. To them the once menacing "Boney" was less a hero than a sucessfully defeated foe. Through the lengthy speeches filled with historical allusions they squirmed visibly. Even Sarah's good friend Graham Robertson had to admit that it was "an overlong prodigy of virtuosity, crashing with beauty and a little boredom . . . a play at which people will yawn and admire. It's like standing before a beautiful waterfall. Pretty soon one wants to leave." Max Beerbohm, who headed his review, "Tame Eaglet; Tame Play," found the evening interminable, lasting as it did from eight until midnight. Also the fifty-six-year-old Sarah Bernhardt's impersonation of the twenty-year-old Duc de Reichstadt left him unimpressed. As he wrote:

> The trouble is not that Mme. Bernhardt looks too old. On the contrary, her youthfulness is astounding. Nor is the trouble merely that to students of history she does not look like any known miniature of the Duc de Reichstadt, and does look like every known photograph of Miss Nellie Farren as "Little Jack Shepherd." The trouble is that to everyone she looks like a woman, walks like one, *is* one.

In spite of these few adverse notices *l'Aiglon* was the hit of the London season. Crowds gathered outside the stage door, some of them semi-hysterical. One worshipping girl fell in love with Bernhardt, or rather with the Duc de Reichstadt. She attended every matinee, sent a daily bouquet along with a poem of her own composition to the theatre and systematically turned down each suitor; and she had several for she was a very attractive young woman. Her parents in deep concern wrote to the actress, who immediately sent for the girl. She received her in her dressing room, wearing an old and somewhat spotted wrapper and minus a trace of make-up. "Take a good look, *ma chère*," she said. "This is really me. There is no such person as l'Aiglon except on the stage." The girl fled in disillusionment. A month later she married and a year later Madame Sarah was godmother to their first child.

L'Aiglon was equally successful in the United States. This was her sixth American tour — she was to make nine in all. For this jaunt she brought with her fifty trunks, five servants, a secretary and Réjane's masseur. She also brought along Coquelin, as it was a co-starring season for her and her "dear Coq." France's greatest tragedienne and France's greatest comedian each was generous about taking a lesser role when the starring one was the other's *pièce de resistance*. In *l'Aiglon* Coquelin gladly played Flambeau, a character who appears in neither the first nor the last act. And she in turn played the insipid role of Roxane so that he could electrify the American audiences with his Cyrano de Bergerac. In Molière's *Précieuses Ridicules* she again semi-obliterated herself as Elmire. And this required nerve on her part, for comedy was never her forte; but when questioned why she did it, she'd laugh and shrug it off by asking who would ever look at anyone else on the stage while "Coq" was on as Mascarille. As though to make a gallantly reciprocal gesture, Coquelin contented himself playing the first Grave-digger in *Hamlet*. In *Tosca* they shone in equally fine roles, although some claim that Guitry's Scarpia had been better. Sarah adored Coquelin, who was both a great artist and a fundamentally simple, good man. Off stage wearing his quaint spectacles, he looked like a village notary. Commenting on his comical nose, she claimed that it was ever sniffing up the joy of life. Theirs was a warm and happy camaraderie. Whenever they played a performance of *Tosca*, the moment places were called for the third act with its murderous supper scene, she'd spring up with alacrity and call out *"Allons tuer Coq!"* And often in the letter scene of *La Dame* when Coquelin as the elder Duval had given a particularly fine performance, sitting at the desk as the heartbroken and lachrymose Marguerite, she'd write in the page before her, "Splendid, my Coq!" and address the envelope, "To Coquelin."

Like all her United States tours, this was a series of triumphs. Critics were again loud in their hosannahs and that American Sappho, Ella Wheeler Wilcox, composed one of her most gushing poems, which was syndicated in every Hearst paper throughout the country. It was all most satisfactory.

She returned with a barrow full of those gold coins and before she shoveled every one of them out the window in Paris, she went for her annual respite in Belle-Isle.

More and more with each passing year, Madame Sarah looked forward to her Belle-Isle summers. The moment she stepped off the little ferry onto the island, she started with nostrils a-quiver like an excited horse breathing in lungs full of the clean salt air, her head raised high, her green-blue eyes following the swooping move-

ments of the planing gulls. Then when her rattling surrey
rounded a bend of the rough road and she caught sight of her Fort
rising on the rocky promontory and waving welcome from the top
of a flagpole a white banner with its gold and blue device of an
"S.B." entwined above a gay *Quand Même*, her soul soared with the
gulls and she shed her eccentricities, her off-stage play-acting, and
became as much of a happy, unaffected woman as it was possible for
her ever to be. Suze Rueff in her book, *I Knew Sarah Bernhardt*,
wrote:

> The heroine of so many great first nights, who had impersonated
> countless characters and varied types of womanhood, here threw
> herself heart and soul into the role of hostess, mother, friend. She
> brought to these the same sure touch, the same perfection of tech-
> nique, the same burning enthusiasm as to all her creations, and the
> result was something unique and unforgettable.

The place was always swarming with guests. Those in residence
every summer were Maurice and his family and Sarah's faithful
three, Georges Clairin, whom she continued to call her "dear
Jojotte," while his name for her was always "Dame Jolie," Louise
Abbéma, who Maurice Rostand says was yearly growing to look
more and more like an elderly Japanese admiral and, of course,
Madame Guérard, who was aging rapidly and before too many
years was gently to depart this life. Sarah continued to love her
p'tit dame dearly although the poor soul's blind devotion was at
times exasperating. The old lady had a way of urging Sarah to
repeat some familiar anecdote, then laughing inordinately long before the point.

Beside those in permanent residence would be a continual coming and going of other visitors: authors, artists, musicians, politicians
and persons who merely had the invaluable asset of being amusing.
Sarah, in her impulsive fashion, would occasionally invite someone
months in advance to come for a visit, then later regret it. When
one August an elderly British spinster, the Honorable Miss Cadogan,
sent a wire saying she was arriving next day, there were cries of

pain from the hostess and groans from her immediate entourage. Then she hit on a plan. When the Honorable Miss Cadogan drove up to the Fort, Madame Sarah welcomed her in the most effusive manner then, lowering her voice, informed her that unfortunately at the moment she had staying with her a cousin who was quite, quite mad. An hour later, as they were having tea in the "Sarah-torium" Clairin, impersonating the madman, appeared at an upper window. Maurice, dressed as a male nurse, and old Geoffroy, as an attendant, were on either side and one of them shouted down that their patient was about to go into one of his more violent attacks and they were going to have to put him into a strait jacket. Shortly thereafter, Clairin, having made an escape from his "keepers" suddenly rose from behind some tamarisk bushes leering wildly. The Honorable Miss Cadogan departed the following morning.

Occasionally a foreign notable might turn up. There was one memorable day when the British royal yacht anchored off the Pointe des Poulains and Madame Sarah's old friend, by then King Edward VII, came across in a launch with a bodyguard of sailors, puffed up the steep steps from the little jetty and paid the lady of the manor an agreeable visit.

Those concrete steps up which His Majesty came panting had been the cause of a local contretemps. Bernhardt had had them constructed to serve as an easy access to a little beach below. When the mayor learned about their going up, he called on Madame Sarah in a state of agitation and protested that they constituted a menace to the island if not a threat to France itself. To her astonished, "Why?" he answered, "They'll facilitate the landing of the enemy." In still greater astonishment she demanded to know what enemy and the little man replied, "Why, the English navy, of course."

Usually in residence for the summer would be some worshipful girl of nineteen or twenty, a budding actress, painter or musician, in whom the great lady was interested as a protégée or, as she put it in her expansive fashion, her "adopted daughter." For a year or two a person named Saryta, an actress, served as volunteer secretary, errand runner and happy slave. It was said that Saryta was the daughter of Jeanne Bernhardt. The identity of her father seems not to have mattered. She was a strange little thing who tripped restlessly about on high heels, smoked incessantly and seldom talked. The young woman who became practically a fixture of Sarah's household was Suzanne Seylor. A well-born girl from the provinces, she had come to Paris, starry-eyed to go on the stage, had found a job in the Bernhardt company and had stayed on as a permanent member both of that corps and of the actress' home entourage. She lived in the boulevard Péreire house as well as the Belle-Isle manor, accompanied Madame Sarah on tour, taking smaller roles in some plays and the rest of the time acting as companion, secretary, courier and permanent lady-in-waiting.

Sarah Bernhardt loved the company of young people. It stimulated her to hear of their interests, to share their enthusiasms. At Belle-Isle to watch them running on the tennis court, diving into the clear water or setting out in a sailboat against a stout wind gave her a wistful pleasure during the years when her torturing knee was forcing her closer and closer to immobility.

Two teen-age visitors who spent several summers at the Fort des Poulains were the Rueff sisters. They came from a Dutch family prominent in the musical and artistic circles of London and their parents were close friends of Madame Sarah. Suze has left us some happy glimpses of the actress' rural routine, as has Yvonne Lanco, another young visitor at the time.

Usually Madame Sarah rose at six and, gun over shoulder, went out onto the promontory to shoot ducks or, failing any game birds, she'd bring down a seagull just for the hell of it, which does seem rather deplorable sportsmanship. One author wrote of arriving for a visit via the early morning boat from Quiberon, approaching the Fort past a formidable guard of two immense ceramic pelicans and crossing the drawbridge just as the chatelaine of the keep emerged dressed in fisherman's jacket and pants, a white beret on her touseled hair, her bare feet in coarse espadrilles. She was armed with a shotgun and accompanied by two colossal mastiffs and a tiny Negro boy. By way of a greeting she fired the gun into the air, a seagull fell and the little blackamoor retrieved it.

Mornings were spent in whatever pursuit each guest fancied. The artists painted, the writers wrote, the musicians practiced, the sports-minded sailed, swam or rode shaggy little ponies about the windswept island. Sarah herself might work on some project in her studio or take a bath in seaweed, which was thought to be highly salubrious. Or perhaps, accompanied by a number of dogs, she'd go for a walk along the path that led through the cyclopean rocks out onto the high promontory overlooking the sea, always using a stout cane on which she became more and more dependent. Eventually she had iron hand rails installed along the steep stretches and at one point a resting place carved out of the rock. This became known as "Sarah Bernhardt's armchair" and is still a visiting site for island tourists.

Often she would organize a shrimping expedition. Net in hand, wearing a great flopping hat anchored by a flowing white veil, her skirts looped up above her knees, she'd wade out into the chilly water and often return with a good haul for lunch.

Her menus were delicious and as carefully planned as those in her Paris house. Attractively served on gay Brittany plates, the food was mainly local produce, much of it from her own estate. For she had purchased the neighboring farm of Penhoët, which provided her with eggs, milk, chicken and butter — although occasionally she'd take it into her head to make her own butter, or, to be more precise, persuade a compliant guest or two to work the churn to the point of exhaustion. She grew her own potatoes and fresh vegetables, also a fair supply of wheat, oats and barley, to be ground at a local mill. She owned a few sheep. There was also a small herd of cattle which she thought it picturesque to have pastured in a nearby field until the guests looked out one day to behold Louise Abbéma, who, wearing a red jacket, had strolled into the enclosure and was barely making it to the opposite fence ahead of an onrushing bull.

That most significant of all French repasts, the midday meal, would be served promptly at one. Once in a while there would be a picnic by the shore or under trees in a meadow. These were no torturous occasions when sitting on the ground one consumed dry sandwiches, gray hard-boiled eggs, sand and small insect life. At a Bernhardt *pique-nique* wooden tables and chairs would have been set up, plates, cutlery and wine glasses laid out and the food, piping hot, would be brought out by farm wagon at exactly the proper hour. Every lunch whether indoors or al fresco would automatically be followed by the mass siesta in the "Sarahtorium." When she'd done with her hour of murmuring to the world at large that she was sleeping, she'd come out from her doze with the bound of a fireman at the first sound of the alarm and order everyone to the tennis court.

Sarah Bernhardt's tennis game had its own rules and they were hardly those of the International Tennis Association. It was an unwritten law that her side had to win. When it came to any game, for that matter, she had to be the winner or else go into the sulking of a neurotically spoiled child. She was a bad loser and the first to admit that she frequently cheated at cards. "But," she'd say, flashing that electrifying smile, "since I'm frank about cheating, it can't be real cheating, can it?" In tennis she always played doubles, taking a stand whenever possible close to the net. Any return balls had to be placed well within her reach, otherwise she'd throw down her racquet and walk off the court. Although more and more hindered by her knee, her enthusiasm remained unmodified. Even up to a few years before her amputation, she'd have herself wheeled to the tennis court and, barely able to totter, take her stand at the net, and the opposing players always saw to it that Madame Sarah won her set.

Evenings at Belle-Isle were simple and relaxed. One played cards or dominoes, sometimes there were charades, often childish games and always good talk. Occasionally a singer or pianist might feel inclined to perform or a poet to read aloud his latest verses.

Reynaldo Hahn, who as a young man was a frequent guest at Belle-Isle, tells of one evening when Sarah jumped up, pushed him off the piano stool and asked if he'd care to hear her one musical composition. This was a terrible little piece called "The Dance of the Bears" which she'd made up to amuse Maurice when he was a child. "You see?" she said with pride, "the left hand doesn't move at all. It just keeps on repeating the same notes."

Hahn remembers another evening when he happened to start playing and humming the *Habañera* from Carmen. Maurice seized his mother's scarf and went into a Spanish dance, his two small daughters imitating him. Clairin grabbed up a fat lady guest and whirled her madly about the room, while old Geoffroy wheezed about in a wild fandango. It ended up with everyone going into convulsions of laughter. "We hold our sides, we moan. Sarah, her head in her hands, weeps with laughter, hiccoughs, sobs. She gasps and lies back, her eyes closed, palms down, then is once more doubled up with glee."

Sometimes when the tide was right, they would all go down to the shore to watch the fishermen haul in their nets filled with a glimmering, slithering haul. On moonlight nights when the sea was tranquil, Sarah would spend a full hour out on the rocky point, drinking in the soft air, the view and the immense peace. Yvonne Lanco says that "her friends kept silent and she, dressed in white, made one think of a Druid priestess listening to the waves."

With all this relaxation, the Bernhardt compulsion for work did not slacken. She was continually reading new plays or going over old ones. Maurice Baring, who paid her a visit in 1901, reports that at the time she was studying a Shakespearean role in English and that he's not sure that it wasn't Romeo! Maybe he was afraid to find out.

At times she'd concentrate on her sculpture. One year she

modeled some "art nouveau" ornaments shaped like flowers and small beasts. They were subsequently cast in metal and exhibited at the 1900 Paris Exposition. It is said that Lalique copied some of these for his jewelry. She made a model for a small paperweight in the form of a fish, had it copied in gold with eyes of opal and gave it to Rostand. Even after she was confined to a wheel chair, she had to find outlet for her energies and started modeling four statues intended to be likenesses of Maurice, his wife, Simone and Lysiane, which she wanted placed about her tomb. That mournful resting place, she designated to be out on a favorite promontory. The request, as is known, was not carried out, and Sarah Bernhardt today lies in Père Lachaise.

The island folk adored this woman. They called her "La Bonne Dame" and with reason. Whenever she drove through the small village, they came out in droves to greet her. She was always laden with cakes and preserves to distribute among the inhabitants and large bags full of hard candies for the children. She chatted with the farmers and fishermen, inquired after their welfare, and her concern was genuine. She had only to hear of a ship's master whose cargo had been ruined in a storm or a fisherman who'd lost his nets or his lobster pots and she'd dive into her purse to help him out, and she paid visits of condolence to every family who might have lost a man at sea.

The mayor of the little town was also the local priest and great would be his astonishment on those rare occasions when "La Bonne Dame" showed up for mass. Bernhardt was an enthusiastic but careless Catholic. But she loved the simplicity of the little village church and spoke often of being moved during the "Pardon" services by the sight of the bowed heads of the young Breton girls and their vulnerable necks below the white native bonnets all rising and falling in rhythm.

After service the congregation would crowd about her carriage. Yvonne Lanco tells of one small boy who was lifted up onto his father's shoulder to see the great lady. The child stared at the strange personage, who by then was well advanced in years, at her yards of white veiling which protected the made-up face from the sun, and piped out, "Is that Mme. Sarah Bernhardt? Why she's ugly!" Sarah burst out laughing and pressing a gold piece into the child's grubby little hand said, "That's for telling me the truth!"

Even in Paris the Belle-Islanders were in her thoughts. The winter of 1911 was a cruel one with bitter cold and innumerable storms, disastrous to the fishing fleet. She organized a large benefit performance, pressed the leading stars of the theatre to take part and cleared a vast sum which she sent to the local *Syndicat* for distribution among the needy.

Tourists were frequently coming over to the island. They would gather on a certain hill that commanded a good view of the Bernhardt property and stare through field and opera glasses hoping to catch a glimpse of the great actress. Sometimes an obliging lady guest would manage to disperse them by putting on her hostess' hat, swathing herself in white scarves and waving briefly from an upper window and the group would go away satisfied.

Some five hundred meters across from the Fort was a large manor house belonging to a local baron. Shortly before the First World War the baron died and a promoter took it over to turn into a twenty-room hotel. Horrified at the prospect of a stream of summer vacationers cluttering up the primitive little island, Sarah purchased the building from the owner, a move doubtless counted on by the man to begin with, and turned it into a further residence. She also bought up all the land within view to protect the property, sinking in all about four million francs into this Brittany establishment. Then in 1922, obeying one of her quick decisions, she sold the whole place without a quaver of sentimental regret. Even at seventy-eight, this indomitable woman never looked backward.

GRAND WORLD TOUR
1891–1893

Repertoire
Adrienne Lecouvreur
Cléopâtre
La Dame aux Camélias
Fédora
Froufrou
Jeanne d'Arc
Le Maître des Forges
On ne Badine pas avec l'Amour
Caroline Blanchard
Théodora
La Tosca
Gringoire

February, 1891	New York	*May*	Honolulu
March	Boston		Samoa
	Washington		Aukland
	Philadelphia		Sydney
	New Haven	*June*	Melbourne
	Norwich		Adelaide
April	Albany	*July*	Sydney
	Rochester		
	Syracuse	*August*	Sydney
	Montreal		Aukland
	Detroit		Tutuila
	Indianapolis		Honolulu
	St. Louis	*September*	San Francisco
	Denver		Los Angeles
	San Francisco		Fresno

September	Portland	February	Forth Worth
	Vancouver		Dallas
	Tacoma		Houston
	Seattle		Galveston
	Spokane		New Orleans
	Butte		Memphis
	Duluth		St. Louis
	Minneapolis		Omaha
October	St. Paul		Sioux City
	Chicago		Minneapolis
	Louisville		St. Paul
	Cincinnati	March	Chicago
	Dayton		Milwaukee
	Columbus		Grand Rapids
	Detroit		Saganaw
	Toronto		Toledo
	Niagara		Detroit
	Buffalo		Cleveland
November	New York		Akron
			Buffalo
December	Philadelphia		Pittsburgh
	New York		
	Providence	April	Brooklyn
	Worcester		Philadelphia
	New Haven		Boston
	Springfield		Winesburg
	Utica		New York
	Albany	May 1–23	Paris
January, 1892	Montreal	June and July	London
	Washington		
	Richmond	August	Paris
	Norfolk		Brussels
	Charleston	September	Brussels
	Savannah		Charleroi
	Atlanta		Antwerp, Ostend
	Chattanooga		Lille
	Macon		Liège
	Mobile		Antwerp
	Meridian		Gand

September	Roubaix	*March*	Lyon
	Amsterdam		Turin
	Utrecht		Milan
	The Hague		Geneva
	Rotterdam		Paris
	Haarlem	*April*	Budapest
October	Namur		Bucharest
	Antwerp		Galatz
	Luxembourg		Sulina
	Nancy		Varna
	Zurich		Constantinople
	Prague		Athens
	Varsovic	*May*	Marseilles
November	St. Petersburg		Toulon
	Moscow		Avignon
December	Moscow		Montpellier
	Krakow		Gette
	Kief		Marbonne
	Odessa		Barcelona
	Lemberg		Perpignan
	Kralow		Toulon
January, 1893	Vienna		Bordeaux
	Trieste		Lisbon
	Venice	*June*	Rio de Janeiro
	Bologna	*July*	São Paolo
	Florence		Santos
	Rome		Buenos Aires
	Naples	*August*	Montevideo
February	Palermo	*September*	Rio de Janeiro
	Monte Carlo		Dakar
	Nice		Lisbon
	Cannes		Bordeaux
	San Remo		
	Marseilles	Home September 29, 1893	

I2.

~~~~~~~~~~~~~~~~~~~~~~~~~~~~~~~

LATTER-DAY MIRACLES

NEW PRODUCTIONS followed one another at the Théâtre Sarah Bernhardt, among them *Francesca da Rimini* by Marion Crawford and Marcel Schwob, Daudet's *Sapho* and a spectacular French Revolution drama by Paul Hervieu called *Théroigne de Méricourt*. There was one ghastly mishap in the way of a dreadful adaptation of *Werther* by Pierre de Courcelle, a second-rate writer of novels and melodramas. In this disaster Sarah portrayed Goethe's melancholy hero to empty seats for thirteen dismal performances. It is best not to dwell on the subject.

In 1903 came the last "Two S's" show piece, *La Sorcière*, a somber drama typical of what Shaw called "the claptraps which Sardou contrives for her": slickly skillful dialogue, unreal characters, preposterous situations and enthralling theatre. The setting was Toledo at the time of the Spanish Inquisition, and Sarah's written-to-measure role was that of Zoraya, a Moorish gypsy accused of sorcery and condemned by the Holy Office to the stake. It offered her a chance to put on what Shaw again called "the whole Bernhardtian range of sensational effects . . . effects so enormously popular and lucrative that, though their production is hardly more of a fine art than lion-taming, few women who are able for them can resist the temptation to devote their lives to them." De Max as Cardinal Ximenes, the Grand Inquisitor, was fiendishly magnificent and *La Sorcière* had a long run.

Not content with playing eight performances a week, this fifty-nine-year-old woman decided to put on some extra *matinées classi-*

ques. One was of Racine's *Andromache,* and in this she alternated her roles, playing Andromache one week and Hermione the next, and playing them both superbly.

The most imaginatively re-created classic was Racine's seldom seen *Esther.* The piece had been written in 1684 by order of Madame de Maintenon. Racine who, after writing *Phèdre,* had fallen prey to qualms of conscience over what his enemies called "the wicked incestuousness" of that drama, went into an unproductive period of brooding piety from which he was eventually roused by Madame de Maintenon, who commissioned him to write a play on a biblical subject. That devout morganatic wife of Louis XIV had founded the Saint Cyr Academy for young girls, a charitable and religious institution for the education of the daughters of impoverished noble families. She wanted a play suitable for the students to perform, and *Esther* was the result. Bernhardt revived it in the manner of its first production with sets taken from seventeenth-century prints and the incidental music originally composed for it by Moreau. De Max as Louis XIV and whoever impersonated Madame de Maintenon came on with a retinue of courtiers, took their places as spectators and the play was performed before them. All the parts, even the male ones, were taken by young actresses, and at one side a group of small girls from a nearby orphanage made up a touching chorus. Sarah herself acted not the title role but that of Assuérus, King of Persia, and she did so in the endearingly awkward manner of a schoolgirl trying her valiant best to give an authentic impression of a bearded potentate. The over-all effect was charming and the *Esther* matinees were repeatd several times.

In spite of these artistic triumphs, the Théâtre Sarah Bernhardt was by no means playing to capacity. The Paris public, that "sacred monster," continued to blow hot and cold. To them she was still "their Sarah" but they were beginning to take her for granted. At the same time, they resented her successes in foreign countries, overlooking the fact that those successes were redounding to their own country's credit. For years they ignored her value as an ambassadress. James Agate's sister May said, "Only when her health was beginning to fail and they felt she was slipping from their grasp did they awaken to the fact that she had done more for France than all their diplomats put together."

That public for some inexplicable reason especially resented her great London following. The possessiveness the British felt about France's leading actress struck them as presumptuous. Notwithstanding the objections of her compatriots Sarah Bernhardt went to perfidious Albion year after year and nearly always played to packed houses. When Madame Sarah came to town during the season, it was An Event, like the pantomimes during the Christmas holidays. Her increasing age seemed to bother no one. In 1904 Max Beerbohm notes, "She is still lightly triumphant over time." There was an excitement about going to see her. Audiences arrived at the theatre in states of anticipatory elation and waited breathlessly for the play to begin and the moment when "The Divine" would make her entrance. The critic and essayist Arthur Symons said, "One's pulses beat feverishly before the curtain had risen; there was a kind of obscure sensation of peril, such as one feels when the lioness leaps into the cage."

And yet not everyone continued to fall under the Bernhardt spell. Sarah by now had lost her excessive thinness. Due to an abdominal operation which had weakened her stomach muscles she had developed a definite little paunch which she did nothing to conceal as she refused ever to wear a corset. Arnold Bennett complained in his Journal as early as 1896:

> This season she is positively obese. But most of the women in her company have waists even larger than hers. Query: is this an accident or has she carefully engineered it?

Bennett of course, like Shaw, was no "Saradorer" and he was exaggerating preposterously. Sarah was thick in the middle, but her arms and upper torso retained the same willowy grace.

The talk of the 1905 London season was Maeterlinck's *Pelléas and Mélisande*, in which Sarah Bernhardt played the romantic hero and Mrs. Patrick Campbell the lovelorn heroine, and the talk was generally good. Maeterlinck was *the* thing at the time with the European and British intelligentsia. Octave Mirbeau hailed him as the Belgian Shakespeare and London critics read obscure meanings into his dream-filled symbolist dramas. Mrs. Patrick Campbell had already played Mélisande in the English version. For this production she had to learn the part in French, and she played it remarkably well with hardly a trace of accent. The press was excellent with the exception of one Dublin critic whose entire review was: "Mrs. Campbell played Mélisande, Mme. Bernhardt Pelléas; they are both old enough to know better." Max Beerbohm, again offended at Bernhardt's appearing as a man, refused to see the show saying, "Sarah is a woman and Mrs. Campbell is an Englishwoman and by these facts such a performance is ruled out of the sphere of art into the sphere of sensationalism. If Maeterlinck were a sensationalist that would not matter."

The play had a good London run and in the course of an ensuing tour of the British provinces, the two stars struck up a joyous and lasting friendship. Sarah warmed to Stella Campbell's expansive and independent nature. She was endlessly amused by her blunt, often outrageous remarks. And Mrs. Pat saw beneath Sarah's complex exterior the essentially human woman. They felt completely relaxed in each other's company. At times they behaved like giddy schoolgirls. On one occasion Stella, seeing a tobacco pouch shaped like a fish in a shop window, bought the thing, painted it in lurid colors and that evening prior to the scene when the two lovers are leaning over the well and Mélisande's wedding ring falls into the supposed water, she placed it on the floor at the bottom of the stage well. The moment came, Sarah immediately spotted the dreadful-looking fish and, without batting an eye, started an improvisation about *"ces poissons là"* that was worthy of Maeterlinck himself. When an actor plays a trick on another, often as not it's he who breaks up and not his victim. Mrs. Pat, the stately, the classical beauty, was so convulsed by her own prank she was unable for minutes to utter a line. A few nights later during the Cave scene when Pelléas guides Mélisande over the rock, Sarah broke a raw egg into Stella's outstretched hand. In addition to the egg, she broke herself up quite hopelessly. Her company was stunned. Madame had never tolerated, much less played, any tricks on stage. They told her co-star with awed solemnity, "She must love you very, very much."

She did and Mrs. Pat loved her. In her memoirs the latter wrote, "The world knows her genius and her colossal courage; but not everyone knows the thought and affection she has always ready in her heart for her friends."

Shortly before this joint venture, Bernhardt had found herself in one of her not infrequent states of needing money. She had appealed to Mrs. Pat, who, although she had only a hundred pounds in the bank at the time, sent the entire amount to Sarah. When *Pelléas and Mélisande* was well launched, after one matinee Mrs. Pat was receiving callers when Madame Sarah walked into her dressing room and in front of the unknown visitors, presented her with a small silver casket which proved to contain her full debt all in five-pound notes.

Throughout the ensuing years, the two kept up an affectionate if intermittent correspondence. In 1916, when Mrs. Campbell was in the United States, she received a cable from Bordeaux:

> Doctor will cut off my leg next Monday. Am very happy. Kisses all my heart.
>
> Sarah Bernhardt.

In 1905–1906 there was another trip to the United States, announced in advance as "The Farewell American Tour of Mme. Sarah Bernhardt." (There were to be three subsequent "Farewell American Tours.") The announcement was made by her new producers, those enterprising and then young Shubert brothers,

Sam Lee and Jake. The tour was booked for the South and the Southwest and not much later the Shuberts issued the further announcement that "Madame Bernhardt will play Texas in tents." This was a bold and desperate move on the part of the Shuberts, for they were bucking the all-powerful Theatrical Syndicate which was composed of the three partnerships, Klaw and Erlanger, Frohman and Hayman, Nixon and Zimmerman, a mighty trust that had a stranglehold on most of the theatres and opera houses throughout the country. The Syndicate dictated what companies were going to play what towns in which theatres, and specified the duration of each stand. They flatly refused to allow "The Bernhardt" to appear in any of their theatres or opera houses except under their auspices and the Shuberts flatly replied very well, she'd appear in other auditoriums even if they had to be make-shift ones. Consequently she played Atlanta, Augusta, Savannah, Tampa and Jacksonville in skating rinks.

Then the company set out for Texas. Some time previously the Shuberts had approached their star and not without trepidation. They explained to her that due to the Syndicate, there was no available theatre in Texas. Even the skating rinks would be closed to them and they came forward with the astonishing proposition that she play under canvas. To their amazement she was childishly delighted with the prospect. It would be an adventure, she said, a genuine "Yankee" adventure — not that the Lone Star State exactly came within Yankee domain.

A special round-top was constructed for them in Kansas City. It had a hundred-and-fifty-foot spread and could accommodate four thousand five hundred spectators. The stage was made in movable sections, the seats folded up, the dressing rooms were like canvas bath houses and there were any amount of further circus inconveniences. It was all like a Barnum and Bailey show. At each stand, the tent would be set up on some local fair grounds. Hastily laid out tracks led from the nearest railroad lines and special trains bringing audiences from all over the state would draw up alongside

"The Bernhardt Tent." Parked on a nearby siding was the company train which most of the time served to house actors and personnel.

It was tough going for everyone. Living quarters were the essence of discomfort and theatrical facilities primitive in the extreme. Weather was always playing alarming competition. Sometimes rain pelted down on the taut white-top with the noise of a hundred snare drums. At other times the savage wind of a Texas "Norther" would tear loose the tent flaps. Actors had to shout themselves hoarse and audiences had to strain to hear the words few of them remotely understood. On one occasion a drunken rancher upon being refused admission knocked down a policeman barring his way, fired off his six-shooter and yelled, "I'm gonna see this Bernhardt gal an' her song-and-dance act better be good!" Players and public somehow survived the ordeal. The Shuberts and their star made a mint of money and Bernhardt's "Yankee adventure" reaped a spread of publicity that reached even the European press.

From Texas they traveled to the West Coast. The Syndicate relaxed their stranglehold and they played legitimate theatres in San Diego and Los Angeles. San Francisco, still in smouldering ruins from the great Fire, was unplayable but the earthquake had not crossed the Bay and they performed in the Greek open-air theatre at Berkeley. Sarah herself volunteered to give a recital for the prisoners of San Quentin. What she performed was a lugubrious little item entitled "A Christmas Night during the Terror," which hardly seems a cheery selection. She was greatly moved by the sight of the row after row of men in black-striped uniforms. What the men in black-striped uniforms thought of the strangely exotic-looking woman who acted for them in an incomprehensible language has not been handed down in the annals of San Quentin.

Before leaving the country, Bernhardt had a short New York engagement at the Lyric Theatre. Her performances played to capacity and the daily box-office line-up stretched clear to 6th Avenue. New York welcomed back "The Bernhardt" and invitations poured in. Hostesses of the Four Hundred who twenty-five years previously had closed their doors to the notorious French actress now fought to entice The Divine into their drawing rooms. Stage-door fans were more clamouring than ever and on one or two occasions she was literally mobbed.

In an unguarded moment she had accepted an invitation to be guest of honor at a reception given by the pupils of the Francis Fisher Powers School of Acting. It was to be held in a Carnegie Hall studio and, being familiar with the harsh lighting of most studios, the cautious actress had visited the place the day before, arranged for a red shawl to be stretched across the dingy glass of the skylight and stipulated that the only illumination come from pink-shaded candles. The effect was becoming in the extreme and the reception started off well enough. The great tragedienne, after receiving an enormous bouquet, addressed a few words of advice to the prospective young actresses, who then came up timidly one by one to shake her hand. The chaos started when one girl asked for a flower from her bouquet. The next two followed suit, then the rest, like maniacal harpies, descended upon the bouquet and completely demolished it. Those who failed to come off with a flower descended upon Madame Sarah herself. They snatched pins out of her hair, tore bits from her voluminous veiling and tried to rip off the ruffle of her silk petticoat. Those in authority were unable to restore order and not until the arrival of the building janitor and the corner policeman was the besieged woman able to make an escape.

The battered chamois bag and the brass-bound strong box were filled to bursting point with American gold pieces when she drove to the pier to catch the ship for France. She was in a fever to get back to Paris "to embrace my son," she told a reporter, and doubtless to part with a fair number of those gold coins in order to meet his debts, an item she didn't volunteer to tell. She was also in a fever to get back to work in her own theatre. Even if she made far less money there than on her tours, even if the French critics were more severe than the foreign gentlemen of the press, to play in her native city was a challenge and at sixty-two she still thrived on challenges. "Paris is a springboard," she said. "I come back to get a fresh *élan*."

The challenge grew more formidable with each passing year. Other and younger actresses with newer attributes had already arrived at the fore in the French theatre. There was the elegant Julia Bartet, who was such a fashion-plate it was said, "Hand Bartet Racine and she'll give you back Paquin," the sparkling Gabrielle Réjane, who after her delicious *Mme. Sans-gêne* had all Paris at her feet, the seductive Jeanne Granier, "her bosom swollen with talent," who was one of the charmers in whom the Prince of Wales was "interested." They might have played a powerful opposition, but Sarah Bernhardt had long established herself in a position apart and exalted. The playwright Robert de Flers declared, "She is no longer an actress. It would be as absurd to assign her a place on the roster of French actresses as to list Molière among our dramatic writers. Like the author of *Le Misanthrope*, Sarah is beyond all classification."

The Paris public recognized her unique value and in 1907 there was held another "Journée Sarah Bernhardt." Not as elaborate as the great celebration in 1896, this consisted of a gala held at the Théâtre Femina. Speeches were made, poems read, short scenes acted, floral wreaths presented and further distinguished if somewhat tiresome tributes manifested. People lined the streets as she rode in state to this function in an open flower-blanketed Panhard-Levassor which was pulled by a gaily decked horse as a precautionary measure against a possible breakdown of the motor.

As the leading actress of France, public and press every few years clamored for her to return to the Comédie Française. The foreign critics periodically deplored her wasting her great talents with generally inferior plays on her incessant tours. A. B. Walkley kept begging her to repent and make a prodigal's return to the fold, and as early as 1896 G. B. Shaw had complained:

I confess I regard with certain jealousy the extent to which this ex-artist, having deliberately exercised her unquestioned right to step down from the national theatre in which she became famous to posture in a travelling show, is still permitted the privileges and courtesies proper to her former rank. . . . Madame Bernhardt has elected to go round the world pretending to kill people with hatchets and hairpins, and making, I presume, heaps of money. I wish her every success; but I shall certainly not treat her as a dramatic artist of the first rank unless she pays me well for it. As a self-respecting critic I decline to be bought for nothing.

Bernhardt turned a deaf ear to these pleas. The memories of her Français days were not among her happiest. Moreover, she took a dim view of the players and *sociétaires* who were the current occupants of the House of Molière. She felt they were too self-satisfied, too stultified by their overly sanctified tradition. One afternoon she happened to be driving past the stage door at the hour a matinee was letting out. Louis Verneuil was with her and she asked him the meaning of the large crowd that was standing about. Verneuil said they were waiting for the Français actors to come out. "What for?" said Sarah, "to hiss them?"

For a brief time Madame Sarah taught at the Conservatoire but soon gave it up. She found that venerable Institute, like the Comédie Française, too tradition-bound. Its conventional routines, she claimed, nipped any pupil's spontaneity in the bud. Instead she formed her own classes, teaching a limited number of young aspirants and, with true French economy, utilizing them as extras and bit players at no pay. James Agate's sister May, who as a girl got her theatre training in one of the classes, wrote:

There was magic in Madame Sarah's teaching as in herself . . . I wonder what this magic was. How did she convey her knowledge of acting to us? We did no exercises, read no tomes, absorbed no conventions. In fact "la Tradition" (words spoken by her with an infinite scorn) was her *bête noire*. She admitted nothing that did not spring from truth and sincerity.

She was lavish with encouragement to a pupil with intelligence and bluntly harsh to a stupid one. She told one cocky youth: "If there were a single moment in your handling of that speech which showed you had thought about what it means, if there were the germ of an idea you were trying to convey, I would say 'That's good, but it can be better.' As it is, you have been taught like that because it has been recited like that for generations. But it won't do . . . go home and next time bring me back something which *means something*." Bernhardt would undoubtedly have been contemptuous of the theorizing of some of our present-day schools of acting. Once when she told a certain aspirant to play a short scene in a certain fashion, the young thing put up an objection saying, "I don't feel it that way, Madame Sarah, therefore I can't do it that way." To which Madame quickly and firmly rejoined, "If you're going to be an actress, my girl, you've got to be able to do it that way or any other way!"

In addition to these classes, Bernhardt put on special matinees of poetry readings in her theatre, a project she shared with the symbolist poet Gustave Kahn, and that veteran Parnassian, Catulle Mendès. These were distinguished, slightly eclectic occasions when actors and authors came out and read their choice selections. Players of the old school declaimed Victor Hugo and Lamartine. That excellent actor Firmin Gémier, who was by then running the Odéon, recited the light *Histoires Naturelles* from the humorous pen of Jules Renard or the ironical *vers libre* of Jules Laforgue. Edouard de Max, with his tormented allure of a fallen angel, intoned the mysterious stanzas of Baudelaire or Poe. And Sarah herself took part. Her entrances on these occasions were worth the price of admission. She'd come on through a doorway center back, pausing for several seconds with one hand held high leaning on the door frame for support, wearing one of her pale-colored "street dresses" which on her looked like a classic robe. The actress Beatrix Dussanne of the Comédie Française, who has written much about the French theatre, often watched those entrances:

The acclamations that greet her give her ample time to come down toward the footlights. Her eye always clear, ever ready to spark, wheedling and triumphant, her head bent to one side over her clasped hands, then her arms suddenly stretched forth in enthusiastic oblation . . . one feels that she is encased in her formulas for seduction as in a long worn garment.

These matinees were highly distinguished and, like most such projects, highly unprofitable.

More profitable, if not all of them were as highly distinguished, were the further productions put on at the Théâtre Sarah Bernhardt. Her choice of plays was based upon the variety of roles they offered her. In Lavedan's *Varennes* she appeared as Marie Antoinette. In Catulle Mendès' *La Vierge d'Avila*, though it was hardly a case of type casting, she impersonated Saint Theresa. Not content with Scribe and Legouvé's *Adrienne Lecouvreur*, she dramatized her own version of that story. Inept drama in six interminable acts though it was, she was none the less pleased with it and kept it in her repertory.* In 1907 she produced *Les Bouffons* by Zamacoïs. In this romantic fantasy she played a hunchback jester named Jacasse who wins the heart of a lovely princess then in the end proves that he himself is none other than a prince in disguise and, flinging off his cloak along with his hump, stands before her handsome and dauntless. A childish contrivance that might have come out of a Perrault fairy tale, but the lines had poetic appeal and Sarah played the hunchback Prince Charming with the grace of a Renaissance ballad singer.

Bernhardt was to interpret further masculine roles: In a special benefit performance she played the Poet in Alfred de Musset's *Nuit de Mai* opposite Julia Bartet's Muse, in Richepin's adaptation of Sem Benelli's *La Beffa* she impersonated a young Florentine, and

---

* About the same time she wrote another play called *Un Coeur d'Homme* with no role in it for herself. Some manager was short-sighted enough to produce this at the Théâtre des Arts, where after three lamentable performances it mercifully floundered. Of the reviewers the critic of the *Journal des Débats* was the kindest, saying simply, "Is Ingres any the less great for having tried to take up the violin?"

in a horrendous opus called *Judas* written by an American named John de Kay, she appeared as that unfortunate apostle and that whole affair was unfortunate. She might have done yet another, for Rostand was said to have been working on his own version of *Faust* with Sarah in mind for Mephisto when the project was cut short by his death.

A simple yet deeply moving play was done in 1909. This was Emile Moreau's *Procès de Jeanne d'Arc*, which dealt with the trial and martyrdom of Joan of Arc. It was quite a scholarly piece, the material having been based on historical fact and authentic documents. Sarah Bernhardt was by then sixty-five and people shook their heads over the rash audacity of her attempting to give any impression of a girl of nineteen. On opening night audience and critics came to scoff. They remained to wonder. She appeared in only two acts but when she was on she created for those who saw her emotions which almost amounted to a mystical experience. She seemed the embodiment of the Maid of Lorraine, a rough peasant yet a visionary, staunchly devout, naïvely innocent and touchingly young. One particularly moving moment came during the tribunal scene, when Joan after being led in and, requesting that the heavy iron fetters be removed from her aching wrists, stood to face her accusers. The Grand Inquisitor started off with the routine questions regarding name and age.

"*Quel est ton nom?*"

"*Jeanne,*" she replied.

"*Ton age?*"

Then, quietly turning toward the audience and in a voice clear as spring water she answered:

"*Dix-neuf ans.*"

There was a gasp from the house. Not a gasp of incredulity but one of wonder and admiration, then breathless silence for a moment and after that thunders of applause. The same thing happened every time she played this scene. The age discrepancy between actress and character wasn't noticed. Even when she was really old and minus a leg, making Music Hall appearances whenever she re-enacted this amazing moment, that latter-day miracle of Saint Joan took place.

The *Procès de Jeanne d'Arc* had such religious and patriotic appeal that the educational authorities were urged to order all schools to close in turn for one afternoon so that the pupils might attend a matinee and see their national actress reincarnate their national heroine. (Joan was not yet their national saint.)

At sixty-five Madame Sarah continued to spend twelve, sometimes fourteen hours a day in her theatre, rehearsing her repertory, auditioning players, teaching her pupils, reading scripts, consulting with her English wig-maker or her stage designer whose paper models for forthcoming sets she'd completely rearrange, snipping bits off with a pair of scissors here and placing them there to the despair of the designer and the improvement of the set. In spite of the strain on her knee she'd climb up to the fitting rooms on the fifth floor to oversee the progress of costumes and encourage the seamstresses or give them hell according to how she found their work.

With all this, she continued to entertain in her backstage dining room with late supper parties or meals between matinees and evening performances. Sometimes, especially as her leg grew worse, she'd spare herself the stairs to her dining room and hold a luncheon on the stage itself. Hostess and guests would sit at some large prop table placed amid a setting of scenery especially put up by apparently willing stage hands who, having yet to be unionized, didn't know the meaning of overtime. The scenic effects varied according to the season. In winter they might dine in one of the sunny *Cléopâtre* sets, in hot weather the surroundings might be suggestive of cold and snow.

In her boulevard Péreire *hôtel* her dinners and luncheons were kept up as lavishly as they had been for the last twenty years. Each meal was a banquet over which she presided like royalty on a sort of coronation chair at the head of a table that was heaped with flowers summer and winter. At her place was a chiseled gold goblet of Holy Grail proportions, a gift from the Lord Mayor of London. From this she'd take an occasional sip of champagne. Guests were given several kinds of wine but Madame Sarah's only alcoholic intake was Veuve Cliquot in minute quantities.

Although she herself ate practically nothing, she was exacting about the food that was passed to her guests. She'd taste a morsel or spoonful of every dish, every sauce, every crouton served, and if any item failed to come up to her standard she thought nothing of summoning the cook and berating the poor wretch in front of the present company. It need hardly be stated that Sarah Bernhardt's cooks came and went in a constantly passing parade.

Invitations to meals *chez Sarah* were sought after by many and afforded only to the choice. Her guest lists, still kept by the aging Emile, must have read like pages from an international Who's Who with such names as Clemenceau, d'Annunzio and the politician Aristide Briand. And right out of the *Almanach de Gotha* came repeatedly the name of that extravagant dandy, the Marquis Boni de Castellane, then at the height of his costly glory made possible by the American dollars of his dismal wife Anna Gould. In 1904 Sarah put on a play written by Boni called *Le Festin de la Mort*, which apparently didn't make enough of an impression for any biographer to mention. The United States ambassador Myron T. Herrick was a regular and so, whenever he came to Paris, was Theodore Roosevelt. Bernhardt and Roosevelt had been great friends for years. Her admiration for him was boundless and she announced to one group of acquaintances, "That man and I, together we could rule the world!" Members of her "Court" were ever present and she welcomed rising young artists and writers such as the dancer Ida Rubenstein or the exquisite poetess Anna de Noailles, whose entry into a room has been described as that of "an Oriental princess descending from her palanquin."

For years Pierre Loti had tried to gain entrée into the house on the boulevard Péreire. The gifted and eccentric author had adored "la Divine" ever since he had seen her in *Hernani* at the age of twenty-seven. He was then in the Navy and his cabin on the vessel "Moselle" cruising the Orient was cluttered with photographs of Doña Sol. During the '90's after Loti was well established as a successful novelist, he wrote Madame Sarah a small masterpiece in the form of a letter of admiration which she never bothered to answer and may well have never bothered to read. Then he dedicated a book to her and she paid no attention to that either. One day her major domo announced that a Japanese gentleman was calling and Sarah, her curiosity piqued, told Emile to show him in. The "Japanese gentleman" was Loti in elaborate make-up and kimono. Sarah sent him about his business. Loti finally crashed the gates by having himself rolled up in a magnificent Persian carpet and delivered by two stalwart Arabs as a gift to be laid at the feet of the lady. The Arabs unrolled the heavy cocoon, Loti half smothered emerged, Sarah screamed with laughter, and after that the author of *Madame Chrysanthème* was a regular guest.

As at Belle-Isle, Bernhardt was a gracious hostess and occasionally a childish one. Jules Renard, whose large Journal is a gold mine of *Belle Epoque* chitchat, wrote of their first meeting. He was taken by Rostand and when they arrived luncheon had already started. As they entered the dining room, Madame rose from her chair and "in a voice joyful, young and adorable said, 'Oh, how happy I am! He's just what I thought he'd be, isn't he, Rostand? Monsieur, I am your admirer!'" Renard was like a schoolboy with his first crush. "I already have a great gratitude in my heart for her, a desire to admire, to love her, and the fear of letting myself go." And in another entry he states, "I would follow her to the end of the earth . . . with my wife." At table he sat on the hostess' right and was so awed he couldn't open his mouth even when a serving man took away his napkin. He did everything wrong, ate his meat with his fruit knife and placed his sucked asparagus stems on his knife rest. Conversation got around to the subject of palmistry and Sarah picked up Renard's hand to study it. To his dismay he saw that his nails were rather dirty. Then Maurice Bernhardt upset a vase of flowers inundating Renard with water and at that Sarah dipped her fingers into the spilled water and rubbed his forehead while she screamed with laughter — which for some reason seems to have delighted Renard. After they returned to the fur-strewn salon, their hostess held forth about the things she had always wanted to do — scale mountains, write poetry, compose music. These wistful yearnings were cut short by the entrance of her newest pet, one of four pumas she'd just purchased. It was brought in on the end of a leash and introduced to the guests one at a time. When the creature sniffed at Edmond Haraucourt's watchfob, that poet closed his eyes and appeared to go into deep prayer. After this, two ferocious-looking mastiffs bounded in but turned out to be playful puppies. Renard winds up his account of the day by saying that as he left, he didn't look for his hat (it happened to be on his head) but left serenely carrying away someone else's.

Most of the boulevard Péreire gatherings were gaily informal. It never bothered Madame Sarah if she made any social blunder. On one occasion, realizing that she had placed a prominent banker at table directly opposite his ex-wife, she forestalled any embarassment by announcing cheerfully, "You two have just been divorced, haven't you? What a lot you must have to tell each other!"

Bernhardt's cooks may have come and gone continually, but her other servants seem to have stayed on with unwavering loyalty in spite of their employer's disregard of their paydays. Sometimes she'd be weeks, even months late with their salaries, then she'd give them lump sums with added bonuses as compensation. Her maids must have had their problems. They had to put up with Madame's sudden rages which were invariably followed by baffling gestures of contrition. After screaming at one, even shaking her in violent fury, she'd all at once assume the expression of a repentant child and present her with a brooch, a bracelet or some other expensive and quite unsuitable gewgaw.

Old Emile, the major domo who had come as an eighteen-year-old house boy and had remained for forty-five years, was long past his usefulness. With age he became deaf, somewhat senile, semi-intoxicated and chronically somnolent. He'd take up his post on a chair in the foyer, go into a profound doze and if he were roused to announce some caller, would growl, stretch and shuffle off muttering imprecations. At Belle-Isle Emile was entrusted with the marketing. The old boy would fill the farm wagon with provisions enough to feed a regiment. Much of it subsequently went to waste. More than once when a suspiciously strong-smelling piece of meat was brought to the table, Emile received a well-aimed biff on the head with a flying roll and he'd barely make it into the kitchen before the meat followed the roll. Sarah was well aware of Emile's complete inefficacy but she kept him on like some crotchety old relative with whom she found herself saddled.

Madame Sarah's watchdog for many years was a fussy little bald-headed man with a walrus moustache named Pitou who acted as secretary, courier and general whipping boy. Pitou was exasperating, stubborn and rather idiotic. His lengthy excuses for the innumerable blunders he committed were more irritating than the blunders themselves. Often when his mistress could no longer endure the high-pitched voice explaining ad infinitum some ridiculous oversight, Pitou would be the target for some projectile, a paperweight and once even an inkwell. But Pitou was adept at either dodging or keeping a half-open door between himself and the barrage and all the time he'd continue to explain. Pitou devoted his drab life to Madame Sarah. He argued with her. Sometimes they fought with the spitfire of a couple of tomcats, but he stayed on and she put up with him.

Lysiane Bernhardt tells of the occasion when her grandmother sent the stubborn little man on a special mission to Aix-la-Chappelle for the purpose of delivering a letter by hand to an important functionary of the town. The regular post would have served just as effectively, but now and then Sarah enjoyed making a gesture in eighteenth-century courier style. Pitou boarded a train, got off at Aix and found the house of the functionary, who proved not to be home. At that, he put a stamp on the letter, dropped it in a mail-box and returned to Paris cheerfully confident that his mission had been accomplished.

After Sarah Bernhardt's leg amputation she entrusted Pitou with all her papers: letters, notebooks, contracts and programs, to put in order and file in an expensive cabinet she had purchased for their storage. Pitou spent weeks over the job, then one day proudly informed his employer that everything was in meticulous order, she could peacefully face posterity. Sarah, who had no intentions of facing posterity just yet, ordered him out of the room. When Lysiane was gathering material for her book, *Sarah Bernhardt ma Grand'mère*, directly from "Great" and wanted information about the Seige of Paris and the Odéon *ambulance*, her grandmother called for Pitou to get her diaries and letters written at that period out of the filing cabinet. They should be, she said, under *G* for *Guerre*. After an interminable wait, Pitou returned in a state of extreme agitation and announced that he'd been able to find only Madame's papers relating to the recent 1914 war. Sarah then yelled at him to look under the "A's" for *ambulance*, which proved as fruitless as the "O's" for *Odéon*, or the "B's" for *Bombardements*. Sarah was on the point of hopping into the adjacent library for the purpose of assassinating Pitou when, with a cry of triumph, he appeared brandishing the 1870 documents. "*Mais naturellement!*" he explained, "I had them under the 'M's' for *Malheurs* [misfortunes] along with your fire in the rue Auber, your mother's death, your marriage to M. Damala . . ." His listing was interrupted by a hurtling vase of flowers which, barely missing his head, crashed on the wall beyond, as with infuriating persistence Pitou droned on the dismal category of *Malheurs*.

For all the exasperation he caused her, Madame Sarah seemed to feel the need of Pitou. In Paris he was ever at her beck and call to perform the duties she imposed on him, and stubbornly determined to do them his way. On tour, he aired her dogs, ran countless errands for her and kept her accounts. He looked after her finances. When the chamois bag or the brass-bound strong box came near overflowing with gold coins, it was he who took the surplus to a bank to have exchanged into bills. One time in San Francisco, driving in a taxi from the station up that precipitous hill to the Fairmont Hotel, Madame ordered Pitou to close up a window. Pitou leaped to obey and yanked at the wrong handle, thereby opening one of the doors. Sarah then ordered him to tell the driver to stop, but Pitou stubbornly kept hold of the handle in a frantic struggle to swing the door shut. This ended with him swinging out with the door and landing on the street. The famous strong box also swung out and exploded on the corner of California and Powell and gold coins shot forth rolling every which way. A few disappeared down the open slots for the cable cars. Sarah screamed, Pitou jibbered endless explanations and shopkeepers emerged to help gather up bits of the golden shower.

On sleeper jumps after the star had got to bed, it was Pitou's nightly duty to hear her read the lines of a role. Sometimes she would add a new play to her already formidable repertory and she had an idea that relaxing on her five pillows and drowsily murmuring the words would subconsciously fix them in her memory.

Although it is a matter of record that Sarah Bernhardt was never known to forget a line, she was not beyond interpolating a line of her own if something went wrong in a scene. Once during a performance of *Phèdre* a sudden icy draft blasted across the stage and in perfect Racinian alexandrines she said, "If someone doesn't close that door, I shall come down with pneumonia before the end of the act," then continued letter perfect with the text and the audience never knew the difference. To be sure it was an American audience.

By 1910 the diseased knee was causing her untold anguish, not only in one spot but up and down her entire leg. She described it as "an animal gnawing my nerves and tendons." It hampered her movements on stage and she was frequently obliged to lean for support on furniture, solid pieces of scenery or some steady arm or shoulder. At home she was considerably curtailed in her physical activity.

She started cutting down her menagerie because of her young granddaughters, who came almost daily to visit her and were in the habit of running all over the house. She gave away her pumas as being too dangerous and her monkeys because, as she put it, they were too "exhibitionist."

During their growing years Lysiane and Simone Bernhardt were a constant delight to her and she to them. Impossible as it was for Sarah Bernhardt not to act off stage as well as on, there was no sham to her family devotion and her love for her grandchildren was almost equal to that which she lavished on their father. Several times a week she'd take them for lovely long drives in the Bois, stopping off for an ice at the Cascades. She'd give them picnics in her garden and often entertain them and their playmates after a matinee in her dressing room, delighting their hearts and upsetting their stomachs with babas, petits fours and further delicious in-digestibles sent in from a nearby *pâtisserie*. Sacha Guitry was al-ways invited to Madame Sarah's children's party at Christmas. In his book, *If Memory Serves*, he recalled the fabulous tree blazing with a hundred candles and, around it on the floor, fifty presents for fifty young guests. Sarah would hold out a grab bag from which each child drew a number indicating a present. He also re-called that through some trick of prestidigitation, she always saw to it that Simone and Lysiane pulled numbers for the best presents.

Sacha Guitry often came to young people's luncheons in the boulevard Péreire, as did Edmond Rostand's son Maurice. These were gay occasions during which Madame Sarah kept her small guests amused, often in squeals of mirth. Rostand remembers one child asking Madame if her hair were naturally curly, and Madame pouring a glass of Heidsieck Monopole onto her head to prove that it was.

When Maurice Bernhardt's delicate wife Terka died, Simone and Lysiane moved in to live with "Great." If Sarah was an ar-dently loving grandmother, she was also a good disciplinarian and a stimulating influence in their development. She instilled in them some of her extraordinary energy, taught them never to be idle, always to be creating something with their minds or their hands. During the rare periods when she was not completely tied up with her theatre or a tour, she took them on trips about the country or even as far as Switzerland in her elegant, chugging Daimler — for Bernhardt was an early motor enthusiast. And every evening she'd call on the girls to recount what they had seen and learned during the day.

Simone Bernhardt, the older sister, married an Englishman and Lysiane lived on with "Great." The bond between the two was tender and lasting. Even when she was away on tour Sarah, who seldom answered a social note, wrote her frequently. Excerpts out of a letter written from America to Lysiane, who was traveling in Italy with a chaperone, are characteristic:

My Lysiane,
I am happy to think of you in lovely sunshine and above all, in that atmosphere of beauty which pervades all Italy . . . I regret not being the one to lift the mysterious veil of infinite beauty . . . Take in much with your grave eyes, with your spirit and hold onto it; for it is in the light of beauty that the soul bathes and bathes again ever. Take care not to catch cold in the churches and museums. Keep your furpiece about your neck. Evenings on your friend's little balcony watch the sunsets, they must be magnificent; sketch a bit of what you see in that garden of poetry. Look at the great screen of black cypresses, look down on the little pond so ancient and charming.
My stay here has been admirable, never have I had more triumphal success. I think often of your father, of you of your home and my heart goes out with a bound to you all; I think too of my little ragamuffin so far away and tears come to my eyes . . . Think of your Great who loves you and who waits with impatience for the moment when you spring onto her bed with a lusty "Bon jour." That will be for Belle-Isle.
I hold you to my heart.

Great.

In their zeal to chronicle the eccentric Bernhardt "legend" the biographers are prone to gloss over her human side. After her death the London critic, A. B. Walkley, wrote in the *Times*: "Mme. Bernhardt as I knew her off-stage showed no caprice. She struck me as a sensible, shrewd, kind-hearted woman, with a keen sense of humor and modest for all her fame." To be sure certain obvious gestures of kindness, such as her daily presentation of a coin to the corner street-sweeper, may have been a calculated act. But her consideration for small tradesmen, some of whom she continued to patronize out the sheer charity, was not for the benefit of any public. The local storekeepers loved and respected her. When she gave up painting, the owner of her art supply shop said sadly, "It's not her clientèle I'll miss . . . it's shaking her hand." She could be sincerely solicitous over employees. Once when a stage hand was badly injured by a falling piece of scenery, and a doctor was unavailable until morning, she stayed up all night in the theatre taking care of the man and tending to his wounds with the skill she'd acquired in 1870. One day at a dress rehearsal, she noticed a child who was playing an extra limping painfully and paused to ask him what was the matter. The small boy tearfully replied that one of the new shoes allotted him by the wardrobe mistress was stiff and hurt his foot. Sarah ordered him to take it off and she held up rehearsal a good fifteen minutes while she bent and worked the offending shoe until it was comfortable.

People were continually coming to her for help: former retainers, down-and-out actors, friends who were on their uppers, and they seldom went away empty-handed. She was indulgently accessible to relatives. Suze Rueff was in her dressing room after a matinee when a doddering Dutch woman, some distant cousin, came in to prattle interminably about family connections that Sarah didn't remotely remember. When at long last she rose to leave she looked about at the profusion of flowers and asked if she might have just one rose as a souvenir. Sarah, in relief at getting rid of her, cried, "Take the lot!" piled a massive load onto her outstretched arms, and sent her on her staggering way jibbering ecstatic thanks. When the old girl was out of earshot Sarah said, "She'll sell the whole lot by nightfall."

With age she was becoming more conscientious about promises made. Prior to a London engagement she had promised the Duchess of Newcastle she'd recite on a certain afternoon at a benefit for a children's hospital. Her London manager, unbeknownst to her, had booked a matinee in Wimbledon for the same date, and the house was already sold out. A friend reminded her about her commitment to the Duchess of Newcastle and without a qualm she canceled the Wimbledon date although it would have meant big money to her.

In the London season of 1910 she appeared for the first time in a Music Hall at the Coliseum, playing short scenes from her repertory, and the public flocked to see her. Her English following, loyal as ever, applauded, tossed bouquets, stood outside stage door or hotel entrance to watch her comings and goings. She was still regarded in a magic light as a creature from another world. One contemporary writer, watching her driving in a victoria past Hyde Park Corner, noted, "As she leaned back in the carriage, extravagantly pale and with lamp-black an inch thick under her eyes and on her eyelids, she looked lovelier than the fairest beauty of the season. She took you into a world where fresh senses were accorded. Did one love this woman? Yes, but as that passion may be conceived on some other planet. What one felt began with admiration and ended there. One desired her just as much and just as little as one desires Cleopatra or Helen of Troy."

By 1910 the gentlemen of the London press had become less loyally devoted than Bernhardt's public. They accused her of becoming stale and overmannered. One critic said that she gave the impression of burlesquing herself and another said, "She is no longer an artist but an international institution." Eleonora Duse with her profound simplicity was coming to the top. The Italian woman's lack of any guile, along with her lack of any make-up and "overacting her underacting," came as refreshing relief after the Frenchwoman's brilliant virtuosity. Bernard Shaw, as we know, was never able to take the latter seriously. Speaking at the Malvern Festival in 1938 he said, "I could never, as a dramatic critic, be fair to Sarah Bernhardt, because she was exactly like my Aunt Georgina; but I could not say this at the time, because my Aunt Georgina was alive."

Octave Mirbeau, who was known for being an outspoken man, once asked Madame Sarah point blank at what age she intended to give up love.

"With my dying breath!" she answered. "I intend to live as I have always lived." And not long after making this statement she proved that she meant what she said.

In the early autumn of 1910 she set forth on her second "Farewell American Tour" with an old repertory and a new member of her company, who was to become her leading man for three years. This was Lou Tellegen, a young man born in Holland of Greek-Dutch parents. His body was a flawless specimen of male beauty. "I was powerfully built," he wrote, "and my legs were steel sinews." His head, however, was contrastingly small and, incidentally, quite empty. His hair was blond and wavy, his eyes languidly blue, his features well formed and his profile, not unlike John Barrymore's, was perfect. After he became an actor he managed to keep it turned toward the audience much of the time. His life had been a tempestuous one, his early youth having been squandered drifting about Europe, getting into colorful scrapes and taking up various careers. He had spent a month in a Russian prison for selling birth-control pamphlets. For a brief time he'd been a trapeze artist with a Berlin circus and he'd eked out a living in Brussels as a cab driver. Eventually he wandered on to Paris where he became a sculptor's model. To quote his own modest words, "My young body was dedicated to the progress of art." Someone gave him a letter to Auguste Rodin, who monosyllabically ordered him to take off his clothes, looked him over and hired him. Tellegen lived for several weeks with the Rodins at Meudon while the master was using him as the model for his well-known "Eternal Spring-time." He then became a professional prize fighter, but when he began to have ambitions for the stage gave it up for fear of impairing his delicate face with a broken nose or a cauliflower ear. He made money gambling with Montmartre apaches, learned knife-throwing, decided to become an actor and entered the Conservatoire.

How Lou Tellegen ever got into the Conservatoire is as much of a mystery as how he subsequently got an engagement at the Odéon, for he was a lamentably incompetent actor and never overcame a strong Dutch accent. The Odéon engagement ended abruptly. After winning a rapidly squandered fortune at Monte Carlo, he went to Brazil and roamed for a month about the jungles, then he worked his way back to France as a stoker on a freighter.

And all this time, according to his own account, he had been steadily seducing women. The man was as vain as a peacock and fancied himself a Don Juan with whom every female fell in love at first sight. Many apparently did, if one were gullible enough to judge by the statements in the preposterous autobiography he wrote in 1931. Its title is *Women Have Been Kind* and *Vanity Fair* in its satirical "Hall of Oblivion" series nominated it for oblivion and remarked that the title should have the additional words "of dumb."

During Tellegen's Odéon days, he was befriended by the actor de Max who, dazzled by the young Dutchman's looks, assured him of a brilliant dramatic career. Shortly after his return from the Brazilian safari Tellegen got into a scrape — involving a lady, of course — and upon being unjustly accused of robbery was clapped into that flea bag of a jail which goes by the interesting name of La Santé, "health." De Max, who happened to be in North Africa at the time, upon receiving an SOS from Tellegen, hastened back to Paris and by pulling the proper wires obtained the release of his handsome protégé. He then proceeded to present the actor with a letter to Sarah Bernhardt.

There are various versions of his first meeting with Bernhardt.
In his own book Tellegen blandly states that he called on her and
that she engaged him on the spot as her leading man. A more
authentic version would seem the one told to me by José Ruben.
That delightful gentleman and excellent actor had then just joined
the Bernhardt troupe for the American tour. He was very young
at the time. The star herself always referred to him affectionately
as *le Jeune des jeunes.* He says that Tellegen presented his letter
during a rehearsal which Madame was conducting from a seat over
the prompter's box. She was exasperated by the interruption and
was all for sending the intruder away, until she looked at the letter
and saw the signature of de Max, of whom she was extremely fond.
She also got a good look at Tellegen and told him to stay around,
she'd see what she could do. Except for his physique, Lou Tellegen
wasn't much to look at that day. He had been completely broke
for weeks. His shoes were shabby and José Ruben says that his suit
shone blindingly under the lights.

At the finish of rehearsal Madame instructed Pitou to give the
young man two hundred francs and tell him to get himself some
presentable clothes, as she intended to take him to America.

Tellegen got together what remaining wardrobe he had not
pawned, and packed it in a secondhand steamer trunk so battered
it burst apart as it was being toted to his cabin. Word of this disaster reached Sarah who, already somewhat smitten, ordered a piece
of her own luggage to be emptied out and sent to him.

Bernhardt had no specific leading man at the time. The actor engaged for the leads at the last moment had backed out of the tour
because Madame Sarah refused to take along his mistress as an
extra player. This would have meant an extra salary and the great
star was penurious when it came to paying her cast. The leading
male roles were allotted to different actors in the troupe. But by
the time they reached America, most of them had been taken away
from the different actors and allotted to Lou Tellegen. She had
rehearsed him constantly during the voyage, given him a stack of

scripts — her repertory was made up of eleven plays — told him to memorize them, and when he stammered that he couldn't possibly do it in so short a time, she had fixed him with a steady blue eye and given the simple command, "Work!"

It is somewhat unpleasant to speculate in any detail upon the relationship between this great artist of sixty-six and the conceited ass who was almost young enough to be her grandson. Lysiane Bernhardt makes no mention of Tellegen, and Louis Verneuil, who was in a way a member of the family, having for a time been married to Lysiane, protests disbelief that any physical affair ever took place and claims that Sarah's possessive interest in the man was purely of a motherly nature. Other biographers give other opinions. Certainly during their three-year partnership they were inseparable. During the 1910 tour he had his own compartment in Madame's private car along with the other honored occupants, the company manager, Madame's personal doctor and that ever-present first lady-in-waiting, Suzanne Seylor, who, it is said, greatly resented the intrusion of Tellegen.

José Ruben recalls an incident during this tour when the "Bernhardt Special" was racing across the Western plains. Late one night the train came to a sudden halt with such a jamming on of brakes a few passengers were jolted out of their berths. Looking from his window, José could see no station, no lights. They appeared to be standing still in a vast expanse of desert. From outside on the tracks came loud sounds of excited argument. The French actors had read translations of Zane Grey and seen early Westerns on the flickers and several of them armed themselves with souvenir tomahawks purchased at the last Fred Harvey counter. José went down onto the tracks to find out the meaning of the commotion. He joined the conductor, brakeman and company manager who were standing directly under Madame Sarah's window. Her light was turned on, the shade went up and there appeared an apparition in white night attire of ruffles and lace, her red dyed hair standing in wild disarray. She struggled with the window until Lou Tellegen, who had put on a brocade dressing gown, reached across and opened it for her. In the voice of some eerie spirit she piped out, "*Q'est-ce qu'il se passe?*"

The company manager, taking the cigar from his mouth, hastened to reassure her. "It's nothing at all, Madame Burrrnard, nothing at all, just a couple of vagrants flagged the train to try for a free ride. Nothing to worry about!"

"*Alors,*" she uttered, "*ce ne sont pas des* bandits?"

"No, no, just harmless hoboes."

"*Quel dommage,*" she sighed wistfully. "*Ça aurait été une impression!*" and she lowered the curtain.

In every city Tellegen was Madame Sarah's escort at all parties, receptions and public functions. She allowed him to take part in her press interviews. The two would go on hunting expeditions together — for Tellegen was an expert shot and often brought down a bird that Sarah would later claim as her trophy.

In his company she became oblivious of anyone else and even neglectful of members of her troupe. Jules Renard's one critical comment about this woman was, "She lives too hard to have any time for thought or sensitivity. She devours life. It's a form of gluttony." In the company was a girl of good breeding whose parents had been extremely apprehensive about the dangers of touring in far-off America. Bernhardt had assured them that their daughter would be completely protected, that she personally would look after her. Tellegen joined the expedition and Bernhardt forgot all about the girl. The unfortunate young thing was receiving a pittance of a salary and in order to save money she put up at a filthy boardinghouse in Philadelphia where she caught some deadly virus and died. It is unpleasant to have to report that the great star did nothing about it and that the company took up a collection in order to ship the girl's body back to her parents.

Bernhardt petted and spoiled her new favorite and was constantly concerned about his health and comfort. She was motherly with him and at the same time capricious. She was also jealous of other women. When they were playing San Francisco she found out that Lou had a rendezvous with a pretty little widow after a matinee and she stymied that by giving a dinner in his honor to which she had hurriedly rounded up some local notables, and Tellegen was forced to obey the royal command.

At times she treated him like an irresponsible child. In an attempt to stop his constant gambling, she saw to it that every week he received just enough pay for his living expenses while the remainder of his salary was sent off' for deposit in the Credit Lyonnais. Incidentally since being taken into the company, he had received a number of raises in that salary.

Madame Sarah, blind to his shortcomings as an actor, kept insisting that he was extraordinarily gifted. As Armand in *La Dame* he was not too bad and in *Phèdre* there was a certain attraction to his Hippolyte, due partly to the fact that being half naked he could display his magnificent physique. Sarah bestowed further favors on him by allowing him to wear, as Hippolyte, her famous jewel-encrusted gold belt at each performance. In every other part he was just a handsome amateur, and most critics were justifiably harsh.

When it came to letting Lou Tellegen play in Paris, Bernhardt was cautious. The first few times he appeared there with her, he had cut a ludicrous figure and the audience had giggled at his rendering the ringing couplets of Racine with a strong Dutch accent. In foreign countries such failings went unnoticed. And diction didn't matter when he played Lord Essex opposite Bernhardt's Queen Elizabeth in the silent film produced by Adolph Zukor in 1912.

The Bernhardt-Tellegen affair, or partnership — whatever it was — continued on through a year back in France and England, where in 1912 the British gave Bernhardt a National Tribute to celebrate her fifty years on the stage. An official scroll was presented to her containing a hundred thousand signatures from every part of the

Empire including Fiji. Then came another "Farewell American Tour" in 1913.

That season they played in vaudeville doing single acts from the Bernhardt repertory on the Keith-Orpheum circuit under the management of Martin Beck, which was an exacting one. She brought her old ardor to this tour. Mrs. Martin Beck told me that her husband approached Madame Sarah with some trepidation to tell her that in certain cities, Chicago in particular, the houses called for Sunday performances. Expecting her to react with fiery protestation, he was vastly relieved when she said, "But Monsieur Beck, the theatre is my life. Of course I shall play on any Sunday!" The tour ended up with a triumphant engagement in New York at the Palace Theatre. After that, Lou Tellegen stayed on in the United States and Sarah Bernhardt returned alone to France.

There is no doubt that this actor, silly as he was, had strong feelings of respect and admiration for Sarah. "I should have been a much happier man had I remained with her until the end of her career," he wrote. "Every moment that I worked with her, I knew the best that the theatre can give and, remembering the most glorious four years of my life, my eyes fill with tears and my heart again cries out, 'Madame! Grande Madame! I am so alone, without you!' " *

* Lou Tellegen enjoyed a brief career as a matinee idol and a hero in silent movies. His chief claim to fame is that in 1916 he married Geraldine Farrar, who divorced him five years later. In 1934, ill and penniless, he committed suicide by stabbing himself with a pair of scissors.

THE GLOWING TWILIGHT

I N DECEMBER, 1913, Sarah Bernhardt scored another hit with a play called *Jeanne Doré* by the humorist Tristan Bernard. There was nothing very humorous about this drama, however. In it she played the mother of a youth condemned to death for murdering a man who has seduced the girl he loves. The final scene takes place outside the prison cell the night before his execution. The mother comes to exchange a few final words with her son. Having to communicate in the dark through the barred peephole of his door, the boy fails to recognize his mother, thinks she's his faithless girl who has returned to him and pours out his love in a torrent of impassioned words while the mother keeps silent and never disillusions him. As the stricken women Sarah was superbly poignant.

On March 16, 1914, Sarah Bernhardt at long last was made a Chevalier of the Legion d'Honneur. The presentation ceremony took place on the stage following a performance and beforehand there was great excitement in the house. Everyone in the company knew about it and the ushers as they seated people murmured breathlessly, "Did you know that Madame is to be decorated tonight?" During the intermissions the audience rushed out and denuded the neighboring flowerstalls, at the finish of the performance bouquets were pelted across the footlights and one inspired enthusiast hurled a streamer of red ribbon symbolic of the *ruban rouge*, which wafted down gracefully at Sarah's feet. The final curtain fell, the cast and theatre personnel gathered on stage and a government emissary came forward, pinned on her France's most coveted medal and gave her the *accolade* on either cheek. During the brief ritual she stood head held high with a proud and youthful stance as though she were playing *l'Aiglon*. Afterward she tried to speak but the words would not come forth. The tears, however, did and with golden dignity she hobbled off to her dressing room.

It was fortunate that *Jeanne Doré* was making money, for as always she was in need of it. Her expenses were as heavy as ever, her economies nonexistent and during past months a necklace, a pin or a ring had more than once been exchanged for cash at the Mont de Piété. She made no bones about this. "I can't see anything shameful in saying one has pawned one's jewelry," she said. "It's borrowing from the government and you pay enormous interest."

She had made her son director-manager of the Théâtre Sarah Bernhardt at a salary he hardly warranted. Maurice was fifty by now, a distinguished-looking man with prematurely gray hair. He had married again, but that hadn't improved his sense of responsibility, possibly because he didn't have any to improve. He was still a spendthrift, still an inveterate gambler. A special telephone in the box office had a direct line to the star's dressing room. Sometimes it would ring during an intermission and the agitated voice of the ticket seller would be heard saying, "Madame Sarah, Monsieur Maurice is here and he wants us to hand tonight's receipts over to him. What shall we do?" And in a tone of hollow weariness Madame Sarah would answer, "Let him have them."

After a profitable tour of the provinces with *Jeanne Doré*, in the early summer of 1914 she went for a vacation in Belle-Isle with her family: her son and his wife, Lysiane and Simone, who had come across from England with her young offspring. Suzanne Seylor was in attendance and the old guard was on hand: Clairin, old Geoffroy and Louise Abbéma. Everyone was enjoying a favorite pursuit and existence seemed as happy and serene as the smiling Brittany sky.

On June 29 they were all relaxing in the "Sarahtorium" when

Emile came puffing back from town with the usual overload of
provender and the day-old Paris papers. It was the custom for
Suzanne Seylor to read excerpts of news aloud each day to Madame
Sarah. That afternoon she read of the assassination of Archduke
Franz Ferdinand and his wife Sophie in a place named Sarajevo.
Amid the peace of Belle-Isle the tragic incident seemed like distant
melodrama. It was sad, of course, but how could one be seriously
concerned about what happened in the Balkans? The Balkans came
considerably nearer when one month later Austria-Hungary declared war on Serbia, and when on July 29 the German Kaiser declared war on Russia, menacing clouds seemed to darken the Brittany sky and the vacationers on the Pointe des Poulains became
tense with unspoken forebodings.

On August 1 Bernhardt, in a fever for news and unable herself
to make the nine-kilometer carriage trip into the little town, dispatched Lysiane and Simone to find out what they could. They
raced off in the trap and joined the crowd of townspeople and
fisherfolk who were staring with apprehensive disbelief at an official
proclamation posted on the door of the mayor's house. It was
President Poincaré's order for general mobilization. With heavy
hearts the young women drove back to convey the grim tidings to
"Great." Lysiane writes that her reaction was to murmur heart-
brokenly, "Dear God! Why does civilization keep on receding!
Each war, even if won, is a fresh defeat to our intelligence." Three
days later across the Channel Sir Edward Grew uttered his prophecy: "The lights are going out all over Europe. We shall not see
them lit again in our lifetime."

The Belle-Isle holiday came abruptly to an end and Madame
Bernhardt returned to Paris with her entourage. During the next
month news from the front was worse each day. Belgium had been
devastated and the Boche had crossed the frontier into French territory. Some units had penetrated to the outlying towns of Com-
piègne and Meaux, and each day the massed hordes of spike-hel-
meted, gray-uniformed men advanced implacably. The occupation

of Paris seemed inevitable. Barricades were set up in the streets and the government, considering discretion the better part of valor, moved its headquarters to Bordeaux.

Bernhardt's friends implored her also to get out of the city, but she flatly refused to, saying that she'd remained there during 1870 and she had no intentions of running away in 1914. In early September a man from the War Ministry called with an official request that Madame Sarah Bernhardt leave the capital and take up residence in a safer part of the country. It has been said that this had been brought about indirectly by her good friend Georges Clemenceau. The Tiger of France was then running an outspoken newspaper called *L'Homme Libre*, "The Free Man," a name which after strict wartime censorship curtailed its editorials, he changed into *L'Homme Enchaîné*, "The Man in Chains." Through influential sources Clemenceau, who had access to certain espionage reports, had found out that Sarah Bernhardt's name was on the list of hostages the Kaiser wanted brought to Berlin as soon as Paris fell.

Sarah was amused by the thought of being on a hostage list. She was also rather flattered. But she couldn't take it seriously. Then the man from the War Ministry appealed to her on the grounds that she was a national figure for whose safety her country could take no risks — a persuasive argument which worked with the lady, and she decided to leave shortly for Andernos-les-Bains in the Gironde.

They were to go by train. The morning of her departure she sent Emile out to hail a taxi. After a considerable time he returned with the news that there were no taxis to be had. Maurice, who had also gone in search, came back with the same information. Finally a battered old vehicle was rounded up and family and baggage crowded in. Madame Sarah had to sit with her leg stretched out before her, as by now the doctors had resorted to the drastic therapy of immobilizing her entire limb in a plaster cast. With a dismal fear that she might never again see Paris intact in all its loveliness, she told the driver to go by way of the Champs Elysées.

Turning onto that gracious thoroughfare they were confronted with the astonishing sight of countless lumbering camions and, following them as far as one could see, line after line of taxis loaded with soldiers. These turned out to be those intrepid Taxis of Paris that transported an entire battalion of reinforcements to the Fifth Army bringing about the Miracle of the Marne. Lysiane tells that an officer stopped their driver and demanded why he hadn't lined up his machine with the others. Opening the door, he ordered the occupants to get out then and there.

"Then he stopped short," she writes, "his eyes fixed on Sarah Bernhardt, who was listening without saying a word, her poor leg rigidly stretched out. The officer raised his hand to his képi and saluted.

"'I beg your pardon, Madame, I didn't know! Go chauffeur, take Mme. Sarah Bernhardt to the station, then come back and put yourself at our disposition.'

"Then he turned a second time to my grandmother.

"'Go with a tranquil mind, Madame. *They shall not pass!*'"

They spent the next five months in a pine-surrounded villa overlooking the tranquil Bay of Arcachon. The stay was anything but tranquil for Madame Sarah. She, the normally physical stoic, at times cried out in agony. An eminent Dr. Pozzi, who was a good friend, journeyed down from Paris and removed the cast, only to discover that gangrene had developed and was rapidly spreading. He, Sarah, everyone knew that amputation was inevitable. Pozzi balked at doing it himself. So did another physician, who refused to perform so drastic an operation on a woman approaching seventy-two who suffered from chronic uremia. Physicians were scarce, most of them having enlisted in the Medical Corps. Finally, a Dr. Denucé in nearby Bordeaux agreed to undertake the risky job.

In the bleak early morning of February 22, 1915, Lysiane, Maurice, Suzanne Seylor and Clairin sat silent and stricken-faced in the hospital waiting room. The stretcher bearing their adored Sarah paused briefly at the entrance. She waved at them cheerfully, called out, "*Allons, enfants, un peu de courage!,*" then with mock bravado she hummed the opening bars of the "Marseillaise" as she was wheeled on down the corridor.

News of the Bernhardt calamity flashed about the globe and messages of condolence swamped the Bordeaux Postes et Télégraphes. One gruesome communication came from .the impresario of the P. T. Barnum freak show, who cabled an offer of $10,000 to display the severed leg in his exhibition.

Convalescence was long and critical and for a time Madame Sarah's life hung in the balance. Slowly, however, her strength returned and she was able to try a wooden leg. Her own had been taken off high up on the thigh, almost at the hip, and the artificial contrivance that was sent had to be attached by means of a heavy girdle that fitted about her hips and stomach. Never in her life had she worn any sort of corset and she didn't intend to now. After trying unsuccessfully to attach the cumbersome contraption by some other means, she flew into one of her old rages and ordered the thing to be thrown into the fire.

The public speculated as to how Madame Sarah would get about from now on. The majority believed she'd wear a wooden leg. Some thought she'd depend upon crutches. An outrageous quip is attributed to the usually kind Tristan Bernard when he attended the first performance she gave after the amputation. Upon hearing the three hammer strokes on wood signaling the rise of the curtain, he remarked to his companion, "*Tiens!* Here she comes!"

She never made any attempt to try crutches and the idea of a wheel chair filled her with contempt. What did they take her for, she snorted, an ancient invalid? Her solution was a specially designed litter chair with two horizontal shafts by which she could be borne about. She stipulated that it be finished in Louis XV style, painted white and ornamented with gilt carving on the sides. Being Sarah Bernhardt she dramatized the situation wherever she was carried, assuming the attitude of an empress in a procession.

Again there were outrageous quips from the insensitive boulevard wags certain of whom nicknamed her *"Mère La Chaise."* Elizabeth Finlay Thomas watched her being taken through her stage door: "Her arms full of roses, the shining fuzz of her hair crowned with her usual capote of flowers, her mutilated figure a mass of velvets, she was the personification of undaunted courage."

If people had any idea that Sarah Bernhardt was finished as an actress, she was going to show them *quand même.* She returned to Paris in October, 1915, the Germans having fallen back sufficiently to mitigate the risk of her being taken as a hostage, although the idea still rather intrigued her. Soon after she was back she put on a bill of three one-act plays and appeared in the final one, which was a sort of tableau with dialogue. This was *Les Cathédrales* by Eugène Morand, a piece described as a "scenic poem" in which various actresses, symbolizing the chief cathedrals of France, recited heroic couplets about the Patrie, la Gloire, the recovery of Alsace-Lorraine and further sentiments calculated to wring tears and cheers from a wartime audience. The last tableau revealed Sarah as the embodiment of Strasbourg Cathedral. Enthroned on a dais, she remained almost motionless as she uttered a long speech; then at the end, she raised her arms and in some superhuman way also raised herself until she was standing on her one leg, managing to balance by leaning against the heavy arm of the chair and her voice in all its power rang forth, *"Pleure, pleure, Allemagne! L'Aigle Allemand est tombé dans le Rhin!"* * Sarah Bernhardt had shown her sacred monster that she was anything but finished.

In 1914 the popular prediction had been, "The men will be out of the trenches by Christmas." But the war went on and on, week after week, month after month, and ever more and more men slogged it out or perished in the mud and misery of those trenches. Early in 1915 the Théâtre aux Armées was organized by an enterprising group of actors and actresses for the purpose of sending performers up behind the lines to entertain the weary *poilus.* Sarah

---

* "Weep, weep Germany! The German Eagle has fallen into the Rhine!"

Bernhardt was fired with the idea that she, too, would travel to the Western Front and carry her art, if necessary, into the trenches themselves.

The authorities were aghast, but at her insistence finally agreed to send her. They stipulated, however, that she must go in company with another player, and they appointed Beatrix Dussanne. Dussanne was then one of the youngest comediennes at the Comédie Française. In future years she was to become one of the leading authorities on the French theatre. Dussanne was discouraged by the instructions that she must accompany Great Sarah — "she with her flowers, her furs, her luxuries of a sovereign . . . and her fragility." She had never met Bernhardt personally and felt considerably awed when she was summoned to the boulevard Péreire to go over plans. In her book, *Reines de Théâtre,* she wrote that she was ushered into a white boudoir, "where I see in the depths of a huge armchair an extraordinary creature: a thousand rumples of satin and lace topped with a tousled red coiffure, ageless features whose wrinkles are caked over with make-up . . . an impression upsetting and a bit sad; she seems so small, so damaged, the great, the radiant Sarah! A little heap of cinders . . ."

Then, Dussanne goes on to say, they started going over their prospective program and the Bernhardt miracle took place: "For two hours the little heap of cinders never stopped emitting sparks! I feel this has occurred ever since she came into this world, and it will continue forever. Beneath the painted and tinseled decrepitude of the old actress there burns an inextinguishable sun."

A few days later, the two boarded a train at the Gare de l'Est. Military regulations forbade any of Madame's customary entourage to go along. Even the men who carried either end of her litter chair were hired porters, trainmen and eventually delegated *poilus.* During the journey she laughed and chatted gaily. They got off at Toul and motored over a rutted road to a nearby town half-shattered by bombs.

The first performance was in an open marketplace where a

crude stage had been set up. Makeshift footlights flickered un-
certainly and a flimsy curtain flapped sporadically in the chill gusts
of a damp wind. The audience seated on benches or squatting on
the ground was made up of over two thousand men, wounded men,
men fresh out of action, men about to go for the first time into the
hell of vermin-infested trenches, barbed wire, no-man's land and
mustard gas. Dussanne and a few others performed their acts first.
Then it was announced that they were about to see Madame Sarah
Bernhardt. The announcement met with dead silence. The flimsy
curtain fluttered open to reveal a wisp of an aging woman propped
against pillows in a shabby armchair. Then the wisp of a woman
began to speak the lines of the patriotic piece she had selected and,
"The miracle again took place; Sarah, old, mutilated, once more
illuminated a crowd by the rays of her genius. This fragile creature,
ill, wounded and immobile could still, through the magic of her
spoken word, re-instill heroism in those soldiers weary from battle."
When she wound up her recitation with a clarion, "*Aux armes!*"
the two thousand men rose to their feet cheering and some of them
sobbing.

In three days they performed in six other villages, some of them
less than a half mile from the Argonne and Verdun. They recited
in barns, in hospital wards, in mess tents and on the terrace of a
deserted chateau. Living accommodations were primitive, but Bernhardt's verve never flagged. They shared the same room, Dussanne
helping the cripple maneuver as best she could. Sarah had become
remarkably adept at hopping and as she'd make her way from bed
to washstand she'd crow with laughter and say, "Look! I'm a
guinea hen! I'm a guinea hen!"

Dussanne sums her up: "An old woman heroically and insanely
determined to ignore time, pain and physical laws, smiling and joking to forestall being pitied, shedding on the public the warmth of a
radiance that never goes out. Greater perhaps in this glowing twilight than in the sparkling days of her apogee."

A number of weeks later, accompanied by Lysiane, she went on another mission for the Théâtre aux Armées playing in three towns along the Marne. At Reims she was placed on a platform outside the semi-shattered cathedral and the soldiers had the thrill of hearing her recite her Strasbourg speech from *Les Cathédrales*. She insisted upon going to Pont-à-Mousson on the Moselle, a site shelled daily by the enemy, but no bomb happened to fall that particular day. At one point she told a general that she wanted to recite for the men in the front-line trenches. The general, somewhat taken aback, said he couldn't give her permission unless he accompanied her. "But wouldn't the Boche recognize your rank and fire?" she asked. "Probably," he answered. "Then let us go back," she said. "France has need of her generals!"

A later reply she made to Lord Kitchener was in the same vein of histrionics. She'd been playing a brief engagement in London and wanted to return to France by the shorter route on a troop ship scheduled to land at Boulogne. She wrote Kitchener, whom she knew well, asking for a permit. Her letter was so highly perfumed it caused consternation in the war office. The hero of Khartoum wrote back that he could not allow her to take such a risk, as that part of the Channel was infested with enemy craft. *"Mais alors!"* was her reaction, "it would be a matter of dying with our soldiers! *Quelle gloire!"*

It will come as no surprise that in 1916 Sarah Bernhardt again was short of funds. She made two movies, those "ridiculous photographed pantomimes," as she called them, one taken from *Jeanne Doré* and the other a war film called *Mothers of France*, both of which brought her in some money. But as always her El Dorado lay in the United States. This was really to be her final "Farewell American Tour." It was financially rewarding and physically back-breaking, lasting as it did for eighteen months. Again she appeared in scenes from her regular repertory, varying the bill with a few new one-act playlets, two by her son and one by herself. The best new item was *Au Champs d'Honneur*, a war piece written by a young soldier then serving in the French Army. The setting is on

a deserted area of the battlefield, and she impersonated a youthful
standard bearer, a former actor and poet, mortally wounded yet
determined to save his battalion's flag from enemy hands. Sarah in
dramatically tattered uniform, face and throat meticulously bloodstained, was especially appealing when she spoke the line, "The
sword of the soldier pierces the flesh, the word of the poet is still
to dominate the spirit." The finale was a mounting vocal crescendo
of vilification of the enemy ending with, "Do not forgive them,
for they know well what they do!" followed, needless to say, by
the standard bearer's death, the flag clutched to her heart. The
reaction to that passage can be summed up in a remark overheard
by José Ruben. No longer in her company, he had stopped by
Madame's dressing room to pay his respects and, finding that she
was still on the stage, had stood in the wings to watch the finish
of *The Field of Honor*. Standing there also were a policeman and
the theatre fireman apparently rapt by words completely unintelligible yet mesmerically exciting. At the end of the last "tirade,"
the policeman and the fireman, at a loss for words, merely uttered
in a hoarse whisper, "Christ!"

The "Lusitania" had been sunk the previous spring. America was
becoming more and more emotionally involved with the war and
people were speculating as to how soon we too would become involved. The Preparedness League was growing in membership, and
advocates of Peace-at-any-Price were being handed white feathers
as pro-German slackers. In her off-theatre hours, Sarah Bernhardt
worked passionately to further the Allied cause. She spoke at Red
Cross rallies, she recited the "Marseillaise" at benefits for French
war widows, Belgian orphans and starving Serbians.

To the utmost of her capacity she became a rabble-rouser, and
the American public regarded her as a heroine in the cause of
Liberty and Justice. An article in the October, 1915, *Theatre
Magazine*, signed "Her American Manager," says:

> She has created in herself a national figure, so that wherever
> Sarah Bernhardt appears, she personifies the flag of her country

. . . she is the embodiment of the national ambition in France, which aspires to the highest culture, to unwavering courage, to infinite tenderness. Sarah is the heart and head of France.

And G. W. Smalley of the *New York Tribune* called her "The greatest missionary whom France or any other country has sent abroad." Her arrival in most cities was greeted by brass bands that alternated "Tipperary" with "Madelon" and "The Stars and Stripes Forever." In San Francisco some official, having learned that Bernhardt's husband had been a Greek, was inspired to have her escorted by an honor-guard in Greek evzone uniforms. It was a nice idea, but someone blundered, for what the guard turned up wearing were uniforms of the Turkish infantry. Turkey, of course, was fighting on the side of Germany.

On April 15, 1917, President Wilson proclaimed, "The supreme test of the nation has come," and the United States entered the war. Sarah sent off a cable to Maurice which said simply, "Hip, hip, hooray." A few days later she received one back from him. It was a request for money.

Margaret Mower, then just beginning her stage career, had been engaged in the Bernhardt company to appear before each scene and give the audience a synopsis in English. Bernhardt liked the lovely-looking American girl and often sent for her to visit in her dressing room. The young actress was there when the company manager delivered Maurice's cable. Madame read it and groaned, threw wide her hands, then asked the manager to advance her some money. The man, in considerable embarrassment, told her he had instructions from the New York office not to advance her any more. Then the weary woman scooped some rings out of a silver bowl on her dresser and handed them to the manager. "He took the rings," Margaret Mower recalls, "bowed and left without comment. Madame's gesture had been in the grandest of grand manners, but one sensed the grimness behind it."

Another grim occasion, again according to Miss Mower, occurred one evening when they were playing at the Brooklyn Academy of Music. Word came back that Lou Tellegen and

Geraldine Farrar were in the audience. Their seats were far down front and Sarah could see them all too clearly from her position on the stage. The handsome couple had been married barely a year, and they were obviously happy and still very much in love. Sarah acted her heart out that evening. She resorted to every one of her tricks including her ability to give an impression of youth and infinite beauty. After the performance she issued instructions that she'd receive only the Tellegeñs. And arranging herself in the proper pose she waited for them in her dressing room. We know what Tellegen had meant to her, and she had always considered Geraldine Farrar a close friend. She waited. For nearly an hour she waited and they never showed up. They didn't even send back a note. The snub cut Bernhardt to the quick. For many days afterward, à propos of nothing she would say, "He never came around to see me. He never came around."

Throughout the tour, she'd been having intermittent attacks of uremia and upon reaching New York she was rushed to Mt. Sinai Hospital for an emergency kidney operation. She took this fresh disaster in her usual stride. "They can cut out everything," she said, "as long as they leave me my head." Letters, wires and further tributes poured in and a cable of affection and concern from Queen Alexandra constituted a nice display on her bureau for visitors to read.

Lysiane came over for her slow recovery at Long Beach. Even as a convalescent Madame Sarah kept mentally busy. She wrote a few short stories and novellas which the *Annales* and the *Gaulois* were indulgent enough to buy. She also did a little dress designing if one is to judge by an article on the fashion page of *Theatre Magazine*: "Mme. Sarah Bernhardt whose high heart knows no fears is an enthusiast about the aeroplane, and it is only a matter of time when she will elude the lynx-like vigilance of her retinue of managers, secretaries, physicians and 'dames de compagnie' and make her maiden flight. But if you think the great and gracious Frenchwoman will make herself hideous to cleave the clouds, you are quite wrong. The Divine Sarah is an apostle of beauty, and she has devised the most fetching and feminine of flying costumes during her hours of summer idleness at Long Beach." There is an accompanying photograph which shows the "Divine Sarah" in her "fetching and feminine flying costume," which appears to consist of a long loose coat worn over a white silk dress, and a large hat covered with a flowing veil that reaches to the ground. The mental picture of anyone wearing such regalia while cleaving the clouds in the open one-engine bi-plane of those days is an interesting one.

When she was well enough, she undertook another extensive vaudeville circuit tour, then, in the late autumn of 1918, she decided to return to France. News from Europe was much more hopeful. The big Allied offensive was on and enemy forces were at long last retreating toward the Fatherland. But German U-boats still menaced North Atlantic shipping and friends begged her not to risk the crossing. She brushed aside warnings and waved gaily from her litter chair as she was carried aboard the steamer. The captain wanted to delegate two seamen to be on hand in case they were torpedoed and had to abandon ship, but she would hear none of it. "They'll be needed elsewhere," she said. "Young lives are more important than my old one."

During the voyage, which was a long one as they had to zigzag, there was one sub scare which proved to be a false alarm. While it was going on she refused to be taken up on deck but remained in her cabin calmly playing dominoes with her granddaughter.

They landed at Bordeaux on November 11 and the town appeared to be in a ferment of celebration. Flags were flying, bands playing and everyone seemed to have gone joyously insane. Madame Sarah thought the Army must have just won a big victory. But as soon as the gangplank was secured, Maurice sprang aboard and burst into her cabin shouting, "*Maman!* The Armistice has been signed! The war is over!"

But Sarah Bernhardt's personal war against ill health and old age was not over. Ill health she ignored. Old age she still would not admit. She never lied about her years, but she clung stubbornly to the self-delusion that in appearance she was younger than most of her associates. During her recent trip she had run across a woman acquaintance whom she'd not seen for some time and who by then was barely approaching sixty, and had later remarked, "That's me ten years from now."

Around this period James Agate wrote of her: "This art, which in its heyday lit up a firmament, moves toward its setting in infinite serenity." It's a pretty statement and one would like to think it was accurate. Her art may have appeared to have taken on an infinite serenity, but she herself was never to enjoy that happy state of soul. This indomitable woman was earning her own living at an age when most people are dozing theirs away. In 1920 she put on another series of classical matinees in which she took part, playing a single act of Racine's *Athalie*. In this she was apparently superbly appealing. The selection included what is known as "Athalie's dream" and contains the lines referring to an aging woman painting her face "in order to repair the irreparable ravages of years." It is a couplet traditionally shouted, but according to Sacha Guitry, Sarah spoke the first line softly, then she paused, opened wide her arms and in a tone of stark admission slowly uttered the desolate words, "*Pour réparer des ans l'irréparable outrage.*" The audience, in a burst of compassionate affection, gave her a standing ovation and she managed to stand also, holding onto the throne, balancing on one leg and with the gesture of a single arm, returning their love.

It must have been a sense of family loyalty which prompted her in that same year to put on *Daniel*, a four-act piece by her grandson-in-law Louis Verneuil. This is the story of two brothers who have loved the same girl. The older brother has won and married her, the younger one, Daniel, has retired to a life of neurotic seclusion and gradual disintegration through drugs. There are further complications of plot too silly to recount. Sarah, of course, played Daniel and appeared in only two acts. The age of this character was meant to be thirty. A first-rate actor named Abel Tarride had been cast as the forty-year-old brother. Rehearsals were well under way when Madame Sarah found out that Tarride himself was fifty. Her reaction was immediately to protest, "Why the man's too old! He'll look like my father!" Tarride was dismissed and a less competent, but younger, actor given the role. Sarah was then seventy-six.

According to the author, the house went wild on opening night, but reading between the lines one gathers that the applause was for the star, not the play. According to Maurice Rostand, Bernhardt herself realized what an appalling vehicle *Daniel* was. He says that her summation of it was *"C'est une foutaise! Une foutaise! Une foutaise!"* a vulgarism which can most politely be translated as "It's a lot of hog wash."

After a modest Paris run, Madame Sarah went on a European tour, including *Daniel* in her repertory. The theatres were packed everywhere, for her public in each country realized they were probably seeing this great artist for the last time. Crowds greeted her arrival in the Madrid station and as she was being carried from the train in her litter, men took off their jackets and spread them on the platform for her bearers to walk on. The old actress burst into tears and kept repeating, "Ah, how good they are! Ah, *les braves gens!*" After Spain she paid her final visit to England.

While she was fulfilling a London Music Hall engagement, she made an extra command appearance for royalty. She and Queen Mary had for years been on a basis of pleasant friendship, and after the performance the two met and chatted of many things. Mary at one point asked her how on earth she could bear up under the strain of acting every day. "Madame," Sarah replied, "I shall die on the stage; it is my battlefield!" That same year she had asked a favor of the Queen. Cochran was about to produce two of Louis Verneuil's plays, when suddenly the censor decided to ban them as immoral. Verneuil appealed for help from Madame Sarah, who was still on the European tour. "Don't worry," she wired him,

"I'll take care of things." Then she sent another wire to Queen Mary:

> My good friend, my grandson-in-law's plays are Parisian, but not immoral. I would be infinitely grateful if you personally would intercede with the censor not to ban them. A thousand affectionate thanks.
>
> Sarah Bernhardt.

Louis Verneuil's plays were put on.

Following London the sick, tired woman dragged herself on a tour of the British provinces playing to audiences that came out of loyalty, pity and admiration. During a Brighton engagement her friend Elizabeth Finley Thomas called at her hotel. Her description of the visit is worth reprinting:

> The page threw open the door . . . a very old woman lay on a huge bed. An elaborate *couvre-pied* hid the lower part of her figure, and I noticed that its folds fell flat on one side. Her blonde hair, streaked by dye, had all its old vitality; but in the crude light from the window her face was ghastly. Instantly, however, the famous smile stretched its double line of red across the large teeth, yellowed by time. Smears of ill-applied lipstick gave her mouth a sanguinary appearance and increased her resemblance to a tigress. Her hands, claw-like and ill-manicured, rested on the counterpane, and the lacy dressing-jacket was soiled and shabby. The impression was both tragic and sinister, but immediately switching on her incantations like a light, she began to speak enthusiastically of her play, passing casually over the physical difficulties . . . Later talking in a matter-of-fact way about her loss of leg, "You remember my motto *Quand Même?* In case of necessity, I shall have myself strapped to the scenery."

Once returned to the boulevard Péreire she put on a brave show of keeping up the old pace. Although her entertaining was no longer on so lavish a scale, every day and all day long she continued to receive an unending stream of callers. She also continued to keep her domestic dog pack of various breeds and she even acquired a final out-of-the-ordinary pet. This was a chimpanzee named Jacqueline who lumbered about the house with an expression of mournful patience and would open and close windows on command.

The authoress Colette who was one of the privileged few to be received by Madame Sarah during her final year, has left us a touching picture of the old actress preparing ground-up coffee in an earthen pot and handing it to her guests. Almost archly she wanted to know if she made coffee as well as Catulle Mendès. Then Colette records;

> The delicate and withered hand offering the brimming cup, the flowery azure of the eyes, so young still in their network of fine lines, the questioning and mocking coquetry of the tilted head, and that indestructible desire to charm, to charm still, to charm right up to the gates of death itself.

By way of a new activity, Sarah undertook a short lecture trip about the country, giving conferences on the plays and poetry of Rostand. In 1921 she produced *La Gloire* by Edmond Rostand and in 1922 *Régine Arnaud*, another Verneuil piece. In the autumn of that year she started rehearsing a Sacha Guitry play, *Un Sujet de Roman*, in which she was to appear with all three Guitrys: Lucien, Sacha and the latter's wife, Yvonne Printemps. The night of the dress rehearsal, while starting to make up, she suddenly collapsed into a coma which lasted about an hour. Her first words on coming to were, "When do I go on?" But she never went on again. The opening was necessarily postponed, another actress found for the part, and the play eventually had a good run at the Théâtre Edouard VII.

Madame Sarah, who adored the part Sacha had written for her, was heartbroken not to be playing it. She kept the script by her bed and every evening she went over it, timing her lines to coincide with those spoken by her replacement. The three Guitrys came daily to see her. She laughed and joked and talked gaily of possible future plays the four of them might do together. The Guitrys also laughed and joked but they could hardly hold back the tears.

For a month or so she lay in bed desperately ill. But she kept mentally alert reading new scripts and she even started to memorize the role of Cleopatra in Corneille's *Rodogune* with an idea of including it as part of her *matinées classiques*. All at once she took a marked turn for the better and it was with characteristic zest that she agreed to take part in a film Sacha Guitry was about to make for a Hollywood company. This was something called *La Voyante*, in which she was cast as a clairvoyant who foretells the future. A striking photograph snapped between shots shows her sitting at her fortune teller's table, the Taro cards spread before her, her eyes protected by dark glasses, the epitome of weariness. As she was still too ill to work in a studio, it was decided to shoot her scenes in her house. Scenery, klieg lights and photographic equipment were installed and she set to work. She told a caller, "They're paying me ten thousand francs a day. It's as good as going to America," then she added brightly, "I wonder when my next tour will be."

On March 21 she collapsed and returned to bed, never to get up again. For five days she was in a state of semi-consciousness. The weather was mild and clear. "It will be a beautiful spring," she murmured. "There will be lots of flowers." And she requested Maurice to see that she was covered with lilacs.

The word spread that Great Sarah was dying, and silent groups stood outside the house like devoted subjects of an ailing monarch waiting for bulletins. On March 25 she asked if there were any reporters outside and on being told that there were, her smile had a touch of its old malice as she said, "All my life reporters have tormented me enough. I can tease them now a little by making them cool their heels." These were her final words. The next day at eight o'clock in the evening Dr. Marot opened the windows, stepped out on the balcony and announced:

"Messieurs, Madame Sarah Bernhardt is dead."

The news, expected though it was, came as a shock. To the people of Paris "Their Sarah" had seemed something as indestructible as Notre Dame. The stark finality saddened everyone. One club man said to another, "Bernhardt is gone. How dark it seems all of a sudden."

The wasted little body lay in her satin-lined rosewood coffin as during the next twenty-four hours thirty thousand persons filed slowly by — persons from every walk of life, eminent celebrities, milliners' assistants, fashionable aristocrats, market women with shawls over their heads.

The government did not see fit to give their greatest actress a national funeral, but the people of Paris gave her one. As many numbers walked behind the hearse, family and official mourners as had at the time of Victor Hugo's obsequies. During the slow journey from the Church of Saint-François-de-Sales the cortege stopped for a minute of silent tribute outside the Théâtre Sarah Bernhardt, then continued on its way.

In the cemetery of Père Lachaise a plain mausoleum bears the single name "Bernhardt." It was, I believe, Jacques Rostand who suggested the more fitting epitaph:

Ci-gît Sarah
Qui survivra.

PARTIAL LIST OF PLAYS AND ROLES
PERFORMED BY SARAH BERNHARDT

BIBLIOGRAPHY

INDEX

PARTIAL LIST OF PLAYS AND ROLES
PERFORMED BY SARAH BERNHARDT

(Titles preceded by an asterisk are those of roles she originated; in certain cases the names of author and roles are not available.)

1862   *Iphigénie* (Jean Racine), role of *Iphigénie*
        Valérie (Scribe and Melesville), role of Valérie
        Les Femmes Savantes (Molière), role of Henriette
        l'Etourdi (Molière), role of Hippolyte
1864   *Le Père de la Debutante* (Barrière), role of Anita
        Le Démon du Jeu (Barrière and Crisafulli)
        Un Soufflet n'est Jamais Perdu
        La Maison sans Enfants (Dumanoir)
        L'Etourneau (Baya and Laya)
        Le Premier Pas (Labiche and Delacour)
        Un Mari qui Lance sa Femme (Deslandes)
1865   *La Biche au Bois* (Coignard *frères*), role of Princesse Désirée
1866   *Le Jeu de l'Amour et du Hasard* (Marivaux), role of Silvia
1867   *Les Femmes Savantes* (Molière), role of Armande
        Le Roi Lear (Shakespeare), role of Cordelia
        Athalie (Racine), role of Zacharie
        Le Testament de César Girodot (Bélot and Villetard), role of Hortense
        François-le-Champi (George Sand), role of Mariette
        Le Marquis de Villemer (Sand), role of Baronne d'Arglade

Le Drame de la rue de la Paix (Belot), role of Julia

1868 Kean (Dumas père), role of Anna Damby
*La Loterie du Mariage

1869 *Le Passant (Coppée), role of Zanetto
*Le Bâtard (Alphonse Touroude)

1870 l'Affranchi (Latour de Saint-Ybars)
*l'Autre (Sand)

1871 *Jean-Marie (Theuriet), role of Thérèse

1872 *Mademoiselle Aissé (Bouilhet), role of Mlle. Aissé
Ruy Blas (Hugo), role of the Queen
Mlle. de Belle-Isle (Dumas père) role of Mlle. de Belle-
Isle
Le Cid (Corneille), role of Chimène
Britannicus (Racine), role of Junie

1873 Le Mariage de Figaro (Beaumarchais), role of Chérubin
Dalila (Octave Feuillet), role of Princess Falconieri
*l'Absent (Manuel)
*Chez l'Avocat (Ferier)
Andromache (Racine), role of Andromache
Phèdre (Racine), role of Aricie

1874 *Le Sphynx (Feuillet), role of Berthe de Savigny
*La Belle Paule (Denayrousse)
Zaïre (Voltaire), role of Zaïre
Phèdre (Racine), role of Phèdre

1875 *La Fille de Roland (de Bornier), role of Berthe
Gabrielle (Augier), role of Gabrielle

1876 l'Etrangère (Dumas fils), role of Mrs. Clarkson
La Nuit de Mai (de Musset), role of the Muse
*Rome Vaincue (Parodi), role of Posthumnia

1877 Hernani (Hugo), role of Doña Sol

1878 *Othello (Shakespeare-Aicard), role of Desdemona
Amphytrion (Molière), role of Alcmène

1879 Mithridate (Racine), role of Monime

1880 l'Aventurière (Augier), role of Doña Clorinde
Le Sphynx (Feuillet), role of Blanche de Chelles

Adrienne Lecouvreur (Scribe and Legouvé), role of Adrienne

Froufrou (Meilhac and Halévy), role of Gilberte

La Dame aux Camélias (Dumas *fils*) role of Marguerite Gauthier

1881 *La Princesse Georges* (Dumas *fils*), role of Séverine

1882 *Fédora* (Sardou), role of Fédora

1883 *Nana-Sahib* (Richepin), role of Djamma

1884 *Macbeth* (Shakespeare-Richepin), role of Lady Macbeth

Théodora (Sardou), role of Théodora

1885 *Marion Delorme* (Hugo), role of Marion

1886 *Hamlet* (Shakespeare-Cressonois-Samson), role of Ophelia

Le Maître des Forges (Ohnet), role of Claire de Beaulieu

l'Aveu (Bernhardt), role of Marthe

1887 *La Tosca* (Sardou), role of Floria Tosca

1888 *Francillon* (Dumas *fils*), role of Francine de Riverolles

1889 *Léna* (Berton-Phillips), role of Léna

1890 *Jeanne d'Arc* (Barbier), role of Jeanne d'Arc

Cléopâtre (Sardou), role of Cléopâtre

1891 *Gringoire* (de Banville), role of Gringoire

1893 *Les Rois* (Lemaître), role of Princesse Wilhelmine

1894 *Izéil* (Morand and Silvestre), role of Izéil

La Femme de Claude (Dumas *fils*), role of Césarine

Gismonda (Sardou), role of Gismonda

1895 *Magda* (Sudermann), role of Magda

La Princesse Lointaine (Rostand), role of Mélissinde

1896 *Lorenzaccio* (de Musset), role of Lorenzaccio

1897 *Spiritisme* (Sardou), role of Simone

La Samaritaine (Rostand), role of Photine

Les Mauvais Bergers (Mirbeau), role of Madeleine

1898 *La Ville Morte* (d'Annunzio), role of Anne

Lysiane (Coölus), role of Lysiane

Medée (Mendès), role of Medea

1899 *Hamlet* (Shakespeare-Schwon-Morand), role of Hamlet

1900   *l'Aiglon (Rostand), role of Duc de Reichstadt
       Cyrano de Bergerac (Rostand), role of Roxane
1901   La Pluie et le beau Temps (Gozlan), role of the Baroness
       Les Precieuses Ridicules (Molière), role of Madelon
1902   Francesca da Rimini (Crawford and Schwob), role of
          Francesca
       Sapho (Daudet), role of Fanny Legrand
       *Théroigne de Méricourt (Hervieu), role of Théroigne
1903   Andromache (Racine), role of Hermione
       *Werther (Goethe-Decourcelle), role of Werther
       Plus que Reine (Bergerat), role of Josephine
       *Jeanne Wedekind (Filippi-Krauss), role of Jeanne Wede-
          kind
       *La Sorcière (Sardou), role of Zoraya
1904   *Le Festin de la Mort (de Castellane), role of Mme. de
          Maujourdain
       *Varennes (Lavedan and Lenôtre), role of Marie-Antoi-
          nette
1905   Angelo (Hugo), role of Thisbé
       Esther (Racine), role of Assuérus
       Pelléas et Mélisande (Maeterlinck), role of Pelléas
       *Adrienne Lecouvreur (Bernhardt), role of Adrienne
1906   *La Vierge d'Avila (Mendès), role of St. Theresa
1907   *Les Bouffons (Zamacoïs), role of Jacasse
       *Le Vert-Galant (Moreau), role of Queen Margot
       *La Belle au Bois Dormant (Richepin), role of Prince
          Charming
1908   *La Courtisane de Corinthe (Carré-Bilhaud), role of
          Cléonce
1909   La Nuit de Mai (de Musset), role of the Poet
       La Fille de Rabenstein (Remon)
       *Le Procès de Jeanne d'Arc (Moreau), role of Jeanne
          d'Arc
1910   La Beffa (Richepin-Binelli), role of Gianetto Malespini

La Femme X (Bisson), role of Jacqueline

*Judas (de Kay-Chassagne), role of Judas

1911   *Lucrèce Borgia* (Hugo), role of Lucrèce

1912   **La Reine Elizabeth* (Moreau), role of Queen Elizabeth

       *Une Nuit de Noël sous le Terreur (Bernhardt-Cain), role of Marion

1913   **Jeanne Doré* (Bernard), role of Jeanne Doré

1914   **Tout à Coup* (de Cassagnac), role of the Marquise de Chalonne

1915   **Les Cathédrales* (Morand), role of Strasbourg (1 act)

1916   **La Mort de Cléopâtre* (Bernhardt-Cain), role of Cléopâtre (1 act)

       *l'Holocauste (Bernhardt), role of the Duchesse (1 act)

       *Du Théâtre au Champ d'Honneur (an unknown French soldier), role of Marc

       *Vitrail (Fauchois), role of Violaine (1 act)

       *Hécube (Maurice Bernhardt-Chavance) role of Hécube (1 act)

       *Le Faux Modèle (Daurelly), role of Madeleine (1 act)

       Le Marchand de Venise (Shakespeare), role of Portia (excerpts)

       *l'Etoile dans la Nuit (Cain), role of Jane de Mauduit (1 act)

1920   *Athalie* (Racine), role of Athalie

       *Daniel (Verneuil), role of Daniel Arnault

       *Comment on écrit l'Histoire (S. Guitry), role of Mariette (1 act)

1921   **La Gloire* (Maurice Rostand), role of La Gloire

1922   **Régine Arnaud* (Verneuil), role of Régine Arnaud

N.B. Revivals are not listed nor are special performances given only once.

BIBLIOGRAPHY

Agate, James. *An Anthology*, ed. Herbert Van Thal (New York: Hill and Wang, 1961)

Agate, May. *Madame Sarah* (London: Home & Van Thal Ltd., 1945)

Arthur, Sir George. *Sarah Bernhardt* (New York: Doubleday Page & Co., 1923)

Baldick, Robert. *The Siege of Paris* (New York: Macmillan, 1964)

Baring, Maurice. *Sarah Bernhardt* (London: Peter Davies Ltd., 1933)

——. *Punch and Judy* (Garden City, N. Y.: Doubleday Page & Co., 1924)

——. *The Puppet Show of Memory* (Boston: Little, Brown & Co., 1922)

Beerbohm, Max. *Around Theatres* (New York: Alfred A. Knopf, 1930)

Bennett, Arnold. *The Journal of Arnold Bennett* (New York: Viking Press, 1932)

——. *Paris Nights* (New York: George H. Doran Co., 1913)

Benson, E. F. *As We Were* (New York: Longmans Green & Co., 1930)

Bernhardt, Lysiane. *Sarah Bernhardt ma Grand'mère* (Paris: Editions du Pavois, 1947)

Bernhardt, Sarah. *Memories of My Life* (New York: D. Appleton and Co., 1907)

Billy, André. *l'Epoque 1900* (Paris: Editions Jules Tallardier, 1951)

Binet-Valmer. *Sarah Bernhardt* (Paris: Flammarion, 1936)

Bradford, Gamaliel. *Daughters of Eve* (Boston: Houghton Mifflin Co., 1930)

Buson, Dani. *Sarah Bernhardt* (Paris: Publications Willy Fischer)

Campbell, Mrs. Patrick. *My Life and Some Letters* (London: Hutchinson & Co., n.d.)

Castelot, André. *Sarah Bernhardt* (Paris: Le Livre Contemporain, 1961)

Colombier, Marie. *Les Mémoires de Sarah Barnum* (Paris, n.d.)

——. *Voyages de Sarah Bernhardt en Amérique* (Paris: C. Marpon et E. Flammarion, n.d.)

Cowles, Virginia. *Gay Monarch* (New York: Harper & Bros., 1956)

Dussanne, Beatrix. *Dieux des Planches* (Paris: Flammarion Collection "1900")

——. *Reines de Théâtre* (Paris: H. Lardanchet)

Ganderax, Etienne. *Souvenirs de Théâtre* (Revue de Paris, III, 1930)

Geller, G. G. *Sarah Bernhardt Divine Eccentric* (New York: Frederick A. Stokes, 1933)

Georges-Michel, Michel. *Un demi-siècle de Gloires Théatrales* (Paris: Editions Andri Bonne, 1950)

Goncourt, Jules et Edmond de. *Journal des Goncourts* (Paris: Fasquelle et Flammarion, 1956)

Gregh, Ferdinand. *L'Age d'or* (Paris: Grasset, 1947)

Guedalla, Philip. *The Second Empire* (New York: G. P. Putnam's Sons, 1922)

Guitry, Sacha. *Si j'ai bonne Mémoire* (Paris: Plon, 1934)

Hahn, Reynaldo. *La Grande Sarah* (Paris: Hachette, 1930)

Hart, Jerome A. *Sardou and the Sardou Plays* (Philadelphia: J. B. Lippincott & Co., 1913)

Huddleston, Sisley. *Paris Salons, Cafés, Studios* (Philadelphia: J. B. Lippincott & Co., 1928)

Huneker, James Gibbons. *Steeplejack* (New York: C. Scribner's Sons, 1909)

Huret, J. *Sarah Bernhardt* (Paris: 1899)

Jullian, Philippe. *Robert de Montesquiou, un Prince 1900* (Paris: Librairie Académique Perrin, 1965)

Keim, Albert. *Le Demi-Siècle* (Paris: Editions Albin Michel, 1950)

Lanco, Yvonne. *Belle-Isle-en-Mer, Sarah Bernhardt Souvenirs* (Paris: Les Nouvelles Editions Debresse, 1961)

Lemaître, Jules. *Les Contemporains* (Paris: Boivin & Cie, 1885)

Lorrain, Jean. *Du Temps que les Bêtes Parlaient* (Paris: Editions Courrier Français, n.d.)

——. *La Ville Empoisonée* (Paris: Editions Jean Cres, 1935)

Magnus, Philip. *King Edward the Seventh* (New York: E. P. Dutton & Co., 1964)

Maurois, André. *A History of France* (New York: Farrar, Straus and Cudahy, 1948)

Melba, Nellie. *Melodies and Memories* (New York: George H. Doran Co., 1926)

Meyer, Arthur. *Ce que je peux dire* (Paris: Plon-Nourrit et Cie, 1912)

——. *Ce que mes yeux ont vus* (Paris: Plon-Nourrit et Cie, 1911)

Moreno, Marguerite. *Souvenirs de ma Vie* (Paris: Editions de Flore, 1948)

Pearson, Heskweth. *Oscar Wilde* (New York: Harper and Bros., 1946)

Phelps, Robert (editor). *Earthly Paradise* (New York: Farrar, Straus and Giroux, 1966)

Pronier, Ernest. *Une Vie au Théâtre* (Geneva: Alex Jullien, 1941)

Ranson, André. *En déjeunant avec . . .* (Paris: Les Deux Sirenes, n.d.)

Renard, Jules. *Journal* (29th Edition) (Paris: Gallimard, 1935)

Robertson, W. Graham. *Life Was Worth Living* (New York: Harper & Bros., 1931)

Rostand, Maurice. *Confessions d'un demi-siècle* (Paris: Jeune Parque, 1948)

——. *Sarah Bernhardt* (Paris: Calmann-Lévy, 1950)

Rothenstein, William. *Men and Memories* (New York: Coward-McCann, Inc., 1931)

Row, Arthur William. *Sarah the Divine* (New York: Comet Press Books, 1957)

Rueff, Suze. *I Knew Sarah Bernhardt* (London: Frederick Miller, Ltd., 1951)

Sarcey, Francisque. *Quarante ans de Théâtre* (Paris: Bibliotheque des Annales politiques et littéraires, 1900–1902)

Scott, Mrs. Clement. *Old Days in Bohemian London* (New York: Frederick Stokes Co., n.d.)

Tellegen, Lou. *Women Have Been Kind* (New York: Vanguard Press, 1931)

Thomas, Elizabeth Finley. *Ladies, Lovers and Other People* (New York: Longmans Green & Co., 1935)

——, ed. and trans. *The Paris We Remember* (New York: D. Appleton-Century Co., 1942)

Trichet, Henry. *Amours et Plaisirs de Paris au XIX* Siècle* (Librairie Astra, n.d.)

Verneuil, Louis. *La Vie Merveilleuse de Sarah Bernhardt* (New York: Brentano's, 1942)

——. *Rideau à neuf heures* (New York: Editions de la Maison Française, 1944)

Walkley, A. B. *Drama and Life* (New York: Brentano's, 1908)

——. *Playhouse Impressions* (London: T. Fisher Unwin, 1893)

Woon, Basil. *The Real Sarah Bernhardt* (New York: Boni and Liveright, 1924)

INDEX

Abbéma, Louise, 95, 111; as member of Bernhardt "Court," 135, 149, 197, 260; Sarah sculpts bust of, 97; at Belle-Isle, 238, 272, 276, 315; portrait of Sarah, 262

Abbey, Henry, 156, 159, 160, 163, 165, 168, 182, 183, 186, 188

Adrienne Lecouvreur, Scribe and Legouvé, 143, 144, 145, 161–62, 172, 178, 195; costume for, 147; Sarah's own version of, 294

Agar, Madame Marie Léonide, 61–62, 64, 200–201, 203, 220

Agate, James, 269, 328

Agate, May, 285, 292

l'Aiglon, Rostand, 63, 107, 264, 265–69

Alexander III, Tsar of Russia, 208

Alexandra, Princess of Wales (later Queen), 133, 144, 214, 326

Alexis, Paul, 243

Alfonso XII, King of Spain, 207

Alixe, 159, 160

Alligators, 189–90

Ambigu Theatre, 216, 220

"America," ship, 149, 152, 197

Anderson, Mary, 195

Andromache, Racine, 103, 284

Angelo, 159, 188, 189, 192, 210, 211, 236

Annunzio, Gabrielle d', 112, 255, 258, 297

Antoine, André, 148

Archer, William, 123

Arnold, Matthew, 128

Arthur, Julia, 262

Arthur, Sir George, 106, 109, 128, 142

Astor, Mrs. William, 156

Athalie, Racine, 54, 63, 328

Auber, 25, 29, 30, 31

Augier, Emile, 140–41

Aurevilly, Barbey d', 23, 24

L'Aventurière, Augier, 141

l'Aveu, 246

Baldwin, Stanley, 1

Balloon, *Doña Sol*, 114–16

Balzac, Honoré de, 5

Banville, Théodore de, xii, 89

Barbier, Jules, 245, 247

Baring, Maurice, xii, 107, 204, 218, 277

Bartet, Julia, 291, 294

Bastien-Lepage, Jules, 95

Bataille, Henri, 253

Baudelaire, Pierre Charles, 182

Beaumarchais, 63

Beauvallet, 29, 30, 36, 39, 55

Beck, Martin, 313

Beck, Mrs. Martin, 313

Beerbohm, Max, xi, 261, 269–70, 285, 286

Beffa, La, Benelli, 294

Bell, Charles, 189–90

Belle-Isle estate, xix, 237–38, 271–79, 315

Benelli, Sem, 294

Bennett, Arnold, 285

Bennett, James Gordon, 165

Benson, E. F., 135

Berentz, Mr., 26, 34

Bernard, Edouard, 2

Bernard, Tristan, 141, 314, 319

Bernhardt, Jeanne, 9, 14–15; as mother's favorite, 18–19, 31, 48; Sarah's early jealousy of, 19; on Sarah's first U.S. tour, 168, 179, 180, 181, 188, 192, 193; and Jacques Damala, 208, 212; morphine addict, 212; death, 212, 228; alleged daughter, 274

Bernhardt, Judith (Youle, Julie), mother of Sarah, 2–4, 6–7, 9, 10, 11, 14, 18, 19, 20, 24; tries to arrange marriage for Sarah, 26, 34; suffers heart trouble, 28, 47–48, 91; and

Sarah's Conservatoire audition, 28; unimpressed by Sarah's talents, 31, 45; has Sarah's hair coiffed, 33; reaction to Sarah's pregnancy, 48; begins to take interest in Sarah, 60; death, 227

Bernhardt, Lysiane, references to her book about her grandmother, *xix*, 20, 23, 26, 46, 57, 111, 113, 142, 183, 190, 236, 241, 260, 300, 301, 310; Sarah starts statue of, 278; lives with Sarah, 303–4; at Belle-Isle, 315, 316; with Sarah during World War I, 316, 322, 326, 327; and Sarah's amputation, 318

Bernhardt, Maurice, *xx*; birth, 48; Sarah's remarks about his paternity, 52; spoiled by his mother, 61, 114, 116, 200; rescued from fire, 66; love for his mother, 149, 151, 197, 243–44, 258; extravagances, 200, 228, 325; reaction to mother's marriage, 213; managing director of Ambigu, 216, 220; infuriated by *Memoirs of Sarah Barnum*, 225–26; in South America, 235–36; at Belle-Isle, 238, 239, 272, 273, 277; meeting with father, 241–42; proclivity for dueling, 242–43; marries, 243–44; and the Dreyfus case, 259–60; on Sarah as Hamlet, 261; at *l'Aiglon*, 269; Sarah starts statue of, 278; director-manager of Théâtre Sarah Bernhardt, 315; cables Sarah for money, 325; mentioned, 60, 299, 317, 318, 332

Bernhardt, Régina, 14–15, 18; and Madame Nathalie episode, 39; lives with Sarah, 48, 60, 65; Sarah starts bust of, 97; has tuberculosis, 100; death, 101

Bernhardt, Sarah, physical appearance, *x, xi, xii;* movies, *x*, 312, 323; voice, *xii-xiii*, 162; legend, *xiii-xx*, 99–102, 136, 155; balloon ascension, *xv*, 144–46; love of animals and exotic pets, *xii*, 16–17, 61, 93–94, 134–36, 139, 189–90, 238, 240, 299, 303, 330–31; birth, 1; parentage, 2; childhood and education, 3–4, 6, 7–9, 10–20; precarious health, 8, 20, 68, 103–4, 138–39, 141, 317, 318, 326, 327; first experiences stage fright, 11–12; baptized, 14; religious devoutness, 15, 18; coffin, 20–21,

100–101; first visit to Comédie Française, 22–24; interviewed by Auber, 25; refuses Berentz's marriage offer, 26; suitors, 26–27; successfully auditions for Conservatoire, 27–32; Prize Day performance, 33–34; auditions and is accepted at Comédie Française, 35, 36; debut, 36–38; earnings, 36, 61, 86, 146, 147, 196, 204–5, 239, 249; performances at Comédie, 38; slaps Madame Nathalie, 39–40; asked to resign from Comédie, 41; lovers, 42–43, 58–59, 188, 210, 211, 221, 223, 232, 234, 250–51, 265, 309–13; at the Gymnase, 43, 45–46; performs at Court, 44–45; goes abroad, 46; and Henri de Ligne, 46–48, 49–52, 241–42; gives birth to son, 48; at Porte Saint Martin, 49; with the Odéon, 53–57; prodigious memory, 57, 302; growing social success, 59–60; and George Sand, 59; grandmother comes to live with, 60; masculine roles, 62–63, 229, 252, 260–61, 266–69, 270, 294–95; performs before Louis-Napoleon and receives brooch from him, 64; impersonation of a corpse, 65; saves son and grandmother from fire, 65–66; benefit arranged for, 66–67; enigmatic nature, 67–68; runs hospital during Siege of Paris, 72–75, 76–77; goes to Germany, 78–79; flees to Saint-Germain-en-Laye, 80; back at Odéon after war, 82; becomes a star, 84–85; receives offer from Comédie Française and leaves Odéon, 85–88; with Comédie Française again, 89–92, 103–10; rue de Rome apartment, 93; famous divan, 93, 94; Clairin portrait of, 94, 262; interest in art and artists, 95–96; as sculptor, 96–99, 132–33, 165, 182, 277–28; builds house, 110–11; "holds Court," 111–13; is made *sociétaire*, 117; signs contract for private recitals in London, 118–20; in London, 121–27, 131–34, 143, 200, 205–6, 228–29, 285–86, 306, 329; and Oscar Wilde, 122–24, 132; and Ellen Terry, 128–29; threatens to resign, 137–38; returns to France, 139–40; resigns from the Comédie, 140–42; in Brussels and Copenhagen, 143–45; theatrical wardrobe, 146–47; plans

U.S. tour, 146–48; sails for America, 149–52; arrival in America, 152–61; New York hotel, 156–57; cartoons of, 158–59, 195, 242–43; American opening, 161–63; curtain calls, 162–63; sensation in America, 163–64; ignored by New York society, 164–66; shopping habits, 166; leaves New York for Boston, 168–70; in Boston, 171–76; and the whale, 174–77; in New Haven, Hartford, and Springfield, 176–77; in Montreal, 177–80; in Philadelphia, 182; in Chicago, 182–84; rigorous tour schedule, 184–88; escapes death in collapse of bridge, 190–93; superstitions, 192, 236; shoots crows in Georgia, 194; ends first U.S. tour, 195–96, 197; appears at Opéra Gala, 201; on tour in Europe, 205–8, 222; and Jacques Damala, 208–16, 218–19, 220, 222–23, 244–45; marriage, 213; takes over Ambigu Theatre, 216; forced to sell possessions, 220–21, 234, 315; arranges for legal separation, 223; and Memoirs of Sarah Barnum, 225–27; on tour in South America, 234–36; injures knee, 236–37, 249; new Paris house, 239–40; on two-year world tour, 248–49, 280–82; takes over Théâtre de la Renaissance, 249; given "Day of Glorification," 255–58; and the Dreyfus case, 259–60; leases Théâtre des Nations, 262–64; and Rostand, 264, 265–69, 278; sixth American tour, 270–71; and Coquelin, 270–71; at Belle-Isle, 271–79, 315–16; farm, 275; as tennis player, 276; burial place, 278, 333; foreign successes resented by French public, 284–85; loses thinness, 285; and Mrs. Patrick Campbell, 286–87; trip to U.S. (1905–6), 287–90; plays in tent in Texas, 288–89; performs at San Quentin, 289; well received in New York, 289–90; 1907 Paris Gala for, 291; urged to return to Comédie Française, 291–92; teaches at Conservatoire, 292–93; puts on matinees of poetry reading; 293–94; attempts at play-writing, 294; as hostess, 296–99; knee bothers her, 296, 302–3, 317, 318; servants, 299–302; and her granddaughters, 303; cuts down menagerie, 303; human side, 305–6; London Press criticism of, 306–7; second "Farewell American Tour," 307, 309–11; and Lou Tellegen, 308–13; third "Farewell American Tour," 313; made Chevalier of Legion d'Honneur, 314–15; during World War I, 316–18, 320–25, 327; suffers from chronic uremia, 318, 326; leg amputated, 319; makes comeback with Les Cathédrales, 320; performs for troops, 321–23; final American tour, 323–27; kidney operation, 326; final European tour, 329; final visit to England, 329–30; lectures on Rostand, 331; final illness, 331–32; funeral, 333.

ALPHABETICAL LIST OF PLAYS PERFORMED, AS MENTIONED IN TEXT (for more complete chronological list, see pp. 337–41):

Adrienne Lecouvreur, 144, 147, 161–62, 166, 178, 294
l'Aiglon, 63, 266–69, 270
Andromache, 103, 284
Athalie, 54, 63, 328
L'Aventurière, 140–41
l'Aveu, 246
Les Bouffons, 294
Brittanicus, 92
Cléopâtre, 247–48
Cyrano de Bergerac, 270–71
La Dame aux Camélias, 50, 147, 148, 166–67, 195, 198, 205, 213–14, 222, 228, 264, 271
Daniel, 328–29
Esther, 284
l'Etourd, 38
l'Etrangère, 138
Fédora, 112, 216–18, 220–21, 222
Les Femmes Savantes, 38, 54
La Fille de Roland, 108
Froufrou, 144, 145, 147, 172, 195, 222
Gismonda, 252
Hamlet, 233, 260–61
Hernani, 109–10, 133, 138, 147, 195, 298
Jean-Marie, 81–82
Jeanne d'Arc, 245, 247
Jeanne Doré, 314, 315
Jeu de l'Amour et du Hasard, 54
Kean, 55–56
King Lear, 54
Léna, 246
Lorenzaccio, 252

Mlle. de Belle Isle, 91
Magda, 251–52
Le Passant, 63
Phèdre, 103, 105–7, 128, 251, 302
Précieuses Ridicules, 270
Procès de Jeanne d'Arc, 295–96
Rome Vaincue, 109
Ruy Blas, 83–85, 88
Sleeping Beauty, 229
La Sorcière, 283
Le Sphynx, 103, 195
Théodora, 231–32, 234, 235
Tosca, 240–41, 271
Valérie, 38
Varennes, 294
La Vierge d'Avila, 294
Werther, 283
Zaïre, 104–5, 133
Bernhardt, Simone, 245, 260, 278, 303–4, 315, 316
Bernhardt, Terka Jablonowska, 244, 245, 260, 303
Berton, Madame Pierre, *xix–xx,* 27, 58
Berton, Pierre, 58, 61, 216, 218, 233; *Léna,* 246
Biche au Bois, La, 49
Binet-Valmer, 99
Bismarck, Otto von, 1, 68
Bonaparte, Napoleon, *x, xv*
Bonaparte, Napoleon III (Louis Napoleon), 5, 13, 45, 61, 64
Bonaparte, Napoleon Joseph Charles Paul (Prince Napoleon, "Plon-Plon"), 58–59, 114
Bonheur, Rosa, 98
Boni de Castellane, Marquis, 297
Bonnetain, Paul, 224, 226, 227
Bouffons, Les, Zamacoïs, 294
Bouillon, Duchesse de, 178
Boulanger, General Georges, 52
Bourget, Paul, 94
Brabender, Mademoiselle, 19, 28, 34
Brandes, Georg, 222
Briand, Aristide, 297
Brittanicus, Racine, 24
Brohan, Augustine, 29, 30, 51
Brohan, Madeleine, *xiii,* 89–90
Bruces, 46, 47
Burne-Jones, Edward, 132

Cadogan, Honorable Miss, 272–73
Café Anglais, 5
Café de Paris, 5

Café de la Régence, 5
Camille. See *Dame aux Camélias*
Campbell, Mrs. Patrick (Stella), 181, 248, 286–87
Canrobert, Marshal, 70, 84, 125, 226
Caruso, Enrico, 67
Castelot, André, *xiii,* 189, 190, 221
Castiglione, Madame de, 23
Cathédrales, Les, Morand, 320, 323
Cauterets, 15, 16
Cavendish, Lady Frederick, 132
Cernuschi, Henri, 234
Chaliapin, Feodor, 253
Au Champs d'Honneur, 323–24
Chekhov, Anton, 203
Cherubini, Maria Luigi, 25
Chic, 158
Chilly, Charles-Marie de, 53–54, 56; and *Le Passant,* 62; reopens Odéon, 81; and *Ruy Blas,* 83; enraged at Sarah's intention of leaving Odéon, 86, 88; death, 88
Chopin, Frédéric, 3
Churchill, Lady Randolph, 126
Clairin, Georges, inspired by Sarah, 18; as close friend of Sarah, 94–95, 111, 135, 149, 197, 318; paints Sarah, 94, 156, 262; bust of, 97; balloon trip, 114, 115, 116; at Belle-Isle, 238, 272, 273, 277, 315; and the Dreyfus case, 260; mentioned, 156
Clarence, Duke of, 52
Claude, valet, 185
Clemenceau, Georges, 297, 317
Cléopâtre, Sardou, 247–48
Cochran, Charles B., 329
Cocteau, Jean, 254
Colette, 331
Colombier, Marie, 180, 181–82, 184, 188, 189, 190, 192, 193, 197–98, 199; *Memoirs of Sarah Barnum,* 51, 224–27
Combermere, Lady, 131
Commune, 79–80
Connaught, Duke of, 124–25
Coppée, François, 62, 256, 258, 259
Coquelin, Constant, 90, 112; in *Valérie,* 38, 137, 181, 253, 255; plays Cyrano, 90, 264; on U.S. tour with Sarah Bernhardt, 270
Cornwallis-West, Mrs., 126
Courcelle, Pierre de, 283
Crawford, Marion, 283
Cri Parisien, 243

Croizette, Sophie, 90, 92, 93, 137; in *Le Sphynx*, 103; made *sociétaire*, 117
Cross, Mr., 134–35
Cyrano de Bergerac, Rostand, 90, 264

Damala, Jacques, 208–16, 218–19, 220, 222–23, 224, 244–45
Dame aux Camélias, La, Dumas *fils*, 50, 107, 148, 166–67, 172, 195, 198, 205, 211, 213–14, 222, 228, 240, 264, 271, 312; Sarah's costume for, 147
Damian, Hortense, 126
Daniel, Verneuil, 328–29
Daudet, Alphonse, 283
Dead City, d'Annunzio, 255
Debay, Madame, 49
Delaunay, Louis, 119, 120
Delavigne, Casimir, 32–33
Denucé, Dr., 318
Deshayes, Paul, 58–59
Deslandes, Raymond, 45, 199–200, 204–5, 216, 249
Dominga, maid, 248, 264
Doña Sol, balloon, 114–16
Doré, Gustave, 95–96, 135, 136
Dorival, 250
Doucet, Camille, 7, 35, 44, 52–53, 61
Dreyfus case, 13, 259–60
Drouet, Juliette, 3
Duchesne, Dr., 74
Dudley, Lady, 119, 126
Dudley, Lord, 126, 127
Dumas, Alexandre, the elder, 3, 5; as friend of Julie Van Hard, 7; and Sarah's first evening at the theatre, 22, 24; coaches Sarah in diction, 27–28; insists Sarah take trip, 46; on Sarah's appearance, 54; *Kean*, 55
Dumas, Alexandre, the younger, *xviii*, 99, 112; Sarah as inspiration to, 18; introduction to Bernhardt 200, 93–94
Duquesnel, Félix, 57; first meeting with Sarah, 53; recommends Sarah for Odéon, 54; as friend and adviser to Sarah, 57, 58; rapturous over Sarah's performance, 56; and *Le Passant*, 62; and Sarah's impersonation of a corpse, 65; arranges benefit for Sarah, 66; reopens Odéon, 81; and *Ruy Blas*, 83; and Sarah's departure from the Odéon, 86, 87; books Sarah for French road tour, 145; mentioned, 233

Dusanne, Beatrix, 293–94, 321, 322
Duse, Eleonora, *xi*, *xvii*, 181, 255, 306

Edison, Thomas, 168–70
Edward, Prince of Wales (later Edward VII), 85, 112–13, 124, 126, 133, 214, 273; caricatured in *Sarah Barnum*, 225
Eiffel Tower, 114
Emile, butler, 112, 297, 298, 300, 317
Escalier, Félix, 110
Essler, Jane, 81, 83
Esther, Racine, 284
l'Etrangère, Dumas *fils*, 133, 138, 148, 195
Eugénie, Empress of France, 22–23
l'Evénement, newspaper, 182, 199, 223
Exposition Universelle, 114

Faille, 53
Farrar, Geraldine, 188, 313n., 326
Farren, Nellie, 270
Faure, Madame Felix, 15
Faure, Uncle Felix, 28
Fédora, Sardou, 112, 203, 204, 213, 215, 216–18, 220–21, 222, 233
Félicie, maid, 112
Femmes Savantes, Les, Molière, 38, 54
Ferry, Jules, 200
Feuillet, Octave, 92, 103
Field of Honor, The, 323–24
Figaro, 136–37
Fille de Roland, La, 108
Fish, Mrs. Stuyvesant, 164
Flahaut, Comte de, 7
Flaubert, Gustave, 59, 112
Flers, Robert de, 291
Foch, Marshal Ferdinand, 77
Forbes-Robertson, Johnston, 122
Fournier, Marc, 49
Frances Fisher Powers School of Acting, 290
Francesca da Rimini, Marion Crawford, 283
Franco-Prussian War, 68–69, 70–79
Franz Ferdinand, Archduke, 316
Franz Joseph, Emperor of Austria, 207
Frederick, Archduke of Austria, 207
Fressard, Madame, Sarah at pension run by, 10–11
Frohman and Hayman, 288
Froufrou, Meilhac-Halévy, 143, 144, 145, 172, 195, 209, 211, 222; costume, 147

Gambetta, Léon, 52, 60, 108, 112; organizes Resistance, 71; allowed to smoke in Sarah's presence, 75; at Opera Gala, 200, 202

Garnier, Philippe, 210, 211, 232, 233; in South America, 234, 236

Garrick, David, x, 131

Gautier, Théophile, 31, 63

Gémier, Firmin, 293

Geoffroy, Edouard, 83, 260, 273, 277, 315

George, Prince of Wales (later George V), 291

Georges-Michel, Michel, xviii-xix

Giffard, Pierre, 114

Girardin, Emile de, 97

Gismonda, Sardou, 252

Gladstone, William, 133

Gloire, La, Rostand, 331

Glu, La, Richepin, 220, 229

Godard, Louis, 114–16

Gordon, Mr., 174–75

Got, Edmond, 137

Gould, Anna, 297

Gounod, Charles, 112

Grand Seize, 5–6

Granier, Jeanne, 291

Grant, Ulysses S., 156

Grau, Maurice, 236

Grévy, President François, 200, 202

Grew, Sir Edward, 316

Guedella, Philip, 7

Guérard, Madame, xviii, 35, 116, 121, 129, 131; Sarah forms attachment to, 15–16, 19; and Sarah's audition and Prize Day recitation at Conservatoire, 28, 31, 34; at Sarah's Odéon opening, 91; as ever-present member of Bernhardt household, 48, 51, 60–61, 72, 135, 136; helps at Odéon hospital, 74, 76, 78; on trip to U.S., 146, 151, 157, 158, 159, 185, 188, 191, 192, 193; at Belle-Isle, 238, 272

Guitry, Lucien, xvii, 181, 252–54; as Flambeau in l'Aiglon, 266, 267–68; in Un Sujet de Roman, 331

Guitry, Sacha, on Mounet-Sully, 137; purchases Sarah's china, 239; on his father, 253; recalls Sunday visits to Sarah, 263; on Rostand, 264; story of l'Aiglon rehearsal, 266–67; recalls Sarah's Christmas party for children, 303; on Sarah as Athalie, 328; Un Sujet de Roman, 331; makes film, La Voyante, 332

Haas, Charles, 60

Hahn, Reynaldo, 251, 277

Halévy, Ludovic, 143

Hamlet, Schwob-Morand version, 261

Haraucourt, Edmond, 258, 299

Harding, Warren G., 1

Harvey, Martin, 131

Heine, Heinrich, 5

Heredia, José Maria de, 258

Hernani, Hugo, 109–10, 133, 138, 147, 195, 298

Herrick, Myron T., 297

Hervieu, Paul, 283

Hollingshead, John, 117, 120, 143, 200

L'Homme Libre, newspaper, 317

Hortense, Agar's maid, 201, 203

Hortense, Queen, 7

Houston, Sam, 1

Howells, Mrs. William Dean, 173

Hugo, Adèle, 3

Hugo, Victor, 52, 112, 148; mistress, 3; in exile, 44, 55; returns from exile, 82–83; Odéon performs Ruy Blas, 83–85, 88; Hernani, 109–10, 133, 138, 147, 195, 298; sends diamond to Sarah, 110; Marion Delorme, 232, 233; death and funeral, 232–33

Huret, Jules, 240

Huysmans, J. K., 100

Ibsen, Henrik, 203

Iphigénie in Aulis, Racine, 36

Irving, Henry, xvii, 112, 125, 130–31, 261

Isabelle, flower vender, 5

Jablonowska, Terka. See Bernhardt, Terka

Jadin, Charles-Emmanuel, 111

James, Henry, 120

Jarrett, Edward, 118–19, 126, 132; arranges exhibit of Sarah's sculpture, 132, 133; proposes U.S. tour for Sarah, 134, 146; on American tour, 148, 150, 152, 153–56, 157, 159, 160, 163, 165, 168, 174, 179, 182, 186, 188, 189, 191, 192, 193, 194; ability to handle Sarah, 153; books South American tour, 234; death, 236

Jay, Mrs. John, 164

Jean-Marie, Theuriet, 81–82

Jeanne d'Arc, Barbier, 245

Jeanne Doré, Bernard, 314, 315, 323
Joinville, Prince de, 5
Jouvin, journalist, 99
Judas, de Kay, 295
Judge, 195

Kabil Bey, 66
Kahn, Gustav, 293
Kay, John de, 295
Kean, Dumas, 55
Kean, Edmund, portrait of, 131
Keppel, Mrs., 113
Kératry, Count Emile de, 43, 72–73
King Lear, 54
Kipling, Rudyard, 131
Kitchener, Lord Horatio, 323
Klaw and Erlanger, 288
Knoedler, Mr., 157

LaBiche, Ernest, 45
Ladies, Lovers and Other People, Elizabeth Finley Thomas, 243
Lady of the Camellias. See *Dame aux Camélias*
Lalique, 278
Lambquin, Madame, 74, 78
Lanco, Yvonne, 274, 277, 278
Langlois, cartoonist, 242–43
Langtry, Lily, 124
Larrey, Baron, 6, 7
Lavedan, Henri, 294
Lavolie, Régis, 6, 14, 22, 24, 43
Léautaud, M., 29–30
Legouvé, Ernest, 32, 178
Leighton, Sir Frederick, 133
Lemaître, Jules, 112; on the Bernhardt voice, *xii;* on Sarah's complex character, *xv;* said to have been Sarah's lover, 250–51; on Sarah as Phèdre, 107; on Sarah as Fédora, 218; on Sarah in *Théodora*, 232; on Sarah's acting, 247; on Sarah as ambassador, 249; *Les Rois*, 250; and day of tribute to Sarah, 256; and the Dreyfus case, 259
Léna, Berton, 246
Leopold, Prince, 133
LePage, Bastien, *xvii*
Lesseps, Ferdinand de, 112
Life of Marie Pigeonnier, 227
Ligne, General de, 50
Ligne, Prince Henri de, 45, 46–47, 49–51, 241–42
Ligne de la Patrie Française, 259

Lincoln, Mary Todd, 151
Lind, Jenny, 153
Liszt, Franz, 131
Lloyd, Marie, 34, 90
Longfellow, Henry Wadsworth, 173
Lorenzaccio, de Musset, 252
Lorne, Marquis of, 178
Loti, Pierre, 297–98
Louis Napoleon. *See* Bonaparte, Napoleon III
Louis-Philippe, 1, 3, 10
Loüys, Pierre, 241
"Lusitania," 324
Lyceum Theatre, 130; Beefsteak Room, 131

McAllister, Ward, 164
Macbeth, Richepin's, 228–29
MacMahon, Maréchal Marie Edmé de, 108
Maeterlinck, Maurice, 286
Magda, Sudermann, 251–52
Magnus, Baron, 144–45
Magnus, Sir Philip, 113
Maintenon, Mmd. de, 284
Maître des Forges, Ohnet, 224
Manet, Edouard, 180
Marivaux, Pierre de, 54
Marot, Dr., 332
Marriage of Figaro, The, 63
Mars, Mademoiselle, 110
Mary, Queen of England, 329–30
Mathieu-Meusnier, sculptor, 96
Mathilde, Princesse, 23, 58, 63–64
Maurois, André, 112
Max, Edouard de, 254–55, 283, 284, 293, 308, 309
Mayer, Franz, 76
Meilhac, Henri, 143
Melba, Nellie, 239
Memoirs of Sarah Barnum, Marie Colombier, 51, 224–27
Mendès, Catulle, 216, 256, 258, 261, 293, 294
Mères Ennemies, Les, Mendès, 216, 218, 219, 220
Methodist, The, 155
Metternich, Pauline, 23
Meunier, Monsieur, 73
Meurice, Paul, 83
Meydieu, M., 14, 27, 28
Meyer, Arthur, 60, 66–67, 120, 143
Millais, John, 126–27

Mirbeau, Octave, 226–27, 259, 286, 307
Mogador, Céleste, 23
Montaland, Céline, 43
Montesquiou, Robert de, 100–101, 115
Montigny, director, 43, 44, 46
Montrin, Ada, 55
Morand, Eugène, 261, 320
Moreau, Emile, 295
Moreno, Marguerite, 102
Morny, Charles, Duc de, 7, 12, 24; promotes theatrical career for Sarah, 22, 25, 35, 36
Morris, Clara, 159–60, 195
Mothers of France, movie, 323
Mounet-Sully, Jean, 101–2; as Sarah's lover, 101–2; in Andromache, 103; in Zaïre, 104; in Phèdre, 105, 106, 127, 128; in La Fille de Roland, 108; as Hernani, 110; protests Sarah's resignation from Comédie Française, 137; at Opéra Gala, 200, 201, 202; mentioned, 181, 254
Mower, Margaret, 325
Mucha, xvii, 262
Murat, Prince, 268
Musset, Alfred de, 3, 5, 29, 59; Lorenzaccio, 252; Nuit de Mai, 294

Nadar, photographer, 230
Nana-Sahib, Richepin, 223–24, 227, 228, 229
Napoleon, Prince ("Plon-Plon"). See Bonaparte, Napoleon Joseph Charles Paul
Napoleon III. See Bonaparte, Napoleon III
Nathalie, Madame, 39–41, 89, 104, 113, 139
Nathan, George Jean, 38
New York Herald, 226, 262
Newcastle, Duchess of, 306
Nilsson, Christine, 235
Nittis, Giuseppe de, 135, 136
Nixon and Zimmerman, 288
Noah, Mme. Lily, 176
Noailles, Anna de, 297
Nuit de Mai, de Musset, 294

O'Connor, Captain, 80
Odéon Theatre, 52; as military hospital, 72, 73–76, 78; reopens after war, 81
Ohnet, Georges, 224

Païva, La, 49–50
Paris Exposition, 114
Paris, Siege of, 70–79; burning of, 80
Parodi, 109
Passant, Le, Coppée, 62–64
Pasteur, Louis, 112
Patti, Adelina, 66–67, 235
Pearl, Cora, 58
Pedro, Emperor of Brazil, 235
Peel, Sir Robert, 1
Pelléas and Mélisande, Maeterlinck, 286–87
Penhoët, farm, 275
Perrin, Emile, 86, 87, 89; and Sophie Croizette, 90, 92; cold, unfeeling nature, 103, 104, 105, 108, 119, 139; and Sarah's balloon trip, 115, 116; and Sarah's resignation, 138, 141, 142
Petit-Bois de la Nieville, Thieule, 2
Phèdre, Racine, 37, 103, 105–7, 120, 127–28, 147, 166, 172, 195, 240, 251, 258, 284, 302, 312
Pierné, Gabriel, 256
Pierson, Blanche, 43
Piron, actor, 192, 193
Pitou, secretary, 38, 190, 300–302, 309
"Plon-Plon." See Bonaparte, Napoleon Joseph Charles Paul
Poincaré, Raymond, 316
Polhes, General, 14
Polk, James K., 1
Pontjest, Mlle., 253
Porel, actor, 81
Porte Saint-Martin Theatre, 222, 223–24, 228, 249
Potin, Félix, 73
Pozzi, Dr., 318
Preparedness League, 324
Princesse Georges, La, Dumas fils, 195
Princesse Lointaine, La, Rostand, 264, 265
Printemps, Yvonne, 63, 253, 331
Procès de Jeanne d'Arc, Le, 295–96
Proust, Marcel, 60, 100
Provost, M., 29, 30, 31, 32, 36–37
Puck, 158, 195
Punch, 261

Queen Elizabeth, film, x, 312

Rachel, Elisa, 5, 22, 32, 106, 116, 162, 199
Racine, and the writing of Esther, 284
Ravachol, 227

Régine Arnaud, Verneuil, 331
Regnier, Henri de, 203
Réjane, Gabrielle, 81, 181, 220, 291
Rémusat, Paul de, 79
Renan, Ernest, 112
Renard, Jules, on Sarah's smile, *xi;* on Sarah's walk, *xii;* on Sarah as inspiration, 18; on Lucien Guitry, 253; at "Day of Glorification" for Sarah, 258; on his first meeting with Sarah, 298–99; one critical comment on Sarah, 310
Richepin, Jean, 220, 221–22, 223–24, 226; adaptation of *Macbeth,* 228; *Sleeping Beauty,* 229; adaptation of *La Beffa,* 294
Rigault, Raoul, 80
Robert le Diable, Meyerbeer, 200, 201
Robertson, W. Graham, *xii,* 123, 129, 132, 269
Rodin, Auguste, 97, 307
Rodogune, Corneille, 332
Rois, Les, Lemaître, 250
Romanesques, Les, Rostand, 264
Rome Vaincue, Parodi, 109, 258
Roosevelt, Theodore, 297
Ross, Robert, 124
Rossini, 7
Rostand, Edmond, 256, 258, 263–65, 266–68, 269, 278, 298; *l'Aiglon,* 107, 264, 265–69; *La Princesse Lointaine,* 264, 265; *Les Romanesques,* 264; *Cyrano de Bergerac,* 264; *La Samaritaine,* 265; version of *Faust,* 295; *La Gloire,* 331
Rostand, Jacques, 333
Rostand, Maurice, 113, 263, 269, 272, 303, 329
Rousseil, Mlle., 105
Rothschild, Baron Adolphe de, 4, 73, 234; bust of, 97
Rothschild, Baroness de, 23
Rothschild family, 126
Ruben, José, 309, 310, 324
Rubenstein, Ida, 297
Rueff, Suze, 272, 274, 305
Ruy Blas, Hugo, 83–85, 88

Saint Cyr Academy, 284
Sainte-Beuve, Charles-Augustin, 3
Sainte-Sophie, Mère, 13, 192, 193
Salomé, Wilde, 123
Salvini, Tommaso, 195
Samaritaine, La, Rostand, 265

Samson, 29, 32–33, 34
San Quentin, 289
Sand, George, 3, 23, 59, 86
Sapho, Daudet, 283
Sarcey, Francisque, 120, 138; on Sarah's debut, 37–38; on Sarah as Zacharie in *Athalie,* 55; on Sarah in *Adrienne Lecouvreur,* 143; on *Le Passant,* 62; changes opinion of Sarah, 89; on Croizette, 90; reviews *Mlle. de Belle Isle* unfavorably, 91; on Sarah's Phèdre, 107, 251; on Sarah as Marguerite Gauthier, 205–6; on the Sarah Bernhardt craze, 215; on *Théodora,* 230
Sardou, Victorien, *xv,* 46, 112, 208, 247; Bernhardt bust of, 97; as playwright for Sarah, 172, 199–200, 203–4, 213, 215–16, 247; as director, 217; *Tosca,* 203, 232, 240–41, 271; *Théodora,* 223, 229–32, 234, 235; *Cléopâtre,* 247–48; version of *Gismonda,* 252; and day of tribute to Sarah, 256; and the Dreyfus case, 259; *La Sorcière,* 283
Sargent, J. S., portrait of Ellen Terry, 131
Saryta, 274
Sassoon, Mr., 110
Saxe, Marshal de, 178
Schneider, Hortense, 69
Schwob, Marcel, 261, 283
Scott, Clement, 241
Scribe, Eugène, 143, 177, 178
Seylor, Suzanne, 274, 310, 315, 316, 318
Shaw, G. B., 203, 252, 283, 291
Sherard, Robert, 123–24
Shubert brothers, Sam Lee and Jake, 287–88, 289
Sibour, Monseigneur, 13–14
Skinner, Otis, *x–xi*
Smalley, G. W., 325
Smith, Mr. Henry, 174–75, 176–77
Sorcière, La, Sardou, 283
Soudan, Jehan, 226
Sphynx, Le, Feuillet, 103, 195
Stebbins, James, 164–65
Stevens, Alfred, 95
Stirtz, Herr Von, 207
Strachey, Lytton, *xiii*
Sudermann, Hermann, 251
Sue, Eugène, 5
Sujet de Roman, Guitry, 331
Sylvestre, Armand, 256
Symons, Arthur, *xi,* 264, 285

Talma, François, 32
Tarride, Abel, 329
Tellegen, Lou, 188, 307–13, 325–26
Tennyson, Alfred Lord, 131
Terry, Ellen, 128–29, 130, 181; Sargent portrait, 131; on Sarah as actress, 205
Théâtre aux Armées, 320, 323
Théâtre de la Renaissance, 249–55
Theatre Magazine, 324, 326
Théâtre Sarah Bernhardt (Théâtre des Nations), 262, 283–84, 293–96
Theatrical Syndicate, 288, 289
Théodora, Sardou, 223, 229–32, 234, 235
Théroigne de Méricourt, Hervieu, 283
Theuriet, André, 81, 82
Thibout, Lambert, 53
Thierry, Edouard, 35, 36, 40–41
Thiers, President Louis, 79
Thomas, Elizabeth Finley, 243, 320, 330
Tillet, Jules de, 252
Tortoni's, 5
Tosca, Sardou, 203, 232, 240–41, 271
Turquet, Edmond, 117

Ugade, Madame, 49
Umberto, King of Italy, 207

Vacquerie, Auguste, 83
Vaillant, xv–xvi
Van Hard, Judith. See Bernhardt, Judith
Van Hard, Mevrouw, grandmother of Sarah Bernhardt, 60
Van Hard, Rosine, 6, 7, 8–9, 10, 11, 12, 79; on the life of a courtesane, 42; gives "Little Duke" to Sarah, 60; caricatured in Sarah Barnum, 225

Vanderbilt, Commodore Cornelius, 167
Vanity Fair, 308
Van Rensselaer, Mrs., 164
Varennes, Lavedan, 294
Vaudeville Theatre, 199, 204, 205
Verneuil, Louis, 50, 51, 101, 241, 292; on Sarah, xvi; on Sarah's initial encounter with Henri de Ligne, 45; on Sarah and Lou Tellegen, 310; Daniel, 328–29; plays banned in London, 329–30; Régine Arnaud, 331
Victor Napoleon, Prince, 268
Victoria, Queen, 1, 124, 205
Viérge d'Avila, La, Mendès, 294
Vincent, Lady Helen, 126
Vitu, Figaro reviewer, 143
Voyante, La, film, 332

Wagner, Richard, 23
Walkley, A. B., 203, 291, 305
Wellington, Duke of, 1
Werther, Courcelle, 283
Whale episode, 174–77
Whistler, J. M., 129, 142
Wilcox, Ella Wheeler, 271
Wilde, Oscar, 112, 122–24, 132
Wilson, Woodrow, 325
Wolff, Albert, 137
Woon, Basil, xix, 27, 38, 51, 95
World War I, 316–18
Worms, actor, 110, 138

Young, Stark, xi

Zaïre, Voltaire, 104, 133
Zamocoïs, 294
Zola, Emile, 98, 112, 148, 259
Zukor, Adolph, 313